Bulgaria, the Jews, and the Holocaust

Rochester Studies in East and Central Europe

Series Editor: Timothy Snyder, Yale University

Additional Titles of Interest

Individualism and the Rise of Democracy in Poland
Tomek Grabowski

Rethinking Modern Polish Identities: Transnational Encounters
Edited by Agnieszka Pasieka and Pawel Rodak

*Seeking Accountability for Nazi and War Crimes in East and Central Europe:
A People's Justice?*
Edited by Eric Le Bourhis, Irina Tcherneva, and Vanessa Voisin

Great Power Competition and the Path to Democracy: The Case of Georgia, 1991–2020
Zarina Burkadze

Toward Xenopolis: Visions from the Borderland
Krzysztof Czyżewski
Edited by Mayhill C. Fowler
With a Foreword by Timothy Snyder

The Universe behind Barbed Wire: Memoirs of a Ukrainian Soviet Dissident
Myroslav Marynovych
Translated by Zoya Hayuk
Edited by Katherine Younger
With a Foreword by Timothy Snyder

Borders on the Move: Territorial Change and Ethnic Cleansing in the Hungarian-Slovak Borderlands, 1938–1948
Leslie Waters

Beyond the Pale: The Holocaust in the North Caucasus
Edited by Crispin Brooks and Kiril Feferman

Polish Literature and National Identity: A Postcolonial Perspective
Dariusz Skórczewski
Translated by Agnieszka Polakowska

An American in Warsaw: Selected Writings of Hugh S. Gibson, US Minister to Poland, 1919–1924
Edited and annotated by Vivian Hux Reed
With M. B. B. Biskupski, Jochen Böhler, and Jan-Roman Potocki

A complete list of titles in the Rochester Studies in East and Central Europe series
may be found on our website, www.urpress.com.

Bulgaria, the Jews, and the Holocaust

On the Origins of a Heroic Narrative

Nadège Ragaru

Translated by Victoria Baena and David A. Rich

UNIVERSITY OF ROCHESTER PRESS

The University of Rochester Press gratefully acknowledges generous support for this publication from the following: the Foundation for the Memory of the Shoah (FMS); the Center for International Studies, Sciences PO; the Scientific Information and Resources Division, Sciences Po; and the Understanding Middle Europe Lab Research Cluster (GDR 3607), National Centre for Scientific Research, all in Paris, France.

Originally published in French as *"Et les Juifs bulgares furent sauvés"* . . . *Une histoire des savoirs sur la Shoah en Bulgarie* by Nadège Ragaru. Copyright © 2020 Presses de la Fondation Nationale des Sciences Politiques

First published 2023

University of Rochester Press
668 Mt. Hope Avenue, Rochester, NY 14620, USA
www.urpress.com
and Boydell & Brewer Limited
PO Box 9, Woodbridge, Suffolk IP12 3DF, UK
www.boydellandbrewer.com

ISBN-13: 978-1-64825-070-5
ISSN: 1528-4808

Cataloging-in-Publication Data available from the Library of Congress

A catalogue record for this title is available from the British Library.

This publication is printed on acid-free paper.

To my mother (1939–2023),
who gave me life and the strength to hold on to it

We oscillate between the illusion of completion and the vertigo of the elusive. In the name of completeness, we want to believe that a unique order exists that would enable us to accede to knowledge from the outset; in the name of the elusive, we want to believe that order and disorder are two of the same words, denoting chance.

Georges Perec, Penser/Classer

From a certain point on, there is no more turning back.
That is the point that must be reached.

Kafka, The Zürau Aphorisms of Franz Kafka

Contents

Illustrations

Maps

Figures

Text Inserts

Full credit details are provided in the captions to the images in the text. The author and publisher are grateful to all the institutions and individuals for permission to reproduce the materials in which they hold copyright. Every effort has been made to trace the copyright holders; apologies are offered for any omission, and the publisher will be pleased to add any necessary acknowledgement in subsequent editions.

Preface

On March 15, 2023, Menachem Z. Rosensaft, general counsel and associate executive vice president of the World Jewish Congress (WJC), made a statement on Bulgarian National Radio (BNR). After recalling the "rescue of the Bulgarian Jews" during World War II, he added:

> We cannot, we simply cannot ignore the fact, and we know the number—it is 11,343 Jews from Greece, from Macedonia who were arrested and who were handed over to the Germans by Bulgarian police, by Bulgarian troops. So, those are the realities, and the only way we will come to term with history is by facing up to it. Now no one is suggesting that anyone alive today bears any responsibility for this. The past is the past. But there is a responsibility to historical truth. By the Bulgarian government, to own up to the truth and to put that as part of its obligation to ensure that the historical record is recorded accurately. No one is doing anyone any favors by distorting history or by suggesting that, oh!, those 11,343 Jews, they are not that important.[1]

A few weeks later, in a much noted article, Rosensaft further elaborated on his previous statement: "To be valid, history must be predicated on absolute, uncompromising truth, not manipulation. Eighty years ago, 48,000 Jews were not deported from Bulgaria—while 11,343 other Jews were cruelly loaded on trains bound for Treblinka, where they were murdered. These are two interdependent realities that cannot be and must not be allowed to be uncoupled."[2]

Rarely had such a prominent representative of the WJC, a highly influential organization in the field of Holocaust remembrance, made so explicit a statement regarding Bulgaria's wartime role and politics of history. Indeed, for decades, across the world, Bulgaria, a former Balkan ally of the Axis powers during the war, was mostly known for its role in what was usually called the "rescue of the Bulgarian Jews"—that is, the nondeportation of about 48,000 Jews holding Bulgarian citizenship, including the remarkable circumstances and actions by Jews as well as non-Jews that had permitted their

---

1   Interview by journalist Irina Nedeva, program *Horizont*, BNR, March 15, 2023, https://bnr.bg/horizont/post/101793639.

2   Menachem Z. Rosensaft, "The Other Side of Bulgaria's Holocaust History Is Needed," *EUObserver.com.*

survival. Most observers were also cognizant of the fact that in the territories of the Kingdoms of Yugoslavia (most of Vardar Macedonia and the city of Pirot in Serbia) and Greece (Western Thrace and Eastern Macedonia) held by Bulgaria between late April 1941 and October 1944, 11,343 Jews had been arrested by the Bulgarian authorities, police and army; interned in temporary detention camps; and deported to Treblinka, where they were exterminated.

In discussing these historical events, however, since the end of World War II, Bulgarian public discourse had systematically lent greater salience to the rescue than the deportations, though the latter issue was never entirely silenced. But in 2023, statements by several Bulgarian officials indicated that the writing about the Holocaust in Bulgaria might be undergoing a dramatic revision, raising concerns over a possible distortion of historical facts. At first sight, this evolution was counterintuitive. The eightieth anniversary of the events of March 1943—when the deportation of an estimated 8,000 Bulgarian Jews was called off, while the Jews of Yugoslavia and Greece under Bulgarian occupation faced deportation—offered the Bulgarian state a unique opportunity to recognize its coresponsibility in anti-Jewish persecutions during World War II. Some observers went so far as to hope that Bulgaria's leaders might follow in the footsteps of former French president Jacques Chirac, who, in July 1995, had publicly acknowledged France's responsibility in the deportations of tens of thousands of Jews to Nazi extermination camps. These hopes were brutally crushed. Instead, Bulgaria's rulers propelled further evolutions in the Bulgarian historical narrative.

First, although in 2003 the Bulgarian government had adopted the designation "Day of the rescue of the Bulgarian Jews, of the Victims of the Holocaust and the Crimes against Humanity" in speaking of March 10, the ceremonies in March 2023 were consecrated nearly exclusively to the "rescue of the Bulgarian Jews." Second, the list of "rescuers" was extended to the *entirety* of Bulgarian society and, even more surprisingly, to the Bulgarian *state*—army and police included—that is, those very institutions that played a crucial role in the successful arrest and deportation of the Jews living in the occupied territories and in the failed deportation of a segment of Bulgarian Jewry. Third, in an astonishing move, the former king, Boris III, who had authorized the deportations from Bulgarian-held territories, was praised for his role in the salvation, while the Bulgarian chief of state, Rumen Radev,[3] a politician close to the Bulgarian left, paid special tribute to King Boris and Queen Giovanna (Joanna). Finally, the blame for the deportations was

---

3   A note on the transliteration of names and patronyms: I have opted for transliteration except for certain individuals who prefer that their names be spelled differently in Romance languages. Those choices, when known, have been respected.

attributed to the Third Reich alone. Television and radio shows, movies and documentaries, exhibitions, conferences, and publications: all contributed to the shaping of this new discourse.

That the Bulgarian authorities were intent on crafting a novel heroic narrative had become evident as early as January 2023 from a statement released on the website of the Bulgarian Ministry of Culture:

> At today's meeting, which was held at the Ministry of Culture, the members of the Initiative Committee for the commemoration of the eightieth anniversary of the rescue of Bulgarian Jews during the Second World War adopted a decision. . . . Today's meeting was led by the minister of foreign affairs, Nikolaj Milkov, in his capacity as deputy chairman of the National Initiative Committee, which is overseen by the president of the Republic of Bulgaria, Rumen Radev. "I am convinced that we will all work together for the cause of showing the significant role of the *Bulgarian state, its institutions* [emphasis added], the Bulgarian Orthodox Church, and the Bulgarian people for this unprecedented act in Europe in one of the darkest years on our continent, when the Bulgarian people and state demonstrated tolerance, empathy, but also will and courage to save their Jewish fellow citizens.[4]

In a similar perspective, on March 9, 2023, Sofia University St. Kliment Ohridski hosted a large conference on "the role of the jurists in the rescue of the Bulgarian Jews," co-organized by the Bulgarian Ministry of Foreign Affairs and Ministry of Culture, the Association of Prosecutors in Bulgaria, the Association of Investigators in Bulgaria, the Federation of the Zionists in Bulgaria, and the Israeli Embassy.[5] A monument featuring a broken Star of David was designed for the occasion. The event's organizers stressed the opposition of the jurists' professional guild to the initial onset of anti-Jewish legislation (in a November 4, 1940, letter) and pointed to the legal background of several prominent public figures who opposed the deportation of Bulgarian Jews in March 1943 (chief among them, Dimităr Pešev, deputy speaker of the National Assembly) as well as the deportation of Jews from the occupied territories (in particular, parliamentarians Nikola Mušanov

---

4   "Iniciativnijat komitet za otbeljazvaneto na 80-ata godišnina ot spasjavanto na bălgarskite evrei odobri nacionalna programa na čestvanijata, kojato šte predloži da se prieme ot ministerskija săvet," January 17, 2023, https://mc.government.bg/newsn.php?n=8589&i=1.

5   See the program of the conference at https://www.uni-sofia.bg/index.php/novini/kalendar/mezhdunarodna_konferenciya_rolyata_na_yuristite_za_spasyavaneto_na_b_lgarskite_evrei; for an official account of the conference, see https://www.uni-sofia.bg/index.php/novini/novini_i_s_bitiya/mezhdunarodna_konferenciya_rolyata_na_yuristite_za_spasyavaneto_na_b_lgarskite_evrei.

and Petko Stojnov). One might have added that those who most doggedly sought the destruction of the Jews also were jurists, including Aleksandăr Belev, a staunch anti-Semite and the head of the specialized Commissariat for Jewish Affairs, in charge of devising and coordinating anti-Jewish policies after September 1942, and Minister of the Interior Petăr Gabrovski, a lawyer and cofounder of the radical nationalist and anti-Semitic organization Fighters for the Advancement of Bulgarianness (*Săjuzăt na ratnicite za napredăka na bălgarštinata*, also known as *Ratnik*).[6]

This new course adopted by the executive power created a deep sense of uneasiness among the Bulgarian Jewish community. On March 4–5, 2023, in Kavala, for the first time in eighty years, the Organization of the Jews in Bulgaria Šalom, led by Professor Aleksandăr Oskar, together with representatives from Bulgarian civil society, took part in the commemoration of the deportation of the Jews of Kavala when it was a Greek city under Bulgarian occupation.[7] As far as the responsibility of the Bulgarian state in these events was concerned, Oskar's statement was shorn of any ambivalence:

> The Jewish community of this ancient and beautiful city, the pearl of the White Sea, was rounded up before dawn. Unfortunately for us, by police officers wearing uniforms of the Kingdom of Bulgaria. This is a fact. A total of 1,484 people from Kavala died in Treblinka. The same thing happened in Xánthi, Drama, and Komotiní. Just like in Skopje, Bitola, Pirot. 11,343 Jewish destinies were shattered across the kingdom's "new lands." It is time to look "in the eyes" at a painful page in our recent history, especially since it precedes and has traced the trajectory of the rescue of Bulgarian Jews.[8]

In an interview to the cultural weekly *Kultura*, Professor Oskar further stated: "It is a good thing that in recent years contemporary authors have conducted an in-depth analysis of these events. I would like to draw attention to the book by the French scholar Professor Nadège Ragaru, who studies in a very detailed fashion the attempts to 'privatize' the rescue of the Bulgarian Jews. Either some take the credit for [being the saviors] themselves or the state becomes the savior. And the second thing is the externalization of guilt: everything is attributed to Nazi Germany alone—something that, in itself, is not true."[9]

---

6   On *Ratnik* and radical nationalist formations in prewar and wartime Bulgaria, see Poppetrov, *Socialno naljavo*.

7   See the remarkable radio reportage by journalist Irina Nedeva, on the BNR program *Horizont*, March 9, 2023, https://bnr.bg/horizont/post/101790785/kavala; https://bnr.bg/horizont/post/101790807/anavi.

8   https://www.facebook.com/photo/?fbid=10160324696741071&set=a.74496591070.

9   Aleksandăr Oskar, "Pamet i moralnata otgovornost," *Kultura*, March 13, 2023, 15.

On March 10, Professor Oskar and his organization also declined to attend the official commemorations of the "rescue of the Bulgarian Jews" that were centered solely on celebrating the role of King Boris III in saving the Jews. The ceremony, whose program was made public at the last minute, started with the inauguration by President Radev of an exhibition on King Boris, a controversial figure, to say the least, at the Bulgarian National Library. Then a delegation led by the president, and comprising members of government, dignitaries of the Orthodox Church, and Simeon II, the son of the former king and himself a former prime minister, laid flowers before memorial plaques honoring King Boris and his wife, Queen Giovanna, as "saviors of the Bulgarian Jews." These plaques had first been installed in Israel on the initiative of descendants of Bulgarian Jews based in the United States but were returned to Bulgaria in the wake of a July 2000 decision by a commission appointed by Yad Vashem and presided over by Polish-born Israeli Supreme Court justice (and president of Yad Vashem's Righteous Among the Nations Commission) Moshe Bejski. The commission determined that the role King Boris played in deporting the Jews from the occupied territories meant that such a monument could not remain in the memorial "Bulgarian forest," not far from Jerusalem.[10] The absence of the leadership of the Organization of the Jews in Bulgaria Šalom, was unprecedented. On that occasion, Professor Oskar publicly relayed the concerns of the Bulgarian Jewish community regarding commemorations that "present[ed] a distorted history of the Holocaust."[11]

Two days later, in his address at the memorial of the 7,144 Macedonian Jews in Skopje, the president of North Macedonia, Stevo Pendarovski, officially asked Bulgaria to publicly acknowledge the historical facts and to apologize for its role in the deportation of Macedonia's Jews during World War II: "The authentic meaning of the word 'justice' in both Hebrew and Macedonian points to what corresponds to the truth. Justice means to recognize and name the truth and for it to be respected by all. Reconciliation requires an apology about the role of the then-profascist government in Sofia in the deportation of the Macedonian Jews."[12] This statement was broadly understood in Bulgaria as part and parcel of an anti-Bulgarian campaign, at

---

10   Ofer, "Tormented Memories," 137–56.

11   David I. Klein, "Bulgarian Jews Skipped an Official Ceremony Marking 80 Years since Their Rescue from the Nazis: Why?," *Jewish Telegraphic Agency*, March 15, 2023, https://www.jta.org/2023/03/15/global/bulgarian-jews-skipped-an-official-ceremony-marking-80-years-since-their-rescue-from-the-nazis-why.

12   "Pendarovski: Za da ima pomiruvanje, Bugarija treba da se izvini za deportacijata na makedonskite Evrei," *Republika.mk*, December 3, 2023, https://republika.mk/vesti/makedonija/pendarovski-za-da-ima-pomiruvane-bugarija-treba-da-se-izvini-za-deportatsijata-na-makedonskite-evrei/.

a moment when the relationship between the two countries had reached a low point.

By June 12, the Bulgarian, Greek, Macedonian, and Serbian Jewish communities issued a statement recalling the historical coincidence, eighty years prior, "of unspeakable tragedy and of overwhelming humanity." They emphasized the duty "to preserve the memory of the Shoah and acknowledge . . . the common threats and opportunities" to its preservation. "A number of public figures are attempting to change, distort, and rewrite the history of the Holocaust by shifting responsibility from pro-Nazi allies and collaborators to the Nazi regime," they further asserted, insisting that "only united as Jewish communities, can our voice and the voices of our ancestors be heard and preserved."[13]

Meanwhile, Bulgarian intellectual milieus have become more divided than ever. While the head of the Institute of History of the Bulgarian Academy of Sciences, Professor Vačkov, insisted in a television interview that "Bulgaria could not oppose sending people to work in the Reich,"[14] three other statements began to circulate in support of the new state policy. The first, released in November 2022, centered on the question of fascism. Denying the existence of such a regime in pre-1944 Bulgaria, the signatories claimed:

> With regard to the implementation of anti-Semitic legislation and the restrictive actions against the Jewish population, the rulers in Sofia are under constant pressure from the German representatives in the country. . . . This universal attitude [the absence of hostile sentiments toward Jews] largely explains the failure of T. Danneker's mission in the spring of 1943 to deport Jews from the old borders of Bulgaria to the camps in Poland. . . . The behavior of Tsar Boris III shows that the anti-Jewish legislation in

13 The Memorandum of Understanding, released on June 12, 2023, was signed by Prof. Aleksandǎr Oskar, president of Šalom; David Saltiel, president of the board of the Jewish communities of Greece; Pepo Levi, president of the Jewish community of the Republic of North Maedonia; Aleksandar Albahari, president of the Jewish community of Serbia; and WJC general counsel Menachem Rosensaft. The text was also read by Professor Oskar at the international conference "Survival of the Jews in Bulgaria and Deportation from Yugoslav and Greek Territories under Bulgarian Occupation: A Divided History," convened by the Mémorial de la Shoah in Paris on June 25, 2023 (with Prof. Nadège Ragaru as scientific organizer of the conference).

14 "Prof. Vačkov: Bǎlgarija ne e možela da se protivopostavja na izpraštaneto na hora na rabota v Rajha," *Lice v Lice*, on the private television channel BTV, March 13, 2023, https://www.btv.bg/shows/lice-v-lice/videos/prof-vachkov-balgarija-ne-e-mozhela-da-se-protivopostavja-na-izprashtaneto-na-hora-za-rabota-v-rajha.html.

Bulgaria was completely imported from outside; it has a conjunctural character and does not reflect the understanding of the main political player in the country—the monarch.[15]

The second initiative, which took the form of an open letter distributed at the end of February 2023 by "citizens and members of civil society organizations"—including several scholars—asked that any March 10 commemoration be held in front of the plaques dedicated to King Boris and Queen Giovanna. This, in turn, would take shape as an "act of recognition, and also an act in the defense of the historical truth and the value of Bulgaria."[16] Finally, the third petition, promoted by eleven historians, mostly from the Bulgarian Academy of Sciences, claimed that the Bulgarian state had been in no position to oppose the deportation from territories under German control.[17]

By contrast, other Bulgarian intellectuals (historians, sociologists, philosophers) penned a strongly worded statement calling on the Bulgarian state to recognize "the responsibility of the Bulgarian state in the persecution and deportation of the Jews during the Second World War from the occupied territories."[18] The call—which before its official release on February 28 already bore the signatures of more than thirty academics, intellectuals, and public figures, including some from the arts—noted that Bulgaria's historical policy could be construed as "negationism" as defined by the International Holocaust Remembrance Alliance (IHRA), an organization Bulgaria had joined in 2018. By March 27, this initiative had collected upwards of 264 additional signatures, mostly from Bulgarian intellectuals and artists.[19] Finally, ahead of the commemorations, Bulgarian journalist Emmy Baruh

---

15   "Imalo li e fašitski režim v Bălgarija? Stanovišteto na 22-ma istorici ot BAN: Fašismăt nikoga ne idva na vlast v Bălgarija, zajavjavat vodešti učeni i pripomnjat istoričeski fakti," *Offnews.bg*, November 23, 2022, https://m.offnews.bg/ news/Istoriia_18809/Imalo-li-e-fashitki-rezhim-v-Balgariia-Stanovishteto-na-22-ma-istori_790134.html; "Stanovište na bălgarski istorici po văprosa: Imalo li fashitki režim v Bălgarija?," https://www.bas.bg/?p=41867.

16   "Otkrito pismo ot iniciativna grupa za dostojno obeljazvane na 80-godišninata ot spasjavaneto na bălgarskite evrei," reprinted by *Dnevnik*, https://www. dnevnik.bg/analizi/2023/03/01/4455522_spasiavaneto_na_bulgarskite_ evrei_diskusiiata_za/.

17   By March 28, the petition has received twenty-seven signatures. https://www. peticiq.com/393491.

18   "Priziv za priznavane ot bălgarskata dăržava na otgovornostta i v presledvaneto i deportiraneto na evreite prez Vtorata svetovna vojna," reprinted by *Dnevnik*, https://www.dnevnik.bg/analizi/2023/03/01/4455522_spasiavaneto_na_ bulgarskite_evrei_diskusiiata_za/.

19   https://www.peticiq.com/392570.

wrote an open letter to President Rumen Radev in which she stated that "what we choose to remember and what we choose to omit when telling our own story is a mark of wisdom, courage, and dignity."[20]

Tracing how the history of the Holocaust in Bulgaria became caught up in such painfully divisive debates, exploring how narrating this past came to serve a diverse array of causes: these are the raisons d'être of the book the reader now holds in her hands. More specifically, this volume aims to explain how, out of a complex past, one single facet—the nondeportation of the Bulgarian Jews, understood as a "rescue"—has become the primary way of narrating the history of World War II in Bulgaria and abroad. In other words, the Holocaust north of the River Danube became, to its south, a "rescue." This book traces the legal, political, and cultural stakes, as well as the multiple local, regional, and international spaces where these understandings of the war were formulated, circulated, and appropriated beginning in 1944. And it shows how Jewish wartime destinies came to constellate around a broad range of (only weakly related) topics and cleavages. Ultimately, this research brings Jews themselves back into the lived experience, writing, and transmission of the historical events.

Against such a background, there is little wonder that this book became enmeshed in the debates that surrounded the eightieth anniversary, and, more broadly, the rewritings of the history of World War II. Initially published in French at the end of October 2020, the volume was released in Bulgarian in October 2022, at the moment when the preparations for the commemoration of the "rescue of the Bulgarian Jews" were gaining momentum. A few days later, on November 2, 2022, Professor Oskar, the head of Šalom, published a photo of himself on his Facebook page reading the book.[21] The professor also spoke at the two book launches organized by the publishing house Kritika i Humanizăm (KH—Critique & Humanism) and moderated by its director, Antoaneta Koleva—one at the Goethe Institute in Sofia on December 2, and the other at the Jewish Cultural House on December 15.[22] Excerpts from the book were reprinted on the human rights website *Librev.bg*, in the cultural weekly *Kultura*, as well as in the daily newspaper *Dnevnik.bg*, the latter attracting around 9,300 readers over a couple of days. Bulgarian journalist Tatjana Vaksberg, who in 2015 had coordinated a new edition of the foundational archive collection originally assembled by Natan

---

20 https://m.facebook.com/story.php?story_fbid=pfbid0fvNqcYMrKyCH
    Zy1v19i1NyQ6cW181FNh9XjyJdhRv84hnqVHSEUTqpz5xsvT3Go5l
    &id=689476667.

21 https://www.facebook.com/photo/?fbid=10160002974306071&se
    t=a.74496591070.

22 https://www.facebook.com/CritiqueAndHumanism/
    videos/613605353785600.

Grinberg in the winter of 1944–45,[23] reviewed the book for the Bulgarian section of *Free Europe* (*Svobodna evropa*) website.[24] Interviews on national television,[25] radio,[26] and in the press followed.[27]

The volume's publication provoked lively discussion and debate. News of its release circulated through social media and by word of mouth, and week after week, between emails to the author and comments posted online, it became clear that many had long awaited a scholarly analysis completed by an external observer—one who was not personally entangled in the controversies between supporters and critics of King Boris III, between former Communists and anti-communists, between and among Jews in Bulgaria, Israel, and other countries. In 2008, the historian Nadja Danova, research director at the Bulgarian Academy of Sciences, had stumbled upon documents relating to the deportations from Northern Greece while conducting research on nineteenth-century Bulgarian history. From the moment she read those records, including the list of Jews by name, young and old, even infants, who were rounded up in March 1943, Danova began to pursue countless studies,[28] as well as a thorough investigation into Bulgarian archives—a task in which she was soon joined by economic historian Roumen Avramov.[29] In 2013, the pair published two volumes of Bulgarian archival records on the deportations from the occupied territories.[30]

However, whereas in the following years the number of documents accessible to the public continued to grow (including through the digitization of archives by the Bulgarian Central State Archives), no Bulgarian scholarly publication ever materialized about Jews' wartime predicaments in territories under Bulgarian control. Of late, several inroads have been made by nonprofessional historians, including documentarist Jacky Comforty and writer and

---

23   Grinberg, *Dokumenti* (2015).

24   Tatjana Vaksberg, "'Po-dobre de ne se govori': Kak Holokosta stana razkaz za nešto drugo," *Svobodnaevropa.bg*, December 16, 2022, https://www.svobodnaevropa.bg/a/32178701.html.

25   On the television show *Kultura.bg*, on Channel 1 of Bulgarian National Television (BNT), and on the show *Istorija.bg*, on Channel 1 of BNT.

26   BNR programs *Horizont* and *Hristo Botev*; private radio channel Darik Radio.

27   "Nadež Ragaru: Bălgarskite vlasti sa bili săučastnici v deportaciite na evreite ot 'novite zemi,'" *Capital.bg*, March 24, 2023; "Nadež Ragaru: Sporăt za 'spasenieto' i 'oceljavaneto,'" *Kultura*, March 13, 2023, 4–8.

28   Nadia Danova, "La Bulgarie et l'Holocauste: État des recherches sur le problème et perspectives," *Études balkaniques*, no. 4 (2012): 18–44.

29   Roumen Avramov wrote on the Aryanization of Jewish properties: Avramov, *"Spasenie" i padenie*.

30   Danova and Avramov, *Deportiraneto*.

painter Martha Aladjem Bloomfield, both of Bulgarian Jewish descent.[31]
Bulgarian Jewish musicologist and writer Lea Koen has also written novels and historical essays on these events.[32] Yet, as the scholar Raymond
Detrez has noted, no study has addressed "the way both the salvation and
the deportation have been presented in Communist and postcommunist
Bulgarian narratives."[33]

This book's invitation to readers—to accompany the author step by step
in the investigation, to judge the material evidence for themselves, and to
take the retelling of this history into their own hands—may have lent a
renewed sense of hope to those intellectuals and human rights activists who,
in Bulgaria and beyond, wish to foster a critical rereading of the national
historical canon. At the time of writing this preface, it is impossible to know
how Bulgaria's politics of history will evolve. But recent developments have
without a doubt confirmed one observation made herein. Controversies do
not simply register the state of affairs; they raise new questions, introduce
new stakeholders, and require that key issues and tactics be redefined.

This discussion is now reaching an English-speaking audience that may
not be familiar with the history of the Holocaust in Southeast Europe and
the (mostly) Sephardic Jews. I would like to thank Series Editor Timothy
Snyder for having accepted this piece as part of the Rochester Studies in East
and Central Europe series that he coordinates, Editorial Director Sonia Kane
for her sensitive and efficient guidance in seeing this project to completion,
editor Robert Fullilove for his outstandingly precise and rigorous copyediting, as well as Assistant Editor Chris Adler-France, and Production Editor
Tracey Engel for their great job on the book. Were it not for the remarkable
translation work done by Holocaust historian David A. Rich and translator Dr. Victoria Baena, the complex narrative strategies of the book could
never have journeyed from French into English. To both of them, my deepest gratitude is due. David provided continued support and encouragement
for the project with a generosity seldom encountered today. I owe him more
than I can say. All my thanks are also addressed to Anastasia Fairchild for her
elegant assistance. Finally, I wish to express my gratitude to the two anonymous reviewers of the manuscript, as well as to Maria Todorova for her delicate and always stimulating remarks.

---

31 Comforty with Bloomfield, *Stolen Narrative.*

32 Koen, *Spasenie, gonenija i holokost*, and *Rafael* (Sofia: Enthusiast, 2017).

33 Raymond Detrez, "Book Review: Nadège Ragaru, *'Et les Juifs bulgares
    furent sauvés': Une histoire des savoirs sur la Shoah en Bulgarie,*" *Colloquia
    Humanistica* 10 (2021), https://ispan.waw.pl/journals/index.php/ch/
    article/view/ch.2608/7313.

In France, Julie Gazier's enthusiastic endorsement of the project at the Presses de Sciences Po gave me full freedom in choosing the kind of investigation and narrative form I wished to deploy. For this freedom, I am immensely grateful. In Bulgaria, publisher, translator, and philosopher Antoaneta Koleva, director of Kritika i Humanizăm, achieved wonders: she cotranslated and meticulously edited the Bulgarian version of the text. All my thanks also go to Roumen Avramov, who cotranslated that volume and wrote one of its two forewords; to Liliana Deyanova, who authored the second foreword and gave graciously of her time in checking sundry sources, dates, and quotations. Were it not for the acumen, rigor, and generosity of archivist and historian Marijana Piskova, the book would not have seen the light of day. All my thanks are also due to Asja Enčeva for her subtle and diligent assistance. The friendship of the "Blagoevgrad group" (Milena Angelova, Anastasija Kirilova, Nurie Muratova, Anastasija Pašova, Kristina Popova, Petăr Vodeničarov, and Sergej Vučlov) and of Vanessa Voisin, Valérie Pozner, and Clara Royer was a tremendous source of hope. I also thank Professor Eyal Ginio, Ilya Grinberg, David Ieroham, Emil Rahamimov, Professor Iris Rahamimov, and Andrea Simon for sharing private archives with me. A note of gratitude, finally, to Maël Le Noc, whose geographic insights allowed me to further explore the visual archive of March 1943 discussed in chapter 3.

For their permission to publish materials from their collections, I wish to express my gratitude and to thank the archivists, librarians, and directors at museums: United States Holocaust Memorial Museum, Holocaust Memorial Center for the Jews of Macedonia, Jewish Historical Museum in Belgrade, and Mémorial de la Shoah in Paris; archives: Bulgarian Central State Archives, Archives of the Committee for Disclosing the Documents and Announcing Affiliation of Bulgarian Citizens to the State Security and Intelligence Services of the Bulgarian National Army, State Military Historical Archives of Bulgaria, Archives of the Bulgarian National Film Library, Archives of the Bulgarian Academy of Sciences, USHMM, State Archives of the Republic of Macedonia (today North Macedonia), Federal Archives of Germany, Hessian Central State Archives, Yad Vashem Archives, Archives of the Ghetto Fighters' House in Israel, Archives of the Jewish Historical Museum in Belgrade, Serbia, Archives of Mémorial de la Shoah in Paris; and libraries—New York Public Library, Regional Library of Munich, Library of the Institute for East and Southeast European Studies in Regensburg, Bulgarian National Library, and National and University Library at Sv. Kliment Ohridski. I reserve a special thanks for Kalina Ančova, Bruno Boyer, Ulf Brunnbauer, Judith Cohen, Angel Čorapčiev, Gudrun Franke, Galina Genčeva, Vanja Gezenko, Frosina Gjurčevska, Mihail Gruev, Radu Ioanid, Borijana Mateeva, Rumijana Nedjalkova, Professor Aleksănder Oskar, Livia Parnes, Marijana Piskova,

Vojislava Radovanović, Goran Sadikarijo, Mario Schaeffer, Carina Schmidt, Milena Todorakova, Vărban Todorov, and Lindsay Zarwell.

I am grateful to the Scientific Advisory Board of Sciences Po for its financial support in carrying out field research in Germany, Bulgaria, the United States, Israel, Macedonia, and Serbia between 2013 and 2018. I also received financial backing for archival and book acquisitions from the French National Agency for Research (ANR) project "WW2CRIMESONTRIAL1943–1991: Nazi war crimes in the Court—Central and Eastern Europe 1943–1991" coordinated by Vanessa Voisin (Alma Mater Studiorum–University of Bologna). Sciences Po's Library, the Center for International Studies (CERI) of Sciences Po, the GDR "Connaissance de l'Europe médiane," as well as the Fondation pour la mémoire de la Shoah (FMS) provided funding for publishing this book as an Open Access digital monograph.

Portions of chapter 1 and chapter 3 evolved from ideas first presented in "The Prosecution of Anti-Jewish Crimes in Bulgaria: Fashioning a Master Narrative of the Second World War (1944–1945)," *East European Politics and Societies* 33, no. 4 (2019): 941–75, and "Bulgaria as Rescuer? Film Footage of the March 1943 Deportation and Its Reception across the Iron Curtain," *East European Jewish Affairs* 50, no. 1 (2021): 36–69, respectively. Material from these publications is used with permission.

Several colleagues and friends have read, discussed, or assisted this research at various times: Natalia Aleksiun, Andrew Apostolou, Emmy Baruh, Rika Benveniste, Martha Aladjem Bloomfield, Xavier Bougarel, Ulf Brunnbauer, Antonela Capelle-Pogăcean, Nathalie Clayer, Emil Cohen, Sonia Combe, Nadja Danova, Stefan Dečev, Jean-Marc Dreyfus, Tomislav Dulić, Gilles Favarel-Garrigues, Jackie Feldman, Catherine Gousseff, Paul Gradvohl, Hannes Grandits, Stilijan Jotov, Krasimir Kănev, Krasimir Kavaldjiev, Éric Le Bourhis, Sylvie Lindeperg, Antoine Marès, Tchavdar Marinov, Nicolas Mariot, Élise Massicard, Yuliana Metodieva, Jaklina Naumovski, Irina Nedeva, Catherine Perron, Sophie Reiter, Sandrine Revet, Menachem Rosensaft, Paul-André Rosental, Jacques Rupnik, Sabine Rutar, the late David Shneer, Johanna Siméant-Germanos, Ilin Stanev, Jolanta Sujecka, Ania Szczepanska, Irina Tcherneva, Maria Todorova, Stefan Troebst, Aleksandăr Vezenkov, and Alexander Zöller.

Finally, I would like to dedicate this book to my mother, to Яна, to Antonela, and to the memory of Pierre Hassner (January 31, 1933–May 26, 2018).

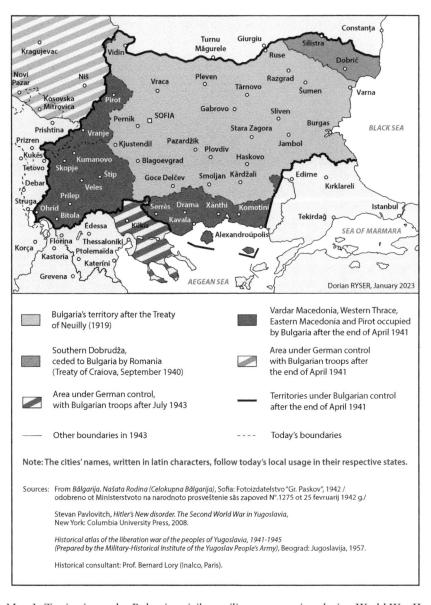

Map 1: Territories under Bulgarian civil or military occupation during World War II.

Introduction

March 12, 2018. The press spreads the news at the very last minute: for the first time, a high-ranking member of the Bulgarian government will take part in a tribute to the 7,144 Jewish victims of the Holocaust in Macedonia (today North Macedonia), land occupied by Bulgaria—a "part ally, part satellite" state of the Third Reich[1]—during World War II. The expectations are high. It is unclear what the tenor of the message to be delivered by Prime Minister Bojko Borisov will be: after seventy-five years, will he recognize the responsibility of the Bulgarian state for the arrests and deportations from the territory that the German victors in Yugoslavia entrusted to its administration, back in April 1941?

In the former Monopol tobacco warehouse in Skopje, where the Macedonian Jews were held before being transferred to Nazi-occupied Poland in March 1943, a narrow strip of red carpet has been placed at a right angle to a commemorative plaque. The Bulgarian prime minister slowly approaches a wreath of white roses wrapped in the national colors of Bulgaria. With a careful gesture, he straightens the satin line, as if by introducing order into the tribute's composition he might straighten the very course of the past. He bows before the monument erected in memory of the victims. Moments earlier, his Macedonian counterpart, Prime Minister Zoran Zaev, made a series of identical gestures: the satin band, the correcting motion, the torso bent forward. Only the bouquet was different, its own reds and yellows taken from the Macedonian flag. The politicians, members of the diplomatic corps, and representatives of Jewish organizations gathered to attend the commemoration follow them with their gaze.

For the span of an instant, the identical, meditative gestures seem to become a synecdoche for the memorial community. Then come the talks of the two prime ministers, which blur the prior sense of proximity between the Macedonians and the Bulgarians. The Macedonian prime minister takes the floor. He refers to the death of the Jewish Macedonians as "the result of inhuman forces against civilization, the world, against love and all that

---

1   The expression is from Hilberg, *Destruction of the Jews*, 2:743. Recently, István Deák has preferred the notion of "politically independent allies" to designate Finland, Italy, Slovakia, Hungary, Romania, Croatia, and Bulgaria, which "all had their own heads of state, ministers, diplomacy, armies, national police and administrations." See Deák, *Europe on Trial*, 7.

is good and human."[2] And he speaks of the future: "Today we draw lessons from the past in order to illuminate a path into a future we will choose together. The acceptance of difference, cooperation, and friendship are values that we accept and that we share in everything that we do, so that this may never happen again." However, the connection between an exhortation to memory and the production of a collective future is the only common thread between his statement and that of his Bulgarian host.

Indeed, the institution of the Bulgarian executive power and the incumbent are present, but the "body of the king"—in Ernst Kantorowicz's well-known formulation—has traveled from Bulgaria without the words that at least a portion of the audience expected.[3] Ironically, a minute detail amplifies the effect provoked by the Bulgarian head of government's speech: there is no simultaneous translation. Foreign guests from the Conference on Jewish Material Claims against Germany, the USHMM, Yad Vashem, and the Mémorial de la Shoah in Paris, among others, stand motionless in their navy blue and black suits before a voice they do not understand, caught in what resembles a foreign film devoid of subtitles. Given the proximity between the Bulgarian and Macedonian Slavic languages, the words of Bojko Borisov are intelligible to nationals from these two countries—but only to them. This shared linguistic understanding, however, fails to bring about a common vision of the past. Members of the audience observe the Macedonian faces in slow decomposition.

Let us listen to the Bulgarian prime minister:

> Today the weather is nice and sunny; we are friends; but if we try for a moment to imagine those men in black uniform, the Nazis who were here and the inhuman acts that they inflicted on living human beings. . . . On Saturday, in one of the largest synagogues in Europe, and certainly the most beautiful in Sofia, there was a ceremony attended by representatives of the world's Jewish organizations, with many dear guests; we honored the memory and bowed humbly before the Bulgarian people, the Church, and the public figures who, in perhaps the most terrible moments, managed to save 48,000 Jews; and for that, the Bulgarian people deserve great consideration. Of course, we feel a great sense of affliction; this is why we are here today, because we must not forget any human lives, none of the men sent to burn in camps not so very long ago. Just twenty years ago, on the territories of the Balkans, terrible events, no less bloody, took place. The meaning [of our presence]—beyond the fact of showing our reverence and our pain before those who were killed—is to draw conclusions, to understand that,

---

2   All translations from Macedonian and Bulgarian are the author's.
3   This point was also underscored by historian Roumen Avramov on the Bulgarian private television channel TvEvropa on March 13, 2018.

in the Balkans, we must build and work together. . . . We have all come to honor this memory and to express our grief together with the Macedonian people for those who did not manage to escape and return alive from the Nazi machine and from Himmler. Thank you for your invitation.

The Bulgarian chief executive has spoken without notes. Though a statement had been prepared, he does not read it. Could this impromptu change of mind account for the missing translation from Bulgarian into Macedonian and English?[4] The head of government has paid homage to the Jews who, according to him, were deported following a decision of "the Nazis." Additionally, mentioning the victims has allowed him to bring to light the exceptional fate of the 48,000 Jewish citizens of Bulgaria who were *not* deported.

On the front steps, a cluster of journalists await the participants. One tense male voice asks the Bulgarian leader:

A citizen of Europe, with a critical question to ask. Is it so difficult for you to ask for forgiveness?

I beg your pardon?

Is it difficult for you to ask for forgiveness? These people want to hear that from Bulgaria.

[Forgiveness] for what?

The Holocaust. Because at the time, the situation was one that you, Bulgaria, were . . .

I can only bow before the Bulgarian people who went up against the system and saved 48,000 Jews. With respect to that other propaganda, not before me.

I'm not talking about propaganda, but . . .[5]

When considering this episode, one cannot fail to recall the date of July 16, 1992, when for the first time a French president, namely François Mitterrand, attended the fifty-year commemoration of 1942 roundups at the Vélodrome d'Hiver in Paris but failed to deliver a speech. It is also hard

---

4   Several sources suggest that an explicit recognition of the role of the Bulgarian state had been considered following discussions between the Bulgarian authorities, the leaders of the Jewish communities of Macedonia and Bulgaria, and the leadership of the WJC. The last-minute decision not to recognize that complicit role would have resulted from bitter differences among the members of the Bulgarian coalition government.

5   Audio file "20180312: Borissov Kommentar," press service of the Prime Minister.

not to remember that three years later his successor, Jacques Chirac, did acknowledge the French Republic's shared responsibility in the wartime persecution and deportation of Jews to Nazi concentration camps.[6] The French and the Bulgarian historical configurations differ, without a doubt: whereas the surrender of the French Third Republic in June 1940 paved the way for German occupation and collaboration by the Vichy regime, the Bulgarian monarchy took the side of the Reich and joined the Tripartite Pact in March 1941, all while refusing to declare war on the Soviet Union. In exchange for letting the Wehrmacht use its territory to launch a military assault on the kingdoms of Yugoslavia and Greece in the spring of 1941, Bulgaria was granted the occupation of most of Vardar Macedonia and Pirot (Yugoslavia),[7] as well as Western Thrace and Eastern Macedonia (Greece) in April 1941,[8] thereby achieving satisfaction of its irredentist aspirations toward its neighbors (see p. xxv).

However, in the two countries the ways of framing questions surrounding wartime events share several common features. Indeed, during socialism, in Bulgarian Communist historiography World War II was presented as a period of de facto occupation by the Nazis. The role of the partisan movement was magnified, while the Bulgarian resistance was heralded as embodying, if not the legal continuity of the state, at least its political legitimacy. In so doing, the Communist narrative relegated responsibility beyond the resistance movement and (by metonymy) the Bulgarian people, confining the burden instead to a handful of "fascist" traitors to the homeland.

Furthermore, as in France, questions of sovereignty have haunted Bulgarian discussions regarding the past since the end of World War II. How should the legal status of the occupied territories be defined? Should they be seen as land incorporated into the Bulgarian state? As regions under

---

6   On France's painstaking attempt at dealing with its wartime past, see, among a plethora of scholarly works, the classic pieces by Henry Rousso, *The Vichy Syndrome* and *Vichy, an Ever-Present Past*; and by Annette Wieviorka, *Déportation et génocide* and *The Era of the Witness*. On the historical facts, see Marrus and Paxton, *Vichy France*; Paxton, *Vichy France: Old Guard*; Joly, *Vichy dans la "solution finale"*; and Klarsfeld, *Vichy-Auschwitz*.

7   Vardar Macedonia—a territory that essentially corresponds to the present-day Republic of North Macedonia—was at that time part of the *banovina* of Vardar, a province of the Kingdom of Yugoslavia created by the 1929 reform of the administrative division of the country. In 1941, although most of the region fell to Bulgaria, Italy obtained the western fringe.

8   In Bulgarian, this area is known as "Belomorie" (with reference to the White Sea, the Aegean); in English, as "Thrace" or "Western Thrace." According to Greek administrative divisions prior to the war, this territory includes "Eastern Macedonia" (Anatoliki Makedonia) and "Western Thrace" (Dytiki Thraki).

temporary administration, where Bulgarian law and bureaucracy, nonetheless, would have prevailed? Or as territories on which Nazi Germany could wield power, ultimately? In contrast to an internationally recognized annexation, would a de facto administration have circumscribed the decision-making autonomy of Bulgaria, vis-à-vis its powerful ally, on the "Jewish question"? And if it is appropriate to speak of Bulgarian responsibility, at what level should such responsibility be located—in the government, in a political regime, or in the state itself?

It is clear just how intricate the arguments were that led the French Council of State to conclude, in two landmark decisions,[9] that the actions of the French state bureaucracy committed between June 16, 1940, and August 9, 1944 (when republican law was restored), did enjoin state responsibility, before specifying that the French Committee of National Liberation and the Provisional Government of the French Republic had remained as the repositories of national sovereignty, ensuring the continuity of the Republic.[10] One country, two states?

In Bulgaria, the complex political, legal, and moral issues regarding the state's complicity in the roundups, internments, and transport of Jews from occupied territories only sharpen upon consideration of what has long been presented as a Bulgarian exception: the "rescue of the Bulgarian Jews."

On the "Rescue of the Jews" and National Exceptionalism: A Riddle of Received Wisdom

During World War II, the policy of the Bulgarian state toward the Jewish population under its control showed two faces: in the "old" kingdom—Bulgaria's borders before April 1941—and the "new" kingdom—the territories of Yugoslavia and Greece occupied after April 1941.[11] In the zones of occupation, in March 1943 an estimated 11,343 Jews—that is, nearly the entirety of the local Jewish communities—were arrested, interned in transit

---

9   Papon Judgment, Conseil d'État [CE], Assembly [ass.], April 12, 2002; Hoffmann-Glemane litigation opinion, CE, ass., February 16, 2009.

10   Conseil d'État, April 13, 2018, no. 410939, Association of the Museum of Letters and Manuscripts. The author wishes to thank Claire Andrieu and Marc-Olivier Baruch for their insights into the French case. See also Baruch, *Des lois indignes?*, 66–99.

11   Chary, *Bulgarian Jews*; Matkovski, *Tragedijata na Evreite od Makedonija*; Hilberg, *Destruction of the Jews*, 1378–1404; Ragaru, "Jews of Bulgaria," 139–75.

camps, and deported to Nazi-occupied Poland,[12] where they were exterminated. The deportations were requested by the Reich, negotiated with the
Bulgarian government through the German legation in Sofia, and finalized
by the Commissariat for Jewish Affairs (*Komisartsvo za evrejskite văprosi*,
KEV), an institution created in late August 1942 to design and supervise
Bulgaria's anti-Jewish policies—under the guidance of Adolf Eichmann's special envoy to Bulgaria, SS *Hauptsturmführer* Theodor Dannecker, who is
infamously remembered today for his role in the deportation of Jews from
France (1942) and Italy (1944). The arrests were authorized by a series of
decrees adopted by the Bulgarian Council of Ministers at the beginning
of March 1943 and carried out by the Bulgarian police in close coordination with the Bulgarian army and occupation authorities. Members of the
German police took part in escorting convoys to the Treblinka extermination camp; the Gestapo was also involved in surveilling temporary internment centers.

Following the signing on February 22, 1943, of an accord between
Dannecker and the Bulgarian commissioner for Jewish Affairs, Aleksandăr
Belev, pertaining to the deportation of 20,000 Jews from the occupied ter-
ritories, the commissioner ordered local delegates for Jewish Affairs in the
country to draw up lists of Bulgarian Jews deemed "undesirable." Both
Dannecker and Belev were cognizant of the fact that no more than 12,000
Jews lived in Bulgarian-held Yugoslav and Greek territories. This allowed for
the inclusion of Bulgarian Jews in the deportation scheme. Belev personally
approved some 8,400 names. The arrests in the "old" kingdom began on
March 8, 1943.

The Bulgarian case was unique, however, in that in the wake of protests by Jews and non-Jews—including local notables, parliamentarians,
and Orthodox Church dignitaries—these deportations, though prepared
and initiated, were subsequently called off. On March 9, 1943, following one or two meetings with a delegation of citizens from the Bulgarian
city of Kjustendil and influential members of parliament, including Deputy
Speaker of the National Assembly Dimităr Pešev, the minister of the interior and public health, Petăr Gabrovski—perhaps after consulting with Prime
Minister Bogdan Filov, members of the chancellery of King Boris III, or
even the monarch himself—gave an order for the arrests to be suspended
and for those already being held to be released. In early May 1943, the
commissioner submitted a new deportation plan. The cabinet granted the
expulsion of Bulgarian Jews from Sofia and other cities, but not their deportation abroad; this was the moment at which German military setbacks were

---

12 Details on estimates of the number of Jews rounded up and deported can be
found in the appendix.

making a Nazi victory in Europe seem more unlikely. Western opinion and a consideration of decisions made in other European countries were gaining import in the regime's calculations and decisions. At that time, other Axis members (namely, Romania and Hungary) had not allowed their own Jewish citizens to be remanded into Nazi hands. Ultimately, some 48,000 Jews holding Bulgarian citizenship—that is, the near total Bulgarian Jewish community—survived the war.

Since the end of World War II, in Bulgaria, the United States, Israel, and various European states, a dominant narrative on the fate of the Jews in wartime Bulgaria has crystallized. This narrative rests on three pillars: first, the Holocaust (in Europe) is translated into the "rescue of the Jews" (in Bulgaria); second, this nondeportation is presented as an exceptional historical fact;[13] finally, the "rescue" is attributed to a supposedly unique Bulgarian quality: national tolerance toward minorities. While there have been loud and bitter public debates, these have mostly revolved around hierarchies of merit in the "rescue of the Bulgarian Jews." Gradually, literary and visual patterns were woven by this loom into a fabric that has remained rather unresponsive to political, social, and cultural transformations, as well as to changes in memory regimes in Bulgaria, in Europe more broadly, and worldwide. No matter the protagonists and episodes chosen, a single story has continued to be told, one that outsources crimes to individuals while nationalizing virtues as collective. Not that the extermination of Jews in the occupied territories was ever entirely obscured. The pattern is even more puzzling: while the deportation for extermination of the Jews from occupied Yugoslavia and Greece was never completely muted, the deportations have been collapsed with acts associated with nondeportation and seem to have thinned out in the process. In public speeches and memory initiatives, in writings by professional and lay historians, in museum exhibitions and artistic works, traces of the destruction of the Jews have lingered in the form of laments over the inability to prevent their fatal destiny.

This book reconstructs the conditions of production and circulation of what have long been considered as true facts—"true" because they were widely believed. In particular, the investigation addresses the following questions: how should we explain that, out of a complex and contradictory past, a single facet—the nondeportation of Jews from the "old" kingdom understood as a "rescue"—has become the primary way of narrating and transmitting Bulgaria's role in the history of World War II not only to Bulgarians, but

---

13 In Bulgaria, the question of whether it is appropriate to place the expression "rescue of Bulgarian Jews" in quotation marks, or to prefer the notion of "survival" to that of "rescue," has been the subject of heated debate. In this work, which constitutes the representations of the past as the object of investigation, the expression will always be written with quotation marks.

to others in Europe, in the United States, in Israel, and elsewhere? Moreover, how ought we understand that the deportations, while not entirely obliterated, were rendered poorly visible under the dazzling light cast on them by the "rescue of the Bulgarian Jews"? How, more precisely, is it possible to fathom that information about these deportations has seemed barely relevant to reconstructing the history of World War II?

For the reader who might doubt that such received wisdom has made its way beyond the Balkans, one can marshal two recent instances, one involving a leading official of an American Jewish organization and the other a French philosopher of Bulgarian origin. In March 2018, on the occasion of the seventy-fifth anniversary of the March 1943 events, the president of the American Jewish Committee (AJC), David Harris, stated in New York: "Bulgaria occupies a very special place in our hearts, and it has for many years. . . . Although Bulgaria was an ally of the Third Reich during the Second World War, this did not prevent some brave Bulgarians—most notably, members of Parliament and the Church—from standing up and refusing to comply with the deportation orders. As a result, nearly 50,000 Jews were saved from the death camps. Now, sadly, not all Jews under Bulgarian rule were protected, but most were, and this act of bravery and brotherhood must never be forgotten."[14]

Equally emblematic is the book *La fragilité du bien: Le Sauvetage des Juifs bulgares* (The fragility of goodness: The rescue of the Bulgarian Jews), published in 1999 by Bulgarian-born French philosopher Tzvetan Todorov.[15] Without overlooking the deportations from the occupied territories, Todorov affirms in a lengthy introduction: "Two countries can remember their history with pride, since the collective protection of Jews was assured even though they were under German control: Denmark and Bulgaria."[16] The author relates his sense of surprise and admiration regarding the reading of Jewish war experiences offered by Hannah Arendt in 1961: "'With the approach of the Red Army,' Hannah Arendt wrote in *Eichmann in Jerusalem*, referring to Bulgaria, 'not a single Bulgarian Jew had been deported or had died an unnatural death.' And she added, 'I know of no attempt to explain the conduct of the Bulgarian people, which is unique in the belt of mixed

14   American Jewish Committee, "AJC Honors 75th Anniversary of Bulgarian Rescue of Nearly 50,000 Jews, Celebrates Friendship with Bulgaria Today," March 10, 2018, https://www.ajc.org/news/ajc-honors-75th-anniversary-of-bulgarian-rescue-of-nearly-50000-jews-celebrates-friendship.

15   Todorov, *La fragilité du bien*. This work was translated into English (Princeton University Press, 2004) and given a more cautious subtitle: *Why Bulgaria's Jews Survived the Holocaust.*

16   It may be worth recalling that Denmark, unlike Bulgaria, was not an Axis member.

populations.' How, indeed, to explain this miraculous accomplishment of goodness? . . . This volume was put together as an attempt to explain this fortuitous event."[17]

Knowledge about the Holocaust: Justice, Fiction, and Controversies

The scope of any investigation into the sites, modes, and agents that created knowledge of the fate of the Jews in areas administered by Bulgaria cannot be confined to the realms of academic or textbook history regarding anti-Jewish persecutions, for one simple reason: writing about the Holocaust has never been the sole province of professional historians. During and following World War II, awareness of the extermination of the Jews progressed at the intersection of Jewish and non-Jewish historians, jurists, artists, activists, and political actors, and among the fields of justice, history, politics, art, and remembrance institutions—as they reverberated upon, mutually influenced, and, at times, clashed with one another.[18]

The architecture of this book reflects such a commitment: throughout the chapters, I consider the production of judicial knowledge during the Bulgarian trials for anti-Jewish crimes of 1945; the negotiation of an "Eastern European" way of rendering fictionally the historical facts at the end of the 1950s; the Cold War circulations across the East-West divide of unique silent film footage showing the March 1943 roundup, transport, and deportation of Jews in Bulgarian-held lands (footage that was successively considered as documentary source, courtroom evidence, and testimony with memorial resonance); and finally, the knowledge requested and fashioned after 1989 within the framework of public controversies. Such a broad focus does not entail eliding differences in the nature, span, and use of these multiple approaches to the past. Nor do I want to suggest that such composite materials could ever be aggregated into a compact whole. Nevertheless, among these heterogeneous productions, situated differently in time and

---

17 Arendt is quoted here from the English translation of Todorov's book: *Fragility of Goodness*, 9–10; Her exact words are as follows: "not a single Bulgarian Jew had been deported or had died an unnatural death when, in August 1944, with the approach of the Red Army, the anti-Jewish laws were revoked. I know of no attempt to explain the conduct of the Bulgarian people, which is unique in the belt of mixed populations." See Arendt, *Eichmann in Jerusalem*, 188.

18 For a similar view of the role of cross-fertilization across social sectors and areas of public life in the forming of knowledge about the Holocaust, see Bohus, Hallama, and Stach, *Shadow of Anti-Fascism*, esp. "Introduction," 6.

space, we can find citations and correspondences that, without producing a single unified vision, outline a realm of the conceivable and the believable. It is within this space and this framework that differences in interpreting the events have been and continue to be formulated.

In defying rigid barriers between historical and lay knowledge, this inquiry also avoids any opposition between written, visual, and sound sources, which would give undue precedence or even exclusivity to the first of these in apprehending history. It is a prosaic observation, one summed up by Sarah Gensburger, that "this historical event [the Holocaust] was, from the start, represented (the unsayable was always visible)."[19] In addition to the production of feature films and visual footage documenting Jewish deportations and photographs (namely, of the end-of-war trials for anti-Jewish persecutions), I also examine the organization of exhibits, museums' staging choices, and the theatrical arena of parliamentary debates.

Recounting tales that have been ceaselessly retold, via mostly referential, but at times also imagined, narratives is the raison d'être of this project. But what status to accord to such narratives—those arts of saying and silencing, acts of constructing and mobilizing the past? In the 2000s, among historians, discussions of the relationship between history and narrative took off once again,[20] following two partially cross-pollinated paths. The first, interrogating and enriching contemporary forms of historical narration, was intended to spur the power of conviction or even seduction of history, within a professional field that had lost a degree of its majesty with the erosion of its readership, owing in part to competition from lay authors and artists who had taken hold of the historical material themselves.[21] Several major pieces have also invited an in-depth reconsideration of the (at times) uncertain boundaries between historical knowledge and personal history, first among them being the "nonfictional memoir" by Daniel Mendelsohn, *The Lost: A Search for Six of Six Million.*[22] In a remarkable essay, *Landscape of the Metropolis of Death,* eloquently subtitled *Reflections on Memory and Imagination,* Israeli historian Otto Dov Kulka, a specialist in the history of modern anti-Semitism and the history of Jews in Nazi Germany, and a Holocaust

---

19 Gensburger, "Voir et devoir voir le passé," 89.

20 A first generation of scholarly debate was prompted by the 1973 publication of Hayden White's *Metahistory: The Historical Imagination in Nineteenth-Century Europe.* One response to White's understanding of historical writing deserves particular note here: Roger Chartier, *On the Edge of the Cliff.* Paul Veyne has also dedicated remarkable pages to the issue of how the past is "intrigued"; that is, known precisely as it is turned into an intrigue, and yet truthful to the historical facts: Veyne, *Comment on écrit l'hisoire.*

21 Boucheron, "On nomme littérature la fragilité de l'histoire," 41–56; Jablonka, *L'Histoire est une littérature contemporaine.*

22 Mendelsohn, *The Lost.* See also Sands, *East West Street.*

survivor himself, challenged further the limits separating personal memory, imagination, and historical knowledge about the Holocaust.[23] Meanwhile, Dov Kulka's work—itself the result of the transcription onto paper of audio monologues recorded earlier—sheds light on how the intertwining between visual, sound, and textual modes of expression may advance our comprehension of the destruction of the European Jewry.

In the field of history of science, whose influence over historical writing among French scholars has significantly increased in the past decade, the second conduit involved the rediscovery of a "classical age" during which written and visual imagination began serving as proof. In the sixteenth and seventeenth centuries, fictional narratives indeed contributed to rendering observations credible, while heaven evaded divine or divinatory sciences.[24] Today, a reconsideration of the historical construction of the dichotomy between "subjectivity" and "objectivity" is called for, alongside an examination of how the involvement of the subject may contribute to the creation of knowledge.[25]

The following pages are indebted to these discussions. I share their aspiration to diversify documentation by varying the theaters of observation as well as to adopt a multiperspective approach in order to restitute the polyphony of the past. I too remain concerned with how literary skills and innovative forms of narration may contribute to historical knowledge. What follows also rests on one core premise. This book was not conceived as an inventory of interpretive mistakes placed in opposition to a single truth of the past. Rather, events and narrative are here seen as coproducers of facts. Chapter after chapter, new sources and new takes on the events serve to deepen both our comprehension of Jewish experiences and the knowledge produced about these experiences. Thereby, the scope of the plausible is gradually reduced, while no claim to a unique truth is made beyond the refutation of certain statements. Within a space delimited by its external borders alone, conflicts between contested meanings remain possible.

Contours of an Investigation

How were the temporal and spatial coordinates of the inquiry defined? The project as a whole is imbued with the notion of a journey. First, it covers a temporal span of seventy-five years, crosses the Cold War borders, and follows Jewish lives as their paths bifurcate in the diaspora and in Israel. Second, the objects whose traces we follow—argument-driven motifs, discursive

---

23   Kulka, *Metropolis of Death.*
24   Aït-Touati, *Fictions of the Cosmos.*
25   Daston and Galison, *Objectivity.*

registers, film footage, visual archives—continue to travel and undergo transformations, being reappropriated in the process. Finally, the movement of the actors narrating the story we are to tell echoes the walking practice of Walter Benjamin, the wandering of the flaneur (*Erfahrung*) understood as a vector of knowledge.[26] Mobility, here, acts as method and parable. It serves to designate the way in which knowledge was created, as well as the composition of knowledge *about* knowledge. Each chapter pauses at distinct sites and distinct moments without presupposing the existence of exclusive links between them. Rather, the contacts and frictions between these vantage points serve to assist the inquiry's progression.

Legal knowledge about the Holocaust—our first incursion into the past— was initially delivered in Bulgaria almost as the events unfolded, even before the end of the war. There was a cost to this concurrence: it distanced a past not yet over from a future nearly at hand, one propelled by the revolutionary momentum of communism. An understanding of days barely gone by was fated to act upon the present in order to advance political change. Page after page, the distance between past and present increases. Our second stop takes place in the late 1950s to early 1960s, a turning point when de-Stalinization was expected to make room for a political and cultural opening, one that the crushing of the Budapest revolution of 1956 nonetheless circumscribed. Those times were obsessed with the denunciation of what was presented as West Germany's failure to address Nazi crimes through the law. The building of partnerships between Soviet states, including in the sphere of (political) art, was intended to strengthen a brittle Eastern European bloc. The topics of World Word II, antifascism, and, incidentally, the Holocaust were some of the themes Bulgaria and East Germany tried to reconcile within the framework of a film coproduction.

In chapter 3, we move from a focus on a single moment (the end-of-war period or the late 1950s) to a time span dictated by our object of inquiry: that is, a few minutes of documentary footage that contain the only recorded images of Jewish deportations from the occupied territories of which any trace has been found to date. As we reconstruct the cultural biography of these film rushes in Bulgaria across the Berlin Wall, the images open up onto the 1960s and 1970s, when the Bulgarian socialist regime sought renewed legitimacy in the nationalization of selected episodes of the past. As socialist dreams began to unravel and failed to deliver on visions of greatness, the history of the "rescue of the Bulgarian Jews" was called upon to buttress a glorious future. The present, for its part, seemed to be slowing down. The slow motion was reassuring to some, but it would soon be met with impatience by the generations that had grown up under socialism. In 1989, the collapse

---

26   Benjamin, *Arcades Project*.

of the Communist regimes once again reconfigured the coordinates of the triangle between past, present, and future, while the new relevance conferred on the Holocaust in Eastern Europe was influenced by, although not a replication of, patterns of Western European collective memory. Situated in this postcommunist era, the two final chapters follow the paths of historiographical and memorial debates and lay out the internal fractures of the period—where revolution and Thermidor merge.

In this volume, the treatment of issues of temporality corresponds to a certain way of thinking about space. The expression "knowledge about the Holocaust in Bulgaria" might in this regard be misleading. Are we considering Bulgarian knowledge or knowledge of Bulgaria—or does the formulation rather refer to the location of the events alone? Obviously, it was impossible to keep to the limits of the nation-state, which, from the nineteenth century on, has striven to wedge history itself into a national frame. The question is, to the contrary, how to identify the sites from which a narrative that claimed to be national has been written, sanctioned, and legitimized and to examine closely the contested meanings associated with these territorial demarcations. Henceforth, instead of taking the grounds of inquiry for granted, we develop them out of observing the agents and their practices. The local, regional, and international scales are defined by the questions asked to the archives, printed documents, and other sources under examination. The degree of overlap between these loci becomes its own object of research. Ultimately, the spatial scope of the analysis emerges from the palimpsest of circulations of people, ideas, and things.

In short, if there is such a thing as Bulgaria—understood here as a space of knowledge production—it is constituted by way of connections whose capture requires that a multiscale perspective be adopted. The bounded territory is like an etching rising in relief from the darkened paper. It is in the number of crosshatched lines, fine or thick—in the ordered chaos of their repetitions—that the image grows legible, emerging in clear relief. We have borne witness to a discontinuous space, where some paths recur more than others, thus enabling some blank segments to recede. As they do so, the spaces indispensable for a survey of knowledge production are stitched together.

This choice of method was not without consequences for source collection. The process stretched from Bulgaria to Macedonia (today North Macedonia), Serbia, Germany, Israel, and the United States, and included exploring archives of sometimes unfathomable depth,[27] as well as examining documents in Bulgarian, Macedonian, Serbian, German, and English, and occasionally in Russian and Hebrew. Interviews with figures from museum

---

27   See appendix for the list of sources.

institutions and actors in the cultural life of Macedonia, Israel, Germany, the United States, and France, as well as with key figures in Bulgarian historiography, round out this material.

Nationalizing the Past, Internationally

The history of the Holocaust in the territories under Bulgarian control has, perhaps uniquely, been integrated into rival national narratives, as the fate of the Jews became a metaphor for the virtue or the suffering of non-Jewish peoples, and a site of political contention. One of this book's ambitions is to demonstrate the intimate links that joined these national appropriations of history to a transnationalizing of Holocaust memory. At the risk of overstatement, one could argue that this transnational process has constituted one mode of, if not a condition for, the increasing nationalization of academic as well as nonprofessional historical writings. It was in turn closely linked to attempts at determining who was entitled, and from where, to tell the story of Jews in Bulgaria and the occupied territories during the war. Changes in the visibility of the extermination of the European Jews on a global scale have also powerfully affected the collective remembrance of the events in Bulgaria and beyond. As we shall see, state actors were not the only agents in this attempt to nationalize the past. Jewish communities originating in the Balkans, as well as the non-Jewish Balkan diasporas, have also contributed in important ways to this process of nationalization through internationalization. Moreover, efforts at retelling Jewish wartime experiences have brought together Jews and non-Jews who shared social backgrounds, political educations, and human experiences.

Prior to World War II, the history of the Balkan Jews had been a story of multiple entanglements, shaped by living in the multicultural Ottoman Empire. Indeed, with the exception of a small Romaniote community that can be traced back to antiquity,[28] the Jewish presence in the Balkans dates mainly from the late-fifteenth-century settlement of Jews expelled from Spain and Portugal who migrated to the territory of the Ottoman Empire, followed by Ashkenazi Jews who fled persecution in Russia and central

---

28 In Bulgaria, these Romaniote communities resided mostly in the northern part of what would become the modern Bulgarian state (Vidin, Nikopol, Silistra, Pleven, and Sofia) as well as in Jambol, Philippopolis (today Plovdiv), and Stara Zagora. On the history of Jews in Bulgaria, see Todorov, Damjanov, and Koen, *Proučvanija za istorijata na evrejskoto naselenie v bălgarskite zemi*; Romano, *Yahadut Bulgariya*; and Keshales, *Korot yehudei Bulgariya*; for a remarkable bibliography, see Eškenazi and Krispin, *Evreite po bălgarskite zemi*.

Europe in the eighteenth and nineteenth centuries.[29] Mainly Sephardic,[30] for several centuries these Jewish communities led imperial lives centered around trade and handicraft. When, in the nineteenth century, the Ottoman Empire began to confront nationalist claims, the Jews were construed as loyal imperial citizens par excellence,[31] even as those promoting competing nation-state schemes urged the Jews to choose between these projects.[32]

Certainly, Jewish lives followed dissimilar trajectories according to the slow retreat and the demise of the Ottoman Empire. In a number of aspiring Balkan nation-states, the dramatic demographic, economic, social, and political changes ushered in by the end of empire witnessed the development of economic and national rivalries between Jews and Gentiles, alongside the spread of modern anti-Semitism.[33] In the autonomous Principality of Bulgaria created in the wake of the Russian-Ottoman War of 1877–78, remnants from old anti-Jewish stereotypes—be they based on religious grounds, associated with the supposed fraternity of the Jews and the Muslims in the Ottoman Empire, or linked to former economic tensions (between peasants and moneylenders, for instance)—lingered in songs, local folklore, and some texts.[34] In addition, the country was not foreign to sporadic anti-Semitic outbursts. Nevertheless, the Jews were not construed as "significant others," unlike the Turks and other Muslim communities, reminiscent of the former Ottoman dominion, or the Greeks, perceived as religious and economic competitors. A small community of less than 1 percent of the country's population at the turn of the twentieth century, the Bulgarian Jews were mostly of humble condition and worked as craftsmen and petty traders. Except for a small bourgeoisie based in Sofia, they did not represent any major challenge to the social ascension of a Gentile bourgeoisie. As Nissan Oren rightfully observed: "While in most other East European countries the urban preponderance of the Jewish population constituted a threat to the rising middle class, in Bulgaria the conflict of interest did not arise. Although moderately influential in the economic life of the country, the Bulgarian Jews played

---

29 Small groups of Ashkenazi Jews settled in Bulgaria as early as the fifteenth and sixteenth centuries, following their banishment from Bavaria.

30 Benbassa and Rodrigue, *Sephardi Jewry*; Phillips Cohen and Stein, *Sephardi Lives*; Todorov, "Evrejskoto naselenie v balkanskite provincii na osmanskata imperija prez XV–XIX vek," 7–20.

31 Phillips Cohen, *Becoming Ottomans*. On Jewish lives in the last decades of the Ottoman Empire, see also Rozen, *Last Ottoman Century*; regarding the Bulgarian case, see Koen, *Evreite v Bălgarija*.

32 Cohen, *Last Century*.

33 Mazower, *Salonica, City of Ghosts*.

34 Todorova, "Evreite v bălgarskata slovesnost"; and "Obrazăt na 'nečestivija' evrein," 10–22.

no political role of any significance."[35] This was all the more true because the Jews were mostly barred from the state bureaucracy and distinguished careers in the army (only a handful rose to high rank). Well into the 1930s, relations between Jews and Gentiles were perceived locally as benevolent, especially when compared to Central and other Southeast European states.[36]

Regardless of the drawing of new political and administrative boundaries, however, long after the fall of the Ottoman Empire, the Sephardic worlds remained united by cultural and religious sensibilities, economic networks, and family relations that could not be limited to national frameworks. In this respect, World War II brought about a violent rupture. It is now an undeniable historical fact: the Jews of Bulgaria and the occupied territories of Yugoslavia and Greece—sometimes linked, before the war, by filial bonds—share (or rather, are divided by) histories that, as a result of the war, came to diverge. Whether they decided to join Israel in 1948–49 or to take part in building socialism in Bulgaria, the majority of the Jews native to this country were born into a legacy of extraordinary survival. In light of this, any suffering related to professional exclusions, to looting, to expulsions from Sofia and other cities in 1943, or to conscription in labor camps long seemed unspeakable beyond the privacy of one's own home. In contrast, images of deportation and extermination haunt the reminiscences and knowledge transmitted to Jews from the former occupied territories, whether they emigrated before the war, escaped arrest, or reached Israel after its founding.

Further adding to these divisions, from the end of World War II on, Jewish communities on both sides of the Cold War were expected to display exclusive national loyalty, to prove how well they had integrated, and to fit their ways of telling and remembering the past into national constraints. In Bulgaria, subscribing to a definition of Jewish experience in terms of "rescue" implied depriving the Jews of agency, except for those who had joined the partisan movement during the war. This point transpired as early as 1945 in the incantatory formula pronounced by one of the prosecutors of the

---

35 Oren, "Bulgarian Exception," 83–106 (here, 88).

36 The extent and nature of anti-Semitism in prewar Bulgaria remains to this day a highly divisive issue in academic and lay circles. There exists no authoritative and comprehensive piece of scholarly research on this question. See Troebst, "Antisemitismus im 'Land ohne Antisemitismus,'" 109–25; Kulenska, "Antisemitic Press in Bulgaria," https://www.quest-cdecjournal.it/the-anti-semitic-press-in-bulgaria-at-the-end-of-the-19th-century/; Kulenska, "Dass wir unser Land"; Krispin, *Antisemitizăm v Bălgarija dnes*, 29–46; Oschlies, *Bulgarien—Land ohne Antisemitismus*; and Brustein and King, "Balkan Anti-Semitism," 430–54. For contrasting views dating from the postwar era, see Arditi, *Hasifrut haantishemit beBulgariya*; and Benvenisti, "Unfavourable Conditions," 177–220.

Bulgarian People's Court at the end of the war. In his final indictment before the chamber responsible for examining anti-Jewish crimes, on March 29, 1945, Mančo Rahamimov proclaimed: "Thanks to the energetic and obstinate involvement by Bulgarian society and the Fatherland Front [*Otečestven front*, OF, a predominantly Communist coalition], which illegally (at the time) prepared the Bulgarian peasants and workers to defend the Jews; thanks to the Bulgarian people, who cherished warm feelings toward them: *we were saved*. Standing here, in my place as prosecutor, and as a delegate of the Central Consistory of the Jews in Bulgaria, I warmly thank the government of the Fatherland Front and all the valiant Bulgarian people for our rescue."[37]

It is difficult to ascertain the extent to which the Jews who committed themselves to the building of socialism in Bulgaria fully believed in the nationalized representations that some of them publicly narrated. During socialism, believing often coexisted with cautious reserve, the use of officially sanctioned discourses to further alternative interpretations of the past, as well as differing remembrance of historical events according to the (public, community, or family) setting. A diversity of forms of adherence thus coexisted, which reflected the existence of multiple social, generational, professional, and political mediations. Furthermore, national frameworks were made far more complex by the bitter divisions between Bulgarian Jews who had decided to settle in Bulgaria and those who chose to leave. Following the creation of the new State of Israel in 1948, an estimated 90 percent of the Bulgarian Jewish community emigrated.[38] This massive departure

---

37   Bulgarian Central State Archives (*Centralen dăržaven Arhiv*) [hereafter cited as CDA], Collection (*fund* [F]) 1449, Inventory (*opis* [op]) 1, archival unit (*arhivna edinica* [ae]) 185, sheet (*list* [l]) 45. We will return to this speech in chapter 1.

38   Between October 25, 1948, and May 16, 1949, 32,106 Bulgarian Jews departed for Israel. For the period of 1948–53, the number grew to 38,651, a modest total compared to those from Romania (122,712) and Poland (104,208), but considerably higher than from Czechoslovakia (18,247) and Hungary (13,986). In proportional terms, Bulgaria, together with Yugoslavia, was among the European countries where the aliyah had greatest reach. Vasileva, *Evreite v Bălgarija*, 125; Hacohen, *Immigrants in Turmoil*, 267. The reasons behind this massive departure have been the focus of scholarly and political contention. The range of factors put forward in the literature include the reluctance of the Bulgarian Jews to see the Bulgarian socialist state expropriate Jewish shops and boutiques again (a few years after the regime of Boris III had done so), the hopes for a new future fostered by the creation of the new State of Israel, and the tight connections among Bulgarian Jewish families and neighborhoods (deemed to account for collective decision-making processes). Some authors, especially in Israel, also see in this wave of emigration

would weigh tremendously upon the stances adopted by Bulgarian Jews, increasingly pressured to conform to the state's discourse. On both sides of the Mediterranean, assessing Jewish wartime experiences involved casting a broader judgment on the Bulgarian monarchy *and* the socialist regime, as well as on the reasons for staying in Bulgaria or opting for the aliyah. The narration of Jewish lives thus became hostage to the political conflict between "Communists" and "Zionists" (to use the oversimplifying terminology of the time) as well as between the Bulgarian and Israeli projects of nation-state building, splitting Jews of Bulgarian descent. For several decades, these battles left little room for the rendering of the diversity of social, cultural, and political sensibilities that existed in prewar and wartime Bulgaria.

However, here again, the Bulgarian and Israeli nationalization processes took place even while historical productions and collective memory remained irreducible to national frames. This is so because contacts between Jews of Bulgarian descent in Bulgaria and in Israel, albeit strongly constrained by the Cold War atmosphere, were not entirely severed.[39] More importantly, the endeavor to give an international audience to the "Communist" and "Zionist" readings of the past required that all contenders in these historical disputes follow closely the scholarly and lay publications released in the two countries. Most surprisingly, perhaps, regardless of the points of discord between them, most Jews who remained in Bulgaria and those who left took a part in developing representations of the war that consigned Jews to the role of victims. On both sides of the Cold War divide, the notion of "rescue" prevailed—albeit attributed to different "saviors"—alongside a vision of the Bulgarians as a people tolerant toward national minorities. In short, the complex and painful comingling of ties and divisions among Bulgarian-born Jews contributed to the transnational circulation of the narrative of the "rescue of the Bulgarian Jews."

In the 1970s, the increasing visibility of the Holocaust in Bulgaria—that is, of the "rescue of the Bulgarian Jews"—constituted one aspect of the patrimonialization of history, a practice shared by several Eastern European states during late socialism.[40] The support that this national(ist) policy gar-

---

proof of the widespread sway of Zionism among the Bulgarian Jews. Still others insist that this choice supports the contention that anti-Jewish persecutions and anti-Semitism may not have been as mild as is often suggested in public speech and academia. Roumen Avramov indicated that each departure had a cost, determined by the Communist Party. See Vasileva, *Evreite v Bălgarija*; Šealtiel, *Ot rodina kăm otečestvo*, 311–412; Avramov, *"Spasenie" i padenie*, 24; and Haskell, *From Sofia to Jaffa*.

39 Marinova-Christidi, "From Salvation to Alya," 223–44.

40 On the Romanian case, see Verdery, *National Ideology under Socialism*.

nered within a cultural elite that enjoyed significant symbolic resources and marks of recognition during late socialism is well known.[41] Few scholars, however, have explored the relationship between, on the one hand, promoting a heroic narrative of the past and broadcasting the "rescue of the Bulgarian Jews" and, on the other, exalting national unity. This very connection further compelled Bulgaria's Communist Jews to mold their retelling of the national past into the frame manufactured by the Communist Party. Fewer still have pinpointed the intricacies of a situation in which promoting the narrative of the "rescue of the Bulgarian Jews" reached the broader world, crossing the East-West divide and going as far as the United States.

In many ways, postcommunism dramatically reshuffled these transnational circulations. Many Jews whose family roots lay in the Balkans found their way back to the land of origin of their forefathers, for a short visit, or several, at times more. At a time when the collective remembrance of the Holocaust had become institutionalized and museums designed to document and transmit the history of the destruction of the European Jews were blossoming, some descendants of Jewish survivors from Bulgaria, Macedonia, and Greece engaged in a number of sometimes divisive memorial initiatives. As earlier, these initiatives were invoked or even convoked to strengthen national dogmas. However, Jewish engagement in memory policies contributed to cross-pollinating political and national identities, ways of relating to one's Jewishness, and transnational senses of belonging.

Reassessing the Cold War Era

Ultimately, studying narratives of Jewish experiences during World War II offers a contribution to the historiography of the Cold War—in two respects, at least. The first concerns awareness of the Holocaust over these four decades; the second, the assessment of the degree of seclusion, competition, *and* international circulations across the East-West divide during the Cold War.

As far as knowledge and remembrance of the Holocaust is concerned, conventional wisdom has long held that there was a homogeneous silence surrounding anti-Jewish persecution in Soviet-influenced states. This was part and parcel of a broader belief that in Eastern Europe and beyond, prior to the Eichmann trial in Jerusalem in 1961—that key moment in the "retrospective perception of an event that took on its true dimension in the aftermath"[42]—the documentation, commemoration, and transmission of the

---

41 Elenkov, *Kulturnijat front*; Kalinova, *Bălgarskata kultura i političeskijat imperativ.*

42 Rousso, *Juger Eichmann*, 13.

memory of the events were deemed to have been confined to the associations of deportees and Jewish community institutions. However, a new generation of research has demonstrated the need for a reassessment of the wartime context and the postwar years (as well as for a more nuanced and diversified view of the ensuing decades). In the Soviet context, for instance, recent literature has shown that there was no failure to document the mass violence against the Jews during the war. Rather the key issue revolved around the framing of the events chosen by Soviet photographers, film directors, and journalists: the exaltation of the struggle against fascism and a universalizing reading of the victims often prevailed over the reconstruction of the unique experience of the Jewish victims.[43] More broadly, a new body of literature has highlighted the extent of the work of documenting the destruction of the European Jews during the war, as well as in its aftermath[44]—both east and west of the emerging Cold War divide.[45]

The judicial prosecution of crimes against Jews in the final months of World War II in Bulgaria, as examined in this volume, offers one more illustration of the complex entanglement between the framing of a universalist discourse, centered around interethnic brotherhood and the heralding of the partisan movement, and efforts on the part of some Communist and left-wing prosecutors, both Jewish and non-Jewish, to collect evidence of the persecution of Jews in Bulgaria and the occupied territories and see that the defendants received their due retribution. That the outcome of the trial should have fallen short of their expectations does not minimize the fact

---

43 Hicks, *First Films of the Holocaust*; Shneer, *Through Soviet Jewish Eyes*; Pozner, Sumpf, and Voisin, *Filmer la guerre*; Voisin, Le Bourhis, and Tcherneva, "Introduction," 1–26; Hicks, "Soul Destroyers," 530–54.

44 On the documentation of the destruction of European Jewry during the course of events, see Kassow, *Who Will Write Our History*. On unique Jewish individuals whose lives were dedicated to recording witness testimonies and collecting data about the extermination of Jews, see Cohen, "Rachel Auerbach," 197–221; Bilsky, "Rachel Auerbach," 74–102; and Yablonka, *Survivors of the Holocaust*.

45 For a transnational perspective on documentation efforts in the years after World War II, see Jockusch, *Collect and Record!*; Cesarani and Sundquist, *After the Holocaust*. See also Aleksiun, "Central Jewish Historical Commission," 74–97; Wóycika, *Arrested Mourning*; Hallama, *Nationale Helden und jüdische Opfer*; and Laczó, "European Fascism," 175–204. For a survey of the intertwining between antifascism and Holocaust memory, seen as entangled and not competitive modes of remembrance, in Eastern Europe, see Bohus, Hallama and Stach, *Shadow of Anti-Fascism*, and esp. Bohus, "Parallel Memories?," 87–108.

that a wide array of material evidence was uncovered in this process and later preserved in archives.

A reconsideration of the nature of the East-West partition has also been called for. From the turn of the twenty-first century, in history as well as in cultural studies, novel scholarship has been disseminated that is no longer hostage to Cold War normative and ideological categories. A transnational history of socialism has formed, one attentive to the circulation of people, ideas, and knowledge across the Iron Curtain.[46] Amid an enthusiasm for rediscovered mobility, however, some of this historiography has yielded to the temptation to substitute an iconography of fluidity for the previous frozen vision of the East-West divide. In doing so, these works have tended to project a globalized present onto socialist pasts.

This book adopts an angle halfway between one reading of Cold War dynamics centered on political and geopolitical competition—eager to see the invisible hand of overpowering states behind each and every decision— and another interpretation focusing on international exchanges. Chapter 3 (the most enigmatic, without a doubt) attempts to seek this balance by studying the multiple journeys and travails of a visual archive. At the start of the investigation, little was known of this peculiar film record, apart from the fact that it was shot in March 1943, and that it shows Jews with their backs bowed, weary, worried, and trudging with bundles on their shoulders, under their arms, in their hands, as they climb into and out of trucks, as they are transferred to trains, wait in detention camps, and end up aboard a steamship in the Danubian port of Lom. During the socialist decades, and in their wake, numerous photograms were extracted from these images and strewn around the world, finding their way into museum collections, exhibition catalogs, and both academic and lay publications.

Chapter 3 approaches the form of a detective story. Without divulging the outcome of the investigation, we can already attest here that these reels experienced multiple social lives. Placed back on the editing table, spliced to other shots and sound, they crossed the Berlin Wall and reached West Germany in 1967, where they were used as judicial evidence. Engraved on a documentary plate in 1977, then in 1986 inserted into a commissioned feature film glorifying the Bulgarian dictator Todor Zhivkov, they provided material for a twilight Cold War plot that took place in the United States— one whose participants included Bulgarian diplomats, intelligence officers, and historians involved in the acquisition policy for the future United States

---

46 "Passing Through the Iron Curtain," 703–10; Faure and Kott, "Le bloc de l'Est en question," 2–212; David-Fox, "Iron Curtain," 14–39; Dragostinova and Fidelis, "Beyond the Iron Curtain," 577–684; Dragostinova, Cold War; David-Fox, Holquist, and Martin, *Fascination and Enmity*; Baulland and Gouarné, "Communismes et circulations internationales," 9–104.

Holocaust Memorial Museum. The case of this film footage offers a unique lens on Cold War rivalries and solidarities. Unstable zones of cooperation did come into existence during the Cold War. Albeit considered by those involved as resulting from personal mediations and favors, these exchanges were not unknown to state actors, and some of their protagonists followed institutional instructions quite closely. Ultimately, the example of the manifold uses of a visual record of the Jewish deportations will suggest just how far East-West patterns of circulation were from abjuring a national framework.

The Way Forward

Let us briefly flip the pages of the book and wander through its chapters. Chapter 1 explores the role of the Seventh Chamber of the Bulgarian People's Court (1944–45)—the first exceptional jurisdiction exclusively dedicated to anti-Jewish crimes in Europe—in gathering evidence about wartime crimes and creating an interpretive framework of the recent past. This first reading of the deportation of Jews from Bulgarian-occupied lands and the nondeportation of Jews from the "old" kingdom is situated within a specific historical moment, one that combines regime change and purges, the ambition to propel a revolution, and efforts to demonstrate Bulgaria's commitment to the Allies ahead of the postwar peace treaties. Building on principally judicial archival documents (preliminary investigations, witness testimonies, oral pleadings by prosecutors and lawyers, the court judgment, and more), the chapter shows the process through which the chamber, whose very establishment seemed to entail the recognition of the singularity of the Jewish experiences, did not succeed in producing a legal statement of the exceptionality of crimes against Jews and ultimately contributed to their euphemization. Several variables account for this outcome. First, the Communist-led ruling coalition of the Fatherland Front expected—indeed, requested—prosecutors and judges to produce an edifying account of the immediate past in order to wedge a political struggle into the present and lay the foundations for a Communist future. The jurists also had to demonstrate, by condemning a limited number of "fascists," the existence of "another Bulgaria," one that was a stranger to the crimes of the Nazis whose occupation it suffered, so as to bargain for vanquished Bulgaria to receive more lenient treatment by the Allies. Second, the approach to anti-Jewish crimes additionally reflected the growing polarization of Bulgarian Jewish worlds between those who believed anti-Jewish persecutions were a historical parenthesis that would be closed once the criminals were sentenced and those who held in distrust the summary justice applied by the Communists, and who hoped for a settlement in Palestine.

Chapter 2 is set at the end of the 1950s, just months before the creation of the Ludwigsburg Central Office for the investigation of Nazi crimes. Zentrale Stelle would play a key role in the launching of a new wave of prosecutions in West Germany, even before the Eichmann trial introduced a new way of relating to the destruction of European Jews worldwide. East of Europe, the crucial topic on the agenda was the denunciation of the purported recrudescence of fascism in West Germany, and the strengthening of the Communist bloc following the Budapest revolution of 1956. The case study chosen to explore this moment and its impacts on the shaping of the "rescue" narrative is the joint feature film production *Sterne/Zvezdi* (Stars; dir. Konrad Wolf; script. Angel Wagenstein), the first and only movie shot in socialist Bulgaria about the deportations of Jews from occupied territories. Drawing on the archives of the bilateral commission in charge of overseeing the production process, the chapter explores how Bulgaria and East Germany, through representing Jewish fates, tried to set the terms for establishing an "Eastern European" way of remembering World War II and the Holocaust, while consolidating (at times conflicting) national readings of history. Leaving the sphere of justice to enter the world of cinema, the exploration of a fictional rendering of historical facts brings into relief the role played by Communist Jews and cinema professionals in the dissemination of representations of anti-Jewish persecutions. The minute analysis of a cardinal sequence in the film—Jews deported from Northern Greece arriving in Bulgaria—from the screenplay to the storyboard and the final cut, serves to illustrate how notions of Bulgarian responsibility in the persecution of Jews were progressively brushed away. Meanwhile, several directorial and authorial choices demonstrate the circulation across the East-West divide of symbolic motifs, chiefly the gendered representation of Jewish suffering and the use of Christian symbols to signify the Jewish tragedy.

With chapter 3, we envision the retellings of Jewish wartime experiences during the Cold War and depict the increasing visibility of the Holocaust in Bulgaria—that is, of the "rescue of the Bulgarian Jews"—from the 1970s onward. The chapter argues that this visibility needs to be understood as the intersection between, first, the growing contention over the past opposing the anti-communist Bulgarians in exile and the Bulgarian Communists, on the one hand, and the Jews who had remained in Bulgaria following the creation of the State of Israel and those who emigrated, on the other. The second parameter concerns the attempt to reinvigorate the failing legitimacy of the socialist project through a search for a heroic past. In order to tell this story, the chapter follows the journeys of a short deportation film shot in March 1943 in the "old" kingdom. While advancing the study of the origins, making, and scenes recorded on these mute frames, the chapter shows how they were used and edited as they repeatedly crossed the East-West divide the 1960s (on the occasion of a trial for Nazi crimes in the Federal Republic of Germany), in the early 1980s (for an exhibit held in West Berlin), as well as in the final years of Bulgarian communism (in the United States). Retracing this film footage's myriad lives evidences the promotion of dictator Todor Zhivkov to the position of coauthor of the "rescue," and the renewed emphasis placed on the collective virtues of the (progressive) Bulgarian people in a diversity of state-promoted publications, exhibitions, and commemorative initiatives.

Leaving socialism for the postcommunist era, chapter 4 explores another site of knowledge production—namely, public controversies and political battles in Bulgaria and internationally. Focusing on the 1990s, this chapter examines the combined effects of the fall of socialism, the opening of international borders, and the reinsertion of Bulgaria into a West European space where the memory of the Holocaust occupies center stage on ways of remembering, commemorating, and talking about Jewish wartime experiences in Bulgaria. In so doing, the chapter makes two points. First, it shows how from the 1990s to the early 2000s, the understanding of Jewish fates became one arena in which partisan identities contested through a discussion of the Communist past and the legacy of the monarchy and "fascism" in post-1923 Bulgaria. Rediscovered on that occasion, the Jewish predicament was marshaled by supporters on the left to denounce the pretense of anticommunists that the pre-1944 era embodied at once civilization and modernity. Nevertheless, in dialogue with an expanded range of actors who felt empowered to speak their truth of the past (memory entrepreneurs, politicians, scholars, etc.), a new memory landscape crystallizes at the turn of the 2000s, one that emphasizes the role of the former "bourgeois" political elite and, in particular, that of then–deputy speaker of the National Assembly, Dimităr Pešev. The "rescue" narrative is not subverted; one merely witnesses a reordering of the list of the deserving. Second, the chapter demonstrates the intimate links that join this new public speech on history to a transnationalizing of Holocaust memory and the role of Jewish communities originating in the Balkans, as well as the non-Jewish Balkan diasporas, in this process.

Prolonging the discussion of public controversies on the Holocaust in Bulgarian-controlled lands during wartime, chapter 5 shifts the focus toward the 2000s–2010s. This period coincides with Bulgaria's accession to the European Union. The EU is a key actor in the field of memory policies and the historical disputes between the Republic of Macedonia (today North Macedonia) and Bulgaria—and the satellitization of issues relating to the Holocaust around these disputes about ethnogenesis, languages, and national heroes—as well as the emergence of public demands for a clarification of Bulgaria's wartime role in the persecution and deporta-tion of Jews. Unlike the course of events in other postcommunist countries (Romania and the Baltic States, for instance), these demands, the chapter argues, did not emerge within the framework of EU accession talks, in part thanks to the successful promotion of the "rescue of the Bulgarian Jews" narrative, in part because the less vocal calls for a criminalization of the Communist past were not seen as concomitant with the rehabilitation of wartime collaborators and war criminals. Rather, they crystallized in a twin context marked by new domestic alliances between the nongovernmental human rights sector and a segment of Bulgarian academia, on the one hand, and the increasing role played by Holocaust museums in the writing of the history of the destruction of Jews and its remembrance, on the other. This evolution has not entirely emancipated members of the Jewish communi-ties in the Balkans, and Balkan Jews settled in Israel, the United States, and elsewhere away from pressures to display exclusive national loyalties and fit their ways of telling and remembering the past into national frameworks. Nevertheless, the chapter shines a light on Jews' engagement in memory policies, and their contribution to a greater awareness of how timely a dis-cussion of Bulgaria's coresponsibility in Jewish persecutions in the "new" and "old" kingdoms may be.

Ultimately, what kind of book is the reader about to discover? A volume on teeming stories of the past, both written and visual, that are continually scattered and reshuffled without any apparent change in the architecture of the narrative. The situation would be burlesque, were it not so tragic: there is something of Charlie Chaplin or of boulevard theatre in this endlessly edited plot, in the way that protagonists, heroes, and traitors step on and off stage at various moments swapping roles, bringing some sequences to life, consigning others to silence, in a wild dance that nonetheless leads all the while to the denial of any agency to the Jews who *were* saved, those living Jews, invited to exhibit only gratefulness—figures absent from their own survival.

This volume also hopes to make a further dent in conventional knowledge about the Communist treatment of anti-Jewish persecutions. What can be observed in the place of continued silence? Certainly, the presence of eclipses and ellipses; certainly, the discussion of an ever-increasing variety of issues through elucidating Jewish fates. Over the past eighty years, the Holocaust has served as a fulcrum for the negotiation of national identities, political allegiances, and projections into the future, while a flurry of protagonists with their own personal stories, professional identities, and contrasting inter-ests added their voices to a chorus of public statements. Certainly, too, the metonymic relationship between the Holocaust (in Europe) and the "rescue of the Jews" (in Bulgaria).

How this miraculous conversion came about is the story to which we now turn.

Chapter I

The Judicial Production of an Account of Anti-Jewish Persecution

The Genesis of a Heroic Narrative

March 29, 1945. The scene was set in the courthouse of Sofia, a huge neo-classical building whose construction was spread over the two decades of the interwar period. With its white facade decorated with twelve monumental columns, the building stood in the heart of the capital, blind to the ruins and to the scree caused by several months of Allied bombardment of "German Sofia."[1] Starting in early March, the palace hosted the hearings before the Seventh Chamber of the tribunal: a chamber set up to judge the alleged perpetrators of the crime of "persecutions against the Jews" (*gonenija na evreite*) in Bulgaria and in the territories it had occupied. At the time of the indictments, the voice of the prosecutor Mančo Rahamimov, a dedicated Communist, rose solemnly in Room 11. Small round glasses on his face, the magistrate wore austere attire that contained a body slightly overweight. Muted, the audience gazed upon him, men—mostly men—shivering in their winter coats:

> For the first time in history, a government has adopted in its supreme law . . . a specific text by which those who have created a racist legislation and those who have cruelly implemented it are declared criminals and consequently liable to prosecution and punishment before a People's Court. The importance [of this trial] extends far beyond the borders of our small country and acquires international significance and appreciation. . . . In decades,

---

1   Nisim Aron Papo, "Antisemitite pred narodnija săd," *Cionističeska tribuna*, 21, March 1, 1945, 1.

centuries from now, historians, scholars, and philosophers from all over the world will come to Bulgaria as they do today. They will leaf through the yellowed pages of the present cases and examine every sentence, every word, and every sign of it to discover the historical truth about bloody and terrible times.[2]

How could one better illustrate than with this quote the extent to which some Communist Bulgarian Jews, even prior to the end of war, were cognizant of the fact that they were thus making a historical contribution and strove to document the persecution of Jews in end-of-war Bulgaria? In fact, the creation, as early as the autumn of 1944, of a Bulgarian jurisdiction exclusively dedicated to anti-Jewish crimes invites us to continue reevaluating efforts to document the Holocaust in close proximity to the events. More specifically, the purpose of this chapter is to explore the way in which justice professionals and witnesses, in close dialogue with the world of the printed word, posed the interpretive frameworks of a past of which they were contemporaries and of which some had been victims. The judicial arena is seen here as a space streaked with social logics coming from outside the courtroom. One of the challenges of the inquiry lies precisely in grasping the modes of importation of political and social divisions within the court.[3] The trial interests us less as a source on events than as the judicial production of a judgment upon those events, without these perspectives being opposed: the objective is to hold together the reconstitution of anti-Jewish policies and the intelligence of the paths by which knowledge and representations of Nazi crimes were elaborated.

That justice was a key factor in the search for evidence, the production of representations associated with the Holocaust, and the historical writing of events is a largely documented fact.[4] Many researchers have also demonstrated how trials, constructed as vehicles of collective memory, helped to shape national identities—Israeli and German, among others—and fueled East-West competition.[5] However, up until recently, in most works the focus

---

2   CDA, F 1449, op. 1, ae. 185, l. 69.

3   A ground-breaking path was opened by Claverie, "Sainte indignation contre indignation éclairée," 271–90.

4   Goda, *Rethinking Holocaust Justice*; Bankier and Michman, *Holocaust and Justice*; Douglas, *The Memory of Judgment*; Bloxham, *Genocide on Trial*; Douglas, *The Right Wrong Man*.

5   On the competition between the Federal Republic of Germany and the German Democratic Republic through the courts, see Weinke, *Law, History, and Justice*; and Weinke, *Die Verfolgung*. On the historical construction of the narrative relating to the German *Sonderweg*, and the role of the trials held in Nuremberg in this process, see Priemel, *The Betrayal*.

was on the emblematic trials of Nuremberg in 1945–46[6] and Jerusalem in 1961,[7] as well as the legal proceedings initiated in the Federal Republic of Germany (FRG) in the 1960s.[8] Knowledge of local trials in the postwar years remains more limited.[9] In this case, the Bulgarian trajectory presents several singularities likely to make it a privileged site for observing the trial of Holocaust crimes.

The first lies in the timing of the prosecutions. Prior to the constitution of the International Military Tribunal at Nuremberg, the decision to bring to justice the presumed perpetrators of crimes against the Jews was taken in November 1944, just months after the Red Army invaded Bulgaria and the Fatherland Front (*Otečestven Front*, OF), a coalition dominated by the Communists, overthrew the "bourgeois" regime on September 9, 1944.[10] On November 24, an amendment was published in the *State Gazette* to the "decree-law creating a People's Court to judge those responsible for Bulgaria's entry into the war against its allies and the crimes related to it" that extended to "persecutions against Jews," the scope of the acts falling

---

6   For a review of the literature on the Nuremberg trials, see Mouralis, "Le Procès de Nuremberg," 159–75. See also Kochavi, *Prelude to Nuremberg*; Heller, *Nuremberg Military Tribunals*; and Mouralis, *Le Moment Nuremberg*. Regarding the Soviet contribution to the trial, see Hirsch, *Soviet Judgment at Nuremberg*; and Ginsburgs, *Moscow's Road to Nuremberg*. On the filming of the Nuremberg proceedings, see Lindeperg, *Nuremberg*. On the subsequent military trials, see Priemel and Stiller, *Nuremberg Military Tribunals*.

7   Yablonka, *State of Israel*; Lindeperg and Wieviorka, *Le Moment Eichmann*; Lipstadt, *Eichmann Trial*. On the impact of the Eichmann trial on Israeli identity, see Segev, *Seventh Million*; Shapira, "Eichmann Trial," 18–39.

8   Pendas, *Frankfurt Auschwitz Trial*; Wittmann, *Beyond Justice*; Weinke, *Die Verfolgung*. For an original perspective centering on the contribution of Jewish agency to the holding of the trial, see Stengel, "Mediators behind the Scenes," 320–49.

9   Among the literature dedicated to Central and Southeast Europe, see Kornbluth, *August Trials*; Finder and Prusin, *Justice behind the Iron Curtain*; Deák, *Europe on Trial*; Barna and Pető, *Political Justice in Budapest*; Frommer, *National Cleansing*; Söhner and Zombory, "Accusing Hans Globke, 1960–1963," 351–86; Person, "Rehabilitation of Individuals," 261–82; Ragaru, "Justice in Mantle Coats," 31–77; Ragaru, "Écritures visuelles, sonores et textuelles de la justice," 275–498; and Ragaru, "East-West Encounters."

10   Alternatively envisaged as a "coup d'état" and a "popular uprising," the September 9 rupture has been the subject of an excellent synthesis: Vezenkov, *9-i septemvri 1944 g.*, and a remarkable historiographical discussion: Daskalov, *Ot Stambolov do Živkov*, 295–430. The Fatherland Front included, in addition to Communists, representatives of the political-military circle *Zveno* (Link), left Agrarians, some Social Democrats, and two independents.

under the exceptional jurisdiction of the People's Court.[11] Examination of the facts was entrusted to the Seventh Chamber. Investigation began in December 1944; hearings started on March 7; the court handed down its verdict on April 2.

Bulgaria thus appears to be one of the very first European states to have created a body specialized in the treatment of crimes against Jews.[12] In concrete terms, this precocity meant that the prosecutors carried out their preliminary investigations in synchrony with the advance of the Red Army westward and the discovery of the Third Reich's extermination camps. Operating in constant back-and-forth between the local and European contexts, the legal professionals faced questions that would haunt subsequent trials of Holocaust crimes: how to argue the capacity of the law to punish and prevent the possible repetition of such human rights abuses? What precedents, what registers of justification could be used? How to qualify crimes of an unprecedented nature and magnitude? The stakes are obviously legal, since it is a question of inventing incriminations and judicial strategies adapted to the exceptional nature of the misdeeds being prosecuted; it is also a political and moral matter insofar as Bulgarian justice professionals are convinced that they are holding a historical trial and a trial for the historical record.

The second element of specificity lies in the position occupied by the Bulgarian state in the economy of World War II. In fact, the prosecution of war criminals saw its coordinates defined by the brutal reversal of geopolitical alliance by Bulgaria, a former Axis member, in September 1944, which led to the launch of a "patriotic war" (*Otečestvena vojna*) against yesterday's allies; the signing in Moscow, on October 28, 1944, of an armistice agreement including a clause relating to the trial of war criminals; and the establishment

---

11 *Dăržaven vestnik* [*State Gazette*, hereafter cited as DV], 261, November 24, 1944.

12 In the USSR, eleven collaborators, mostly auxiliaries of the *Sonderkommando* 10a, had been tried for counterrevolutionary acts committed against "innocent Soviet citizens" in the summer of 1943. In Poland, six SS officials and *kapos* (prisoner functionaries) from the Majdanek camp were brought to trial at the end of 1944, but the Jewish identity of the victims was not mentioned in the indictment, nor was anti-Semitism cited as a motive. The "August trials" (1944) paved the way for a number of judicial proceedings against perpetrators of anti-Jewish crimes, but no special jurisdiction was set up for this particular kind of crime. Finally, two guards from a forced-labor unit appeared before the People's Court in Budapest in January 1945 for the torture and murder of 124 Hungarian Jews and Communists, without a specialized court being established. Deák, *Europe on Trial*, 191–209; Kornbluth, *August Trials*; Finder and Prusin, *Justice behind the Iron Curtain*, 18–24, 29–40.

of an Allied Control Commission (*Săjuzna kontrolna komisija*, SKK) dominated de facto by the Soviets.

Two final introductory remarks are in order. The first concerns the notion of the "narrative" of the recent past. Using this expression to qualify what was played out on the judicial scene does not in any way amount to postulating the existence of unequivocal judgments on responsibility for anti-Jewish persecution, including in Communist circles. Rather, what is at issue is the aggregation of sometimes contrasting sensitivities, know-how, and interpretations. From this plurality, however, emerged a melodic line whose accents—the understanding of the crimes, their perpetrators, their victims as "heroes of history"—were to be the subject of reexposures in the following decades, similar to those musical motifs that appear under the bow of the soloist, whose movements toward the string and wind sections, and then toward the orchestra as a whole, give unity to a concerto.

The second remark concerns the status of the People's Court and the historical treatment of the sources produced by a postwar justice system that has been erected since 1989 as an emblem of "crimes of communism," as the expression goes. Few researchers today could dispute the profusion of attacks on the notions of independent, impartial, and neutral justice that marred the work of the People's Court—in particular that of the First and Second Chambers, which had to deal with the files of regents, royal advisers, ministers, and deputies in power between January 1, 1941, and September 8, 1944.[13] They concerned, among other things, the legal framework of court action (failure to respect the principle of nonretroactivity of the law, lack of appeal), the rights of accused persons (conditions of arrest, detention, obtaining confessions, access to a lawyer), the drafting of indictments and the requisitory speeches, the conduct of hearings and sentencing policy.[14] The difficulty lies elsewhere. Caught in the web of memory controversies, the denunciation of the political justice of the People's Court seems to have dissuaded historians from consulting the archives of the Seventh Chamber;

---

13 Meškova and Šarlanov, *Bălgarskata gilotina*; Kanušev, *Prestăplenie i nakazanie v nacionalnata dăržava*, 287–89.

14 The joint indictment of the First and Second Chambers was drafted by a special commission of the Central Committee of the Bulgarian Workers' Party/ Communists (*Bălgarska rabotničeska partija/komunisti*, BRP/k); Georgi Dimitrov, the party leader and former general secretary of the Comintern, annotated the final indictment from his Moscow exile; the sentences were negotiated between Stalin, Dimitrov, the secretary of the party's Central Committee in Sofia, and the Bulgarian minister of justice. CDA, F 250B, op. 1, ae. 58, l. 1–2; CDA, F 250B, op. 1, ae. 68, l. 1–22; CDA, F 1B, op. 7, ae. 190, l. 14.

the historiography on the judicial treatment of anti-Jewish crimes in Bulgaria thus remains anemic.[15]

Rather than abandoning this documentation,[16] we propose here to construct as an object of research the political, historical, and legal prisms through which the resort to justice attempted to shed light on the crimes committed during the war. The stakes are high; the judicial examination of the persecutions of the Jews in 1945 produced a paradoxical result: the chamber, whose very establishment seemed to be committed to the recognition of the singularity of the Jewish wartime experience, failed to produce a legal statement of the exceptional nature of these acts of violence. Moreover, it contributed to their euphemizing. Anti-Semitism—a motive whose relevance for thinking about anti-Jewish policies could be questioned by historians and sociologists[17]—certainly figured at the heart of the hearings, the requisitory speeches of the prosecutors, and the court's judgment. Nevertheless, insofar as it was seen as an imported ideological-logical product, the fruit of "fascism," the reference to anti-Semitism served to support a narrative of the war organized around two figures of evil, the Nazis and the "fascist clique," and a collective hero, the resistance. Ultimately, the actors charged with assessing individual responsibility took part in the elaboration of a trope of collective innocence that still constitutes the dominant public narrative of the Holocaust in Bulgaria today.

Reconstructing the combination of internal and external factors at the origin of this paradox is the object of what follows. Several parameters will be highlighted. The action of the Seventh Chamber was first of all constrained by the obligation to link three orders of finality: the prosecution of war crimes, the judgment of the old regime, and the impulse of revolutionary transformations. The didactic vision of justice promoted by its initiators required prosecutors and judges to produce an edifying account of the immediate past in order to wedge a political struggle into the present and lay the foundations for a Communist future. The treatment of anti-Jewish crimes then reflected the growing polarization of Bulgarian Jewish worlds. Negotiation of a Jewish and Communist identity, political competition, and differences over the opportunity to build a future in Palestine all influenced the reception of the court's action. Finally, the dynamics of the trial cannot be isolated from the international justice audiences. One of the obsessions

---

15   For a few exceptions, see Sage, "Sedmi săstav na Narodnija săd v Sofija, mart–april 1945," 159–64; Todorov and Poppetrov, *VII săstav na Narodnija săd.*

16   The archives of the trials, kept in the Bulgarian Central State Archives, include the prosecution files, the minutes of hearings, as well as technical and financial documentation.

17   Mariot, "Faut-il être motivé pour tuer?," 154–77.

of the Bulgarian rulers was to distance themselves from the elites in power until September 9, 1944: it was necessary to demonstrate, by condemning a limited number of "fascists," the existence of "another Bulgaria," a stranger to the crimes of the Nazis whose occupation it would have suffered.

Judging in Time of War

On September 17, 1944, a week after the overthrow of the "bourgeois" regime, the new prime minister, Kimon Georgiev, presented his program from the front steps of the Sofia Palace of Justice: the trial of war criminals was part of a political project that included an amnesty for "fighters for popular liberties and victims of exceptional anti-popular laws, a purge of the civil service, and a reform of the justice system."[18] In the construction of the judicial cause, retribution for violence committed against partisans occupied a key place. The temporal horizon of the incriminated acts was not specified, nor was the institutional framework of the judgment—exceptional jurisdictions or ordinary courts?

The announcement gives substance to Communist invocations of justice that had been recurrent since the German invasion of the Union of Soviet Socialist Republics (USSR) in June 1941. Within the Central Committee of the Bulgarian Workers' Party/Communists, the reference to a "people's court" had appeared in September 1941 in an incantatory resolution: "[The fascists] must know that the day is not far off when they will be brought before a people's court and that it will be merciless."[19] On July 17, 1942, the Fatherland Front, in its founding proclamation, announced the institution of a "people's court for those guilty of the catastrophic policy carried out to date and those guilty of excesses against the patriotic fighters and the peaceful population of Bulgaria and the occupied territories."[20] The term "People's Court" (*Naroden săd*) was also included in the December 1943 program of the office of the Central Committee of the Workers' Party, in exile, which drew up a list of future indictees not that dissimilar from the one drawn up in 1944.

The creation of the People's Court by the decree-law adopted by the Council of Ministers on September 30, 1944, and published in the *State*

---

18 *Rabotničesko delo*, 7, September 18, 1944, 1. See the program of the Fatherland Front at http://www.omda.bg/public/arhiv/prilojnia/dokumenti_bkp/publichno_sabranie.pdf (accessed July 16, 2022; no longer active).

19 Cited in Meškova and Šarlanov, *Bălgarskata gilotina*, 43.

20 Ibid., 54.

Gazette on October 6 combined several aims.[21] First, it was to replace private vengeance with a judicial logic. As elsewhere in liberated Europe, the collapse of power led to a flurry of arrests, kidnappings, and summary executions.[22] The actions of certain Communist militants and partisans betrayed the violent skills acquired in clandestine life, as well as the autonomy that some units of the resistance enjoyed, especially since they were poorly coordinated until the spring of 1944. In September 1944, a popular militia replaced the detested police; young partisans joined it, often resisting hierarchical orders and lacking legal knowledge.[23] From the point of view of the BRP/k officials, there was an urgent need to put an end to the "improvisations of authority" by which citizens took justice into their own hands.[24]

The desire to control extralegal violence is in no way incompatible with the use of expeditious settlements to consolidate the new political order—the second objective sought with the creation of the People's Court. The Communists succeeded in taking control of the Interior and Justice Ministries, but they had to deal with a wide range of allies, including the political-military circle *Zveno* (Link), which was known for its art of coup d'état.[25] Purification and the tribunals were arenas where power relations

---

21 D.V., 319, October 6, 1944.
22 Vezenkov, *9-i septemvri 1944 g.*, 367. Vezenkov puts the number of executions between September 1944 and the spring of 1945 in the range of 4,000–7,000. This figure includes the death penalties determined and carried out by People's Court (1,046 according to General Prosecutor Petrov's July 1945 report to the Central Committee of the Workers' Party), as well as the victims of summary killings (the *State Gazette* listed over 2,000 names of people who had gone missing). I wish to thank Aleksandăr Vezenkov for offering a detailed account of his calculation. On Petrov's report, see CDA, F 250B, op. 1, ae. 70, l. 4–46.
23 Komisija za razkrivane na dokumentite i za objavjavane na prinadležnostta na bălgarski graždani kum Dăržavna sigurnost i razuznavatelnite službi na bălgarskata narodna armija [hereafter cited as Comdos], F 1, op. 8, ae. 11, l. 1–14.
24 The expression is borrowed from General de Gaulle.
25 In the government, the Communists also held the Public Health portfolio and a ministerial post without portfolio. The elitist *Zveno* circle had been created in 1928 around an eponymous publication headed by the journalist Dimo Kazasov. Advocating a project of technocratic modernization, the circle had forged close relations with members of the Military League (*Voennija Săjuz*), an influential organization of active and reserve officers. This connection was to make a decisive contribution to the May 1934 coup, a prelude to the establishment of the personal dictatorship of King Boris. The Agrarian government officials gradually became a rallying point for opponents of Communist centralization.

between coalition partners were negotiated. The adoption of legalistic rhetoric gave Georgi Dimitrov, the exiled Communist leader, and Trajčo Kostov, the secretary of the Central Committee in Sofia, a few precious weeks to speed up the purges.[26] The 28,630 arrests, 10,919 indictments, and 9,550 convictions—26 percent of which were death sentences and 12 percent life sentences—decided at the end of 135 trials strengthened the hold of the Communists on the key institutions of the state.[27] Last but not least, the creation of exceptional jurisdictions and the wide publicization of the trials allowed the Workers' Party to undertake the work of supervising its members and disseminating Communist thought at a time when the organization was experiencing an explosion in its numbers.[28]

Placed at the service of an internal agenda, the recourse to justice also constituted the fruit of a global time marked by the international circulation of postwar ideas. Since the Inter-Allied Conference held at St. James's Palace in London (January 13, 1942) had "place(d) among their principal war aims the punishment, through the channel of organized justice, of those guilty of or responsible for these crimes, whether they have ordered them, perpetrated them or participated in them," retribution for war crimes had become a subject of many discussions among the Allies.[29] In November 1942, the Soviet Union created an extraordinary state commission (*Chrezvychajnaya gosudarstvennaya komissiya po ustanovleniyu i rassledovaniyu zlodeyanij nemetsko-fashistskikh zakhvatchikov*, ChGK) in charge of investigating and prosecuting crimes committed on its territory,[30] a model later replicated by the partisans of Josip Broz (Tito) in Yugoslavia. One cannot therefore be surprised that the armistice agreement signed by Bulgaria with the Allies

---

26 Vezenkov, *9-i septemvri 1944 g.*, 359–69.

27 According to the report of Minister of Justice Minčo Nejčev. CDA, F 146, op. 5, ae. 476, l. 84–85.

28 Between the two world wars, the demography of the party underwent wide fluctuations in conjunction with political repression and the internal conflicts of the BRP/k: it went from 30,000 members in 1932–33 to 4,000 in 1934, 7,952 in October 1936, and 6,890 in mid-1940. Oren, *Bulgarian Communism*, 108–9. Richard Crampton offers a conservative estimate of 15,000 members in October 1944 and 250,000 just a year later. Crampton, *Short History*, 146.

29 Kochavi, *Prelude to Nuremberg*. See facsimile of the declaration "Punishment for War Crimes: The Inter-Allied Declaration Signed at St. James's Palace, London on 13th January 1942" and Relative Documents at http://nla.gov. au/nla.obj-648522001.

30 On ChGK's creation and operation with regard to war crimes investigations, see Sorokina, "People and Procedures," 797–831; and Kudryashov and Voisin, "Early Stages," 263–96.

on October 28, 1944, in Moscow included, in addition to the demand for the abolition of anti-Jewish measures, an Article 6 requiring that "the Government of Bulgaria will cooperate in the apprehension and trial of persons accused of war crimes."[31] Although the document says little about the form that this judgment would take, the international requirements were on everyone's mind. When they came to power, the Bulgarian Communists had briefly entertained the illusion that it would be possible for them to preserve a fringe of the territories acquired in 1941. The insistence of the British on making the full withdrawal of Bulgarian forces from Yugoslavia and Greece a precondition for the conclusion of the armistice reduced these hopes to nothing. The Bulgarian leaders now feared that possible Greek claims supported by Great Britain would call into question the territorial integrity of the "old" kingdom (Bulgaria in its pre–April 1941 boundaries). The presence of the Red Army and the authority exercised by the "Soviet viceroy," General Biryuzov, number two on the Allied Control Commission, were further reminders of the precarious status of the former member of the Tripartite Pact.

To deduce that the creation of the People's Court would betray the rapid Sovietization of Bulgarian justice and provide evidence of the subordination of the Bulgarian Communists to their Soviet comrades would, however, be inaccurate for at least two reasons. First, more than Soviet pressure, it is probably more appropriate to speak of socialization and shared Communist representations. After the failed attack on the king at the Sveta Nedelja Cathedral in Sofia in April 1925, Bulgarian Communist militants had been the object of a vast campaign of repression. Considered by the public authorities as a means of stigmatizing political opponents, the judicial arena provided the accused with a space for publicizing their cause. Additionally, the three thousand or so Bulgarian Communists exiled to the USSR in the 1920s and 1930s had opportunity to immerse themselves in a political reading of justice and purges.[32] Finally, Georgi Dimitrov himself knew what his international prestige and career owed to his performance at the Leipzig trial following the Reichstag fire in 1933.[33] In 1944–45, it was in close dialogue with Stalin that the tutelary figure of Bulgarian communism established the

---

31 Cited in Ognjanov, Dimova, and Lalkov, *Narodna demokracija ili diktatura*.

32 Oren, *Bulgarian Communism*, 83–100.

33 The burning of the German parliament building on the night of February 27–28, 1933, served as a pretext for a campaign of repression against the Communists. Arrested on March 9, and charged with arson and attempting to overthrow the government, Dimitrov defended himself with a verve, determination, and strength of conviction that earned him an acquittal on December 23, 1933. The radio broadcast of the trial contributed to the international reputation of the Bulgarian tribune. Ibid., 60–72.

sentences of the First and Second Chambers of the People's Court—prior to their deliberations. From the point of view of institutional architecture, conceptions of law, and personnel, the postulate of a rapid transposition of the Soviet model into the Bulgaria of the Fatherland Front also had to be nuanced. At the time when the decree-law of October 6, 1944, was drafted, the Sovietization of Bulgarian justice was in its infancy.[34] The political break with the bourgeois order took place, at least in part, with the weapons of the defunct world.

The (In)visibility of Anti-Jewish Crimes in the "General Trials"

The decree-law of October 6 provided for "the trial by a people's court of those responsible for Bulgaria's entry into the world war against the allied peoples and for the crimes related to it."[35] However, the ambiguity of the mechanism was apparent in the definition of the acts to be prosecuted and their temporal framework: was it a question of judging "war crimes" or "fascism" as a regime? If the decree-law limited the examination of acts to the three years of world conflict, the desire to take revenge on "twenty years" of "fascist governments"[36] was reflected in the declarations of Procurator General Georgi Petrov[37] and his final indictment for public presentation of the charges, which he delivered on January 24 and 25, 1945.[38] Ten counts of indictment were defined in Article 2, which included alliance with the Third Reich, the declaration of war on the United States and the United Kingdom, the initiation of hostile acts against the USSR, the endangerment of soldiers occupying Yugoslav and Greek territories (and the crimes committed by these same occupying forces against the local populations), abuses against civilians and repression of the partisan movement, and the use of public offices for private enrichment. The accused were divided into three categories: ministers who served between January 1, 1941, and September

---

34 On the reform of the judicial system beginning in the summer of 1945, see Semkova, *Promeni v sădebnata vlast na Bălgarija*, 53–72.
35 DV, 219, October 6, 1944.
36 The year 1923—with the assassination of the Agrarian leader Aleksandăr Stambolijski in June and a Communist uprising in September—marked in the Communist historical imagination the beginning of the "fascization" of the Bulgarian regime.
37 *Rabotničesko delo*, 22, October 12, 1944, 2.
38 See the working version of the indictment: CDA, F 250B, op. 1, ae. 66, l. 1–2, and the speech to the court: CDA, F 1449, op. 1, ae. 7, l. 2672–2894.

9, 1944; deputies of the Twenty-Fifth National Assembly; and "other civilian or military persons." The range of penalties, identical for each crime, ranged from imprisonment to capital punishment. Fines of up to 5 million leva were also imposed.

In the initial version of the decree, crimes committed against Jews were given only a single mention as a breach of public probity. Article 5 thus incriminates "persons who illegally accumulated wealth for themselves or for others during the dark period of the national catastrophe after January 1, 1941, who used their position or their relations with the government and the [so-called] 'Allied States' (Germany, Italy, Japan, Croatia, Slovakia, etc.). Included are persons who received bribes in the form of fees or other bribes, or *who in various ways robbed Jews,* citizens of the occupied territories of Macedonia, Serbia and Greece, and antifascists—prosecuted, accused, and convicted for antifascist activity."[39] Neither deportations, nor spoliation, nor forced labor were specifically mentioned.

Admittedly, "the inhuman persecution of the Jews" acquired new prominence in the indictment for the First and Second Chambers drawn up on December 5, 1944,[40] as well as in Petrov's final indictment, which he presented as an outcome of German will and the "greed" of the fascists.[41] The adoption of anti-Jewish legislation was said to have been "imposed by the German masters."[42] Certainly, when Prosecutor General Petrov discusses the deportations from the occupied territories, he does not refrain from recalling the terrifying conditions Jews were subjected to during the round-ups: "at night, they were dragged out of their homes, herded like cattle into sealed wagons, and driven to the port of Lom. From there they were

---

39 CDA, F 250B, op. 1, ae. 20, l. 5 (emphasis added).

40 The persecutions are dealt with at the end of the list of crimes in a paragraph that mentions the adoption of anti-Jewish legislation "under Hitler's diktat," the Aryanization of Jewish property, and the enrichment of the Fascists, while noting the deportations in one sentence: "About 13,000 Jews were rounded up from Belomorie and Macedonia and taken in sealed wagons to Poland, where they were exterminated in the cruelest manner." CDA, F 1449, op. 1, ae. 1, l. 4v.

41 In his presentation of the charges against former prime minister Bogdan Filov (February 15, 1940–September 14, 1943) and the minister of the interior and public health, Petăr Gabrovski (February 15, 1940–September 14, 1943), the public accuser promptly dispatched the "Jewish question": "The indicted Petăr Gabrovski is the most diabolical enemy of the people's fighters and of the Jewish minority." In the crimes attributed to Filov, "the sinister mockery and robbery of the Jewish minority" are mentioned only in passing. CDA, F 1449, op. 1, ae. 7, l. 2760–61 and 2759.

42 Ibid., l. 2854.

loaded onto ships for their country of birth—Galicia. The fate of this unfortunate Jewish population is known. They were burned alive, and all of them, men, women, youths, and children, in crematoria created on purpose by the German monsters. I do not know whether at least one of them remained alive to tell of the terrible crime committed by the vulgar German murderers."[43] He also underlined the fatal destiny of the children and newborns: "So the Jews were handed over to the German beasts because they did not want the victory of the Axis. And because our country had to be 'cleansed' of 'provocateurs.' So the children, even the babies, who were remanded to the Germans and thrown alive into the furnaces of the crematorium, they too were 'provocateurs' and did not want the 'victory of the Axis'? This is the kind of executioners the Bulgarian people were in the hands of."[44]

The venality and moral turpitude of bureaucrats and officers—"the so-called patriots . . . installed in the Jewish apartments . . . who had bought furniture at derisory prices, including Persian carpets and pianos, etc."—are entitled to more colorful descriptions.[45] Prosecutor General Petrov also recalls "the fire in a Jewish concentration camp, in the Kajluka area, near Pleven, where on the night of July 10–11, 1944, dozens of Jews lost their lives and several dozen others were badly burned." He suggests that the fire may have started as a result of criminal activity: "Their impression was that the fire was caused on purpose, because there were various rogue legionnaires hanging around there, and because the security did not allow them to leave the building and save themselves. Several women were trampled in the commotion and eleven people burned in this fire. After that, the criminal arsonist began to tell that his money had burned."[46]

Responsibility was attributed to the king, the ministers, the "deputies of the majority who voted for the anti-Jewish laws," the commissioners for Jewish Affairs "in concert with the entire anti-Semitic apparatus of the Jewish Commissariat," and finally to "journalists and writers, commandants of forced labor units, defenders of the regime, members of the *Ratnici* and *Brannik* organizations,[47] leaders of the reserve officers, etc." Despite a brief allusion to the "bloody document" signed by Commissioner for Jewish Affairs Belev and the German SS representative, Dannecker, the role of the Bulgarian authorities in the deportations was the subject of a thrifty

---

43 Ibid.
44 Ibid.
45 Ibid., l. 2858.
46 Ibid.
47 On *Brannik*, a youth movement modeled on the German *Hitlerjugend*, and *Ratnik*, a xenophobic and anti-Semitic organization created in 1936, see Poppetrov, *Socialno naljavo.*

description: "Put [the Jews] into the hands of the German executioners."[48] Of the 222 pages of the final indictment, violence against Jews occupied only a handful.

It is around another axis that the pleading is ordered: Prosecutor Petrov intended to give to World War II a genealogy that removed the mortgage of war crimes from the Communist future by converting Bulgaria from an ally of the Reich and an occupying power into a victim of war. The agent of this metamorphosis would be the monarchy. Accession to the Tripartite Pact was presented as the last of three "national catastrophes" caused by the criminal diplomatic choices of Kings Ferdinand (in 1913 and 1915) and Boris III (in 1941). The "great Bulgarian chauvinists," those vassals of German imperialism—itself the son of capitalism and the father of Nazism—were the preferred targets of the indictment. The denunciation of the crimes committed against Communist partisans and activists presented, in a mirror effect, a heroic portrait of those who embodied the continuity of the state in the face of adversity. Jewish questions only appeared in the narrative if they consolidated the plot.

The court's retribution for the crimes confirmed this ancillary position. Although the facts of "persecution against the Jews" were retained against four of the five categories of defendants defined in the court's judgment, the elements that would have made it possible to correlate the evaluation of the acts with the sanctions pronounced are absent. However, the accused's having defended Jews during wartime did not attract the clemency of the judges toward them. The case of the former deputy speaker of the National Assembly, Dimităr Pešev, is emblematic here: this conservative politician, who had voted for anti-Jewish provisions in December 1940, made a decisive contribution to the suspension of the roundups of Bulgarian Jews in the "old" kingdom on March 9, 1943. Pešev also initiated a petition against the government's anti-Jewish policy, signed by forty-two majority deputies, that led to his removal from his position as deputy speaker. In 1945, although the former parliamentarian escaped the death penalty, he nevertheless received a fifteen-year prison sentence.[49] No less tragic is the fate of one of the great figures of the Democratic Party (*Demokratičeska partija*), the jurist and former minster of the Interior and Public Health and former prime minister Nikola Mušanov. This right-wing politician denounced with remarkable constancy, legal rigor, and moral force all anti-Jewish measures, whether they targeted Jews of Bulgarian citizenship or those residing in the

---

48   CDA, F 1449, op. 1, ae. 7, l. 2855.

49   Dimităr Pešev was released after a year in prison and led an isolated life until his death in 1973. In that year he was awarded the title of "Righteous Among the Nations" by the Yad Vashem Institute. See chapter 4.

occupied territories. This commitment did not spare him the verdict of one year's imprisonment common to most members of the Muraviev government (September 2–9, 1944).[50]

How, on the basis of these fragmentary data, can one cast light on the decision to entrust a specialized chamber with a more detailed examination of anti-Jewish crimes? Here, we need to depart the praetorium, to pull ourselves away from the magnet of the courthouse, in order to examine the work of building a case by Bulgarian Communist Jews.

The Construction of a Judicial Cause by Bulgarian Communist Jews

Before the war, the Bulgarian Jewish community was structured around four pillars: the rabbinate, the Central Consistory of Jews in Bulgaria, the Jewish municipalities—which assumed denominational, civil, social, and cultural missions—and the network of Jewish schools. At the end of August 1944, Prime Minister Ivan Bagrjanov encouraged the reformation of the consistory, which the war had reduced to the role of a "transmission belt" for the government and the Commissariat for Jewish Affairs (*Komisarstvo za evrejskite văprosi*, KEV). On September 18, a new team with a Communist majority took control of the Consistory.[51] David Ieroham, a lawyer by profession and an influential figure in the Social Democratic Workers' Party (*Bălgarska rabotničeska social-demokratičeska partija*), became its president; he was assisted by Žak Natan, a self-taught journalist, economist, and Communist activist who had received solid ideological training in the USSR.[52] Among the other members of the Consistory was the lawyer Mančo Rahamimov, future prosecutor of the People's Court.

In the space of a few weeks, a new community framework was formed. A Jewish section (*Evrejski otečestven front*, EOF) was created within the Fatherland Front, which welcomed Communists, social democrats, left-wing agrarians, and members of *Zveno*; it was later timidly opened up to left-wing Zionists. A cluster of cultural and charitable organizations formed around EOF. From the center to the periphery, consanguine relations were established between the EOF's central committee and the Consistory, as well as between the local committees of the Jewish section of the Fatherland Front

---

50 Nikola Mušanov was released on the eve of the general elections in November 1945. He was arrested again in 1947 and died in prison in 1951, officially of a heart attack.

51 CDA, F 622, op. 1, ae. 131, l. 77; Vasileva, *Evreite v Bălgarija*, 11–24.

52 CDA, F 2124K, op. 1, ae. 19 578.

and the Jewish municipalities. Through the straddling of multiple positions—and, in some cases, the use of violent means of persuasion—Bulgarian Communist Jews established control over the centers of Jewish social, cultural, and religious life.[53]

The lives of powerful men of the day followed similar biographical trajectories. Most of them were born or had lived in the multiethnic working-class neighborhood of Jučbunar, the heart of Jewish life in Sofia. They were left-wingers in their youth and experienced upward social mobility through law studies, involvement in the activities of the Jewish cultural houses (čitališta), as well as in the Jewish or progressive press. Several of them had experienced exile. Having opted for an advocate's robe rather than a magistracy subordinate to the political authorities, they defended Communist militants after the 1924 ban on the party. During the war, in forced labor battalions, internment camps for "seditious" people, and partisan units, or during the expulsion of Jews from Sofia in May 1943, many of them formed strong friendships. Having reached the leadership of the Jewish community, they aspired to bring to justice those responsible for the humiliations, privations, and violence to which they were subjected.

On October 30, 1944, in its inaugural issue, *Evrejski Vesti* (Jewish news), the weekly newspaper of the Jewish section of OF, relayed this position. As Natan Grinberg, an active Communist who was commissioned to research the archives of the wartime Commissariat for Jewish Affairs in the fall of 1944, wrote: "[It is] up to the Jewish committees of the Fatherland Front to point out [the fascists] to the militia and, on the basis of the facts, to demand their detention and surrender to the People's Court. If some fascists are detained for other crimes, it is nevertheless appropriate to transfer the material that concerns us Jews in order to obtain a conviction for these crimes as well."[54]

A month later, the secretary of the Social Democratic Workers' Party, Eli Baruh, an accountant by profession, and a former forced worker (and future prosecutor), launched an appeal for witnesses in the columns of the newspaper.[55] The research that Grinberg and the Sofia lawyer Isak Francez, the new commissioner for Jewish Affairs, pursued in the archival funds of the Commissariat[56] confirmed their beliefs: they discovered with horror that Bulgarian authorities had planned thoroughly the "Final Solution" of the

---

53   On this process seen from a "left Zionist" point of view, see Keshales, "Tova se sluči prez onezi godini," File no. 3, 7–17.
54   Natan Grinberg, "Naroden Săd," *Evrejski Vesti*, 1, October 30, 1944, 2.
55   Eli Baruh, "Zašto mălčite?," *Evrejski Vesti*, 5, November 30, 1944, 2.
56   In the spring of 1945, the Jewish Consistory published a selection of documents from the archives of the Commissariat: Grinberg, *Dokumenti* (1945).

"Jewish question" for the whole of the kingdom.[57] On December 1, 1944, in the name of the Consistory, Rahamimov asked the prosecutor general to mention explicitly the persecution of Jews in the indictment against the accused brought before the First and Second Chambers. The deportations of the Jews of Macedonia and Greece were at the heart of his request:

> Mr. Chief Prosecutor,
>
> Within the framework of the fascist regime and the anti-Jewish laws in the country, Bulgarian Jews were cruelly prosecuted, and the Jews of Thrace and Macedonia—11,000 people—were sent to Poland, where they were murdered in the most atrocious manner.
>
> The people's power of the Fatherland Front saved the Jews of Bulgaria.
>
> Now that the racist legislation has been invalidated and abolished, we ask you with the utmost respect—in the draft law prepared by the minister of justice on the prosecution of fascist acts and in the commission in which you participate—to include anti-Jewish crimes.

This will be an act of great political and historical importance, absolutely in harmony with the program of the Fatherland Front, to which the Jews of Bulgaria fully adhere.[58]

However, these advocacy practices are not enough to explain the rallying of Dimitrov, the Workers' Party, and the Fatherland Front to the principle of a separate examination of these crimes. Elsewhere in Europe, at that time, abuses against Jews were in fact judged in conjunction with other criminal acts, without coming under separate jurisdictions. In Bulgaria itself, one might have expected that the creation of a specific category of perpetrators and victims would have aroused the reservations of a fringe of Communist cadres and militants.

The reconstruction of the decision-making process here comes up against the silence of the archives. The coded telegrams exchanged between Dimitrov and Trajčo Kostov, general secretary of the Central Committee of the Workers' Party, remain stubbornly silent on this subject, as does the diary of the Bulgarian leader.[59] One hypothesis is obvious, however, from the reading of the deposition of Žak Natan, the head of the Central Committee of the Jewish section of OF (EOF), before the People's Court on March 16, 1945: "If we want to be presented as a democratic country before the

57   Israel Majer, "Istoričeski dni," *Evrejski Vesti*, 19, March 10, 1945, 1.

58   CDA, F 250B, op. 1, ae. 75, l. 1. The document is annotated by Georgi Petrov's own hand; he asked that it be used to write the "report of the minister of justice."

59   Dimitrov, *Dnevnik*.

entire democratic world when the destiny of our country is decided in an international conference, we will have to demonstrate that . . . anti-Semites are judged because they are fascists and that there are no anti-Semites in the democratic circles of the Bulgarian people."[60]

That the horizon of postwar diplomatic settlements gave a decisive impetus to the judicial treatment of anti-Jewish persecutions appears credible. At the end of World War I, Bulgaria had paid dearly for its support of the Central Powers: the Treaty of Neuilly-Sur-Seine of November 27, 1919, imposed heavy territorial losses, exorbitant reparations, and a drastic reduction in its military strength. The humiliation of Neuilly had fueled Bulgarians' nostalgia for their lost greatness and led to a territorial revisionism based on the principle of the alliance sealed with the Reich in March 1941.[61] Haunted by the territorial question, the new leaders knew that the Allies had promised to take into account the treatment of minorities in peace treaties. On October 27, 1944, on behalf of the World Jewish Congress, Baruch Zuckerman drew the attention of the Consistory to this point. In his missive, he reproduced an excerpt from the appeal written in May 1943 by Jak Asseo, a Bulgarian Jewish merchant who had immigrated to the United States and had taken over leadership of a Committee for the Rescue of Bulgarian Jews in October 1942: "Do not forget that a few weeks ago the President of the United States himself, Mr. Roosevelt, and the British Minister Mr. Eden, stated unambiguously that the behavior of all unfriendly countries toward their Jewish minorities will be taken into consideration when deciding on the fate of enemies of the Allied nations. No excuse will be sufficient to [justify] the inhumane treatment of any minority."[62]

Communist leaders were likely to hear the argument that the prosecution of anti-Jewish crimes could deliver political dividends.[63]

---

60 CDA, F 1449, op. 1, ae. 181, l. 256.

61 Znamierowska-Rakk, "Bulgarian Territorial Revisionism," 102–25.

62 The letter is on file with the prosecution: CDA, F 1449, op. 1, ae. 207, l. 266; and the archives of the Jewish Consistory: CDA, F 622, op. 1, ae. 87, l. 1–4 (here, 3). One learns that the missive reached its addressees with a delay of two months, after a detour by the representation of the Jewish Agency for Palestine in Istanbul because of "the impossibility of communications between your country and America." CDA, F 622, op. 1, ae. 87, l. 5, 12.

63 In August 1945, the Bulgarian delegation to the WJC in London listed the holding of the trial among the facts to be credited to Bulgaria. CDA, F 28, op. 1, ae. 119, l. 43–46.

A Sketch of the Trial Scene

It remained to be determined whom to bring to justice, for which crimes, and before which judges. The decree-law of October 6, 1944, provided that prosecutors would be appointed by the Council of Ministers on the proposal of the minister of justice (Article 5), while conferring a power of initiative on the Fatherland Front. In the end, three of the four prosecutors were of Communist persuasion; the last was a Social Democrat. The names of attorneys Mančo Rahamimov and Boris Bărov were supported by the Workers' Party; that of Eli Baruh was suggested by the president of the Consistory, David Ieroham.[64] Tracing the path at the end of which the lawyer Slavčo Stoilov joined this trio is a challenge; at the most, we can note that he had been legal counsel in Sofia in a high-profile lawsuit brought against several future high-ranking Communist officials. The four prosecutors had one thing in common: none of them had served as prosecutors prior to 1945.

This shift on the chessboard of justice from defense to prosecution is less surprising than it may seem. The autumn of 1944 was the scene of a vast cleansing: as early as October 4, the minister of justice, Minčo Nejčev, a Communist, had a list drawn up of judges, prosecutors, and other professionals he considered compromised. In the months that followed, 145 magistrates out of 618 were dismissed from their posts for their "fascist" past and 33 for "other" reasons.[65] The lack of cadres as well as the search for trusted people enlightened the solicitation of attorneys who had made their mark in the defense of Communist defendants. Their experience as lawyers, active in the interwar era, at a time of intense (and rather expeditious) state repression against Communist sympathizers, in turn influences the definition of their new attributions by the public accusators. In the wake of the abortive Communist uprising of September 1923, the Bulgarian parliament passed the Law on the Defense of the State, which created a range of crimes with severe penalties, entrusted military tribunals with the handling of political cases, and restricted the rights of the defense.[66] In 1934, the indepen-

---

64   Baruh, *Iz istorijata*, 178.

65   CDA, F 1B, op. 6, ae. 67, l. 15. The Ninth Chamber of the People's Court also contributed to purges of the judiciary: twenty-three judges and prosecutors from the Supreme Court of Cassation, regional courts, and a court of appeal appeared for vetting. The chamber delivered its verdict on April 27, 1945.

66   On several occasions, the International Juridical Association (IJA), created in Berlin on December 9–12, 1929, on the initiative of the Comintern, protested against the repression suffered by Communist sympathizers. On the IJA's Bulgarian section, see CDA, F 2123K, op. 1, ae. 1019K.

dence of the judiciary was further curtailed, while government interference in proceedings involving political opponents increased, especially after King Boris III introduced a personal regime in 1935. It is on the strength of this science of judicial rules that the prosecutors of the Seventh Chamber made their entrance onto the scene: with astonishing ease, they borrowed from their opponents of yesteryear the authoritarian tone that the latter had cultivated in their activity in the judiciary.

On paper, the prerogatives granted to public prosecutors were vast: charged with supervising investigations, they had the right to carry a weapon, could order arrests, and could demand "full cooperation from all the military and militia authorities."[67] In practice, the investigation of cases was hindered by the disorganization of the police following massive dismissals in the autumn of 1944 and the incorporation of inexperienced partisans. Relocated to the provinces in the spring of 1944 to flee Allied bombing, government offices slowly returned to Sofia. The repatriation of the archives of the civil and military administrations of the Yugoslav and Greek territories, evacuated in October 1944, was delayed. The civil service lacked everything—paper, telephones, vehicles, petrol—which limited travel abroad or even within the provinces.

The composition of the court also illustrated the confusion of the new era. As in other European states, in the Bulgaria of the Liberation the aspiration for a popular rejuvenation of justice was widespread. Article 6 of the October decree-law required that legal professionals appointed by the minister of justice be joined by laypeople selected by the regional committees of the Fatherland Front. In fact, precedence was given to the latter: they were chosen, in accordance with the instructions of the National Committee of OF, from among individuals "of absolute integrity, who are close to the people, enjoy their trust and prestige, and, above all, are devoted antifascists who have fought or are ready to fight against fascism."[68] Political loyalty prevailed over hastily transmitted legal knowledge.[69] The popular jurors of the Seventh Chamber were workers or peasants.[70] Only the president of the court, Petko Petrinski, was a jurist, with a lackluster career. His hour of glory

---

67 Baruh, *Iz istorijata*, 174.

68 CDA, F 28, op. 1, ae. 112, l. 9.

69 For all chambers of the People's Court, 120 training seminars were organized. CDA, F 250B, op. 1, ae. 68, l. 1–22.

70 Order 426 of March 5, 1945, names Tončo Carvulanov, worker, village of Svoge; Blagoj Gorčilov, worker-welder in Sofia; Leftera Hr. Dimlirova, resident of Svoge; and Nikola Manolov, from Sofia. The profession of the last two jurors is not known. Cvetana Hr. Rusinova, a worker in Sofia, was an alternate member. During the trial, she sat among the jurors. CDA, F 88, op. 2, ae. 26, l. 27.

would come in 1946–47 when he took on the role of prosecutor in several "show trials."[71]

From the outset, the Seventh Chamber's remit constrained the examination of the facts. Only crimes committed by Bulgarian citizens in the "old" (pre–April 1941 boundaries) and "new" kingdoms (with additional and officially "liberated" Yugoslav and Greek lands) were prosecuted. No foreign nationals—and therefore no German war criminals—were brought to justice. Above all, the prosecution had to build its case around two qualifications: Article 2, paragraph 10, of the amended version of the decree-law incriminated "persecutions against the Jews" (*gonenija na evreite*). The nature of "facts, writings, speeches or . . . other" demonstrating an "active and efficacious" contribution to anti-Jewish persecution was left to the discretion of the judges. Article 2, paragraph 4, referred to persons who had used their "connections with those in power or with the combatant states, or their professional position, in order to unlawfully obtain material benefits for themselves or others."[72] Why other charges, such as murder or physical violence, were not included in the indictment is a mystery.

A list of sixty-four defendants was drawn up.[73] It constituted a roadmap of the missions assigned to the Seventh Chamber.[74] The executives of the Commissariat for Jewish Affairs were placed at the heart of the indictment. Eighteen of the one hundred or so agents that the KEV had at the beginning of 1943 were brought to justice. The former commissioner for Jewish Affairs Aleksandăr Belev (September 1942–October 1943) was tried in absentia (although he was probably deceased by the time of the trial). His successor, however, Judge Hristo Stomanjakov (served October 11, 1943–July 1944), deputy prosecutor at the Sofia court of appeal prior to his appointment at the KEV, did appear in the dock. Four former heads of departments were arrested. First came Jaroslav Kalicin. A lawyer by training, Kalicin had been director of the extremely influential Administration Department and responsible for designing the concrete setup of the deportations from occupied Yugoslavia and Greece. In March 1943, Kalicin in person supervised the arrests of Jews in Northern Greece. Penčo Lukov, a former deputy

---

71 Born in 1907 in a poor village in northwestern Bulgaria, Petko Petrinski worked briefly as a lawyer before entering the judiciary. He joined the BRP/k in January 1945, two months before his appointment as head of the Seventh Chamber on March 1, 1945. CDA, F 88, op. 2, ae. 26, l. 14; CDA, F 1B, op. 6, ae. 407.

72 D.V., 261, November 24, 1944.

73 A sentence would be pronounced against fifty-three of them: forty-two appeared in court; nine were tried in absentia, and two were listed as dead by the time of the verdicts.

74 CDA, F 1449, op. 1, ae. 79, vol. 2, l. 17–91.

prosecutor in Plovdiv and director of the Sofia Central Prison, was the second defendant in this group: he headed the Economics Department. In 1943, he was tasked with coordinating arrests in the "old" kingdom. The third protagonist was Zahari Velkov, the nephew of one of Bulgaria's most celebrated authors, Elin Pelin (who himself denounced anti-Jewish persecutions). Velkov was entrusted with supervision of the deportation from occupied Vardar Macedonia (Yugoslavia). Thereafter, he was promoted to head the Economics Department of the Commissariat for Jewish Affairs. Detained in Skopje (Macedonia) in the winter of 1944, he was charged in Bulgaria but did not appear before Bulgarian judges. Finally, Dr. Ivan Popov, another member of the bar, was charged with preparing the Radomir camp intended to receive Jews from the "old" kingdom in March 1943 (as we know, the Bulgarian Jews were not deported in the end). Popov was also asked to coordinate the Jewish expulsions from Sofia into the province in May 1943. Following Kalicin's departure from the KEV in October 1943, Popov took over his position as head of the Administration Department.

The distribution of charges gave special visibility to the deportations (twelve officials of the Commissariat and four officials dispatched to the occupied territories), to the auctions and liquidation of Jewish property (fifteen indictees), to forced labor (fourteen), to anti-Semitic writings (seven), and to the management of internment camps for so-called seditious Jews (four). On this chessboard, however, the white squares are more eye-catching than the black ones. First, absence: beyond the exceptional bureaucracy of the KEV, the Bulgarian state apparatus was largely spared any criminal consequences. It is true that two former employees of the Bulgarian National Bank were prosecuted in relation to the use of violence in extracting money from Jews in the "old" kingdom; a former mayor and local delegate for Jewish Affairs was also accused and his case was examined, despite the fact he was already dead by that time. Moreover, a former vice-district governor (*okolijski upravitel*, deceased) and his right-hand man, once a police deputy chief (in absentia), also featured among the accused. However, when it came to assessing responsibilities for the deportations, the list of members of the state bureaucracy was surprisingly short: the only mayor indicted in connection with the deportations was Angel Čerkezov, who had distinguished himself by proposing to tighten the anti-Jewish provisions designed by the police station in Drama, Greece; a police chief stationed in Serres, Greece, escorted him. The police and intelligence services remained otherwise untouchable. In addition, no representatives of the tax, railway, or public property services were prosecuted. The second major absentee was the army. Some military personnel were arrested for their role in enforcement of forced labor, such as Colonel Mumdžiev, director of the forced labor department at the Ministry of Public Works, and some unit commanders. However, the contribution of the military to securing the roundups was not the subject of any prosecution.[75]

This arbitration was not devoid of political considerations. On the night of September 8–9, 1944, the army's rallying to the coup d'état of the Fatherland Front precipitated the overthrow of the regime. The minister of war, General Ivan Marinov, commander of the occupying forces in Macedonia at the time of the roundups,[76] saw his political instincts rewarded by promotion to the rank of lieutenant general and assignment to the post of chief of staff. The institution was nevertheless regarded by the Communist leaders as an ivory tower. On November 18, fearing that the courts would be used as a pretext for a purge, the new minister of war, Damjan Velčev, from the *Zveno* circle, issued a circular prohibiting the arrest of combatants at the front. Five days later, in spite of Communist protests, the Council of Ministers agreed to circumscribe the scope of arrests: officers, noncommissioned officers, and active or reserve soldiers indicted for actions falling under the jurisdiction of the People's Court could instead request assignment to the front.[77] Those who distinguished themselves there would see their cases dropped; arrests were also suspended. The aim was not to hinder the war effort.

On January 20, 1945, Minister of Justice Nejčev demanded that arrests be halted on February 1, on the grounds that "it will be impossible for officers at the front to accomplish their mission, which is currently of crucial importance, if they find themselves under the permanent threat of being arrested and thrown into prison."[78] The order, reiterated on February 8, circulated to the regional branches of the militia twelve days later.[79] The timing is decisive here: the appointment of the prosecutors of the Seventh Chamber was spread out through December, and the investigations reached their cruising speed only in January. In other words, by the time the accusers were ready to make arrests, the restrictions are already in place. Furthermore, during the trial, proceedings against nine of the sixty-four accused would be suspended for the same reason.[80]

---

75   Comdos, F 13, op. 1, ae. 2, l. 32, 63, 140.
76   The 15th Infantry Division was based in Bitola between June 18, 1942, and September 3, 1944.
77   Comdos, F 3, op. 3, ae. 11, l. 401–3; *Rabotničesko delo*, 67, December 4, 1944, 1.
78   Comdos, F 3, op. 3, ae. 11, l. 166.
79   Ibid, l. 165. About 500,000 Bulgarians took part in the fighting, and 30,000 were injured or lost their lives. Oren, *Revolution Administered*, 87.
80   CDA, F 1449, op. 1, ae. 181, l. 124–27, 179; CDA, F 1449, op. 1, ae. 185, l. 2.

Courtroom 11

The framing is in place. We will soon enter the courtroom to observe how a story of the crimes and their perpetrators, and the "rescue of the Bulgarian Jews," was staged there. The threshold we are about to cross is nothing like the marbled, high-ceilinged splendor filmed by the cameras during the "general trials" in the First and Second Chambers. No mosaic depicting a draped Themis, scales in hand, to dominate the court, the accused, and the public. Courtroom number 11 is austere: a thin line separates the bare white walls from the paneled basement; no telephones, no microphones, no projectors whose intense light might warm the place. Justice is presented in her simplest form: a bell within reach of the president. The four jurors are spread out on either side of Petko Petrinski, with modest piles of documents in front of them. A woman's face catches the attention: her gaze, absent-mindedly, seems lost amidst the audience; her unassuming light pullover contrasts with the dark suits of the other jurors. To the left of the courtroom, an alternate member takes notes, a hand meditatively placed on her forehead (see figure 1.1).

The grandeur of the prosecutors cannot claim any material privilege in these places where their voices will be decisive. They share a narrow wooden table; only the public prosecutor, Boris Bărov, has a lectern, above which his torso barely rises. He crowds onto a chair that one imagines to be too low. Two clerks, with bent backs, transcribe the proceedings; a handful of journalists imitate them. Everything is cramped in this rectilinear space of the 1940s. Faced with these bodies bent over their writings, the recently appointed minister of propaganda Dimo Kazasov, with his elegant white beard and tailored suit, stands at the helm with the ease of the tribune that he is. The moment was captured on March 16, 1945, the date of the statesman's deposition (see figure 1.2).[81]

For the occasion, the room is packed. The public attendees were probably handpicked—the committees of the Fatherland Front, the "Agitation" Department of the Workers' Party, perhaps also members of the Consistory, being assigned quotas. Behind these faces, captured in an eternal instant, lives elude us. Along six rows of wooden benches, the spectators are huddled together, heavily dressed in coats and scarves, gloves for the wealthy. Heating was restricted during that winter. Around the entrance door,

---

81 The pictures are listed as photographs of the Sixth and Seventh Chambers taken on March 15, 1945, in the Bulgarian Central State Archives. The date is incorrect because Kazasov, who is present in one-third of the photographs, testified the following day. CDA, F 720, op. 7, ae. 38, film 45/131 and film 45/132, March 15, 1945, Karl Sakal.

Figure 1.1. Seventh Chamber of the People's Court: The court. *Source:* CDA, film 45/132, no. 14. Courtesy of the Bulgarian Central State Archives.

spectators stand against the wall. Photographed from the journalists' area, the room has a surprising division between the right-hand section, where the tense faces, short hair, and slim bodies are those of men under judicial warning who are guarded by a single soldier, and the left-hand section, itself divided between the front rows with their wealthy audience and a back room containing the socially less well-to-do. Has the theater of justice borrowed from its fictive brother the social distribution of seats? The play of glances, for its part, escapes the contrasts of opulence: some spectators, caught by the witness on the stand, ignore the eyes that freeze them; others address the lens head-on.

We will not learn anything more from this scene. We must be content with this fine tear in the graphical silence of the past. And approach the narrative of events as the praetorium elaborated it, distributing the figures of good and evil. This rests on three touchstones: the definition of the crimes, the tracing of individual responsibility, and the examination of the role of bystanders.[82]

---

82   The notion of "bystander" is from Hilberg, *Perpetrators, Victims, Bystanders.*

Figure 1.2. Seventh Chamber of the People's Court: The testimony of the minister of propaganda, Dimo Kazasov. *Source:* CDA, F 720, op. 7, ae. 38, film 45/132, no. 1. Courtesy of the Bulgarian Central State Archives.

The Germans, the Fascists, and the "Good People": Drawing the Perimeter of Guilt

Tracing the path by which the documentation of anti-Jewish persecutions was placed at the service of a serious narrative of a notion of collective innocence and Bulgarian heroism leads us to pay privileged attention to two kinds of voices, that of the prosecutors and that of the president of the court. Works of recapitulation, ordering and sorting of the material and testimonial evidence presented during the trial, the indictments, and the judgment also draw on the depositions of key witnesses. The pretrial indictment called 333 witnesses to the stand; 321 eventually appeared before the judges.[83] This image of a "trial of witnesses" nevertheless calls for two nuances. In the pretrial courtroom, the pace of the depositions accelerated as the days

---

83 Requests for the appearance of defense witnesses were granted sparingly, with no more than three or four per defendant.

of the hearings passed.[84] Their tempo often reduced the speaking to a simple retelling of their deposition statements, but without the question-and-answer openings. Above all, testimonies were treated differently depending on the political and social status of the speakers. At the beginning of the trial, the floor was given to the representatives of the new ruling class—the minister of propaganda Dimo Kazasov, the minister of social affairs Grigor Češmedžiev, the secretary-general of the Ministry of Propaganda Menahem Fajonov, the new provisional commissioner for Jewish Affairs Isaak Francez, and the head of the Jewish section of the Fatherland Front Žak Natan. There was no question of constraining their speaking time. The general questions that the president of the court addressed to them, and the relevance of their individual experiences, were intended to guide the public toward a "just" interpretation of the war and the trial.

Before proceeding to the examination of the hearings, a final reminder is in order: exposing the judicial construction of the facts does not amount to postulating the existence of an identical understanding of the crimes in the minds of justice professionals. Although the influence of "fraternal" discussions on the writing of the petitions and on the jurors cannot be proven, given the current state of the archival sources, a reading of the minutes of the trial suggests the existence of a contrast between the wealth of evidence collected by several prosecutors and the weakness of the sentences they demanded. The slippage between the indictments and the pronouncement of the verdicts, toward an unexpected clemency, appears even more striking.

By their density, their brilliance too, two indictments stand out: those prepared by Bărov and Rahamimov. Slavčo Stoilov delivered a rather lackluster summary of the charges and indictments; his main case was that against Stomanjakov, commissioner for Jewish Affairs between October 11, 1943 and July 1944. Finally, it was the turn of Eli Baruh, whose ardor in support of the accusation in cases of forced labor came up against an uncertain mastery of legal knowledge. Of particular interest here was the plea of Prosecutor Bărov. Although he was asked to handle a heterogeneous set of cases (those of Commissioner for Jewish Affairs Belev, several authors of anti-Semitic literature, and members of commissions for the liquidation of Jewish property), it was in fact he who set out the political framework for the deportations from the occupied territories and, by correlation, for the nondeportation of Bulgarian Jews.

---

84 Thirteen witnesses appeared on March 16, seventeen on March 17, thirteen on March 19, thirty-one on March 20, forty-eight on March 21, thirty-one on March 22, forty-six on March 23, sixty-five on March 24, and fifty-seven on March 26.

Born in 1896, Boris Bărov received legal training in Leipzig, Germany, and Vienna, Austria.[85] His international experience, his Communist Party credentials and the authority he enjoyed must have argued for the assignment of such responsibility. The indictment he prepared was marked by two questions:

1. Was the deportation of the Jews of Aegean Thrace and Macedonia imposed by Germany in an imperious, imperative way or did the government have some relative freedom of action and, conscious that [the Jews of Aegean Thrace and Macedonia] were sent to a certain death, could it have offered another fate to those people?
2. What was the position of Tsar Boris in particular on the Jewish question? Was he their friend or their enemy? And who saved the Jews of the ancient territories of our country from the furnaces of Majdanek?[86]

Three hours later, the prosecutor delivered his conclusions. The first: "Never have the interests of this monarchy been in harmony with the interests of the Bulgarian people."[87] Judging that the action "on the Jewish question was only partially enlightened within the framework of general policy,"[88] the public prosecutor intended to dispel the illusion of Jews believing "in the psychological conditions in which they found themselves . . . that their rescue had come from the supreme authoritarian potentate in our country, Tsar Boris."[89] The second conclusion was equally clear-cut: "The answer to the question I have raised—who saved the Jews of the old kingdom of Bulgaria from an appalling death in the murderous furnaces of Majdanek and Belzec?—is now clear: the Bulgarian people, Bulgarian society, the Red Army, and no one else."[90]

Before reaching this denouement, several steps were taken. The first consisted of proving that at least some of the "fascist" elites, moved by

---

85 David Koen, "Narodno văzmezdie," *Godišnik na Obštestvena kulturno-prosvetna organizacija na evreite v Narodna Republika Bălgarija* [hereafter cited as *Godišnik na OKPOE*] 20 (1987): 259. Like nine other prosecutors in the People's Court, Bărov would be arrested after the trial on suspicion of financial malpractice. Prosecutor General Petrov reportedly secured his release. Returning to the bar, Bărov joined the board of the Lawyers' Union at the end of 1946, before being appointed to the Court of Cassation. At the same time, he pursued a career as a professor of civil law.

86 CDA, F 1449, op. 1, ae. 185, l. 39–40.

87 Ibid., l. 44.

88 Ibid., l. 22.

89 Ibid., l. 44.

90 Ibid., l. 50. Bărov's information is incorrect: Jews from the occupied territories were exterminated in Treblinka.

ideological convictions or vile ambitions, had indeed adhered to the project of the Final Solution. To this end, Prosecutor Bărov conducted a meticulous examination of the archives of the Bulgarian Foreign Ministry and claimed, with written evidence, that the authorities meticulously monitored the responses of their neighbors—satellite countries, occupied countries, or allies of the Reich—to German demands. Moreover, he argued that "the Bulgarian fascist governments . . . have proved more servile on the Jewish question than those other satellites of German Hitlerism, Romania and Hungary."[91] At the same time, the prosecutor described at length the actions of an intelligentsia deemed to be fascinated by Nazi ideology and infatuated with King Boris. Once the double guilt of the rulers and of certain intellectuals had been exposed, the question of the innocents remained. A real argumentative challenge: it was a question of simultaneously demonstrating the virulence of fascism—in order to obtain the condemnation of the accused—*and* to convince the court that its contagious effect had remained circumscribed. To do this, the prosecutor established a watertight separation between a handful of traitors to the nation and a society supposedly united in its rejection of moral compromises. Above all, he resorted to a tried and tested oratory technique, the relationship of a history of broken filiation. The target of this virtuoso exercise? Jaroslav Kalicin, the former head of the KEV's Administration Department, one of the chief organizers of Jewish deportations from the occupied territories.

In a rhetorical question, the prosecutor asked him during cross-examination why he showed "sentimentality." The answer brought Kalicin's mother into the picture, disowning her son: "Kalicin knows that he is speaking here in front of the Bulgarian People's Court and, consequently, in front of the Bulgarian people. He feels well that his 'great Bulgarian' visions were and remain only his own, and those of his friend Belev and Co., a group, a clique of pseudo-intellectuals who had nothing in common with the views of Bulgarians. He knew that even his mother would speak out against the plans for greater Bulgaria."[92] Bărov continued, broadening the spectrum of analysis: "A policy of persecution of these people [the Jews] was alien to the vision of the nation of our people. Fascist governments, both in the past and in the present war, did not learn any lessons from the national catastrophes and,

---

91   Ibid., l. 43. Although the Romanian state did not authorize the systematic deportation of Jews from the "old kingdom" of Romania, anti-Jewish pogroms took place in Romania, and the state supervised the extermination of 280,000 to 380,000 Jews in Transnistria. Ioanid, *The Holocaust in Romania.* In Hungary, until the German invasion in the spring of 1944, the authorities refused to carry out the systematic deportation of the Jewish population. Braham, *Politics of Genocide.*

92   CDA, F 1449, op 1, ae. 185, l. 20.

instead of rallying to the healthy social feelings of the Bulgarian people and to the views of the people, cut off all contact with them; devoid of principles and a sense of responsibility, they stubbornly followed the instructions of Hitler's *agentura* and the fatal consequences of those for the people."[93]

It should be noted that the accuser was not content to separate the "fascists" from the "Bulgarian people." He proceeded to the extradition of the former in a double national and social register. "National," since as vassals of the Germans they would have abdicated their Bulgarianness; "social," because they belonged to an elite "that lived its own life, foreign to the life of the broad popular masses."[94] "The nationalist organizations," he continued, "remained foreign to the Bulgarian people and never had any importance for them."[95] Once the parasites have been extracted from the collective body, the image of a Bulgaria oblivious of the divisions would assert itself.

To suspend here the analysis of the indictment prepared by Bărov would, however, amount to only a partial image of his work. For, before delivering this sententious conclusion, the representative of the Public Prosecutor's Office discussed a remarkable corpus of material evidence pointing to the existence, *at the very least* within the Commissariat for Jewish Affairs and the Ministry of the Interior and Public Health, of civil servants who had actually planned to deport *all* Jews living in territories administered by Bulgaria. In fact, it was necessary to await the final judgment of the court to observe a quasi-erasure of Bulgarian responsibility. In the verdict pronounced by President Petrinski, the figures of "traitors to the Bulgarian nation and people" faded away in favor of an accentuation of the German contribution, which echoed the indictment of the First and Second Chambers: "*Entirely under Hitler's diktat*, the government of B. Filov began an inhuman persecution of the Jews. . . . Hooligan pogroms against the Jews and their property began. . . . These repugnant persecutions exposed Bulgaria to the eyes of the civilized world. . . . *But this was Hitler's aim: in order to subjugate Bulgaria, it was necessary to expose and compromise it before the whole civilized world. . . . Thus, the anti-Jewish policy of the fascist governments of Tsar Boris was only one link in the great treason that aimed at making Bulgaria an obedient instrument of German imperialism*."[96]

President Petrinski then asserted:

> It cannot be denied that in our country, too, attempts were made to drive out the Jewish minority. What can be said with certainty, however, is that *the anti-Semitic persecutions in our country are not the work of the*

---

93   Ibid., l. 22.

94   Ibid.

95   Ibid.

96   CDA, F 1449, op. 1, ae. 1, l. 4v (emphasis added).

Bulgarian people, but only of a handful of bureaucrats for whom the Gestapo statutes have had a higher value than the honor and dignity of the people themselves. . . .

In March 1943, the Jews of Thrace and Macedonia were deported. The deportation took place solely in the *newly attached lands, which were not even recognized by Germany*. . . . The will of Germany did not impose itself alone on these lands, but in all our country. . . .

The question of the deportation of the Jews was only authorized by Interior Minister Gabrovski and by Mr. Beckerle, minister plenipotentiary of Germany. . . . *The deportation action was German rather than Bulgarian.* . . .

The deportation of the Jews from the new territories took place with unexpected speed. The action was completed before the Bulgarian people understood what was happening.[97]

Three motives emerge here: first, the Bulgarian state would not have exercised its sovereignty over the occupied territories and could not therefore be held responsible for the policies that were applied there. Second, under German control, only a "handful of [Bulgarian] bureaucrats" would have consented to deportations from the occupied territories. This is forgetting that the Bulgarian authorities received full executive powers over the "Jewish question" from the parliament in June 1942 and that the roundups were authorized by a series of decrees of the Council of Ministers at the beginning of March 1943.[98] Finally, attributing the parsimony of Bulgarian social mobilizations against the arrest of Jews in occupied territories to the lack of time and information amounts to omitting the fact that the political, economic, and social exclusion of Jews in the "old" and "new" kingdoms was a process that lasted more than two years.[99]

The conversion of selective responsibility into collective innocence just depicted does not mean that Bulgarian magistrates were indifferent to the ideological convictions that may have underpinned the commission of the crimes. On the contrary, anti-Semitism lay at the heart of the proceedings. However, the elucidation of its role came up against a political framework that ended up leading the prosecutors to crack the factual and interpretive edifice that they themselves had built: in the courtroom, nothing less than

97 CDA, F 1449, op. 1, ae. 179, vol. 2, l. 30–31 (emphasis added).
98 See the decrees organizing deportations, denaturalization of rounded-up Jews, and liquidation of Jewish property (Decrees 29, 113–17, 126, and 127) adopted by the Council of Ministers between March 2 and 5, 1943, in Grinberg, *Dokumenti* (2015), 22–42.
99 Chary, *Bulgarian Jews*, 35–101.

the consolidation of the emerging regime *and* the demonstration of the legitimacy of proceedings that had to deal with only one type of crime, that committed against Jews, was at stake. At the end of the trial, the Jews left the scene as victims, among many.

A Fascist Is an Anti-Semite . . . and Vice Versa

Faced with the challenge of characterizing persecution on an unprecedented scale, Bulgarian prosecutors fell back on a notion, that of anti-Semitism, that provided a legitimate category of understanding in the political worlds in which they operated. On March 7, 1945, the president of the court announced the opening of the first session: "The Seventh Chamber of the Supreme People's Court opens the hearings of criminal trial No. 7, 1945, against the accused who have manifested themselves as anti-Semites. Anti-Semitism, as a political expression of racism and an attack on the human spirit, is for the first time subjected to the judgment of history and to the conscience of the Bulgarian nation."[100]

The indictment prepared by Bărov had retraced the history of anti-Semitism over the long term, declaring its religious, economic, and political motives. But it is in the learned address of Prosecutor Rahamimov that the theme received its most systematic treatment. The requisitory speech he read will serve as a guide to shed light on the way that a sign of equivalence was drawn between fascism and anti-Semitism. The consequences of this coupling are well known: the contraction of the surface of responsibility, the production of an irenic image of those who were not yet called *bystanders*, and the attribution to the antifascist resistance of the meritorious "rescue of Bulgarian Jews."

Charged with supporting the accusations against eight executives of the Commissariat for Jewish Affairs and three others involved in deportations, the prosecutor decided to place the 1945 trial in a prestigious lineage by tieing it to the Hilsner case, in which a Jew had been accused of ritual murder in Bohemia in 1899, and to the Dreyfus case. Seeking to accord credibility to the action of the Seventh Chamber by reference to these scandalous affairs was not without audacity, since it was the commitment of remarkable individuals—Tomas Masaryk, then professor at the University of Prague, and the French novelist Émile Zola—who opened the way to the overturning of those infamous verdicts. The public denunciation of anti-Semitism constituted their bond of filiation. Although the Bulgarian prosecutor prudently underlined

---

100 CDA, F 1449, op. 1, ae. 179, vol. 1, l. 13.

the contrast between the bourgeois struggle "of specific individuals under the pressure of progressive public opinion" and the collective struggle waged in 1945 for "the honor, dignity, culture, and greatness of an entire people,"[101] he readily imagined himself as heir to Zola's work.[102]

Thus, equipped with a chosen past, Prosecutor Rahamimov also situated the action of the public prosecutor's office in a present envisaged on a European scale. His mental cartography of the persecutions was clearly anchored in the East: the stations of Jewish suffering, as reported by Ilya Ehrenburg in the Soviet press, across Kharkov, Lublin, Lwów, and Bełzec. The Bulgarian prosecutor's legal references were firmly anchored in France, where he stayed with his brother in his youth. Reading his speech before the Seventh Chamber, one would think that in March 1945 the opposition between Soviet and Western conceptions of democracy had not yet been internalized, any more than the geopolitical division of Europe outlined at Yalta a month earlier.

In order to convince the court of the "active and substantial contribution" to the anti-Jewish persecutions by the defendants of the Commissariat, the plea highlighted their affiliation with a xenophobic and anti-Semitic organization the Union of Fighters for the Advancement of Bulgarianness (*Săjuz na ratnicite za napredăka na bălgarštinata*, better known as *Ratnik*) of which wartime interior minister Gabrovski and Jewish Affairs commissioner Belev had been active leaders. The logic was transparent: we are not dealing here with civil servants who had benevolently fulfilled their duty, but with anti-Semites determined to ruin Jewish lives. Mobilizing a wide range of material evidence, the prosecutor went further: he asserted that the *Ratnici* leaders had managed to infiltrate the state apparatus and to recruit agents to defend an anti-Jewish line. A fine tactician, Rahamimov used the figure of Commissioner Belev to evoke these processes; it is through the eyes of the latter that he approached the eminently sensitive theme of the extent of Bulgarian support for anti-Jewish measures: "Aleksandăr Belev, who regularly attended the sessions of parliament and followed all the debates with great attention, was not satisfied with the law [i.e., for the Defense of the Nation]. He considered that it was too soft, that the Jews were given too many rights. . . . Thus, the racist agenda of the state began to be implemented in other ministries as well. The Ministry of the Interior, the Ministry of Finance, and the Ministry of Agriculture and Public Property competed

---

101 CDA, F 1449, op. 1, ae. 185, l. 74.

102 Two years earlier, Rahamimov had become the father of a boy whom he named Emil after the author of *J'accuse*. Interview with Emil Rahamimov, Sofia, December 17, 2016.

with each other to introduce legislation and issue regional decrees, ordinances, and orders severely restricting the rights of Jews."[103]

As will be readily noted, the usual rhetoric of the "fascist clique" is missing here. It was indeed a state policy implemented by ordinary institutions that the public prosecutor sought to highlight. The most daring statement, however, was still to come. From the point of view of Rahamimov, the Bulgarian authorities had not yielded to supposed German pressure; they acted on their own initiative in planning the roundup of some 8,000 Jews holding Bulgarian citizenship: "If the Germans had wanted those 8,000 [Bulgarian] Jews, and not only those 8,000 Jews, but the 40,000 Jews, was there a force in the country that could have opposed them? No. Without question, no. But the Germans did not impose their will, nor did they make this question a diplomatic issue; in fact, they did not issue any official request concerning the dispatch of these 8,000 Jews to the German territories in the East."[104]

No other legal professional dared to accuse the Bulgarian government so explicitly. And yet, at the end of his requisition the prosecutor resolved to dismantle stone by stone the architecture of his reasoning. First of all, he enameled his speech with sentences such as "the Bulgarian people . . . are strangers to anti-Semitism and anti-Jewish persecution."[105] Did not civil servants, whose eagerness to execute anti-Jewish orders Rahamimov had previously evoked, belong to the Bulgarian people? When the time came to seek sentences against the accused, the public prosecutor steadily diminished the responsibility of public officials. With a few exceptions,[106] he refrained from specifying penalties, being content to suggest orders of magnitude[107] or to indicate "that he supported the charges" under paragraphs 4 and 10

---

103 CDA, F 1449, op. 1, ae. 185, l. 93.

104 Ibid., l. 139.

105 Ibid., l. 140.

106 CDA, F 1449, op. 1, ae. 185, l. 153–83. In the case of Kalicin, Rahamimov called for the defendant to "bear full responsibility and [be] subject to full confiscation of his property." Against Zahari Velkov, who supervised the deportations from Macedonia and was being tried in absentia, a "life sentence and full confiscation of his property" were demanded; Penčo Lukov, one of those responsible for the roundups in the "old" kingdom, deserved "no less than fifteen years' imprisonment and partial confiscation of his property." CDA, F 1449, op. 1, ae. 185, l. 153–83.

107 Thus, for Marija Pavlova, deputy director of the Administration Department, and a woman of influence: "a medium sentence"; and for A. Belev's personal secretary, Liljana Panica: "a smaller sentence." Both defendants would leave the court free.

of Article 2 of the October 6, 1944 decree-law.[108] Meanwhile, with anti-Semitism reduced to the rank of an appendage of fascism, a metonymic relationship flourished between the antifascist struggle and the defense of Jewish rights.

In the indictment, Rahamimov dwelled at length on societal mobilizations against the Law for the Defense of the Nation, discussed in parliament in November and December 1940.[109] Mention was made of the letters of protest addressed to the authorities by several professional unions; an even greater impact was attributed to the leaflets that the Workers' Party, then clandestine and weakened, had illegally distributed. Then came the mention of the speeches of deputies during the parliamentary debate on the text: the timid concert of hostile voices was reduced to that of the Communist Todor Poljakov; nothing was said about the commitment of the leader of the Democratic Party, Nikola Mušanov—whom the People's Court had just condemned to a year in prison—or the intervention of Petko Stajnov, who in 1945 as the minister of foreign affairs, was officially a nonaligned figure, whose good relations to the *Zveno* circle were, however, known.[110] The variety of interventions in favor of the Jews was credited only to the "antifascists."

Prosecutor Rahamimov's performance resembled a confluence toward which the narrative currents that irrigated the audiences would have converged. In his deposition, Natan, head of the EOF, had stated: "The question of anti-Semitism cannot be dissociated from that of fascism."[111] A few days later, Prosecutor Baruh echoed his words: "These are inseparable concepts—a fascist is an anti-Semite and an anti-Semite is a fascist."[112] At no time would the defense attorneys' plea that the two concepts be kept

---

108 The case of the mayor of Drama, Angel Čerkezov, comes to mind: "By his actions, Mr. Rahamimov asserts, the defendant Čerkezov actively, substantially, and atrociously persecuted the Jews, for which reason he is answerable under Article 2, para. 10, of the Decree-Law for the People's Court." The defendant was finally acquitted.

109 The bill was modeled on the Nuremberg Laws and laid the groundwork for the identification of Jews and their civic, social, and economic marginalization. It was discussed in the National Assembly on November 15 and 19, 1940, as well as December 20 and 24, when it was adopted; signed by the king on January 15, 1941, the law was published in the *State Gazette* on January 23 and, thus, came into force. See DV, no. 16, January 23, 1941.

110 CDA, F 1149, op. 1, ae. 185, l. 87.

111 CDA, F 1449, op. 1, ae. 181, l. 256.

112 CDA, F 1149, op. 1, ae. 185, l. 272.

separate be heard.[113] The possibility that anti-Semitism may have concerned broader strata of society than "fascist circles" was not considered—and for good reason. The absence of anti-Semitism was referred to as a virtue judged to be particular to the Bulgarian nation. The minister of propaganda, Dimo Kazasov, claimed this point before the judges on March 16: "[The passing of the anti-Jewish legislation] represented a gross assault on a special, very old national value—Bulgarian tolerance."[114] This is particularly significant if one recalls that, in 1940, Kazasov had vigorously denounced the adoption of an anti-Jewish law on the grounds that the Jews—unlike the Turkish minority—did not represent a threat.[115] Following in the wake of the minister, Prosecutor Bărov certified that "as far as racial differences and persecutions are concerned, they were never familiar to the Bulgarian people."[116] A social representation that coalesced in the nineteenth century was thus perpetuated, the new ruling elites taking up an antiphon of the "bourgeois" discourse from which they declared they wished to break.[117]

One enigma remains: why did Jewish Communist lawyers agree to paint their discourse on this canvas? Could it be because they were ideally placed to fear the resurgence of expressions of anti-Semitism in Bulgarian society? The hypothesis cannot be ruled out. In the autumn of 1944, the Sofia Jews expelled in May 1943 were allowed to return to the capital city. A decree on housing was to facilitate their resettlement. On November 28, 1944, the Council of Ministers decided to give this text a restrictive interpretation: only homes actually occupied by their Jewish owners before expropriation were to be vacated within a month; the housing shortage in bombed Sofia and the reluctance of those benefiting from the economic and social exclusion measures underpinned this choice.[118] Another piece of evidence can be added to the file: as early as October 1944, the legal counsel of the Ministry

---

113 The lawyer Mihail Stoenčev, who defended Colonel Mumdžiev, tried to use this distinction to exonerate his client from the charge of "fascism," which he considered to be more serious than the accusation of anti-Semitic sentiments. CDA, F 1449, op. 1, ae. 186, l. 31–33.

114 Ibid., l. 182.

115 CDA, F 250B, op. 1, ae. 47, l. 1–2.

116 CDA, F 1449, op. 1, ae. 185, l. 151.

117 In this multiethnic territory, a province of the Ottoman Empire that became a principality in 1878, the consolidation of the social positions held by the Orthodox Slavs took place at the expense of Turkish-speaking representatives of the Ottoman administrative, military, and landed elites, on the one hand, and of the Greek economic bourgeoisie, on the other. Lory, "Strates historiques des relations bulgaro-turques," 149–67; Avramov, "Anchialo 1906," 31–115.

118 CDA, F 136, op. 1, ae. 48, l. 21.

of Justice began to draft a decree-law on the restitution of looted Jewish property.[119] On January 6, 1945, the Zionist weekly *Cionističeska tribuna* announced that the government had passed it.[120] In this case, the announcement was premature because it took a few more months before the text was issued in the *State Gazette* and thereby promulgated (March 2, 1945)—in a variant that aroused discontent even in the Jewish Communist ranks.[121]

A careful reading of Natan's deposition before the court reinforces this hypothesis. The Jewish political figure raised a pressing question about the loyalty of the Jews of Bulgaria:

> With the blood of heroic Bulgarian youth and of our Jewish youth was sealed the sacred union between the Bulgarian people and the Jewish minority in our country and, as a result, we can affirm that today, when we denounce the anti-Semites, we are doing something for Bulgaria, our homeland, and that we are not animated by other considerations. If, in our country, certain elements want to separate the Jewish minority from the just path where the seeds of love for Bulgaria, the motherland, are sown, we are ready to denounce the representatives of chauvinism in our midst just as the entire Bulgarian people denounces great Bulgarian chauvinism. . . . No doubt should remain in Bulgarian society, when we consider a trial of vital importance for our country, with regard to the depositions made before the People's Court; these have no other motivation than the denunciation of the bearers of anti-Semitism who are also the bearers of fascism.[122]

The emphasis on Jewish patriotism and the exaltation of brotherhood in combat suggest the urgency felt by the Communist Jewish elite to convince the majority of its unwavering allegiance. This statement is particularly illuminating in the light of the conflicts that were going on in the Jewish community in the spring of 1945: the investigation of cases, the conduct of hearings, and the rendering of judgment by the Seventh Chamber had as a background an intensification of the struggles for the control of Jewish institutions and the definition of a collective future.

---

119 CDA, F 136, op. 1, ae. 110, l. 30–38.
120 "Văztanovjavat se vsički imuštestveni prava na evreite," *Cionističeska tribuna*, 14. January 6, 1945, 3.
121 The complexity of the procedures, the obligation of the recipients to pay 5 percent of the amounts received to the Central Consistory of Bulgarian Jews, as well as the delineation of the parameters of the restitutions are particularly controversial. See "Naredba-zakon za urеždane imuštestvenite posledici ot otmjanata na protivoevrejski zakoni," DV, no. 50, March 2, 1945, 1–4; Vasileva, *Evreite v Bălgarija*, 22–23.
122 CDA, F 1449, op. 1, ae. 181, l. 257–58.

The Euphemization of Jewish Suffering

In a book published in Israel in 1960, Eli Baruh, the public prosecutor who handled most of the forced labor cases, bitterly evoked the disinterest of Jewish victims in the People's Court: "Unfortunately, Jewish lawyers, did not take much of an interest in the conduct of this historic trial, even less than other people, and did not contribute much to its success. . . . While many commanders of Jewish labor units went unpunished, the blame lies with those hardworking Jewish lawyers who failed to file in time with the prosecution solidly substantiated cases relating to the commanders' actions."[123]

This lament was similar to the appeal for witnesses he had published in *Cionističeska tribuna*, on January 6, 1945: "Did you not hear the spontaneous voice of the people demanding the People's Court for all those who had forgotten themselves in pecuniary greed, dissolute life, and cruelty toward progressive and honest Bulgarian citizens? . . . To date, no solidly and seriously substantiated complaints by Jewish forced laborers against the cruel, brutal, bribe-extorting commanders of labor units have been received. . . . Why are we silent? Could it be that we are afraid that fascism will come back and that we will have to face up to some unpleasantness?"[124]

In 1972, the American historian Frederick Chary offered an alternative reading of this relative (dis)engagement: dispossessed of their lodgings, stores, and boutiques, deprived of means of subsistence, the Jews would have been more concerned with reestablishing a seed of daily normality than with legal proceedings.[125] This socioeconomic context, although essential, does not suffice to explain the Jewish reservations about bringing war criminals to justice. It must be combined with a consideration of internal competition within the Jewish world.

The conflict between "Communists" and "Zionists" (as it was presented during socialism) has been the subject of a rich historiography structured around two opposing points of view, in Bulgaria and Israel.[126] By reducing the dynamics to a confrontation between partisans of a Jewish national project in Israel and defenders of a revolutionary Communist project in Bulgaria, this literature has tended to undermine the indeterminacy of the end-of-war

---

123 Baruh, *Iz istorijata*, 176.
124 Eli Baruh, "Evrejskite trudovi rabotnici i Narod. săd," *Cionističeska tribuna*, 14, January 6, 1945, 2.
125 Chary, *Bulgarian Jews*, 118.
126 Several post-1989 writings have qualified these assessments: e.g., Vasileva, *Evreite v Bălgarija*, 11–24; and Šealtiel, *Ot rodina kăm otečestvo*, 311–412. See also Haskell, *From Sofia to Jaffa*.

and immediate postwar years,[127] the existence of plural political sensibilities within both the Fatherland Front and the Zionist constellation,[128] the
possible coexistence between leftist convictions and dreams of a "national
home" in Palestine, as well as the effects of the acceleration of time in these
labile months. This is all the more so since this literature was written from
a known outcome—the emigration of nearly 90 percent of the Jewish community of Bulgaria to Israel between 1948 and 1952—and influenced by
ideological struggles that did not end with the demise of the Cold War.
Restoring the palette of fears and enthusiasm observed in the winter of
1944–45 goes beyond the scope of this chapter. Nevertheless, a few avenues
may be sketched out.

After a brief moment of relief associated with the receding threat of
deportations, several lines of contention emerged in Jewish circles whose
bourgeois elites, politically close to the conservatives, looked on with dismay, then with growing concern, at the reforms proposed by the Fatherland
Front.[129] Where the Jewish youth who joined OF embarked on a profusion of political, social, and cultural activities and assumed unprecedented
responsibilities in their euphoria,[130] the more affluent fringe of Bulgarian
Jews noted the strengthening of the state's influence on the economy and
the repression of Bulgarian elites among whom they had many social relations. The Communists promised to "revive Jewish daily life and the Jewish
economy."[131] But notwithstanding the sluggishness of the reestablishment
of Jewish professional rights,[132] the worlds of trade, small business, and
handicrafts were among the first victims of state requisitions, price regula-
tions, and the "fight against speculation" implemented by the authorities.
The reports of the militia reflect the frustrations caused by these measures.

---

127 Following the banning of Jewish organizations in April 1942, some activists
     from youth movements (*Ha-Shomer Ha-Tsair*, *Makabi*, and even *Betar*) joined
     the antifascist struggle. Some youths returned to the Zionist organizations
     after the war. Šealtiel, *Ot rodina kăm otečestvo*, 400.

128 On these internal divisions as seen from the left Zionist (*Poale Cion*) viewpoint
     of a person who finally moved closer to the United Zionist Organization, see
     Keshales, "Tova se sluči."

129 The extent of the social contrasts accentuates these judgments: in the eyes of
     a fraction of the Jewish bourgeoisie, the partisans were more undisciplined
     bandits than war heroes, and the Communist comrades (or parvenus) who ran
     the Jewish institutions were not only political opponents, but also unwanted
     company. Mermall and Yasharoff, *Grace of Strangers*, 43–45.

130 Passi, *Imalo edno vreme*.

131 "Na dobăr păt," *Evrejski Vesti*, 4, November 22, 1944, 1.

132 Vitali Haimov, "Tărpim i čakame," *Cionističeska tribuna*, 2, November 4,
     1944, 1.

Welcoming the weak implantation of the Zionists in the Sofia region, agent Kr. Stefanov noted as follows: "In recent times, various well-known circles, mainly among traders affected by the limitation of speculation, have become Anglophile, demanding freedom of trade and profit, etc. But the majority of Jews remain OF, especially among the youth, workers, and craftsmen."[133] Nor did the creation, in December 1944, of reeducation camps, intended to accommodate "criminals, prostitutes, pimps" alongside figures judged to be politically dangerous, escape the attention of Jews, who tended to act reservedly toward the actions of the government.[134] At the same time, a legislative project was being discussed that would constitute one of the pillars of the repressive arsenal of the Communist regime: the Decree-Law for the Defense of the People's Power (*Naredba-Zakon za zaštita na narodnata vlast*). Adopted on January 26, 1945, and submitted to the regents for approval on March 7, the act came into force on March 17—in the middle of the trial before the Seventh Chamber.[135]

Beyond the struggle for control of communal institutions, relations between the Jewish section of OF and the United Zionist Organization (*Edinna cionistićeska organizacija*, ECO), reconstituted in October 1944, were polarized around three questions: participation in the "patriotic war," conceptions of Jewish identity, and the future of Palestine. At the end of October 1944, the Jewish section of OF launched a vast campaign in favor of conscripting Jews into the armed forces, which, closely supervised by the Red Army, worked to drive the Wehrmacht back from Yugoslavia to Hungary and Austria. Fighting "against the murderers of our six million brothers" was one of the slogans of the conference the Jewish section of OF organized in Sofia on November 12. A few days earlier, *Evrejski Vesti* issued an appeal:

> Our active participation in the final destruction of the Hitlerian hydra is a matter of honor and values. . . . The fact that we are ruined cannot serve as an excuse. We enjoy the most precious possession—*the freedom* that gives us the opportunity to devote ourselves to creative productive work and vast prospects for the restoration of what was lost. . . . Let us go to the front with our heads held high! This *right* that we have wanted for so long is now

---

133 Comdos, F 1, op. 1, ae. 96, l. 44.

134 DV, 15, January 20, 1945.

135 The decree-law provided for the introduction of a new range of incriminations for setting up or leading organizations "with fascist ideology": attempted coups d'état, rebellion, terrorist acts, sabotage or damage to public property, dissemination of false information, and so on. Penalties included capital punishment or life imprisonment. See the decree-law at http://www.decommunization.org/Communism/Bulgaria/Documents/ZZNarVlast.htm.

given to us to make use of to avenge every single victim of the Hitlerist beast and their fascist followers.[136]

Should we be surprised to find from Avram Kalo's pen an additional argument in favor of this commitment? "It is only by taking this path, shoulder to shoulder with the entire Bulgarian people in a common struggle against the enemies of humanity—the German fascists—that the hatred of the Jews artificially sown by the Bulgarian chauvinists will be removed and that a healthy brotherhood similar to that which binds the peoples of the USSR and of the new Yugoslavia will be built."[137] While the Zionist press refrained from disavowing the armed struggle against the Nazis, it approached with caution the Jewish contribution to the war effort and focused its coverage on the creation of a Jewish brigade in Palestine deployed in the European theater.[138] Within the Jewish community, of all political persuasions, the call to arms was extraordinarily unpopular, as some forced laborers had only just been demobilized. Physically and morally exhausted, Bulgarian Jews were also unfamiliar with the handling of weapons. The doors to a military career had only narrowly opened to them after the creation of a Bulgarian Principality in 1878, then completely closed during World War II. Sending hastily trained recruits to the front line was virtually tantamount to certain death.[139]

The bifurcation of judgments on the war prolonged the crystallization of contrasting readings of the recent events. From the extermination of the Jews of Europe, the extent of which they were discovering more dramatically every day, the Zionists drew the conclusion that the temptation of assimilation was a mistake. Making his own the maxim according to which "You can live in brotherhood with other peoples, but do not forget your individuality

---

136 Avram Kalo, "Evreite i Otečestvenija Front," *Evrejski Vesti*, 2, November 4, 1944, 1.

137 Josif Baruhov, "Vsiški na fronta!," *Evresjki Vesti*, 2, November 4, 1944, 2.

138 "Evrejskijat narod—vojuvašta strana," *Cionističeska tribuna*, 8, November 25, 1944, 1.

139 The lack of military training for Jews and the prevalence of anti-Semitism in the army was noted in a report by the head of the Department for Work with the Masses of the Central Committee of the Workers' Party in 1945. CDA, F 1B, op. 25, ae. 71, l. 17–18. The Jewish Consistory tried to intercede with the War Ministry to have men born in 1921–24 excluded from conscription. On November 27, 1944, Order No. 9 693 of the General Staff recognized the months spent in labor camps as "military service" and exempted Jews subjected to forced labor from mobilization. CDA, F 622, op. 1, ae. 9, l. 23–24, 26–37, 45.

and its value," Ahad Aam looked without kindness at Germany, "where assimilation had affected 90 percent of the Jews":

> Coming from wealthy strata, they had disavowed Jewish nationalism. But events in this country very bitterly contradicted the theory of the assimilationists [*assimilantite*], who claimed that the Jews had long since ceased to be a people, that they did not exist as a Jewish nation, that only a Jewish religion existed, etc. . . . In practice, even in the most democratic countries, in the best of cases, Jews are treated as citizens of another category, inferior to that of non-Jews. This attitude has nothing to do with our religious affiliation. Today the people among whom we live do not even want to know to which religion we belong. It is important to them to know to which nation we belong.[140]

In the light of the war, Jewish history is reread as a history of uninterrupted persecution since the destruction of Babylon:

> Two thousand years have passed since the Jewish people lost their independence. Since then, the great Jewish tragedy has unfolded throughout the history of mankind up to the present day. For several centuries, Polish, German, Czech, etc. Jews have worked to create cultural and commercial centers, forgetting to learn the lessons of Jewish history—two death storms have shaken the diaspora. Some precursors of the deadly storm warned of the approach of death. [Ber] Borochov, [Theodor] Herzl, [Max Simon] Nordau, etc. shouted: "Leave the diaspora, build your homeland!" But no one paid attention to these signals. And today we are witnesses to the terrible Jewish catastrophe that makes others pale. Majdanek, Trambinka [*sic*] etc. are symbols of the greatest massacre in the history of mankind. . . . Six and a half million corpses of children, women, the young and old were murdered and burned simply because they were Jews. . . . *In vain, the Jews believed that culture and human progress would solve the "Jewish question."*[141]

No recourse to justice could therefore protect Jews from the threat of oppression. Sabitaj Eškenazi, a supporter of Workers of Zion (*Poale Cion*), a left-wing Zionist movement, summed up the general sentiment before the

---

140 Ahad Aam, "Asimilacija," *Cionističeska tribuna*, 3, October 23, 1944, 4.

141 Š. Dembovič, "Evreite v Evropa i Palestina," *Cionističeska tribuna*, 3, October 23, 1944, 2 (emphasis added). *Cionističeska tribuna* offered an estimate of those Jews who had been able to settle in Palestine in 1944: "7,291 Jews, 248 Arabs, 957 others. Of which 1,516 from Romania, 1,257 from Turkey, 913 from Yemen, 521 from Bulgaria, 311 from Czechoslovakia, 300 from Iraq, 270 from Poland, 257 from Germany and Austria, 181 from Syria and Lebanon, 106 from Hungary, 52 from Egypt, etc." See "7,291 imigranti pristignali v Palestina," *Cionističeska tribuna*, 3, October 23, 1944, 2.

national conference of local OF committees and Jewish municipalities in January 1945: "We do not want laws that protect us, we want to write these laws ourselves."[142] More than ever, Palestine was a horizon for the future: "The Jewish State will return to our people the benefit of true humanity: the Homeland, pride, spiritual freedom and the history of a future. This is the only solution to the Jewish question. There is no other."[143]

The visit of David Ben-Gurion, the executive director of the Jewish Agency for Palestine, who crisscrossed Bulgaria (visiting Svilengrad, Haskovo, Plovdiv, and Sofia) December 1–7, 1944, reinforced this momentum.[144] However, contrary to its initial declarations, the Bulgarian government multiplied the obstacles to emigration.[145] At the beginning of November 1944, in a letter addressed to the prime minister, the representative of the Jewish Agency for Palestine in Sofia deplored the refusal by the leadership of the militia to issue exit visas favoring aliyah candidates.[146] On November 21, he denounced the cumbersome procedures.[147] Jews wishing to emigrate had to "renounce their rights" over their property, liquidate it, and draw up an inventory of the property transferred. The height of absurdity, "no municipality can issue such certificates. Not only because verification is a laborious process, but because the law on the restitution of property taken from the Jews has not yet been published and, consequently, this property is not formally returned to the Jews, so that the latter cannot liquidate it." Above all, migrants had now to provide an attestation signed by a public prosecutor confirming "that the person is not under indictment or charge for crimes of a general nature or under the Law on the People's Court." The representative of the Jewish Agency protested: "We believe that, against the Jews, as fully antifascist elements who have been the most affected by this [fascist] regime, charges have not and will not be brought before the People's Court." Could certain Jews, judged too close to the former elite or who had rallied to the "chauvinistic" project of "Greater Bulgaria," fall under the law?

On the subject of the People's Court, *Cionističeska tribuna* initially adopted a significantly more favorable line than we might have expected from the interinstitutional exchanges preserved in the archives of the Bulgarian secret police. On February 20, 1945, the newspaper reproduced a resolution of the local Ruse branch of the Pioneer Youth Organization (*He-halutz*)

---

142 Vasileva, *Evreite v Bălgarija*, 21; CDA, F 622, op. 1, ae. 132, l. 15–18.
143 Dembovič, "Evreite v Evropa i Palestina," 2.
144 Keshales, "Tova se sluči," 57–64; "Baruh Aba!," *Cionističeska tribuna*, 9, December 1, 1944, 1; "Bulgarian Jews in Desperate Plight, Ben-Gurion Reports; No Jewish Property Returned," *Jewish Telegraphic Agency*, December 22, 1944.
145 Keshales, "Tova se sluči," 69–77.
146 Comdos, F 1, op. 1, ae. 53, l. 2–4.
147 Ibid., l. 7–8.

preparing future *olim* for agricultural work, acclaiming the "severe but just" sentences of the First and Second Chambers.[148] Two weeks later, the Central Committee of the Unified Zionist Organization registered the bringing to justice of the perpetrators of fascist crimes to the credit of the Fatherland Front. Gurner signed an apologetic commentary:

> The fascist beasts could not be stopped. And so, in their blindness they went so far as to declare war on the great progressive peoples and provoked our savior—Russia. Only then did the glass of patience overflow. The people rose up, took their destiny into their own hands, caught the entire fascist mafia, brought it before the People's Court, and sentenced it to death. The verdict against those responsible for the third national catastrophe, though severe but just, can in no way redeem the faults committed by the murderers of the Bulgarian people. . . . It only comes to appease the popular conscience and remind all of society's factions that the people are masters of their own destiny.[149]

Likewise, the preparation of the hearings before the Seventh Chamber was evoked in a language that the leaders of the Workers' Party would not have disavowed. On March 1, the attorney Nisim Aron Papo took up the Communist slogan: "The fight against fascism is a fight against anti-Semitism. The victory: a full and final victory over fascism means victory over anti-Semitism."[150] An appeal for witnesses was launched to support the accusation against the expropriators of Jewish enterprises.[151] The only publicly discordant note was the Zionists' insistence on the exceptionality of Jewish suffering, as this telegram to the president of the Seventh Chamber testifies:

> The Central Committee of the Bulgarian Unified Zionist Organization, which brings together the nationally minded Jews in the country, welcomes the efforts of the People's Court to clarify and establish the criminal acts of Hitler's agents in the country, who sent 12,000 Jews from Belomorie and Macedonia to their deaths, inflicted great spiritual suffering, and completely ruined Bulgarian Jews and, in so doing, exposed and sullied the name of Bulgaria and its tolerance of the country's Jewish minority. The Bulgarian Jews await a severe and just sentence in order to satisfy and appease the upset spirits of the first and greatest victim of Hitlerism in the country—the Bulgarian Jews—and thus to restore the integrity and reputation of the Bulgarian people.[152]

---

148 *Cionističeska tribuna*, 18, February 20, 1945, 2.
149 Š. Gurner, "Narodnata prisăda," *Cionističeska tribuna*, 17, February 10, 1945, 1.
150 Papo, "Antisemitite pred narodnija săd," 1.
151 *Cionističeska tribuna*, 21, March 1, 1945, 2.
152 "Telegrama na Edinnata cionističeska organizacija do VII săstav na Narodnija săd," *Cionističeska tribuna*, 23, March 17, 1945, 1 (emphasis added).

Yet, after a flamboyant opening article,[153] *Cionističeska tribuna* remained silent on the judicial arena during the hearings: no transcriptions of witness statements, nor extracts from the prosecutors' requisitions or the court judgment. Even more astonishing was the fact that the Zionist leaders' interventions in the courtroom—the head of the Unified Zionist Organization, Vitali Haimov;[154] the attorney and leader of the Jewish municipality of Plovdiv, Žak Levi; the former vice president of the Central Jewish Consistory, Nisim (Buko) Levi, also a lawyer; the former head of the Jewish Agency for Palestine during the war, the lawyer Jako Baruh; and others—received no echoes.[155] Levi appeared in court as a defense witness, taking up the case of the head of the Department of Forced Labor in the Ministry of Public Works, Colonel Mumdžiev, who was charged with "anti-Jewish persecution."[156] Nisim Buko Levi came to testify on behalf of Liljana Panica, Commissioner Belev's personal secretary, who had brought him in on the secret of the deportations.[157] Summoned to give an account of the mobilizations against the deportation of Bulgarian Jews, Baruh, who was at the time in the process of breaking off his allegiance with ECO and had initiated a rapprochement with the Fatherland Front, denounced Stomanjakov for his role as the commissioner for Jewish Affairs; he also exposed the alleged misdeeds (misappropriations, concussions, abusive proximity to former rulers) of the president of the Jewish municipality of Ruse, Fiko Levi, one of the targets of the Jewish section of the Fatherland Front.[158]

Could the internal divisions within Zionist circles and the distribution of Zionist testimonies for and against certain defendants explain the public silence in the Zionist print press regarding the course of the trial? The acceleration of political time provides an additional explanatory variable. On February 20, 1945, *Cionističeska tribuna* devoted a double issue to

---

153 S. Farhi, "Edna godišnina," *Cionističeska tribuna*, 22, March 10, 1945, 1.

154 Reflecting the tensions between Communist and Zionist Jews in the spring of 1945, Vitali Haimov was only allowed a brief deposition, late in the hearings (March 23), against the commissioner for Jewish Affairs, Stomanjakov; a senior KEV official, Dr. Ivan Popov; and Marija Pavlova, deputy director of the Administration Department. CDA, F 1449, op. 1, ae. 183, l. 236–37.

155 CDA, F 1449, op. 1, ae. 182, l. 124.

156 The colonel is said to have agreed to the request of a delegation of Jews from Plovdiv, led by Žak Levi, not to demobilize Greek Jewish forced laborers in October 1943, in order to protect them from possible deportation. Prior to the roundups of March 1943, the Commissariat for Jewish Affairs had demanded the demobilization of former Yugoslav and Greek forced laborers present in the "old" kingdom. CDA, F 1449, op. 1, ae. 184, l. 177–81.

157 CDA, F 1449, op. 1, ae. 183, l. 30–35.

158 CDA, F 1449, op. 1, ae. 182, l. 78–85.

Palestine, the tone of which evoked the radiant happiness of 1930s Soviet propaganda.[159] Shaken by state repression, the emigration of a fringe of its leading cadres during the war, and the conflicts surrounding the issuance of certificates for Palestine, the Zionist movement was going through a phase of reorganization.[160] In the autumn and winter of 1944, a conflict arose between Sofia attorney Jako Baruh, the main interlocutor of the Jewish Agency for Palestine and its Istanbul branch, and the leader of the Unified Zionist Organization, Vitali Haimov, over the future of the Zionist constellation, relations with the Fatherland Front, as well as the management of the Jewish cultural house, the cultural and social center of the community. The discord ended with the marginalization of Baruh, who was also considered too close to the Communists. The struggle for Jewish self-determination could thenceforth attract the full attention of the Zionists, at the price of deteriorating relations with the Communists.

On March 8, 1945, Radenko Vidinski, head of the commission for minorities at the Central Committee of the Workers' Party, opened the hostilities. "One should not believe that today, in Bulgaria, everything is allowed, including sowing 'great national' ideas among minorities."[161] The Zionist reply that arrived nine days later was scathing: "The elementary demand for normal national life, for the creation of conditions favorable to a just historical development similar to that of all other peoples, is not and cannot amount to spreading 'great nationalism.'"[162] To these intrigues, the courtroom was hostage.

The view of the Communists and their social democratic allies of the judicial process was deduced as if by transfer from that of the unified Zionists. From the point of view of the members of the Fatherland Front, equal rights and justice—not emigration—had to provide an answer to the Jewish question. The social democratic lawyer David Ieroham, the new president of the Jewish Consistory, reminded us of this: "The whole OF program relies on the law, on justice. . . . Where equality prevails, there is no Jewish problem."[163] Punishing the perpetrators of crimes would demonstrate that fascism constituted a parenthesis, attributable to a handful of "traitors," and that this parenthesis was now closed. Under the pen of Žak Natan, *Evrejski*

---

159 *Cionističeska tribuna*, 19–20, February 20, 1945, 1–5.

160 On these interpersonal, institutional, and generational tensions, see Šealtiel, *Ot rodina kăm otečestvo*, 195–201; and Keshales, "Tova se sluči."

161 "Nacionalnite malcinstva i Očestvenofrontovska Bălgarija," *Otečestven front*, 134, March 8, 1945, 3.

162 C. M. Lazar, "Nacionalnite malcinstva," *Cionističeska tribuna*, 23, March 17, 1945, 1.

163 David Ieroham, "Po koj păt?," *Evrejski Vesti*, 1, October 30, 1944, 4.

Vesti proclaimed it loud and clear: "The division sown by fascist domination must be erased. The Bulgarian people are our best defenders and friends."[164]

From the advances of the Seventh Chamber of the People's Court, *Evrejski Vesti* proposed without surprise much broader coverage. The publication also did an impressive job of transcribing archives[165] and reproduced photographs of the arrest and detention of Jews in the "new" kingdom (the occupied territories) from the holdings of the Commissariat for Jewish Affairs. In the courtroom, most Communist Jews also supported the accusation. Their desire to argue the possibility of intercommunity coexistence was reflected in a topography of societal divisions that did not set Jews against non-Jews but rather, within each cultural group, the defenders of the "chauvinistic" project against the supporters of brotherhood. The formulation reached perhaps its most accomplished version in the statement of Žak Natan, a member of the Central Committee of EOF: "A malevolent atmosphere [settled] in our country from 1941, a malevolent atmosphere that cost the Bulgarian people a great deal, that brought misfortune not only to the Jewish minority in Bulgaria, because of which the Jewish minority suffered in Bulgaria along with the Bulgarian people, who were fighting against fascism and in many respects suffered more than the Jewish minority in Bulgaria, since they were actively fighting against fascism."[166]

Let us concede that this syntactic elaboration is somewhat tortured. At the beginning of the paragraph, the singularity of the Jewish experience of the war fades away behind the postulate of a shared cruel destiny. At the end of the statement, the configuration is reversed: from a grief that had affected the various parts of society in equal measure, one has moved to a minimized Jewish suffering when measured against the trials and tribulations of non-Jews.

It was Rahamimov who was entrusted with the presentation of the summation. By specifying that he intervened as prosecutor, member of the Consistory, and victim, the public prosecutor highlighted the porous boundaries between the roles assumed by Jews involved in the retribution of crimes. His tribute to the ruling coalition also leaves one dubious: "Thanks to the energetic and obstinate intervention of Bulgarian society and the Fatherland Front, which at the time illegally prepared the Bulgarian peasants and workers to defend the Jews, thanks to the Bulgarian people who

---

164 Žak Natan, "Našite zadači," *Evrejski Vesti*, 1, October 30, 1944, 1.
165 As early as December 1944, *Evrejski Vesti* reproduced the agreement concluded on February 22, 1943, between Theodor Dannecker, Adolf Eichmann's special envoy in Bulgaria, and Belev, the commissioner for Jewish Affairs, for the deportation of 20,000 Jews.
166 CDA, F 1449, op. 1, ae. 181, l. 257.

had warm feelings for them, *we were saved*. And I, here, from this place, as prosecutor and as delegate of the Central Consistory of the Jews of Bulgaria, warmly thank the government of the Fatherland Front and all the valiant Bulgarian people for our rescue."[167]

Ultimately, the aspiration to defend coexistence, transcending cultural boundaries, thus led Communist Jews to inscribe their description of war experiences into the Communist interpretive matrix and to participate in the euphemization of anti-Jewish persecution. As for the Seventh Chamber, created specifically to deal with anti-Jewish crimes and thus, incidentally, to make their uniqueness known, it was deprived of the means to accomplish this task by being subordinated to the production of a narrative of interethnic solidarity.

The Posterity of the Court: A Central Elision

On April 2, 1945, the court handed down its judgment. Under Article 2, paragraph 10 (persecution of Jews) and Article 2, paragraph 4 (prevarication and influence peddling), the defendants risked a "fixed sentence of temporary or life imprisonment, or the death penalty, and a fine of up to 5 million *leva*." Twenty of the fifty-three defendants were acquitted. Two were sentenced to death; three to life imprisonment; and three to sentences of ten to fifteen years in prison. The other prison sentences ranged from one year (nine defendants, *of which seven were conditional*), two years (seven), five years (five), six years (one), and eight years (one). The notion of "active and substantial" contribution to persecution was limited to acts related to the organization of roundups and deportations. The Aryanization and liquidation of Jewish property was punished primarily in cases where public officials misappropriated sums intended for the public treasury for their own benefit, or else when financial extraction from Jews was obtained through resort to sadistic and violent means. Forced labor as such was not qualified as an infringement of Jewish rights: sentences punished the acceptance of bribes by unit chiefs—in exchange for "favors" granted to forced laborers— or an exercise of physical violence deemed disproportionate and, therefore, discriminatory. How can such leniency be understood, especially when one remembers the sentencing policy applied by the First and Second Chambers of the People's Court at the end of January 1945, which handed down 103 death sentences for 166 defendants, and no acquittals?

---

167 CDA, F 1449, op. 1, ae. 185, l. 147 (emphasis added).

Several testimonies suggest that intercessions influenced the court's assessment of the evidence. In a report addressed to the Central Committee of the Workers' Party in July 1945, Prosecutor General Petrov deplored the pressure exerted on the judges in the case of Marija Pavlova, deputy director of the Administration Department of the Commissariat:

> The case of Pavlova—cousin of Dr. Hr[isto] Kabakčiev,[168] who was the first assistant of the executioner Belev and is coauthor of the most serious crimes. The argument was that it was necessary to save the name of comrade Hr. Kabakčiev. I thought that his name and spirit would have been better defended by liquidating such a criminal and traitor of the people with a heavy sentence. . . . This unjustified sentence is the reason for the discontent of the Jewish comrades and of society up to the present day. I did not agree with it, but some people interceded directly with members of the Court.[169]

Other witnesses at the time suggested that the outcome of the trial had been determined by political considerations. Samuil Arditi—the son of Benjamin Arditi, a Jewish merchant born in Vienna, who established himself in Bulgaria in 1916, became a leader of the small Revisionist Zionist movement in interwar Sofia, then settled in Israel after the war—reported comments that his father had confided to him: "On the day of the judgment, Mančo Rahamimov came out of Petrinski's office angry and agitated; some of the accused had been exonerated, the death sentences were not going to be carried out. The sentences imposed were minimal. The party spoke out against further death sentences. Much blood has already been shed. It opposed harsh sentences in order not to stir up society."[170] The assertion, although it cannot be supported by archival sources, appears plausible. At the end of long months of dramatic legal proceedings, at the beginning of April 1945 the priority of the Communist leaders was a (temporary) demobilization of the

---

168 Hristo Kabakčiev (1878–1940), a lawyer by training, publicist by profession, was one of the most renowned leaders of the Bulgarian Communist movement in the interwar period, as well as the editor in chief of *Rabotničeski vestnik* (Worker's newspaper). After spending two and a half years in prison for his role in planning the September 1923 Communist uprising and being sentenced to twelve years imprisonment in 1925 (only to be released shortly thereafter), he immigrated to the USSR, where he was to fall victim in 1938 to the Great Purge. He died shortly after his release from a Soviet prison in October 1940.

169 CDA, F 250B, op. 1, ae. 68, l. 13–14.

170 Samuil Arditi, "VII-jat săstav: Edna goljama farsa," July 9, 2004, http://forums.f-e-n.net/viewtopic.php?p=425301&sid=cb20d72bcb85c37fdb65f713883d2fb6 (accessed February 19, 2020; no longer active).

masses, the management of social discontent, and a calming of interpartisan relations. Preparations for the general elections, initially scheduled for August 1945 and postponed to November, polarized attention: in the expectation of a severe political struggle, the priority was to seek consensus. In this case, it could not be ruled out that certain high officials of the state and the party were hostile to the pronouncement of sentences whose severity would, in their view, have betrayed an abusive singling out of Jewish victims.

That such an outcome was felt in Jewish Communist circles as a failure can be inferred from an oblique reading of the debates of the Central Jewish Commission of the Central Committee of the Workers' Party concerning the appointment of the secretary of the Jewish municipality of Sofia in January 1946. Natan Grinberg, who is remembered for having carried out research in the archives of the Commissariat for Jewish Affairs in the autumn of 1944, was a candidate for the post.[171] Several votes were opposed, including that of Betty Danon, a former partisan: "Grinberg bears responsibility for the *failure of the Jewish trial* at the People's Court."[172] And the Communist lawyer Israel Majer continued: "From the moment he [N. Grinberg] was invited to the Commissariat for Jewish Affairs, he locked himself up alone there, to write his book; he is one of the people responsible for the failure of the trial, because he kept to himself documents not handed over to the popular militia that would have been important for the trial."[173]

In May 1946, the conduct of the "trial of the anti-Semites" was nevertheless put forward by the Bulgarian delegation at a London meeting organized as part of the peace negotiations. A declaration of the Central Consistory of the Jews of Bulgaria was made public there:

> Immediately after the changes of September 9, all decrees and laws restricting the rights of Jews were abolished. A fact of great importance for the future democratic development of our country should be strongly emphasized here. All the culprits and propagators of fascism in our country have been brought to justice before a Special People's Court. The regents; the ministers of all the fascist cabinets; the members of parliament who passed the racial and fascist laws and declared war on the allied peoples; the military, journalists, writers, professors, agents of the administrative apparatus and the police; etc. received severe but just sentences.
>
> Particularly important and significant is the fact that independently of the abovementioned chambers, a special chamber of the People's Court

---

171 CDA, F 622, op. 1, ae. 127, l. 33–39.
172 Ibid., l. 32 (emphasis added).
173 Ibid., l. 50 (emphasis added).

was created to examine the criminal acts of all anti-Semites who actively and substantially contributed to the implementation of the racial laws in the country. *Bulgaria is one of the few states in Europe where fascist criminals have been convicted and the only one in which anti-Semites and anti-Semitism as an ideology have been stigmatized and tried.*[174]

The text was intended as a refutation of the report on the situation of the Jews of Bulgaria published by the Anglo-American Commission of Inquiry into the Problems of European Jews and Palestine[175] in April 1946:

The Jews at home greeted with astonishment and rejected the findings of the Anglo-American Commission for Palestine concerning the situation of the Jews in Bulgaria.

1. In Bulgaria, of the Jews who died as a result of Nazi persecution, there were none, except for those who fell as partisans. The number of Jews in our country has not decreased; on the contrary, it has increased.

2. All Jews in the country enjoy the support of the government. There are no Jews in Bulgaria who are worried. Absolutely no difference has existed between Jews and Bulgarians since September 9. It is true that the Jews have on the whole become poorer, but this is due to their dispossession under the fascist regime. Now, in parallel with the economic recovery of the Jewish people whose properties have been stolen by the Germans, the situation of the [Bulgarian] Jews is recovering.

3. The assertions according to which the Bulgarian government would prevent Jews who wished to do so from leaving the country do not correspond to the reality of the facts.[176]

---

174 The statement of the Central Consistory of Bulgarian Jews of May 12, 1946, originally published in *Evrejski Vesti*, 80, May 12, 1946, 1, and reproduced in "Priloženie kăm arhivnija fond," *Godišnik na OKPOE* 19 (1985): 345–49 (emphasis added). It is followed by a translation into Bulgarian of the World Jewish Congress's reply, which stated that due to the nondeportation of Bulgarian Jews, no clause concerning Jews should be included in the peace treaty.

175 *Report of the Anglo-American Committee of Enquiry Regarding the Problems of European Jewry and Palestine*, Lausanne, April 20, 1946, Cmd 6808, Pro 30/78/30, The National Archives (Kew), https://www.bibliotheque-numerique-aiu.org/viewer/16089/?offset=#page=16&viewer=picture&o=bookmark&n=0&q=.

176 *Godišnik na OKPOE* 19 (1985): 348 (emphasis added).

Insisting on the status of the Bulgarian trial, the declaration did not attempt to link the judicial treatment of anti-Jewish crimes in Bulgaria with the work of incrimination, qualification, and judgment of Nazi crimes carried out by the International Military Tribunal at Nuremberg at the same time. It is within another referential framework that the trial before the Seventh Chamber is inscribed: that of the condemnation of racism and anti-Semitism, a key theme of Bulgarian public discourse in the spring of 1946. Above all, the Consistory declaration took up several obligatory figures from the Seventh Chamber in relation to the crimes committed. Bulgaria was presumed to be a victim of Nazi Germany. Cautiously, however, the notion of "occupied people" was preferred to that of "occupied country": "The fascist governments did not dare to send Jews to their deaths whereas the governments of the other *occupied European peoples* gave their authorization." The theme of Bulgarian victimhood was prolonged by the assertion that "in Bulgaria there were no Jews who died as a consequence of Nazi persecution." The outcome was predictable: "The Bulgarian people, together with the Bulgarian Jews who constitute an inseparable part of it, are fighting in the name of the principles under the flag of which the Allied peoples fought. . . . And we are convinced that, if these facts are correctly appreciated, just decisions will be reached."[177]

From the spring of 1946, the narrative of Jewish suffering and Bulgarian heroism thus received the form that it would largely retain until the fall of communism. Is this the reason why the legacy of the People's Court disappeared from public space in a matter of months, like a mold broken once the imprint of a sculpture has set? As elsewhere in Europe, a Cold War atmosphere spread over Bulgaria during 1947. The hardening of the regime under the leadership of Vălko Červenkov, a fan of "show trials," the anti-Semitic campaign of late Stalinism, and emigration to the new State of Israel encouraged the Jews remaining in Bulgaria to adopt a low profile. At the time when Žak Natan published his memoirs in 1971, the judgment of anti-Jewish crimes was only entitled to laconic appraisal: "We had to take part in the judgment of the anti-Semites, of leaders, and of organizers of anti-Jewish persecutions."[178] Nothing survived of the terror caused by the discovery of the destruction of the Jews of the "new" kingdom and of Europe.

Admittedly, the official silence was in some instances broken by public reminiscences: on the tenth anniversary of the verdict of the Seventh Chamber, in 1955, the court's judgment was the subject of bitter debates among Bulgarian Jews living in Israel. During the Eichmann trial (1961),

---

177 Ibid., 349 (emphasis added).
178 Natan, *Pametni vremena*, 290–91.

the Bulgarian authorities praised themselves for having judged anti-Jewish crimes at an early stage. In the 1980s, finally, the patrimonialization of the "rescue of Bulgarian Jews" led to a timid reevaluation of the action of the People's Court. However, the essential lies elsewhere: obliteration is not tantamount to oblivion. In the following chapters, we will show how a harmonic scheme, composed in 1944–45, crossed the decades and the East-West frontiers, traveling in the form of notes transmitted orally or in written mentions to unpublished sources. It is possible to go so far as to argue that the heart of the cultural, rhetorical, and historical productions devoted to Jewish destinies during the socialist era resided in the silent dialogue they established with the founding moment of a process whose centrality was renewed by its very elision.

Chapter 2

Deportation of the Jews, from Belomorie to the Screen

Negotiating a "Socialist" Reading of the War

Hristo Radevski (poet): What's at the heart of the film?
Emil Petrov (film critic): At the heart of the film is, I think, the relationship
between Ruth and Walter.
H. Radevski: Between a Greek Jew and a German soldier? Why
make such a film?
E. Petrov: You would have to ask the producers; that question
is irrelevant in evaluating the artistic work as an artistic production.
Nikola Mirčev (painter): Bulgarian Jews weren't sent to Auschwitz.
H. Radevski: On the other hand, we are making a film that will
help strengthen Bulgarian-German bonds.

—Meeting of the East German–Bulgarian Artistic Council,
January 5, 1959[1]

January 5, 1959. We are back in Sofia, fourteen years after we left it. In the
city center, the zeal of the builders of socialism has consigned all traces of
the war, as well as the prewar era, to dust. Now, Stalinist neoclassicist buildings surround the Largo, a vast triangular square where streets of shops once
wound in and around Jewish-owned businesses. Crowned by a red star, the
Headquarters of the Bulgarian Communist Party (*Bălgarska komunističeska
partija*, BKP) towers over the view, facing left toward the future presidency
building, right toward the gleaming Central Universal Mall (*Centralen
Universalen Magazin*, CUM)—Bulgaria's first shopping mall, built in 1957.

---

1   CDA, F 404, op. 4, ae. 130, l. 27.

Bulgarian socialism has entered the age of consumption, its arrival hailed by singer Lea Ivanova in a jazzy popular song "Cum! Cum! Cum!"

Let us continue our stroll. A few strides away from the capital city's political center, the East German–Bulgarian Artistic Council holds its meetings (a brief excerpt from one can be found in the epigraph). As in other European cities, in the final quarter of the nineteenth century Sofia had developed by unfurling out from a large central avenue: blanketed, in 1907–8, with a distinct swath of small, straight, bright yellow cobblestones. The street, opportunely renamed Lenin Avenue, now runs along the party headquarters before greeting the mausoleum of the departed socialist leader G. Dimitrov, his embalmed body maintained with scientific care. White, massive, and angular, the memorial stands opposite the former Bulgarian Royal Palace, now an art museum, where—though few passersby would recall it—the Ottoman governor of the Sofia district once resided. Turning right, one continues alongside the Rakovski Street cinemas—some of which were converted into theaters in the 1940s—before weaving in and out of side lanes to reach Slavejkov Square, known in the prewar period for its buzzing cabaret nightlife. Following the tracks of the tramway and the emblematic Holy Seven Saints Church, there appears Šišman Street, named after one of the medieval khans who ruled over Bulgaria. (The city's histories have not all been effaced to an equal extent.) Here, the national Bulgarian cinema company, D. P. Bălgarska Kinematografija (Bulgarian Cinematography), a public monopoly created in 1948, has installed a projection room where artists, producers, directors, and party leadership representatives gather. On the docket: socialist art and ideological correctness.

> *Object of investigation:* the film *Zvezdi/Sterne* (Stars), coproduced by the Studio für Spielfilme of the Deutsche Film Aktiengesellschaft (DEFA) and the Bulgarian *Studija za igralni filmi* (SIF Bojana), directed by the East German filmmaker Konrad Wolf, from a screenplay by the Bulgarian Angel Wagenstein.[2]

> *Mark of distinction:* the first—and only—Bulgarian socialist film to address the deportation of the Jews from the Greek territories under Bulgarian occupation during the war.

> *Critical response:* the work was entered into the Cannes Film Festival in 1959 under the Bulgarian flag—a geopolitical necessity, given that the German Democratic Republic was not recognized by France[3]—where it

---

2   Note on transliteration: Angel Wagenstein's name is spelled in its usual English variation, except in connection to texts written in Bulgarian.

3   The rule to be followed was that the selected works must stem from nations with which France, as the host country, had diplomatic relations. In 1955,

was awarded the Special Jury Prize, while François Truffaut's *Four Hundred Blows* won the Grand Prix, heralding the start of the "New Wave."

Plot: the story of impossible love between a young German commissioned lieutenant and a Greek Jewish teacher, detained with her fellow Jews in a transit camp in southwestern Bulgaria. Walter, a painter whom the war has thrust into the heart of the fighting, lives out the conflict in a state of disengaged disillusionment; transformed by the amorous encounter, he will attempt, ultimately in vain, to save the woman he loves, before deciding to join the Bulgarian resistance—choosing humanist (and Communist) values over murderous national loyalty.

We enter the history of the film's shooting at a turning point: January 5, 1959, the final meeting of the East German–Bulgarian Artistic Council. The German team has arrived in Sofia with some apprehension. Rumors have been circulating: while the East German studios have recently approved the movie, the leadership of Bulgarian Cinematography is said to hold certain reservations about it. From the outset of the bilateral meeting, the intentions of its representatives are loud and clear: recommending to the Science, Education, and Arts Department of the Central Committee (*Otdel Nauka, obrazovanie i izkustvo*) that the film be banned.[4] It falls to Hristo Radevski, a conservative poet recently replaced by the even more doctrinaire Georgi Karaslavov at the helm of the Writers Union (*Săjuz na pisatelite*),[5] to launch the debate.

Bluntly, Radevski asks, "We have arranged for a film about Greek Jews to be directed by German and Bulgarian filmmakers. But shouldn't our German comrades make their own film on these Jews? Why should we get involved?"[6] When the tense deliberations come to a close at 11:30 p.m., the attendees are still divided.[7] The waiting begins. On January 16, Albert Wilkening, director of Deutsche Film AG (DEFA)'s Studio für Spielfilme, bids his Bulgarian counterpart Georgi Jovkov "to communicate to us as soon

---

West Germany had adopted the Hallstein Doctrine, according to which, as the sole legal representative of Germany, it would break off diplomatic relations with any nation that recognized East Germany. France established diplomatic relations with East Germany in 1973.

4   CDA, F 404, op. 4, ae. 130, l. 6–53. According to Wagenstein, the German delegation had been advised upon its arrival in Sofia that a special commission of the Bulgarian Communist Party's Central Committee had decided against distributing the film. Vagenštajn, *Predi kraja na sveta*, 261.

5   Hristova, *Spesifika na "bălgarskoto disidentstvo,"* 190–205.

6   CDA, F 404, op. 4, ae. 130, l. 56.

7   Ibid., l. 59. The Bulgarian members of the Artistic Council were divided— some for, some against, and some with qualified support for the film.

as possible your point of view on the question [of whether *Zvezdi/Sterne* should be submitted to international festivals]," a proposition approved by the East German vice minister of culture. He adds, equivocally, "Obviously we would be thrilled if our two countries could present this film together, but we would be prepared to present it on our end alone."[8] The thought that the DEFA might benefit from the collectively created work may well have convinced the Bulgarian authorities to approve the release of the feature film.[9]

The previous chapter described the legal framing of crimes against the Jews as World War II drew to a close. Here, our focus shifts from knowledge and representations of the past, as formed in the judicial arena, toward those created via fictional reconstructions of the war. In the earlier setting, the trials remained haunted by the Germans, absent from the defendants' bench despite having presumably inspired the acts committed by their Bulgarian vassals. Now, "flesh and blood" Nazis, if such a term can apply to bodies onscreen, take center stage in a dialogue between East Germans and Bulgarians. Still, the paths of our protagonists involve dodges and feints, with each striving to produce a self-promoting national narrative—and in so doing to elude responsibility, perhaps, for the appalling events of the recent past.

Construing the production of *Zvezdi/Sterne* as a historical object is a less straightforward enterprise than it may first appear. In Eastern Europe, the art of film was considered an instrument of mass education, as well as a diplomatic weapon. This chapter takes shape in conversation with a body of scholarly works that have, of late, sought to problematize visual accounts of the Holocaust, whether in film, television, photography, or, more recently, comics.[10] Questions regarding the legitimacy of representations of the destruction of European Jews have largely dominated the scholarship: are

---

8   Ibid., 1. 335–36; see also Georgi Jovkov's acceptance letter, January 31, 1959
     (ibid., 1. 333). The required changes included the deletion of the image of
     the newborn at the start of the film, a cut in the market scene, and the amend-
     ing of the symbol of the cross. The Artistic Council's meeting minutes in
     Sofia have been preserved in Bulgarian; those of the Babelsberg meetings, in
     Bulgarian and in German. Unless otherwise mentioned, all translations here
     are from the Bulgarian.

9   The work first appeared in theaters in Sofia on March 23, 1959, then once
     more after the announcement of awards at Cannes. With 1,579,913 tickets
     sold, the film was among the period's box office successes. Janakiev, *Cinema.
     bg*, 298.

10   Hirsch, *Generation of Post-Memory*; Struk, *Photographing the Holocaust*;
     Schandler, *While America Watches*; Kleinberger and Mesnard, *La Shoah*; Germa
     and Bensoussan, "Les écrans de la Shoah," 21–620; Maeck, *Montrer la Shoah à
     la télévision de 1960 à nos jours*; Gundermann, "Real Imagination?," 231–50.

not representations a kind of re-creation, one that threatens to substitute for the absences that such work seeks to account for?[11] In an effort to broaden the purview of historical research by abjuring internal cleavages within the profession, an ever greater number of authors have recently begun to interrogate the conditions in which visual documents, fictional or not, can enrich our interpretation of the past. In doing so, they have turned the visual history of the Holocaust into a fascinating subfield in the historical discipline.[12]

As a film, *Zvezdi/Sterne* has been the subject of multiple studies (figure 2.1). Seen from an auteurist perspective, the work has been described as one stage in the career of East German director Konrad Wolf.[13] The solitude of man in the face of his fate, identity dilemmas, and the entanglement between political commitments and the crossing of national borders—all have been identified as persistent motifs. Yet in considering such themes as beholden to the artist's biographical trajectory, this strain of writing overlooks how art worlds (to borrow Howard Becker's formulation[14]) are enmeshed with a web of individualities and professions. Especially in coproductions, specific motifs cannot be reduced to the intention of a single artist. Alternatively, the film has been interpreted as a keystone in cinematic representations of World War II, antifascist resistance, and the Holocaust in East Germany.[15] This discovery of connections between East German and West German productions, while belated, has shown how the arts contributed to the rivalry between two inheritors of a divided Germany; it has tempered a view of East Germany's commissioned works as unwaveringly silent on the Holocaust.[16] In analyzing the movie's fictional content, however, the focus has largely been on the prominent themes, the main characters and their motives, and, less often, the visual aesthetics.

The concerns of this chapter lie elsewhere. The aim is less to evaluate the artistic qualities of *Zvezdi/Sterne* than to use the feature film as a prism onto a specific moment in recounting anti-Jewish persecutions, one located at a particular junction. Considered from a national perspective, the film offers

---

11   On the polemic between documentarian Claude Lanzmann, director of *Shoah* (1985), and historian Georges Didi-Huberman relative to the use of images of the Holocaust, see Didi-Huberman, *Images in Spite of All*. See also Chéroux, *Mémoire des camps*; and Crane, "Choosing Not to Look," 309–30.

12   Milton, "Images of the Holocaust—Part I," 27–61; Milton, "Images of the Holocaust—Part II," 193–216; Shneer, *Grief*; Lindeperg, *"Night and Fog"*; Bruttman, Hördler, and Kreuzmüller, *Die fotographische Inszenierung des Verbrechens*; Ebbrecht-Hartmann, "Trophy, Evidence, Document," 509–28.

13   Elsaesser, "Histoire palimpseste, mémoires obliques."

14   Becker, *Art Worlds*.

15   Bathrick, "Holocaust Film," 109–34.

16   Pinkert, *Film and Memory*.

an angle on the consolidation of socialism, fifteen years after it was established, as it vacillated between professional artists' quest for autonomy and a continuation, even intensification, of political control over artistic creation. Viewed from the standpoint of accounts and remembrance of the Holocaust on a global scale, however, *Zvezdi/Sterne* takes shape within a moment of transition: two years later, the arrest of Adolf Eichmann in May 1960 and his subsequent trial in Israel in 1961 would transform public knowledge of the extermination of the European Jews worldwide. Two years earlier, in 1956, the withdrawal of Alain Resnais's film *Night and Fog* from selection at Cannes had provoked a shock wave in Western *and* Eastern European artistic milieus. The East German–Bulgarian coproduction thus frays the edges of long-standing depictions of this period (1949–61), in both East and West, as rendering anti-Jewish crimes poorly visible—depictions that, as we shall see, may call for a reconsideration.

More specifically, this analysis of *Zvezdi/Sterne* aims to retrace the intertwined movements by which two Eastern bloc countries attempted to produce, simultaneously, a national vision of (partially) divided pasts *and* an "Eastern European" reading of the war. To do so, they had to employ all resources that circulated internationally and that transcended the cleavages of the Cold War. Unfolding in three parts, the investigation first interrogates how a coproduced film contributed to crafting competing nationalist readings of World War II. Bulgarian and East German cultural leaders expected two distinct narratives from *Zvezdi/Sterne*: whereas DEFA officials were awaiting "a film on Jewish tragedy and German Guilt," in the words of director Wolfgang Kolhaase,[17] the Bulgarian Cinematography directors, for their part, were not met with the mainstream antifascist work that they had anticipated. In their eyes, the film was meant to prove the existence of Communist resistance to the German "occupier," thus exempting Bulgarians from responsibility in the occupied territory roundups. From the East German point of view, the goal was to demonstrate the existence of "another Germany" innocent of Nazi crimes, while leaving room for the re-creation of Jewish suffering during World War II and, incidentally, interrogating present-day attitudes toward Nazi crimes in both West and East Germany. Whereas the German cultural elites, in Berlin, were in search of shades of gray, in Bulgaria only the black stains of Nazism could confer the desired relief on the partisan movement. The opposing judgments that the two partners would cast on the film can be traced back to this foundational misunderstanding.

---

17   CDA, F 404, op. 3, ae. 130, l. 161 (trans. from German). On December 31, 1958, in Babelsberg, director Kurt Maetzig had praised a work that "tells the tragic fate of the Jews and, with it, the tragic fate of Germans in the era of fascism." CDA, F 404, op. 4, ae. 130, l. 102 (trans. from German).

Second, *Zvezdi/Sterne* offers a vantage point onto the negotiation of a concordant reading of history, on the part of the states that would come to be known as the "Eastern bloc." In this case, the fact that the collapse of the partnership between Bulgaria and East Germany was only narrowly avoided suggests that these dialogues were not always as straightforward as has been assumed. The configuration is unsettling in another respect: unlike, for instance, Romania and Hungary, Bulgaria and the GDR had never maintained intricate historical relations. There is no equivalent, here, to the situation of East Germany, Poland, and the Soviet Union, which had to move beyond their former status as enemies and find ways of becoming allies. Both Bulgaria and East Germany had inherited a fascist past from which they wished to escape. From this surprising parallel was born a bilateral cooperation that would contribute to fashioning an Eastern European way of rendering Nazism. Yet this East-East solidarity only developed by overstepping its bounds. Far from being limited to two protagonists, the collaboration between the Bulgarian and East German studios was peopled with actors who would, subsequently, be cut in the editing process—chiefly, those from West Germany and the USSR. Ultimately, the production of a shared interpretation of the recent past saw its coordinates defined by, but not limited to, divisions between East and West.

This brings us to a third and final point. Beyond the dynamics of nationalization and the formation of a geopolitical order, *Zvezdi/Sterne*'s representation of the genocide of the Jews borrowed from visual and symbolic repertoires that, around the time the movie was shot, were being formed on a global scale. Whether they concerned definitions of Jewish agency—and the recourse to gendered categories to describe it—or the religious resonance of the catastrophe, these codes fractured the East-West borders that narratives like *Zvezdi/Sterne*'s were meant to bolster. What emerges here instead is thus a concomitant coproduction of national, regional, and international scales. Rather than opposing national dynamics to international processes, or, failing that, presuming as self-evident the transnational circulation of visual and historical imaginaries, we will discover instead a diverse array of transmissions, varying across territories and time.

In introducing and discussing *Zvezdi/Sterne*, we have taken some artistic liberties. The camera was initially set inside the meeting hall of the East German–Bulgarian Artistic Council. Though beginning with the decisive meeting of January 5, 1959, sample shots were taken from earlier meetings, in a syncopated back-and-forth between the production of the film and those earlier events.[18] In the gaps between these exchanges, the manufacturing of the reels carried on. Later, the lens absconds, shunning the meeting room in order to capture aspects of the shooting, which was mainly carried

---

18   January 6, April 30, July 10, and December 31, 1958, respectively.

Figure 2.1. German poster (working copy) of
the film *Sterne/Zvezdi*. *Source:* Deutsche Film
Aktiengesellschaft © DEFA.

out in Bulgaria, in the bucolic region of Pirin. Finally, a third angle on the
film emerges, like a cutaway scene, from the crosscutting of an excerpt from
the screenplay, the storyboard, and the images that would ultimately be displayed. Juxtaposing these three variants of a specific scene will serve as a
corrective to the belief that the final visual and sound product of the film
was entirely molded by the Artistic Council and that the wordy transcripts
of the meetings preserved in the archives suffice to illuminate the diversity of
human crafts, techniques, and sensitivities involved in its making. Working
over the maladjustments between the three layers will enable us to restore
the work of hands and voices, which do not all feature in such accounts.
This chapter adopts its narrative structure as a response to the dilemma of
inscribing images that the reader does not see, and can only speculate on, in
lingering over the written word.

Cinemas on Unequal Terms in Bulgaria and East Germany

Bulgaria and Germany's Soviet occupation zone entered the end of the war with contrasting cinematic traditions and with partially divergent national stakes. They did, though, share a definition of the role of art. In the modest-sized Balkan country, a taste for moving images had been manifest since the interwar period, fed by American, German, and French films,[19] though without the development of its own film industry. When the Fatherland Front came to power, the Bulgarian catalog counted forty-six titles.[20] Vălko Červenkov, who chaired the Committee on Sciences, Arts, and Culture, decided to give a priority role to the large screen in "the political and cultural education of citizens, particularly the youth."[21] To do so, he needed to create a national cinema: in 1948, any private production, distribution, or operation was forbidden. A new national company, D. P. Bălgarska Kinematografija, was put under the authority of the Committee on Sciences, Arts, and Culture. Young filmmakers, screenwriters, and technicians were sent abroad for their degrees, mainly to the USSR and Czechoslovakia; the infrastructure benefited from Promethean investments, as the number of movie theaters grew from 213 in September 1944 to 1,045 in 1951.[22]

Ordinance No. 91 of the Council of Ministers, of January 31, 1952, strictly defined the requested film repertoire: "Bulgarian cinematography must primarily produce films devoted to the socialist construction of our country that show images of the new man on screen—the heroes laboring in factories, mills, and mines, machine-tractor stations, and TKZs [collective farms], our border guards, the Dimitrovian youth, works in the domain of our socialist culture."[23] The narratives are sketched on a standardized canvas: the heroes are clearly distinguished from the villains; group dynamics are preferred to the description of individuals, who, for their part, are meant to blend in to a collective history. Although the notion of sacrifice may be elevated, the tone of the works is tasked with promoting an optimistic and linear vision of time. A screenplay must respect the rules of "socialist realism," which, though never as uniform and exclusive as it has often been described,

---

19   In 1924–25, 358 films were distributed in Bulgaria, including 31.6 percent from Germany, 29.3 percent from the United States, 24.3 percent from France, 6.1 percent from Italy, 2.5 percent from Denmark, and 1.1 percent from the USSR. Janakiev, *Cinema.bg*, 62.

20   *Bulgaran is Gallant* (*Bălgaran e galant*), the first Bulgarian film of Vasil Gendov, came to screens in 1915.

21   Quoted in Deyanova, *Nacionalno minalo i golemija dekor*, 3.

22   Garbolevsky, *Conformists*, 15–64.

23   *Kino* 2 (1952): 1–4 (here, 2).

nonetheless designated a strict system of constraints.[24] The repressive climate of the Červenkov era (1949–54) and the lack of trained creative and technical personnel led to anemic levels of production.[25]

In 1950, artistic councils (*hudožestveni săveti*) were created at studio headquarters.[26] These were intended to stimulate filmmaking, all while reaffirming political control over the process. This Bulgarian institution was similar to the Soviet Union's, which had come into being ten years earlier.[27] Composed of cinema professionals (producers, directors, operators, screenwriters, editors, etc.), a secretary from the Communist Party, and sometimes also external consultants (literary critics, journalists, etc.), these bodies were responsible for overseeing the projects from the screenwriting through the final shooting. They were to survey the production plans, discuss the scripts, direct the choice of actors, watch the finished films (in addition to, at times, the rushes), and submit their views on the artistic and ideological quality of the works. Gradually, these councils would become avenues of professionalization for the cinema branch. At the same time, they never overcame a muddled connection between aesthetic conformity and political conformity. Juxtaposed to collegial relationships were love affairs, professional and generational rivalries, and multiple artistic sensibilities. Mobilizing ideological arguments sometimes became a way to assert artistic points of view; aesthetic criteria, a means to defend political choices.

Far from limiting itself to banning or tinkering with the films—"retouches" imposed on the script, during shooting, or at the moment of release—such control was registered in the material embodiment of the film process itself. Every artist knew what it was like to have a scene, editor, or actors imposed; to fail to obtain the desired cameras, reels, or editing schedules; or to receive a disappointing number of copies and a too-brief release in theaters. Censorship was its own coproduction, delegated in part to artists who attempted to circumvent the constraints of the period they lived in, in the name of principles they had internalized.[28]

Although shaken by the destruction of war, food rationing, and a Soviet occupation that most people did not exactly welcome as a liberation, the German zone of Soviet occupation (1945–49) entered the postwar period under better auspices. It inherited the basic film infrastructure of the Third Reich, from the workshops of the Universum-Film Aktiengesellschaft (UFA), the Terra-Filmkunst, and the Tobis, to the film production plants

24　Kărdžilov, "Filmi razdeli," 96–111; Pozner, "Le 'réalisme socialiste,'" 11–17.

25　Yanakiev, *Cinema.bg*, 297–311.

26　CDA, F 404, op. 3, ae. 2, l. 3, 3a.

27　Laurent, "Le Conseil artistique du ministère soviétique du Cinéma," 71–80.

28　On the Soviet model, see Godet, *La Pellicule et les ciseaux*.

Kodak and Agfa.[29] Despite the lack of equipment and film, a rapid uptick in production was enhanced by the May 1946 creation of the Deutsche Film Aktiengesellschaft, which was financed and controlled by the Soviet Military Administration in Germany (*Sowjetische Militäradministration in Deutschland*), and the Central German Administration for the People's Education (*Deutsche Zentralverwaltung für Volksbildung*).

The Soviet authorities made the "reeducation" of the masses through culture a priority. Officers and civil attachés in Berlin, who happened to be great admirers of German culture, reopened theaters, concert halls, and opera houses. Promoting a Cultural Alliance for the Democratic Rebuilding of Germany (*Kulturbund zur Demokratischen Erneuerung Deutschlands*), the Soviet administration advocated broad antifascist front policies.[30] The first Congress of German Writers organized in Berlin in October 1947 illustrated this ambition—one that, paradoxically, it would put to an end. That is, behind the debates on humanism and antifascism emerged a split: between artists who, under Nazism, had made the choice of interior exile and those who had opted for armed struggle or emigration. Before the war, this divide originally spanned the boundaries between Soviet and Western occupation zones; it would be reconfigured as an East-West line of demarcation in the Cold War.[31]

Finally, the beginning of the shooting process benefited from a relative continuity between the UFA and DEFA in terms of technical and creative staff.[32] The paradox is evident, if familiar: revolutionary times are experienced and felt as more radical when those who craft them are able to mobilize visual imaginaries, cultural references, and knowledge borrowed from defunct eras. Beginning with the creation of the GDR in October 1949, the East German Communist Party nonetheless strengthened its grip on the cinematic industry. Thematic outlines valued heroic figures turned toward the future; ideological instructions were as indecipherable as they were imperative, which lent a certain languor to the production process. In this context,

---

29   Moine, "RDA (1946–1990)," 167–72.

30   Genton, *Les Alliés et la culture, Berlin*.

31   Agocs, "Divisive Unity," 56–78.

32   Feinstein, *Triumph of the Ordinary*, 19–44; Schenk, "Auferstanden aus Ruinen," 476–81. Joshua Feinstein has underlined some of these continuities: Friedl Behn-Grund, director of photography for *Die Mörder sind unter uns* (The murderers are among us) and for *Ehe im Schatten* (Marriage in the shadows), had in 1941 directed *Ich klage an* (I accuse), a Nazi-commissioned film justifying the politics of euthanasia. Wolfgang Zeller composed the music for the propaganda film *Jud Süss* (Süss the Jew, 1940) before *Ehe im Schatten*.

the USSR's crushing of the Berlin uprising of June 1953[33] had an ambivalent effect; if the decision to resort to repression contributed to reinforcing political surveillance throughout the creative spheres, it also resulted in a stabilization of structures, leaders, and commands addressed to the film industry. A venue was opened, too, for more popular, commercial cinema.

Until 1953, the horizon of German reunification had continued to inhabit the East German imaginary. The intensification of the Cold War and the integration of West Germany into NATO in 1955 gradually led to the conviction that the East-West divide was there to stay: East Germany would have to invent another way of being German. As pivotal actors in shaping this new identity, the arts were enjoined to portray, at once, German historical continuity, a rupture with the Nazi past, and a demarcation between West and East German identities. While claiming the legacy of German high culture, the new German Democratic Republic would not tarry in shifting the blame for the Nazi age, though lived in common, onto its capitalist neighbor. In the meantime, political pressures sharpened: in 1957, at the end of a show trial, Walter Janka, former director general of the DEFA (1948–49), and Wolfgang Harich, a philosopher, were condemned to five and ten years of prison, respectively, for "counterrevolutionary conspiracy." The fact that the former was freed in December 1960, following an international campaign of support, and found employment once again as literary secretary in charge of finding and reading scripts at the DEFA in 1962, did not diminish the force of the message addressed to intellectuals attempting to think freely, albeit on the left.[34]

In Bulgaria, the years 1957–58 also hosted a scene of more stringent control. In the wake of the Khrushchev report, the Central Committee meeting of April 1956 ousted Červenkov from his leadership positions in the Communist Party and the Bulgarian state. A duo took his place: from it would emerge the nimble figure of First Secretary Todor Zhivkov.[35] This handover of power left some room for hopes of a liberalized cultural sphere, in the model of Polish, Hungarian, and Yugoslavian reforms. In the Union of Writers, members of the new generation denounced the routine of formulaic writings and clichéd storylines.[36] The revolt soon spread to film circles, where certain creatives, trained abroad and familiar with the world's

---

33 On June 16, 1953, a protest movement by construction workers against an increased rate of work and low salaries broke out in East Berlin and quickly spread to all of East Germany, before being repressed with the support of Soviet tanks. Spittmann, "Dr 17," 594–605.

34 Hoeft, *Der Prozess gegen Walter Janka und andere.*

35 Hereafter the name of the Bulgarian Communist leader will be spelled using the usual English transcription.

36 Dojnov, *Bălgarskijat socrealizăm*, 128.

contemporary masters, were keen to espouse the tenets of Italian neorealism.[37] The repression of the Hungarian Revolution of 1956 brought this quest for freedom to a brutal halt. In the spring of 1957, Armand Baruh, former chairman of Bulgarian Cinematography's screenplay commission, deplored the recent scripts' "poverty of ideas."[38] A few months later, two plays were taken off the bill for having failed to portray antifascist resistance with all its proper luster. On April 8, 1958, the first secretary criticized the filmmakers: "For several years, the [Bulgarian] Cinematography has proposed a series of apolitical films bereft of ideas and with a deformed vision of life in our country. . . . Some workers in the cinema sphere, cut off from life and endowed with poor Marxist-Leninist preparation, have yielded to 'innovative' outside modernist influences, diverging from the method of socialist realism and realist traditions in our own art, and have created inappropriate films. It is now obvious that the Central Committee and the government cannot but intervene in the work of the Cinematography."[39]

Five films were subject to censorship, one of which was banned outright. Shot in 1957 by two artists known for their commitment to socialism and their role in the antifascist resistance, Binka Željazkova and her husband, Hristo Ganev, and entitled *Life Flows Quietly By* (*Životăt si teče tiho*), this film recounted the betrayal of the antifascist legacy by former partisans whose social success and attraction to a consumerist way of life had estranged them from their former political vision.[40] In the film crew, three names stand out: Željazkova, who, upon the signing of the East German–Bulgarian agreement in the spring of 1958, was to be first assistant director for *Zvezdi/ Sterne*—a decision later canceled;[41] Isaak (Zako) Heskija, who would nonetheless be recruited as assistant cameraman for the film; and camera operator Vasil Holiolčev (whose path we will cross again in chapter 3). The vice director of Bulgarian Cinematography, Martin Ginev, defended the ban: "Those who decided on the film's fate . . . are no less attached [than the filmmakers] to the national cinema, nor do they understand our reality any less."[42] His statement did not put an end to expressions of discontent amid the artistic milieu. On July 5, 1958, the Central Committee ordered the return

37 Janakiev, *Cinema.bg*, 219–26.
38 Ibid., 213.
39 *Kinoizkustvo* 5 (1958): 4–7.
40 "Životăt si teče tiho . . . ," in Genčeva, *Bălgarski igralni filmi*, 2:103–5; Ragaru, "Unbearable Lightness," 240–48.
41 See below in this chapter.
42 Marin Ginev, "Za pozicijata, iskrenostta I . . . greškite," *Narodna Kultura* 33, no. 16 (August 1959).

to "clear Communist ideas and adherence to the party line."[43] Directorial turnover was quick to follow. During the summer of 1958, Trifon Trifonov handed over management for the studio for feature films to G. Jovkov—just as *Zvezdi/Sterne* was being filmed.

Elusive Presences of the Holocaust on the Screen

In the film representations of anti-Jewish persecutions, there is a striking contrast between Bulgaria and East Germany. German filmmakers in the immediate postwar period felt an urgent need to understand the origins of Nazism, people's devotion to Adolf Hitler, and the ravages of the war. Several works, semiautobiographical in nature, addressed the recent past head on.[44] Their creators were filmmakers, screenwriters, and actors who had suffered from Nazism; some had been imprisoned (Erwin Geshonneck), while others had survived in hiding (Kurt Maetzig, a "half-Jew," according to Nazi terminology); still others had been forced into exile (the physician and politically active writer Friedrich Wolf, father of Konrad Wolf, among others). In their interrogation of German responsibility, they addressed a collective "we" that glanced back to a time before a rupture between East and West.

The list of notable titles included Wolfgang Staudte's iconic *Die Mörder Sind Unter Uns* (The murderers among us, 1946), a project that had been submitted to the American and British occupation forces before receiving Soviet support. Filmed with expressionist accents, the work recounts a military doctor's return to a devastated Berlin, as he is kept alive by the hope of avenging a captain's order of the assassination of Polish civilians. His love for a concentration camp survivor will dissuade him, at the last minute, from enacting justice. The accommodation, if not complicity, of witnesses is at the heart of the plot; the (possible) Jewishness of the hostages is never made explicit. Shortly thereafter, K. Maetzig released *Ehe in Schatten* (Marriage in the shadows, 1946), a film inspired by the life of actor Joachim Gottschalk, who killed himself with his Jewish wife and their son in 1942 in order to escape arrest by the Nazis. German introspection also burrowed into deeper historical grooves, tracing the warning signs that would anticipate support for the Führer's racial theories. *Die Affäre Blum* (The Blum affair, 1948), directed by Erich Engel, was inspired by a true story, the tale of a Jew falsely accused of murder in Magdeburg in 1926. The creation of the GDR nonetheless tuned down efforts at critically investigating issues of responsibility up until the second half of the 1950s. While the mentioning of anti-Jewish

---

43 *Kinoizkustvo* 8 (1958): 4.
44 Mückenberger, "Anti-Fascist Past," 58–76.

crimes did not disappear, nor did attempts at reckoning with the Nazi past, but these endeavors increasingly had to be inscribed within a framework structured around an opposition between West Germany, considered essentially fascist, and East Germany, an altogether different regime with irreproachable citizens.

One searches in vain for similar interrogations in postwar Bulgarian cinema. World War II was certainly omnipresent on-screen: it took its place amid a reinvented historical continuity where revolutionary fervor, having reached maturity in 1944, could be traced back to the anti-Ottoman struggles of the nineteenth century, before continuing with the abortive Communist uprising of September 1923 (*Septemvrijci*, Septembrists, Zahari Žandov, 1954), the defense of Dimitrov at the Leipzig trial in 1933 (*Urokăt na istorijata/Urok istorii* [A lesson in history], a Soviet-Bulgarian coproduction codirected by Lev Oskarovich Arnshtam and Hristo Piskov, 1956), and, finally, resistance during the war. Heroism shattered in its prime took on the features of Nikola Vapcarov, a poet and member of the resistance who was executed in July 1942 (*Pesen za čoveka* [Song of man], Borislav Šaraliev, 1954), or a collective portrait of groups of partisans, minus those who, though ready for individual sacrifice, would risk hindering collective progress (*Zakonăt na moreto* [The law of the sea], Jakim Jakimov, 1958). Nevertheless, these narratives functioned within a cultural and educational system that muted anti-Jewish violence in Bulgarian-held territories.[45] In the rare instances when moral questions were sketched out, they were entrusted to the elites of the now-sunken monarchical world. In this regard, *Trevoga* (Alarm, 1950) was emblematic. An adaptation by Angel Wagenstein and Orlin Vasilev of the eponymous play by Vasilev, the feature, which is often described as Bulgaria's first antifascist movie, explored the ethical dilemma of the father of a young gendarme who had rallied to fascism; meanwhile, his son-in-law has espoused the Communist cause. The rendition of this triangular plot was entrusted to the safe hands of a dedicated Communist, an experienced film director: Zahari Žandov; however, this spared him neither criticism from the party nor an alteration of the film's final scene.

The meager production output in Bulgaria (thirty-six films between 1950 and 1957) is not sufficient to shed light on the silence about the predicament of Jews during wartime. The emigration of some 90 percent of the Jewish

---

45   Liliana Deyanova has underlined the contrast between, on the one hand, the high school history textbook of 1946, which mentions the adoption of the Law for the Defense of the Nation and the deportation of "11,410 Jews" from the "new lands" while concluding that "the Bulgarian people were opposed to this extraordinary crime," and, on the other hand, the 1954 textbook, where the events are condensed into a single line. Deyanova, *Očertanija na mălčanieto*, 160.

community to the new State of Israel understandably shrank the Jewish presence in the cultural sphere.[46] Nonetheless, young Communists were beginning to reach renown, from the screenwriters Baruh and Wagenstein to the camera operator Isak Šekerdžijski. The explanation must be sought elsewhere. The aliyah increased pressure for compliance among the Bulgarian Jews who chose to remain in Bulgaria. By the beginning of the 1950s, the institutions that had ensured the reproduction of Jewish identity had either been dissolved or subordinated to the central government: on May 19, 1947, the Jewish section of the Fatherland Front was transformed into a democratic Jewish committee deprived of any influence.[47] Most Jewish municipalities were closed after the emigrations of 1948–49, and the Jewish Scientific Institute of the Central Consistory lost its autonomy in 1951. A glance toward Stalin's anti-Semitic campaign—the shelving of *The Black Book of Soviet Jewry* on anti-Jewish crimes, compiled by Ilya Ehrenburg and Vasily Grossman; the termination of the Jewish Antifascist Committee in the winter of 1948–49; the arrest of over a hundred figures of the committee; the trial of fifteen of them in May–July 1952; and execution of thirteen committee members, among them five Yiddish writers, in August of that year[48]— encouraged Bulgaria's Jewish artists to adopt a low profile in their homeland. Against this background, references to the fates of the Jews who had not survived the war seemed inopportune. And yet they would occur several years later, in a country newly keen on improving its international standing.

One Coproduction, Two Institutions, Several Agendas

In the Bulgarian film industry, the technical and personnel needs were immense. In September 1944, the Bălgarsko Delo Foundation, which produced Bulgaria's newsreels, owned a mere four cameras and one editing table; two years later, the numbers had reached eleven and seven, respectively. One struggles to imagine the lengths to which the Bulgarians had to go in order to overcome that deficit. In 1946, they agreed to barter with Hungary: Bulgaria would furnish furs and cigarettes in exchange for Aeroflex

---

46 Vasileva, *Evreite v Bălgarija*, 125; Hacohen, *Immigrants in Turmoil*, 267.
47 CDA, F 1B, op. 6, ae. 306, l. 1.
48 On the Jewish Antifascist Committee and the trial of May–July 1952, see Estraikh, "Life, Death, and Afterlife," 139–48; and, more broadly, the special section "The 1952 Trial of the Jewish Anti-Fascist Committee in the Soviet Union," with additional contributions by Anna Schur, Harriet Murav, Alice S. Nakhimovsky, Alexander Nakhimovsky, and Ber Kotlerman, https://www. tandfonline.com/toc/feej20/48/2?nav=tocList; as well as Redlich, *War, Holocaust, and Stalinism.*

cameras, Leica instruments, projectors, and projection lamps. Alas, judged to be of poor quality, the furs were turned back at Hungarian customs, while 110 kilograms of cigarettes disappeared under mysterious circumstances in Vienna. Those may well have ended up in the gratified hands of the French occupying forces.[49]

Bulgarian cultural officials had first turned to the Soviet Union: in November 1944, June 1946, and June 1947, Soviet task forces came to Sofia, with disappointing results. Promises of technical assistance were reiterated in a bilateral agreement on cultural cooperation in 1948. After long and protracted negotiations, filmmaker Sergey D. Vasilyev came to Sofia to film an epic celebrating the role of Russia in Bulgarian emancipation from "Turkish oppression." *Heroes of Shipka* (*Geroite na Šipka/Geroi Shipki*) promulgated echoes between the first (1877–78) and second (1944) "liberation" of Bulgaria—first by Russians, then by the Soviets. Packed with spectacular scenes of battle, the film won the Best Director Award (in a tie) at the 1955 Cannes Festival.[50] In order to reduce their cultural isolation, Bulgarian authorities also encouraged imports from West Germany, Czechoslovakia, Hungary, Poland, and Romania; East German and Hungarian Film Weeks were organized in the Bulgarian capital. Links with the West expanded: beginning in 1952, a Bulgarian delegation attended Cannes each year.[51] The proportion of Western films in theaters increased significantly, going from 0.14 percent in 1952 to 31.12 percent in 1957.[52]

All the conditions were in place to encourage a possible partnership with East Germany, which would have the double advantage of an imagined continuity—dictated by the prestige of antebellum German culture—as well as novelty. East German leaders reached a similar conclusion via other avenues. Early on in their rivalry with West Germany, they began to seek keenly after Western partners. Between 1956 and 1960, the DEFA aroused the interest of French left-wing artists such as Gérard Philippe (*Bold Adventure*, Gérard Philippe and Joris Ivens, 1956), Simone Signoret (*The Crucible*, Raymond Rouleau, 1957), and Jean Gabin (*Les Misérables*, Jean-Paul Le Chanois, 1958).[53] Several Communist sympathizers, including the documentary filmmaker Ivens; the writer, translator, and screenwriter Vladimir Pozner; and the film historian Georges Sadoul, fostered these connections. Although an accumulation of political challenges eventually slackened such momentum,

---

49   Garbolevsky, *Conformists*, 22–23.

50   Piskova, *"Geroite na Šipka."*

51   Garbolevsky, *Conformists*, 35.

52   Imports from "capitalist countries" fell sharply (15.51 percent in 1961) after the crushing of the Budapest uprising. *Kino i vreme* 5 (1973): 15.

53   Val, *Les relations cinématographiques entre la France et la RDA.*

the Babelberg studios achieved their goal: they had demonstrated their ability to manage multinational productions.[54] Though rather less impressively, the signing of an agreement with Bulgaria belonged to the same quest for recognition. As Kolhaase declared before the Artistic Council on January 5, 1959, geopolitical barriers to East German influence could be circumvented: "Today, in Western societies, under the effect of the shared threat of war arising from West Germany, public opinion is being reborn, in the sense that the GDR, after being refused recognition for years, is increasingly entering the public eye. We are currently organizing a DEFA Film Week in London, which will replace the UFA Film Week initially planned. We cannot underestimate the fact that with films like *Zvezdi*, which raise a number of issues, we will reach a vast audience with highly diverse viewpoints."[55]

On May 31, 1957, in Babelsberg, the DEFA and D. P. Bălgarska Kinematografija signed a framework agreement laying out a foundation for future collaboration, which would begin with the making of a film tentatively titled *Zvezdi/Sterne*. The joint work was to be enacted under financial (point 2, I) and artistic (point 3, I) parity: "The two countries should contribute to the entire artistic development to approximately the same degree." Although the "country that provides the director assumes responsibility [for the coproduction], . . . the screenplay will be approved by both parties" (point 10). The operation expenses and per diem payments would be the responsibility of the country of origin (point 12, I). One final guideline was of particular note: "the film will be shot as follows, in one sole version: the Bulgarian actors will speak Bulgarian, and the German actors, German" (point 4, II). Two negatives would be made; Bulgaria would retain the distribution rights for Bulgaria, while the DEFA would hold the rights for East *and* West Germany (point 4, I).[56]

On March 12, 1958, the project was further specified: it would be a 2,800-meter film whose screenplay, entrusted to the Bulgarian Wagenstein, would be reworked with Wolf. The calendar was carefully defined: the script had to be finished by the end of May 1958, with distribution approved in Sofia by May 5 and in Babelsberg by the 15th. The sets and costumes were to be ready by May 31, the shooting scheduled by June 5. The goal was to complete the shooting in five months (June 15–November 5), editing in two months (November 6, 1958–January 2, 1959), and to submit a first version of the film to the German and Bulgarian studio directors on December 5 and 10, respectively. The final approval was fixed for January 5, 1959—that is, three days after the soundtrack recording.

---

54   Buffet, *Défunte DEFA*, 115–19.
55   CDA, F 404, op. 4, ae. 130, l. 46.
56   Ibid., l. 149–53.

A more careful reading of the agreement nonetheless indicates an asymmetry between so-called equals. The East German Cinematography proposed three title roles: German second lieutenant Walter, Captain Kurt, and the young Jew Ruth.[57] The more marginal figures would come from the Bulgarian studio: resistance member Baj Petko, young partisan Blaže, and a fascist policeman. If the shooting was to take place in Bulgaria, the Germans would provide the cameras, film, and sound equipment; Babelsberg would be responsible for the sound engineering and development of the negatives. Despite the appointment of two production managers—Vălčo Draganov and Hans-Joachim Schöppe, the latter eventually to be replaced by Siegfried Nürnberger[58]—the Bulgarians seemed like feeble understudies. The director Wolf would be supported by a Bulgarian assistant: Ganeva/Željaskova, whose name was subsequently removed; the German director of photography (Werner Bergmann), by a second Bulgarian operator (Todor Stojanov); the German production designer (Alfred Drosdek), by an assistant provided by the Bulgarians (José Sancha); and so on.[59] Furthermore, it was decided that only one negative, co-owned by the DEFA and the Bulgarian studio, would be preserved in Babelsberg.[60] In exchange, Bulgaria would receive two release prints (a double negative and a reserve copy), a certified copy calibrated to the Bulgarian version, a soundtrack (excluding voice), and a master copy for the creation of a 16mm version.[61] Finally, on July 1, 1958, the financial indicators for the coproduction were confirmed. Bulgaria would contribute 60 percent; Germany, 40 percent.[62] For the nascent Bulgarian cinema, this was nonetheless a success: in these few pages, the disparity between unequal film histories seemed to diminish.

---

57   CDA, F 404, op. 4, ae. 130, l. 127.

58   Ibid., l. 127.

59   Multiple other changes came later: Isak Heskija was designated assistant director in February 1958 (CDA, F 404, op. 4, ae. 130, l. 180), followed by Rangel Vălčanov in August 1958 (ibid., l. 182). The latter would appear in the credits as "consultant to the director." On October 5, Nenčo Červenkov and Ivan Karadžov were hired as assistant producers (ibid., l. 181).

60   In April 1958, Albert Wilkening noted that, "for artistic reasons," the replies from the German characters would be subtitled and not dubbed. Ibid., l. 353.

61   Ibid., l. 131. A rider to the coproduction agreement, dating to February 25, 1959, replaced the provision of a master copy by the granting of three hundred meters of film.

62   By the end of 1958, the question of exceeding the budget had led to spirited debates, with the DEFA calling for a revision of the July 1, 1958, agreement. On March 24, 1959, the initial division of expenses was confirmed. Ibid., l. 173.

Konrad Wolf and Angel Wagenstein, a Dear Friendship

Located at a juncture between two countries, *Zvezdi/Sterne* was also the result of an encounter between two men. During their studies at the Gerasimov Institute of Cinematography in Moscow, Konrad Wolf and Angel Wagenstein (1922–2023)[63] embarked on a friendship that would end only with the death of the German director in March 1982.[64] Their biographical trajectories are remarkably parallel. Both artists were born in the 1920s in leftist Jewish families; Wolf's father was a doctor as well as a famous Marxist writer. Wagenstein's origins, in Plovdiv, were more humble as he came from a family of artisans.[65] Experiences of exile and war nonetheless muted the power of these social contrasts. The Wagenstein family fled to France to escape the wave of arrests of Communist militants following the failed assassination attempt on King Boris in April 1925; they would remain there from 1928 until 1934. After the Nazis came to power, the Wolf family escaped to Austria, Switzerland, and then France in 1933, before reaching Moscow in 1934, where the young Konrad spent his childhood.[66] During World War II, both men took part in the antifascist struggle: Wolf joined the ranks of the Soviet army, in particular as a translator-interpreter; in May 1945, he entered liberated Berlin as a lieutenant.[67] Incriminated in a resistance action, Wagenstein was arrested in Sofia in December 1943 and condemned to death (see figure 2.2).[68] The Red Army's invasion of Bulgaria and the overthrow of the wartime regime in September 1944 saved his life.

The fact that these two men met around the aspiration of bringing anti-Jewish persecutions to the screen is not surprising. As the project was being launched, Wolf had already distinguished himself with *Lissy* (1956), a film that related the story of a young woman divided between her loyalty to her husband, a member of the Nazi Party, and her Communist brother. The director had also just finished shooting *Sun Seekers* (*Sonnensucher*, 1958), a

---

63 Wagenstein was part of the first group of Bulgarian students sent to Moscow in 1947 alongside two screenwriters, two directors, one photographer, and two film editors. *Kinorabotnik* 5, 1980, 10.

64 Besides *Zvezdi/Sterne*, their most notable collaboration, Wolf and Wagenstein also cooperated on other projects, including an adaptation of a Lion Feuchtwanger novel, *Goya*, coproduced with the USSR (1971), and an adaptation of *The Little Prince* for East German television (1966).

65 Vagenštajn, *Predi kraja na sveta*. On his trajectory, see also the documentary by Simon, *Angel Wagenstein: Art Is a Weapon*.

66 Arnold, *Die Revolution frisst ihre Kinder*.

67 Wolf told the story of this experience in *Ich wahr neunzehn* (I was nineteen), RDA, DEFA, 1968. See also Werner, *Konrad Wolf*; and Wedel and Schieber, *Konrad Wolf*.

68 CDA, F 2123K, op. 1, ae. 5744, l. 111–14.

polyphonic representation of German-Soviet relations whose plot unfolds in the uranium mines of Wismut, property of the USSR. Lacking the idealism usually ascribed to representations of German-Soviet friendship, the film was met with an icy reception by officials of the DEFA and the Socialist Unity Party of Germany. Two weeks before the filming of *Zvezdi/Sterne*, Wolf had to reshoot several scenes of *Sonnensucher*.[69] Despite this political setback, exploring the stakes of multiple identities and conflicting loyalties would continue to motivate the director's creative energies.

A similar sense of urgency and inner necessity preoccupied Wagenstein. To the history narrated in *Zvezdi/Sterne*, he had been a direct witness: during the war, Wagenstein was mobilized into a Jewish forced labor battalion. Because he could read and write, having been trained as a construction mechanic, he was tasked with overseeing the building of the road railway Krupnik-Demir Hisar (Sidirokastro) that controlled access to occupied Northern Greece. It was in this capacity that he saw the passing convoys, in March 1943, carrying Thracian Jews to the Gorna Džumaja transit camp, as re-created in *Zvezdi/Sterne*. In 1945, during the preliminary investigations of the Seventh Chamber of the Bulgarian People's Court, the aspiring artist had reported these facts to the militia: in close proximity to the events (and, possibly, with a view to the specific political situation at war's end), Wagenstein blamed the deportations on the Germans alone.[70]

That the Bulgarian–East German coproduction was also, and perhaps primarily, the result of a human encounter, is beyond doubt. One point, however, remains to be clarified. Had Wolf and Wagenstein seen *Night and Fog* when they conceived of *Zvezdi/Sterne*? Might Alain Resnais have influenced their approach? We know that the making of the documentary was in cooperation with the Polish Cinematography; however, *Night and Fog* was only distributed in East Germany in June 1960 following translation controversies, which have been brilliantly reconstructed by Sylvie Lindeperg.[71] Among Polish and East German movie professionals, nonetheless, the film received wide acclaim even before its official release. According to Perrine Val, Wolf "saw the film for the first time in East Germany no later than the first half of 1957, when the DEFA proposed a new translation of the commentary."[72] A fine expert on the director, Thomas Elsaesser, for his part, has claimed

---

69   In October 1959, as a result of the intervention of the Soviet ambassador, the film premiere in East Berlin was canceled: Buffet, *Défunte DEFA*, 111–14.

70   CDA, F 1568K, op. 1, ae. 138, l. 192–93. The future screenwriter was featured among the witnesses listed in the indictment, but he did not testify before the court. After 1989, Wagenstein offered a novel reading of the events. This time, he assigned the Bulgarians as exclusive a role in the deportations as he had given the Nazis in his 1945 account.

71   Lindeperg, *"Nuit et brouillard,"* 191–200.

72   Val, email correspondence, June 10, 2018.

Figure 2.2. Shot of Anžel Rajmond Vagenštajn arrested by the Bulgarian police (1943). This photograph features in the police file put together after his arrest in Sofia, on December 2, 1943, for "attempted theft in the Armenian cooperative and attempted murder of a second lieutenant." *Source:* CDA, F 2123K, op. 1, ae 5744, l. 111–12. Courtesy of the Bulgarian Central State Archives.

to have identified motifs of *Night and Fog* in *Zvezdi/Sterne* (for example, the strings of barbed wire, the presence of a young girl at the entrance to a passenger wagon). One may not follow him on this track.[73] For now, let us suspend such lingering questions.

---

73   Elsaesser, "Vergebliche Rettung," 73–92. I agree with Perrine Val that the widespread use of such figurative codes as barbed wire makes it difficult to ascertain the existence of a direct influence—all the more given that the train scene echoes a shot of the actual deportations of the Greek Jews filmed in

Shooting Notes and Other Digressions

The digression that follows will lead us into the path of a shooting process where international and national scores would play out.

1. The storyboard is approved on July 17, 1958, on the condition that the remarks of the Artistic Council on the return of the "Bulgarian line" be taken into account."[74] The shooting begins one week later in the charming town of Bansko, in southwestern Bulgaria. Located in the Pirin area, this market town borders the Rhodope Mountains, whose summits are dusted with snow throughout the year. Typical last-minute defections are in order. One actor, for instance, leaves the production in a huff after realizing that he is to play a simple blacksmith and not the heroic resistance character he had imagined.[75] How to select the actress who would play Ruth is a challenge of another order entirely. The choice ultimately alights on the young Saša Krušarska, then a student at the Institute for Theatrical Studies of Sofia (*Viš institut za teatralno izkustvo*). Her name is confirmed on July 29, five days after the start of shooting. "The actress who has been hired does not have the requisite experience," warns Draganov, the producer, in a letter addressed to the studio director on August 3, 1958; the director insists she remain in Bansko so that he could practice during her free time. "We have given our agreement," Draganov notes, before adding, "Given that this was not specified in the production budget, there is a real risk that we might exceed the planned budget under 'fees' and 'operations.'"[76] The calendar must be revised: the scenes between Walter and Ruth are postponed to the end of August.[77] This temporal compression will be reflected in the film: what seems like an unmoving present of conversations is superimposed onto the linear progression of the plot. Otherwise, the shooting is uneventful; for the film crew, the anniversary of the "revolution of September 9, 1944" is a day off; Wolf falls ill for a short time. Nothing out of the ordinary.

2. Nonetheless, on set there prevails what we might call a meteorological issue. In summer, the south of Bulgaria is awash in brazen sunlight. Yet the deportations of Jews from Northern Greece had taken place in

---

March 1943, which Wagenstein had shown to Wolf and his photography director, Werner Bergmann. His intent in so doing was precisely to help his colleagues offer an authentic rendering of this scene.

74 CDA, F 404, op. 4, ae. 130, l. 69.
75 CDA, F 404, op. 4, ae. 130, l. 221, 223.
76 Ibid., l. 212.
77 Ibid., l. 357.

March, in a cold that made the conveyance of the Jews arrested in the early hours of the day particularly dreadful. Unable to reproduce such a cruel cold, the director and his director of photography, Bergmann, decide to film the boarding of the trains under a torrential rain.[78] In mid-October 1958, the crew returns to Sofia, where a water cannon is employed as a remedy to the imperfections of reality. In the finished work, the contrast between the daylit, summertime world and the final night of deportations has great power of suggestion. Might these weather-related challenges explain why the filmmakers will situate the deportations in October 1943 (and not in March)—the camera lingering over the sign "10.1943" appended to the cars? Or should this dating be seen as a minute shift that heralds entry into a fictional world?

3. If the Bulgarian production file is to be believed, bilateral cooperation proceeds smoothly. Citizens—ordinary or not (for who would dare to adjudicate this point in the absence of robust proof?)—seem to have determined to give their own high appraisal of the advance of East German socialism over its Bulgarian counterpart. The file notes, for instance, the disappearance of a few expensive cameras: on October 21, 1958, during a shoot in Bansko, assistant director Michael Engelberger is divested of his Exakta Vare, lens 326741, showpiece of the famous Ihagee company in Dresden, with unquestionable technological quality, elegance, and price.[79] Two days later, at Zemen station, the daydreaming lieutenant Walter, alias Jürgen Frohriep, declares the "loss" of a Super Ikonta Zeiss Ikon, with a Tessar lens, leading product of another large German company based in Dresden, Ziess Ikon.[80]

4. Let us leave the world of image to venture into that of sound. *Zvezdi/ Sterne* involved finely honed work on intonations, languages, and melodies. The story is narrated by voiceover. Melancholy and supple in the German version, as if to imitate Walter's bearing, in Bulgarian it is dull and cold. At the meeting of the Artistic Council, the choice of the male voiceover on the newsreel is deplored. Its impeccable ideological correctness clashes with the narrative of tragic love. Around this first voice, however, interweaves a garland of languages—Bulgarian, German,

---

78 Bergmann, trained in photography before the war, then as assistant photographer for the Boehner company in Dresden, covered front operations for the German newsreels before a serious accident, in 1943, that led to the amputation of one arm. Employed by the UFA, then the DEFA, he met Wolf during the filming of a documentary by Joris Ivens in 1951; their collaboration resulted in twelve films and a friendship that lasted twenty-five years.

79 CDA, F 404, op. 4, ae. 130, l. 235.

80 Ibid., l. 225.

Greek, and Ladino[81]—whose shimmering hues will brim over into the images. The voiceover and linguistic mosaic, in turn, are fringed by the song "S'brent/Undzer shtetl brent," adapted from a poem by Mordechai Gebirtig composed after the pogrom in Przytyk, Poland, on March 9, 1936.[82] Written in Yiddish, but sung here in German, "Our shtetl burns"[83] opens and closes the film, fostering a sense of alarm that rings like a call to arms. If a spectator were to listen to *Zvezdi/Sterne* with her eyes closed, before looking at the images with the sound off, she would have a singular experience: wherever the visual content most aligns with the conventions of the "antifascist film" genre, the sound choices resolutely anchor the work in the realm of fictional renditions of the Holocaust. Were the filmmakers aware of these layering effects? Be that as it may, both had expressed their desire to offer an "internationalist" vocal rendering of Jewish fates—a choice possessing a certain boldness, only a few years after the latest campaigns against "cosmopolitanism."

Script, Storyboard, and Film: Effects of Cutting and Framing

In order to illuminate how the film came into being, including the choices made by the film crew, one artifice consists in isolating a specific scene and its unfulfilled possibilities, thereby revealing the subtle transformations and minute variations through which its narrative was crafted. Here, the chosen scene is that of the Jews' arrival in a small Bulgarian town after they were rounded up in Greece. Within the filmic economy, central to our purposes, it opens with Captain Kurt and Second Lieutenant Walter gazing with carefree contemplation at mountains backed by the frame of a blue sky.

The reader will encounter, in what follows, three consecutive rewritings. The first, within a black frame, stems from the literary screenplay in the version published by Wagenstein in 2002.[84] The second, within a dotted line, is excerpted from the storyboard (*regisjorski scenarij*) preserved in the Bulgarian Central State Archives (CDA).[85] The repartition of stage directions and dialogues figures in the original document. Finally, the third rewriting, with a gray background, retranscribes the dialogues of the completed film—translated from German—together with a description of the

---

81   Romance language spoken by the descendants of the Jews expelled from Spain in 1492.

82   In the film credits, the song appears with the German title "Es brennt!" ("It's Burning!") and is attributed to "Mordechai Gebirtik [*sic*]" "ermordet 1942" ("killed in 1942").

83   The notion of "shtetl" refers, literally, to a village or small town, and by extension a neighborhood, where the majority of the population is of Jewish origin.

84   Vagenštajn, *Tri scenarija*.

85   CDA, F 404, op. 4, ae. 128, l. 175.

images. Several sentences have been bold-faced in order to emphasize how the three forms evolved. From one version to the next, the material words grow sparser, eroding amid the turn to the image: in making the film, the dialogue was progressively cut, any unnecessary words gradually pruned. Through these travels, however, the narration also underwent a major shift: the men and arms who once framed the convoy of deportees were gradually erased until giving the impression, in the finished film, that the deportees are moving forward in disarray with only a handful of policemen on horseback by their sides.

Literary Script, Wagenstein

Scene 10.

Daytime. A hill above the town.

It is almost twilight; the firs are casting long shadows over the valley, as between them, the winter roses and fresh needles work their way toward the light. Opposite, the mighty mountain range is still white with snow; below, at the very bottom, in the valley sheltered from the winds, the first fruit trees are already in bloom.

Lieutenant Kurt Müller is lying down on the grass, half-clothed, while Walter whistles and works away at the activity most strictly forbidden to him—drawing.

Kurt stretches leisurely, with an almost animal pleasure under the heat of the sun, the crystalline air, and simply the feeling of being alive.

– Walter, you know what I was just thinking?

Walter stops and looks astonished.

– You're saying you sometimes think?

Kurt is not offended; he throws a small object in the direction of his friend and continues:

– Yes, this is my soldier's philosophy: too much thinking gives me a stomachache! . . . But, suddenly I remembered where we were before. Leningrad!!! . . . Brrr, you remember?

Walter raises his eyes from the drawing, where he has portrayed the snow-white mountain with a small village below in the valley. His eyes have lost their usual smile; a deep, hopeless sadness cloaks his face.

– Yes, I remember. So?

Kurt tears off a twig, begins to chew at it, and lies down again, hands under his head, gazing happily up at the blue sky.

– And here, a silent and wild refuge. Here there is no war. Such calm! Listen, listen . . .

Somewhere above, though invisible, planes roar in the distance.

– The Yankees! They pass over and *goodbye*!

The lieutenant shakes a fist up at the sky, though in a friendly way, as if they could see him from above. Then he goes on:

– The only bad thing about the situation here is the women. It's not that they don't want it, but they're ashamed. It's the Orient—you know how it is! . . . Ideas are ideas, Walter, but in wartime the most important thing for a man is to save his skin . . . No, no, I'm happy!

Walter keeps drawing and speaks without lifting his head:

– Because you're a chimpanzee . . . you're really to be envied, Kurt. For two million years humanity has been creeping up, only to go back to where it started. It's too bad—all these efforts gone to dust!

Kurt replies casually:

– In times of war, everyone is a chimpanzee. Look, here's a little monkey! . . . When I see kids, I always think of the three of mine in Bavaria . . . Monkey, come here, come here, I'll give you some chocolate!

These words are addressed to a shepherd who has led his flock to the hill. The boy gets scared and runs away with his goats.

Kurt laughs happily:

– No, it's incredible, what a backward country: the children don't even know what chocolate is.

Suddenly, Kurt springs to his feet; annoyed, he spits to the side and begins to pick at the threads of his uniform jacket.

– Damn the war, and the Jews who started it!

In the folds of the lower peaks, like a dark snake, winds an ornamental line over which a small train is crawling slowly—something like a children's toy, with small, open cattle cars, full of people.

Walter points with his pencil at the children's cars, as they move along, guarded by Bulgarian policemen—before each wagon stands a policeman with a pistol.

– What is that?

– Greek Jews, may the Devil come and take them one and all! . . . I have to go meet the convoy, no way around it.

With a truly poetic flourish, he makes a sweeping farewell gesture:

– Goodbye, tranquil and verdant hamlet!

And, buttoning up his jacket, he speeds down the slope to meet the human transport.

Walter starts to whistle; the question of the Jews has clearly not interested him; and, under his pencil blooms a small village cradled within the white mountain.

We turn to the ancient steeple . . .

Storyboard (l. 26–30)

Scene 11. 125.5 meters
A steep slope above the city
(Outdoors—Nature—Razlog—
daytime—a sunny afternoon).
Characters: Walter, Kurt
Minor characters: the young shepherd.
Extras: Greek Jews – men – 480
  Greek Jews – women – 420
  Greek Jews – children – 100.
  German soldiers – 30.

Cinematic technique: a small crane

53 – 16 m.
Panorama. From a long to medium shot   The dialogue is in German.
(small crane)
And before us stands the majestic
mountains, bathed in colors from the
sloping afternoon sun
The camera moves, *legato*, through a
panorama.
Already, yellowed fields, some plowed,
stretch down the side of the mountain
to the city that extends below us,
dappled by the afternoon sun.
We now see that we are atop a
precipitous hillside.
A steep trail weaves and winds up to
the city.
On the hillside grazes a small herd of
goats. Beside him, a shepherd plays with
a large dog. In the foreground arise the
ends of tobacco stalks, almost full of
mature leaves ripe for harvest.

We leave behind the field and into the
frame enters a black withered branch,
an officer's cap hung upon it.
Behind the top of a tree appears the
lieutenant. He is lying down, happily
stretched out on the grass, with an
almost animal joy at the sun, the air, and
simply the feeling of being alive. Kurt
sits up, leans on his elbow, and says:

– Walter, you know what I was just thinking?

The camera now turns toward Walter,
seated, his back half-turned to his friend,
exactly at the edge of the hill; he whistles
and is doing what the captain has strictly
forbidden him from doing: drawing.

– Don't tell me you think!

54. – 12 m.
Mid-angle shot.
Kurt is not offended, he picks up a
pebble, throws it in the direction of his
friend, and laughs good-naturedly.

– Listen, Rembrandt! Don't you know that this is the military principle: You should not think too much because that hurts the stomach!

A distant roar of airplanes can be heard more clearly

Then his face becomes expressionless.

– When I look at this paradise . . . I suddenly remembered where we came from, you and me. Leningrad! Do you remember?

55. – 4 m.
Mid-angle. (steep from below to cloudy sky)

Walter looks forward with unseeing eyes that have suddenly lost their usual sneer, his face stiffening for a moment. Then he relaxes again and turns to Kurt.

– Yes.

– So what?

56. – 23 m.
<u>Crane shot, from a large shot (the steep path seen from above) to a medium shot.</u>
Kurt tears off a twig, begins to chew at it, and lies down again, hands under his head, gazing happily up at the sky.

– What?... Leningrad! And here—a calm and wild small island. There is no war, none! Such silence!

<u>The camera pulls back slowly</u> and behind Kurt captures the vast landscape with lots and lots of sky above him. Kurt takes the twig out of his mouth and points upward:

– American planes... They pass over and *goodbye*!

He sits up again and scratches a bit behind his ear:

– The only bad thing about the situation here is the women! My God, it's not that they don't want it, but they're ashamed.

He turns to Walter once more, excited by an idea that has just gone through his mind:

– We should organize something at the *krắčma* [bistro].

Since Walter doesn't react, he lies back down on his back and, to conclude, says:
...

– No, Walter, I'm happy!

57. – 11 m.
(<u>like in 55</u>)
Walter smiles, sarcastically, still occupied

by his drawing:

– Because you're a chimpanzee!... You're really to be envied, Kurt. For two million years humanity has been creeping up, only to go back to where it started. It's too bad—all these efforts gone to dust!

And concludes dryly:

– A shame, such work carried off by the winds!

The voice of Kurt, who always knows better:

– In times of war, all men are chimpanzees.

58. – 9 m.
Mid-angle.
Medium shot.
In the foreground, slightly below the summit, the young shepherd has just taken hold of a goat that had gotten away. The boy and the dog try to get it back up the hill.

Standing out against the background of the mountain, Kurt has sat up, and cries out:

– Ah, look, a little chimpanzee!

The child stops and turns around.

Kurt:
Then he shouts in the child's direction:

– Like the **three of mine at home.**
– Chimpanzee!

The child draws the goat close to him and runs away fearfully. The dog, as if to defend his little master, begins to bark loudly.

– Dog barking –

59. – 13 m.

Medium shot. Seen from below (low-angle shot)

Kurt quickly rummages through the pocket of his jacket, thrown on the grass: He takes out a piece of chocolate, shows it to the shepherd, waving his hand:

– Hey, chimpanzee, come here!

– Come on! I'm giving out chocolate!

The boy runs down the slope even faster.

– The barking subsides –

Kurt turns, disappointed, toward the camera, and, with a short, embarrassed laugh, mutters:

– Damn, what a backward country! The children don't even know what chocolate is.

His gaze wanders off, then suddenly becomes attentive; he sits up.

60. – 10 m.

Wide-angle, distant, general.

In the foreground, an arrangement with the black branch and the officer's cap on it stand out in the composition.

The other side of the hill is not so steep. Here, before one's eyes opens the broad plain that detaches itself brusquely from the peaks of the high mountains in the sky.

From the mountain in the distance up until the foot of the hill winds a dusty road.

Over the road stretches an endless

Kurt's exasperated voice:

– Damn it!

column of people, guarded on both sides by policemen on horseback. A cloud of dust floats down into the valley.

61. – 1.5 m.
(as in 55)
Walter looks over his shoulder and asks:

– What is it?

62. – 11 m.
Wide-angle—distant general shot
(as in 60).
Kurt enters the frame:

– Greek Jews . . .

He takes his cap, puts it on his head and leaves:

– . . . The devil take them. I have to watch them until the freight cars arrive.

He leaves the frame.
Along the road the column of Jews marches endlessly, painfully.

63. – 8 m.
Medium shot.
In the foreground, Walter is shot from behind.

Kurt has already crossed (while buttoning his jacket) part of the mountain path. He turns once more to Walter and yells over to him, back to his simple, goodhearted joviality:

– Goodbye, Rembrandt! Enjoy our little paradise, at least you can.

He then continues down the slope.
On the way, he sings loudly:

Some lines from a German song, such as "You, My Silent Valley"
("*Dich, mein stilles Tal*")
(Im schonsten Wiesengrunde)

The Finished Film[86]

Several white clouds scatter over a mountain revealed in a slow panorama shot from right to left, with a background of birdsong and bells. The camera glides over a cap hanging on a branch, as Kurt's stretched-out body enters the shot, partly reclining, a cigarette in his hand, then stops at the blond lieutenant, in a white T-shirt, who is drawing in black pastel the landscape before him.

– You know what I'm thinking about, Walter?

– You're thinking?—well then.

– Hey, listen, Rembrandt, thinking too much hurts your stomach. You know, what we can see here, it's paradise (he draws a puff on his cigarette). When I think about where we've come from, Leningrad (with a grimace).

His shirt is open, his hair is brown, soft, captured by the midtorso-level lens.

– You remember? When we were captured?

The camera films Walter's face, still drawing; his gaze fixes the lens, then hardens for a moment. The noncommissioned officer is seen from a low-angle shot, the drawing's cardstock cutting out a black geometric space on the blue sky.

– So?

– So? Stalingrad, and this silent and wild island. (Kurt, cigarette in his mouth, stretches out on the grass). No, no, there's no war. Without a doubt. There's nothing; only silence.

The scene is interrupted by the noise of airplanes in the sky. Kurt rises up:

– Americans, they're flying over us...and *goodbye*.

With his right hand as a visor, he stares at the sky; Walter's back remains in the frame. Kurt gives a short wave.

– The only bad thing about the situation here is the women. **It's not that they don't want it, but they put on airs.** Say, Walter, what if we organized something in the *krăčma* [bistro]?

---

86   The dialogues have been retranscribed from German and the images described by the author.

Stretching between two remarks, he turns back jovial, toward Walter, whose back is still turned.

– I'm happy.

The camera has lingered over Kurt's good-natured face. Walter's voice can be heard.

– Because you're a chimpanzee.

The second lieutenant's face appears.

– Oh, Kurt, I envy you. Civilization has crept forward for two million years only to return to where it started. It's too bad, what a waste!

– In times of war, everyone's a chimpanzee. Look, over there, too, there's another little chimpanzee.

Below, a young daydreaming shepherd appears in the foreground, leaning over a wooden stick, his flock behind him. Kurt calls out: "Hey, chimpanzee!" The boy turns around: "Come here, chimpanzee," then, in bad Bulgarian, "Come on! I'm going to give you some chocolate." His slender body leaps up in a movement that seems to bring him closer to the Germans, before branching off toward the herd, which he hastily gathers back. The sound of bells accompanies this disorderly movement.

– What a backward country! The children don't even know what chocolate is.

Cigarette in his mouth, Kurt seems to notice something. **Over a dusty dirt path, a vehicle is leading a column of deportees, who are heading forward by foot, slowly, painfully, sagging under the weight of their luggage.**
   Annoyed, he throws down his cigarette:

– By God!

He stands up; Walter hadn't moved, at most making a slight movement of the head to the left before asking:

– What is it?

Kurt's torso, which occupies the left third of the screen, partly conceals the column, as does the cap hanging on the branch, to the right.

– Greek Jews.

Cap in hand, Kurt pulls up the suspenders hanging over his pants.

– **The Devil himself should come and get them,** he says, adjusting his cap. I have to manage them until the trains come and collect them.

The column is difficult to see behind Kurt's broad figure. A careful viewer might discern a few isolated policemen on horseback, too distant and shadowy—in contrast to the dusty-white dirt—for their uniforms to be identified with certainty by an untrained eye. No reaction has been filmed on Walter's face.

From script to storyboard to film, we witness a fascinating process of refining and paring down. With the shooting and the editing, Kurt has forgotten that he was the father of three children in Bavaria; but the throwing of a cigarette has replaced the moment when he spits to the side. As for Walter, the T-shirt and his turned back have taken center stage. There are no more exoticizing and/or culturalist evocations of the landscape: the leaves of tobacco, one of the region's major crops with its mostly Bulgarian-speaking Muslim workforce, no longer offer their brown contrast to the white mountain. A mention of "oriental" female reticence toward liberated sexuality has also disappeared. Above all, the meaning of the scene has been reshuffled: guarded by Bulgarian policemen the rounded-up Jews no longer arrive by train; they enter the town on foot in a column rendered almost abstract by being filmed from a distance, blurring the individual figures. If the storyboard called for the presence of "30 German soldiers" and portrayed policemen on horseback, the lens only ended up filming four or five Bulgarian agents of order on horseback, only one of whom can be seen, and briefly at that. At what point were these changes decided on? Archival documents do not allude to them. It is nonetheless difficult to imagine that budgetary constraints led to this contraction: in a planned socialist economy, it only cost a modest sum to provide extras, who were paid at most a nominal fee. It is also hard to dismiss the role of political variables, given how central ideological control over films was at the time, judged in strategic terms. One would be curious to know when the version of the script that Wagenstein offered for publication in 2002 dates back to, given that it explicitly includes the presence of Bulgarian policemen.

Two Very Different Wars: The Bulgarian Lens

Equipped with these questions, we can now return to the tumultuous meeting of the East German–Bulgarian Artistic Council in January 1959. As in the three variations of the scene of the deportees' arrival, reconstructing these clashes will serve to place three disputes into relief: competing endeavors aiming at the nationalization of the past, the delicate negotiation of a "socialist" understanding of the Nazi era, and the symbolic restitution of anti-Jewish persecutions.

The Bulgarian Cinematography officials had agreed to the making of an antifascist film. The result, a movie on the deportations of Jews from occupied Greek territory, left them speechless. The recounting of historical events was strongly criticized, particularly the reconstitution of the war, relations between Bulgarians and Germans, and the partisan movement:

> If the film deals with the great ideas of the war and fascism as social evils, with the need to fight against them, since the action takes place in our Bulgarian situation, the way this situation is rendered, how the participation of the Bulgarian people and its point of view on these questions are shown, is of particular importance to the Bulgarian viewer. . . . First, here the direct consequences of the war, of the factual occupation of Bulgaria by German soldiers during this period do not transpire. The result is thus that in the one or two crowd scenes we see, somehow the Bulgarians and Germans live much too peacefully, and much too well.[87]

In this statement of January 5, 1959, Venelin Kocev, director of the *Narodna Mladež* (Popular youth) publishing house and representative of the Cinematography management within the Artistic Council,[88] exposed a Bulgarian leitmotif.[89] In order to extract itself from the legacy of fascism, Communist public discourse conventionally presented Bulgaria as a state subjugated to the Reich. Against this background, to choose a languid village in the slumbering splendor of snowcapped mountains in order to conjure up the war was seen as inappropriate. And what to make of the market, brimming with supplies, that was recorded on camera?[90] Defending the film, the director Borislav Šaraliev deployed a wealth of ingenuity to suggest at once the realism of the plot *and* its political inadequacy: "At first glance, it cannot be said that things weren't that way, since, even during the most difficult years in 1943–44, in the villages chickens could be found on the

---

87   CDA, F 404, op. 4, ae. 130, l. 14.

88   Venelin Kocev would have a career as a party ideologue, becoming successively secretary of the Central Committee (1966–71), deputy member of the Politburo (1972), and vice president of the Council of Ministers (1972–74).

89   Taking part in the meeting were the Bulgarian members of the Council, the secretary of the party organization within the studio (Ivan Dimitrov), several representatives from the DEFA (Willi Brückner, Wolfgang Kolhaase, and Wolf), as well as outside guests (Vălčo Draganov, Isaak Heskija, Borislav Šaraliev, Rango Vălčanov, Wagenstein, and A. Zajdel). The poet Hristo Radevski was the chair. CDA, F 404, op. 4, ae. 130, l. 6–7.

90   Ibid., l. 14.

market, even eggs and butter could. But if, logically thinking, we reflect, one cannot possibly follow the writer and director into the market scene. . . . [This scene] gives the viewer the sense of an overly calm life, one that has remained almost untouched and unaffected by the war."[91]

Beyond the privations of war, the very nature of relations between Bulgarians and German "occupiers" came under debate. In this case, filming the second lieutenant Walter sketching in chalk a female nude on a trailer, before a coterie of young Bulgarians looking on appreciatively, seemed clearly inappropriate. To be sure, the complicity between the Bulgarian fascist chief of police and Captain Kurt was portrayed in the intoxicating atmosphere of the *krăčma*, inhabited by women of easy virtue with sensual attributes and of dubitable sobriety. The exaggerated characterization respected the standards of the era: gluttony and sexual avidity were traits often ascribed to fascists. However, the enemy was considered to have been insufficiently condemned in the film. During the meeting on April 30, 1958, the film critic Jako Molhov had even insisted that *Zvezdi/Sterne* amounted to a rehabilitation of fascism.[92] Ginev grew indignant in turn. Wolf retorted: "In my feeling—I always allowed myself to be stung by this feeling—the film should not end with compassionate tears, as abstract humanism does, but with a strong fighting feeling of hate and love. . . . This is not abstract humanism. This is, in my opinion, a humanism of combat."[93] The major concern of Bulgarian Cinematography was nevertheless to be found elsewhere: in the representation of the Bulgarian antifascist struggle.

Since the first meeting on January 6, 1958, the meetings of the Artistic Council condemned with metronomic regularity what they considered to be a picturesque treatment of Bulgaria, as if the territory was a kind of colorful backdrop to an exclusively German plot. Through a metonymic effect, the Bulgarian people themselves were to be rendered ornamental. Thus would result a face-to-face encounter between Nazis and Greek Jews, which would reduce, even evacuate, any Bulgarian contribution to the antifascist fight. On January 5, 1959, Dako Dakovski, director of the patriotic *Pod Igoto* (Under the yoke, 1952), condemned the ease with which Bulgarian resisters put their fates into the hands of a German, in this case Walter:

> For me, the greatest weakness . . . lies in the presentation of our resistance movement. In this section, according to me the film absolutely does not correspond to reality. Here the question is no longer on the place given to the Bulgarian partisan movement. It is about something much more serious—the erroneous historical perspective of the relationship to Hitler's

91 Ibid., l. 33.
92 Ibid., l. 80.
93 Ibid., l. 49.

occupation soldiers. For me, today as last time, the scenes in the forge still sound absolutely false, artificial. In the first place, when Walter goes to Baj Petko, and Baj Petko reveals to him that they tried to steal weapons. . . . I think we have no right to lie to our German comrades by letting them believe that the relations between Hitler's occupation soldiers and the Bulgarian partisans can be represented and developed in this way.[94]

Hampered by the waves of exile in the 1920s and 1930s, the internal purges of the Communist Party, and the marginalization of the radical wing in the name of the Fatherland Front policy, the Bulgarian partisan movement during World War II was only consolidated relatively late. Decades of literary, poetic, cinematic, and theatrical production would strive to compensate for this fact. All the same, *Zvezdi/Sterne* included only a few combat scenes, reduced to one nocturnal theft of medicine for resisters holed up in the mountains and Jews interned in the camp. Two characters were to embody the partisan movement: Baj Petko, the archetype of the clever, deceptively good-natured Bulgarian; and Blaže, a blond adolescent who would be abused by a cruel police chief. In the eyes of the film censors, the invitation of a (non-Bulgarian) Jewish family to hide Ruth, with the possibility of her escape, was a further failure.

From the first discussions on the script, Wagenstein had developed a line of defense: his goal was not to provide a representative vision of the resistance, but rather to tackle antifascist combat through the history of a missed encounter. One might have forgiven the relatively minor weight given to heroism. But how to make up for a representation that failed to assert the ideological roots of the struggle? The writer Pavel Vežinov, a member of the Artistic Council, protested against the motivation given for Walter's joining the antifascist combat—love and humanism:

> Actually, the dramatic conflict unfolds between Walter and Ruth. Walter is a nice person endowed with a certain degree of integrity—he dabbles in philosophy to present himself as a good person and closes his eyes to the crimes committed around him. Ruth is the one who has a certain influence over the mask he wears. And it's through general humanist positions that she weighs on him. . . . It would be good for the author to find some small means, some marginal changes in the script, to give the sense that the Bulgarian revolutionary movement also influences Walter's ethical position, his moral position in these relationships.[95]

---

94   Ibid., l. 39.
95   CDA, F 404, op. 4, ae. 130, l. 63.

Two changes were considered essential: highlighting the fraternal relationship between partisans, and showing that Walter embraces resistance and faith in communism in the same breath.

The German guests generally listened to these (intra-)Bulgarian jousts with studied patience and reservation. However, at times they reminded their colleagues that the coproduced film was meant to reflect an actual historical situation: the collaboration of Bulgarians with the Third Reich. On December 31, 1958, during a meeting organized in Babelsberg in the presence of the Bulgarian producer Draganov, screenwriter Wagenstein, and composer Simeon Pironkov, *Zvezdi/Sterne* had an enthusiastic reception, a prelude to its approval by the East German authorities. During the conversation, however, Wilkening, the director of the German film studio, had explicitly invited his "Bulgarian friends" to embark on a process of reckoning critically with the past: "The film will leave many people with a feeling of profound sadness, but that type of sadness that can lead [the audience] to a greater consciousness of what they might have done, what they should have done and did not do. . . . *In this film, we also show the culpability of those who collaborated, through the character of the chief of police. For this reason, [the film] will be of great significance to our Bulgarian friends too.*"[96]

The day after the Babelsberg meeting, in a letter to the Bulgarian studio, German production director Nürnberger was quick to welcome "the central artistic and ideologically correct conception [of] a film that exerts a strong emotional influence and that, through its resonances, will lead the audience to reflect and to activate their support to our common struggle for peace." He had no difficulty in presenting the film as a work on fascism *and* anti-Jewish persecution, in the tradition "of a series of good films from the DEFA such as *Ehe in Schatten, Der Mörderer sind unter uns,* [and] *Der Rat der Götter* [The council of the gods, K. Maetzig, 1950]," before concluding: "We believe that the making of this film, precisely in this moment, as West Germany is making great strides toward a restoration of fascism *and the open persecution of Jews,* has contemporary political significance."[97]

At the time of the January 5, 1959, meeting, the Bulgarian Cinematography officials had the minutes of the Babelsberg meeting at their disposal. Yet, for them there could hardly be a question of Bulgarian responsibility for the deportation of Jews from Northern Greece. The storyboard had planned to represent the repressive Bulgarian system via a chief of police and a unit commander of forced laborers. Annoyed that a Jewish carrier had spilled water on his boots, the commander would hit him in the face and

---

96   Ibid., l. 96 (emphasis added).
97   Ibid., l. 112.

leave him in a heap, covered in blood.[98] But this scene disappeared from the finished film. Above all, an elision was enacted in the sequence of the convoy's departure for Poland, identical to that in the scene of the deportees' arrival.

Opening the valve via flashback, *Zvezdi/Sterne* begins and closes with shots of a train station, railroad, and cars. Shot at night, the boarding area shimmers in lustrous black. All while cursing at the Jews "*Schneller! Schneller! Schneller!* [Faster! Faster! Faster!]," Captain Kurt, rain streaming down his uniform, helps a child to climb aboard a wagon, and holds out his hand to Ruth, who refuses it. Erased from this scene is the shot where "German Wehrmacht soldiers, soaked with rain, occupy the entire length of the ramp. In their eyes, there is neither cruelty nor compassion—instead, indifference and fatigue. A soldier, with raindrops dripping down his cap, whispers to his neighbor, 'When is all this going to be over? I'm falling down, I'm so tired.'"[99] The "endless line of soldiers' boots," contained in the script and storyboard, has been dispersed: what remains is only a brief "I'm tired" that the lens records while the camera prepares a high-angle shot over the deportees. No Bulgarian policemen enter the shot: in *Zvezdi/Sterne*, Nazis accompany the convoys. However, as for the protagonists of this sequence shot, the storyboard had offered the following description:

First scene. 159 meters, including 60 caption meters.

Railway ramp

(Outdoors—nature, Sofia and a combination of night, wind, rain).

Characters: Ruth, Walter, Kurt, Ruth's father.

Background characters: an old Jew with a violin, a young boy with a backpack, an old Jewish woman, a young Jewish mother, an unshaven Jew, a Jewish woman with a young child, 1, 2, and 3 German soldiers, a person ill with fever.

Extras: 500 in total, including 430 Jews (180 men, 170 women, 80 children), 30 German soldiers, 30 Bulgarian policemen, 10 railwaymen.[100]

So where did these "30 Bulgarian policemen" go? At what point in the production did they peter out? The poet and writer Valeri Petrov, son of the famous Communist lawyer Nisim Mevorah, went so far as to express surprise that the camp had not been placed under the responsibility of a significant number of German officers: "For example, what makes an impression is

---

98   CDA, F 404, op. 4, ae. 128, l. 19.
99   Vagenštajn, *Tri scenarija*, 13.
100 CDA, F 404, op. 4, ae. 128, l. 1b.

the fact that, if I am not mistaken, or at least in the viewer's memory, only three Germans remain—Walter, Kurt, and this Amur, the one who follows them, and a captain who appears at the beginning and then suddenly disappears never to return. Such a thing, from the organizational point of view of the Wehrmacht, was not possible—that such a camp should not have been guarded by so few people, even if our gendarmerie was there too. There are only three people there."[101] These choices in the film's pictorial outfit were nonetheless not enough to satisfy the Cinematography officials. They would have wished to see Bulgarians express faultless solidarity toward the Jewish victims. The ideologue Venelin Gocev was deeply upset: "Another problem is in the way in which the attitude of our people toward the anti-Semitism that at the time was manifested is concretely shown in the film. The fact that a few individuals show compassion and help the victims of fascism with all they can—in this case, a group of Jews who are to be sent to Poland—is weak, very bland, and insufficient in essence. We believe that in this respect if the film is not corrected, the Direction of the Cinematography will insist that it is not released on screen."[102]

Having remained silent during the critical moments of the debates, Wolf tried to defuse the conflict: "I feel uneasy," he noted in his final speech, "when [a coproduction] is placed on a scale and we begin to weigh the German percentage, the Bulgarian percentage. Up until now, I had been skeptical about certain coproductions. And what made me happy about this film was that national aspirations hadn't been sidelined, but rather were subordinated to a common cause."[103] His rhetorical art was impeccable; the reference to internationalism, unassailable. What the German filmmaker failed to recognize was that the East German partners were also advocating a political agenda. The negotiation of the appearance of Nazis *and* Germans would be a particularly acrimonious affair.

Negotiating an East-East Reading of Nazism: German Polychromy?

The screenplay had proposed two figures of Germanness: the first was found in the features of Captain Kurt, a bon vivant Nazi officer of unthinking, almost careless obedience. Indifferently cruel toward the Jews, he is not insensible to his friend Walter's melancholy. During the first discussion of

---

101 CDA, F 404, op. 4, ae. 130, l. 20.
102 Ibid., l. 14–15.
103 Ibid., l. 51.

the script in the Artistic Council on January 6, 1958, Wagenstein had used a pastel scheme to portray this character, drawing on his own memories:

> This film will for the first time depict Germans in formally unoccupied territories.[104] Kurt is not that fascist German army officer who tears people from their homes and shoots them—he will even go so far as "to carefully hand a child into the wagon," and he is very loyal toward the Jews. He belongs to the type of German officer that procures a woman for Walter or does a few favors for him; because it is forbidden to keep medications in camp, he throws them out, etc. The Germans in Bulgaria used to go to Ashinger [a restaurant in Sofia] with women of easy virtue (*damički*) who only knew a few words in German; they jealously maintained their personal hygiene, brushed their teeth, and shaved every morning, etc.[105]

This characterization is far from the outrageous visions of the Wehrmacht usually proposed in Bulgarian film. The second image of Germanness is embodied by Walter, a slender young man with soft blond locks and a leisurely gait. Structured around this binary, the film's plot follows Kurt's progression toward actions that his refusal of reflexivity makes inevitable, and opposes him to the transformation that Walter undergoes as a result of love.

On January 5, 1959, Ginev caustically condemned the construction of the two German characters: "Either they're overly good, or they're excessively naive, or else the whole thing is a joke. It seems to me that neither one, nor the other, nor the third can be true. We know the Hitlerites; we know how cynical, capricious, and brutal they were, and how they acted to allow such things to flourish in their garden. So my first note in this regard is about the general atmosphere that emerges from this fascist camp, which is really very strange."[106] Here bubbles up the propensity for Bulgarian Cinematography officials to trace a line of continuity between "German" and "Nazi," ready to impute to the German people in its entirety (East *and* West) responsibility for Nazi crimes.

From the point of view of DEFA's leadership, this was precisely the line that could not be crossed. How to align with a verdict that yoked (East) German identity to the East German state project? In *Zvezdi/Sterne,* they saw a film of combat, in the conflict that opposed them to West Germany. Against a West Germany accused of having promptly turned the page of Nazism, East Germany claimed a capacity to embody a German moral conscience. In the immediate postwar period, support for a legal reckoning

---

104 It should be noted that this is the only mention, in these terms, of the wartime position of Bulgaria during the debates.
105 CDA, F 404, op. 4, ae. 130, l. 93.
106 Ibid., l. 11.

of Nazi war crimes was constitutive of East German identity.[107] From the mid-1950s, the press continuously condemned the presence of former high-ranking Nazi officials in the inner circle of Chancellor Konrad Adenauer. The Ministry for State Security (*Ministerium für Staatssicherheit*), or Stasi, did not hesitate to procure the support of Polish intelligence services in order to prove the involvement of high-ranking West German officials and military officers in Nazi crimes.[108] For director Kolhaase, the plot of *Zvezdi/ Sterne* was notable in introducing an analogy between the passivity of the early 1930s, at the birth of Nazism, and the present inertia in the face of West German revanchism: "Today, West Germany is undergoing a phenomenon of restoration, particularly through the postmortem rehabilitation of all the fascist criminals of the era. This restoration is also being carried out through cinematic means. There are dozens of films that have no other purpose than to demonstrate that [fascism] was not so bad after all. We must fight against this political rehabilitation of fascism by all means possible. And we think that this film offers one such weapon."[109]

The insistence on this battle was not devoid of tactical considerations: because Bulgarian attacks targeted the understanding of the past, East German comrades responded by situating the film in a present horizon, that of a struggle for world peace—for they knew that, if sanctioned by the USSR, it could not be publicly disowned by their counterparts. It was by proclaiming Kurt's obvious current-day relevance that Kolhaase defended the character:

> This film has above all been shot with a gaze toward the future, not toward the past. . . . We nonetheless believe that there is no rehabilitation, here, of the two main German characters—Kurt and Walter. Kurt, this joyful, unscrupulous bon vivant, a criminal, is today making his happy return in West Germany. Such people are still held to be "good guys." They are organized into various associations and await the repetition of what they failed [to achieve] the first time. The unveiling of this type of man, not only before the German audience but for all peoples, is associated with a warning: do not let yourself believe in this kind of modern mask.[110]

The condemnation of West German "fascism" nonetheless had another dimension: it involved an intimate, painful introspection. Thus, it was from a position of concern—the events of June 1953 were not far off—that Kolhaase broached the question of political regression in East Germany:

---

107 Fulbrook, *German National Identity*, 28–35.
108 Weinke, "Der Kampf um die Akten," 564–77.
109 CDA, F 404, op. 4, ae. 130, l. 44.
110 Ibid., l. 45.

As for Walter. I believe that the most important fact in the image of Walter is that he, too, is recognized as guilty in this film. . . . And if today there are people like Kurt in Germany—I am speaking above all about West Germany, *but this is a common national problem here*—there are also Walters who are hostile to it, who are good people, who feel ill at the notion of what is brewing, but who don't do anything in response. And we must show them the question of the past so that they can understand that silence is a crime.[111]

The very nature of East German exceptionality was at stake: to what moment in the past could this difference in German ways of being be traced? How could historical continuity be maintained if it excluded the Nazi era? Placing a fragment of history in parentheses, as a foil, did raise the double problem of filiation and affiliation. Emerging from a fault line in linear German history, weren't East Germans risking being relegated to the margins of the national narrative? In *Zvezdi/Sterne*, references to classical German culture proliferate—a culture that the Jews condemned to extermination shared with their executioners: to thank Walter for having brought a doctor into the camp, Ruth's father gives him a book by Heinrich Heine. The pre-Nazi philosopher also makes his way into the conversations between the two young people, united at least in part by the world of letters. The centrality of Walter's character, in the eyes of the East German filmmakers, can undoubtedly be understood in this light: it is up to him to prove the possibility of a historical bifurcation. The catharsis he experiences is what authorizes, at once, a rootedness in the German past and an unbinding. This helps to explain the intense dispute that staked conservatives Radevski and Ginev against Wolf, while the painter Nikola Mirčev tried to occupy a mediating position:

Radevski:	That Walter, we're wondering if he's hostile to Hitler?
Mirčev:	Why would he be pro-Hitler! Can we say that all Germans are pro-Hitler?
Ginev:	We're not talking about the German people. . . . It seems to me that all this anti-Hitlerism isn't represented in the way that not only we, but all of Europe, know it; that this Kurt, described with all his qualities, is an image stitched together from the very same white threads that we can see in dozens of places, that this Walter neither can nor should in any way exist.
	. . .
Mirčev:	But should an artistic production be so beholden to the realistic?
Ginev:	It's a question of true things as artistic representations of reality.
Radevski:	This is the question: is reality reflected rightfully?

---

111 CDA, F 404, op. 4, ae. 130, l. 45.

Wolf:	I would have liked to ask you, when dealing with such central, such crucial remarks, not to proceed so abstractly, but rather to refer to examples from the film. On the topic of Walter, allow me to make a remark *to the extent that we do, in spite of everything, have something in common with the German people and with German fascism, and we thought about that when we made the film.* If some claim that Kurt is not the prototype of the fascist officer, that may only be a claim, but it has not been proven. . . .
Ginev:	I feel that we could debate this question for a long time. I don't think that Walter never could have existed. I think that *in this pro-Hitler atmosphere, in this pro-Hitler milieu, he could not have existed in this way.*
Wolf:	*Why is that?*
Ginev:	He would have had another fate.
Wolf:	*Why?*
Ginev:	Because neither Kurt, his captain, nor the Bulgarian fascist police would have allowed such a flower to grow.
Wolf:	*In that case, there would be no German Democratic Republic today. No! I don't share your opinion. I think that in the former fascist army, there were Walters.*[112]

Wolf drew on his esteemed past in order to defend this position: "I lived through the war and fascism. For four years, I was in the Soviet army, and during those four years, day after day I accomplished work that put me in contact with the most different representatives of the fascist army. I can't let one statement only remain, and I can't let it be said that the fascists that we see [in the film] rather resemble soldiers and officers from World War I."[113] Yet, the balancing act remained tense. All the more, given that the double operation of insertion into the *longue durée* and rupture on the short-term basis took place by borrowing from the visual and narrative codes of inter-war cinema. In Babelsberg, on December 31, 1958, one of the participants praised "the bold sentimentalism" of *Zvezdi/Sterne.* He might also have underlined that the film was part of a genre, sacrificial melodrama, popularized by the UFA. In many respects, Wolf's film participated in an all-German cinematic history. In the reading it offered of the persecution of the Jews, the work nonetheless overflowed its edges.

---

112 Ibid., l. 42–43.
113 Ibid., l. 48.

Jewish Fates, in a Minor Key

During the 1945 anti-Jewish crime trials in Bulgaria, there was a palpable tension between rendering Jewish experiences of war singular or shared. Fifteen years later, the pattern was repeated. Approached by the leadership of Bulgarian Cinematography as an antifascist drama, *Zvezdi/Sterne* was not supposed to single out the specificity of Jewish fates, but rather to make of them the instrument of condemnation of Nazi cruelty; Jewish victims were shown in a merely illustrative way. Viewed as a reflection on the "tragedy of the Jews and the responsibility of the Germans," as Kolhaaase said,[114] the filming acquired a very different scope: the movie illuminated a specific Jewish destiny. Wagenstein was the only Bulgarian participant in the Artistic Council to attempt to reconcile these two perspectives, by making crimes against Jews the very quintessence of fascism:

> In our film, fascism is not expressed through the character of Kurt alone. Fascism is also expressed through these 8,000 Greek Jews sent to Osviencim [Oświęcim, Auschwitz]; out of that group, only one woman returned to Greece, sent to a brothel. This is fascism. If during the war people like Walter could not change the course of events, any more than our Walter manages to stop the train, [it is because] they realized far too late that the train had to be stopped before it started. Because it is not enough to want something not to happen; you have to do something so that it does not happen.[115]

The Bulgarian officials did not agree to this statement. In the first place, their criticism targeted the way the "Jewish masses" were featured in the movie—that is, the absence of Communist activists among them, and the

---

114 CDA, F 404, op. 4, ae. 130, l. 96.
115 CDA, F 404, op. 4, ae. 130, l. 53. In so doing, Wagenstein, who was familiar with the East German context, may well have borrowed a rhetorical device employed by members of the East German cultural elites, as they drew on the framework of antifascism in order to disseminate information about the Holocaust and mold its remembrance within the GDR. In a remarkable essay, Stefan Stach has convincingly argued that in the late 1950s and the 1960s, memories of antifascism did not necessarily compete with frameworks that stressed the destruction of Jews. Nor could the reference to the Holocaust be seen first and foremost as a ploy to denounce the revival of fascism in West Germany. Instead, the predominance of the narratives of antifascism and (West) German failure to break with the Nazi past offered many East German artists a venue to broach the question of Jewish annihilation. Stach's study of several documents and diaries about the plight of Polish Jews during the war, translated from Polish into German, serves to make this point. Stach, "Jewish Diaries," 273–301.

fact that their portrayal as victims failed to abide by one of the tenets of anti-fascism: that all characters, Jewish or non-Jewish, should be seen as combatants with a fighting spirit. Beginning with the April 1958 meeting, the vice director of Bulgarian Cinematography, Ginev, spoke out against the "overly stereotypical representation of the Jewish camp."[116] In January 1959, he clarified his accusation by deploring the absence of Communists among the rounded-up Jews. The words of journalist Nikola Aleksiev were even more explicit: "Why was it necessary to show Greek Jews here when in our antifascist struggle we have so many heroic images of Jews—Communists and antifascists—of whom any antifascist movement could be proud? These luminous images of antifascist Jews did not come out of nowhere; they are deeply linked to all the work that our party accomplished in this segment of the Bulgarian population too."[117]

Critic Emil Petrov attempted to mitigate the seriousness of this failure: "What does resistance to fascism and Hitlerism amount to in this film? On the one hand, the resistance of a group of Jews, who are leaving for a concentration camp; on the other, the Bulgarian line of resistance, the line of active Communist fighters, revolutionaries, opposing fascism. . . . It would be a normative demand to insist absolutely in this concrete production that there be representatives of the Communists among the group of Jews. The Communist point of view is present in the film, and this is sufficient."[118]

In May 1959, the journalist Nešo Davidov, son of the lawyer David Ieroham, who had been president of the Central Consistory of Jews in Bulgaria until 1952, once more lingered over the portrayal of Jewish victims deprived of (Communist) agency, in one of those didactic reviews familiar to socialist readers:

> If we discount Ruth for the moment, no prominent image emerges from the Jewish masses. . . . The mother, the elderly people, the children—they are all reduced to a crowd of people, beaten down, stripped of individual traits, who have lost all their capacity to manifest human dignity, rumbling resigned and submissive like cattle to the slaughterhouse. . . . The viewer is appalled. He longs to see a sign of resistance, however tenuous it may be, in these people. Even a man condemned to death, when he is led to the guillotine, has a momentary recoil, does he not? But these people, they go on, they go on.[119]

---

116 CDA, F 404, op. 4, ae. 130, l. 60–77.

117 Ibid., l. 15.

118 Ibid., l. 25–26.

119 Nešo Davidov, "S dălboka čovečnost i čuvstvo za mjarka," *Kinoizkustvo*, May 1959, 7–15 (here, 11–12).

The critic contrasts a disarmed and powerless Jewish community to the exemplary Jewish Communists. His pen then slides toward the anecdote of a lived experience in 1943 in Somovit, in an internment camp for Bulgarian Jews deemed "seditious," where internees had decided to reserve the best food rations "for the young and healthy," who had the best chance to survive. "This story is true and, I believe, heroic," Davidov writes.[120] The triple displacement from non-Bulgarian Jews to Bulgarian Jews, from supposed passivity to collective action, from fiction to reality, is of a piece with the canonical narrative that the publication of the book *Jews Fallen in Antifascist Struggle* had recently consecrated.[121]

One point in the journalist's review nevertheless catches the reader's eye: if the opposition between valiant Communists and Jews deprived of agency bears the mark of socialism, the image of the "cattle ready for slaughter" was hardly limited to the Eastern bloc. Let us continue studying his piece, which warrants further consideration. Davidov regrets that Ruth fails to offer a counterpoint to Jewish passivity:

> She might have and should have filled the void in the Jewish group. She is young, she is smart. In her, the desire to live cannot be easily extinguished. . . . We understand her, and we even believe that, if a possibility presented itself, her active position would grow into a fight. That is why we quickly come to love her. But then come the long walks and conversations with Walter. In a melodramatic and theatrical tone, she speaks of the people, those people of the future who will be good, of crickets, of stars. . . . And that is it. . . . All she does in the film is to reinforce the sense of tragic inevitability that awaits the entire Greek Jewish group.[122]

Did the choice of a young woman to symbolize Jewish suffering predispose the film to delineate the themes of fatalism and powerlessness? What spatiotemporal horizons would we need to encompass in order to account for the movie authors' narrative choices? To answer this question, the borders of Bulgaria may prove too narrow.

Jewish Passivity: A Question of Gender?

A brief foray into debates on the choice of the actress to play Ruth can begin to lift the veil over these issues. The Bulgarian and East German crews delivered their own visions of the role of the Jewish teacher, as well as of gender

120 Ibid., 13.
121 *Evrei zaginali v antifašiskata borba.*
122 Davidov, "S dălboka čovečnost," 12–13.

identities. In 1957, at the Karlovy Vary festival, Wolf had noticed a young Israeli actress, Haya Harareet, who had appeared in the Italian film *La donna del giorno* (Woman of the year; Francesco Maselli, 1956). Debated in the Artistic Council in April 1958, his proposal to hire Harareet to play Ruth had received the qualified support of Šaraliev, another director and member of the council: "As an actress, I like Haya Harareet, but for me the character of Ruth is not only associated with moral purity, but also external purity. I imagined Ruth as a very beautiful, very charming young woman, not necessarily very young. Yet here, I don't have the sense that I'm seeing a charming young woman. It's possible that, later, under the proper light, her face makes a different impression and certain defects are concealed and attenuated. I, however, would not be against a good and significantly more beautiful actress."[123]

Wolf's dry reply: "The question of beauty, particularly for a woman, is obviously a question of taste. I find Haya Harareet beautiful, on the inside as well as on the outside."[124]

Wagenstein continued, in a tone not devoid of misogyny: "It's difficult to find a woman who's at once very beautiful and very smart."[125]

Rereading these lines provides a useful reminder: many an interpretation verges on overinterpretation, especially as it attributes a reflexiveness to actors that might be foreign to them. We should bear in mind, nonetheless, the image of a young woman of virginal purity: we will find our way back to this metaphor. When she was invited to join the East German–Bulgarian production, the Israeli actress was negotiating a contract with Hollywood that would soon bring her glory, together with Charlton Heston, in William Wyler's *Ben-Hur* (1959). Casting thus had to be quickly resumed and extended to Poland, Czechoslovakia, Hungary, and the USSR—a challenge summarized by Ganev: "We have to have in mind that, from a strictly mechanical and arithmetical point of view, Ruth doesn't have a very important role in terms of the reel: for that reason, we must choose a very brilliant actress who will remain in the mind of the viewer and will make her influence over Walter be perceived as a subtext."[126] The hope of convincing Tatiana Samoilova, the protagonist of the sumptuous *Letyat zhuravli* (The cranes are flying; Mikhail Kalatozov, USSR, 1957), which won the Palme

123 CDA, F 404, op. 4, ae. 130, l. 74.
124 Ibid.
125 Ibid.
126 CDA, F 404, op. 3, ae. 21, l. 170.

Figure 2.3. Ruth (Saša Krušarska) in a deportation convoy (*Zvezdi/ Sterne*). *Source: Zvezdi/Sterne*, Konrad Wolf, 1959 © Lotte Michailowa.

D'Or at Cannes in May 1958, to accept the role quickly dissipated. Saša Krušarska thus became a fallback (figure 2.3).[127]

What role was Krušarska to assume? In the film, Ruth appears in fourteen out of sixty-nine scenes (*kartini*), mostly at Walter's side. The love that arises between them is constructed less as a tool of conversion than of inverted identity: the German second lieutenant undergoes a kind of rebirth (figure 2.4). Whereas at the end of the first promenade, the young soldier reclines as he listens to Ruth, whose ample bust stands out against the white clouds of evening, over the course of their encounters he learns to stand up, both physically and metaphorically.[128] The young teacher, for her part, marches toward an acceptance of her fatal destiny. She makes an autonomous decision at only two occasions: when she flags down the lieutenant from the fenced-in camp courtyard so that he might fetch a doctor to assist in a difficult birth; and when she tries to distract children terrified by the pregnant woman's cries by organizing a teaching session in the camp. Apart from that,

127 Warmly received in Cannes, Saša Krušarka would soon marry Rangel Vălčanov, "director's consultant" in *Zvezdi/Sterne*. She later moved to Italy, where she abandoned acting as a career.

128 Pinkert, "Tender Males," 193–210.

Ruth is acted upon by others: it is Captain Kurt who, to cheer Walter up, brings her into the bistro where he is drinking heavily. She is also escorted back to the camp after each long walk, her nocturnal absences leading to a suspicion among the other internees that she might be peddling her beauty to survive. In love as in death, she will be sought out and fetched; one might write, paraphrasing the journalist Davidov, "She goes on, she goes on."

The camera choices reinforce this sense of a character who is a repository for external intentions, primarily via the overlay image effects. As the cries of the newborn ring out, a gushing waterfall from the depths of the forest covers Ruth's angelic, immobile, and radiant face. In an even more dramatic fashion, when the deportation convoys leave the station, the young woman is filmed in a close-up behind bars, gazing in expectation, though she knows it to be in vain. Over her face scroll the lyrics for "S'brent/Undzer shtetl brent."[129] Were the director and cinematographer aware of the associations that they had created by opting for such an inscription?

As Daniela Berghahn has noted, "The chief function of women in the films' narrative economy was to heighten the trope of self-sacrifice around which the fascist genre is structured."[130] Until the 1960s, there were few East German films recounted from a female perspective. Yet, should the film's narrative scheme be traced to this legacy alone? Adopting a comparative perspective suggests a supplementary hypothesis: in the films of the 1950s and 1960s, women regularly serve as allegories for Jewish suffering.[131] Several months after *Zvezdi/Sterne*, *Deveti Krug* (The ninth circle; Yugoslavia, 1960) reached screens in Yugoslavia, a project of France Štiglic whose plot bears remarkable similarities to *Zvezdi/Sterne*. *Deveti Krug* is a bildungsroman at the end of which a young, non-Jewish Croat, Ivo, decides to oppose the anti-Jewish persecutions.[132] After a sham marriage to a young Jewish woman, Ivo slowly grows attached to the woman—also named Ruth—whom he has married against his will, and exchanges his adolescent trappings for the courage of a grown man. He will go to the length of sneaking

---

129   The passage appears in white text, thus recalling the annotations chalked onto the convoys: It's burning! Brothers! Oh, it's burning! / If you want to save our shtetl / Fetch buckets, put out the fire! / Put it out with your own blood / Show that you can! / Don't stay put like that / Don't let this happen / Our shtetl is burning / It's burning, burning, burning.

130   Berghahn, "Resistance of the Heart," 167.

131   Lewis, *Women in European Holocaust Films*.

132   On March 27, 2014, Nevena Daković, from the Faculty of Arts at the University of Belgrade, proposed a discussion on the work shown at the Paris Holocaust Memorial (Mémorial de la Shoah).

Figure 2.4. The meeting between Ruth and Walter, the German second lieutenant, across the barbed wire fence of an internment camp (*Sterne/Zvezdi*). *Source: Sterne/Zvezdi,* Konrad Wolf, 1959 © Lotte Michailowa.

into the extermination camp where his beloved is being held; yet, battered by the experience of the concentration camp, she cannot find the force to flee. Once more, women serve as a foil to men whom they accompany in the development of a political conscience; Jewishness is represented with feminine features, sweet and condemned. The main difference between Walter and Ivo is that Ivo, refusing to abandon the woman he loves, dies as he tries to help her regain freedom.

Five years later, in Czechoslovakia, these gendered stereotypes would unfold in a filial mode in *Obchod na korze* (The shop on Main Street, 1965), a film by the directors Ján Kadár and Elmar Klos. The screenplay, written by Ladislav Grosman, tells of the Aryanization of Jewish properties and roundups of Jews in a small town in Slovakia. The breathtakingly beautiful work was awarded the Academy Award for Best Foreign Film in 1965. Jewish suffering, here, takes on the features of Rozália Lautmannová (the great Polish actress, Ida Kamińska), an old woman whose deafness seems to symbolize the refusal of Jews to heed the warning signs. Once again, it is a Christian, the carpenter Tono Brtko, who, named manager of Aryanized

Jewish dry goods, grows attached to this woman, who could be his mother, and becomes aware of the horror of the anti-Jewish persecutions. The denouement is tragic: wishing to prevent Rozália from being discovered by the police, Tono inadvertently causes her death and commits suicide, breaking one of the prohibitions of "socialist realism" (the film was released in 1965, a liberal parenthesis that will not outlast the repression of the Prague Spring).[133]

Zvezdi/Sterne is thus not alone in connecting gender stereotypes (female passivity) and cultural stereotypes (Jewish passivity). One final piece can be added to this file of internationally circulating symbols of Jewish suffering: not content to feminize passivity, the film envelops the Jewish martyr with a Christian covering. This choice—surprising for Jewish Communist artists— borrowed from an emerging repertoire that transcended the borders of the Cold War.

Christian Signs for Jewish Suffering? A Transnational Symbolic Repertoire

In *Zvezdi/Sterne*, Ruth wears a dark dress; her hair is most often hidden under a black scarf that outlines a delicate oval around her face. Bergmann, the director of photography, chose to illuminate her face with an intense white light, such that her features are erased behind a deep, dark gaze, reminiscent of the saints of Byzantine iconography. The three-quarter-angle shots, with her face stretched skyward, suggest all the same pictorial references with a religious connotation: Ruth radiates a saintly clarity. Even more explicitly, Christian symbols frame the emergence of her love for the German lieutenant. Their first promenade has them wander alongside a cemetery, as we learn that the Jewish baby born in the camp has not survived. Moreover, the encounter, which seals their secret connection, takes place under the protective shadow of a church, refuge of their hopes. Between two shots of the heavenly canopy and the star on Ruth's chest, the lovers draw close in a fleeting kiss, before resuming their walk toward the church. The camera follows them, a tender couple beneath a massive Orthodox cross.

On January 5, 1959, the display of this symbol aroused an intense reaction from director Văljo Radev.[134] A richly oblique dialogue ensued between Petrov, whose father, the Communist lawyer Nisim Mevorah, had converted

---

133 The censors, however, insisted that a final scene be added, during which Tono and Rozália, bathing in an atmosphere of glimmering unreality, would fade into the distance, dancing, accompanied by fanfare music.

134 CDA, F 404, op. 4, ae. 130, l. 36.

to Protestantism; Molhov, a Jewish screenwriter, author, and critic; and Mirčev, whose wife was the Jewish actress Lisa Leon:

Petrov: I have to say that symbols are so heavily marked in some moments, which perhaps in the design did not assume a symbolic character, but now begin to sound symbolic. For instance, during the promenade of the two main characters, when they are approaching the church. That image of the cross that the two characters—the man and the woman—approach, and the fact that this is at a very important moment, without text, suggest perhaps more things than the authors of the film had intended them to; it's closer to a line—you clearly see which one I mean—that is not desirable at the moment. . . .

Molhov: . . . The cross to a certain extent unites two people who already love each other—the cross isn't the most appropriate symbol, neither for the situation, nor for what we would like to say about these two people.

Mirčev: Surely a five-pointed star should have been put here!

Molhov: This won't do, this cross is not appropriate.[135]

None of the speakers mentioned the displaced nature of representing a Jewish tragedy by means of Christian symbols. They only related their discomfort regarding the use of religious symbols to socialism's general distrust of confessional markers. Neither did they anchor their remarks in a personal trajectory. Could such avoidance have been the result of a time when making Jewish identity explicit was not a welcome avenue?[136] Wolf's

---

135 Ibid., l. 18, l. 22.

136 Although Bulgaria never faced anything close to the anti-Semitic campaign of late Stalinism in the Soviet Union, the early 1950s were a period of fear and uncertainty there too. Bulgaria's Jews learned to carefully parse what they could say to different people, in different places, at different times. Any hint of Jewishness or interest in the wartime predicament of the Jews could only be discussed in a safe and trustworthy environment. By the end of the decade, such cautions had still not been forgotten, despite the relative easing of the regime. Some observers, including an anonymous reviewer of this manuscript, have suggested that Jewish identities were of minor import to Bulgaria's Jews in those years, and only acquired significance several decades later. In this respect, it may be worth recalling that in the fall of 1944, Valeri Petrov coauthored with illustrator Marko Behar a short theater play designed to popularize the achievements of the People's Court. Petrov was the son of renowned Communist jurist Nisim Mevorah, who had converted to Christianity in the late 1930s. The play delineated several "types" of criminals and victims—and Jews were one of the categories the two authors singled out. Several drawings

reaction was equally unexpected: in his concluding statement, the filmmaker conceded the inopportune nature of the metaphorical choice, no more. On January 16, 1959, listing the modifications envisioned by the German party, Wilkening returned to this point: "In the double exposure shots before the church, we will try to manipulate the angle to distance the cross from the church, or, at least, to fade it out so that it doesn't emerge so distinctly."[137] For the contemporary viewer, the sfumato effect is very inconclusive.

Recurring use of Christian iconography to depict anti-Jewish persecutions was, at the time, not limited to Bulgarians and East Germans. In a remarkable article, Stuart Liebmann has traced the emergence of visualizations of the Holocaust in the immediate postwar period.[138] Comparing documentaries and fictional films made in the East *and* the West, the historian notes the recurrence of Christian motifs in works made by mostly Jewish filmmakers, producers, and screenwriters. Such a semiological register was perhaps meant to facilitate a broad public's identification with Jewish suffering by proposing a supposedly universal reference. It might also have been meant to counter the risks of anti-Semitic responses to allusions to the Holocaust in Poland, the USSR, and even the United States. Historian Sylvie Lindeperg mentions, in this sense, "the symbolic combat between the two crosses, Nazi and Christian, which erased the Jews from the memory of deportation" and underlines "the inability to represent deportation according to a secular symbolic system."[139] Fifteen years later, the power of evoking Christian symbols seemed to succeed in triumphing over Cold War divisions as well as Eastern European atheism campaigns.

At first blush, it might seem a counterintuitive exercise to trace the footsteps of *Zvezdi/Sterne*, since this very object of study appears to demonstrate par excellence the existence of an "Eastern bloc"—only to trouble any serene vision of the latter. By analyzing the making of the movie, however, we have uncovered the bitter labors that governed the creation of intersecting (though hardly unified) understandings of the recent past. From the outset, Wolf's work invited a challenge to any reading of film history solely in the terms of the cultural Cold War or the confrontation between East and West Germany. The discussions in the closed space of the Bulgarian–East German Artistic Council have offered a prism onto the resurgence of lived

---

were explicitly dedicated to Jewish suffering. As noted in chapter 1, however, emphasis on unique Jewish war experience came to be downplayed with the dawn of the Cold War. Such avoidance in public does not mean that Bulgaria's Jews forgot their memory of anti-Jewish policies. See Petrov and Behar, *Naroden sǎd*.

137 CDA, F 404, op. 4, ae. 128, l. 337.
138 Liebmann, "Les premiers films sur la Shoah," 145–82.
139 Lindeperg, *Clio de 5 à 7*.

experiences and a montage of a narrative chiseled by the present of the late 1950s. Conceptions of war, fascism, anti-Jewish violence, national identities, and socialism were all at play. Examining these exchanges underlines, in topographical relief, the fact that contemporary resonances of World War II were a result of Bulgarian and East German cultural elites seeking ways to affirm continuity with the national past, all while overseeing a rupture with the bourgeois order. Finally, as we have seen, bilateral cooperation was striated by spatial coordinates that were not confined to the East-West divide.

It is often said that a text is the result of its contexts, both of writing and of reading. The developments above suggest a visual variation of this maxim: the images cannot be viewed outside the words through which they were produced and spoken; even in an authoritarian regime, the cinematic object cannot be reduced to a compilation of commands. The film has been seen in its multiple identities, despite—or perhaps as a result of—the efforts deployed by its authors and censors to confine its possible meanings. This statement is in line with the path followed throughout this book: retracing the genesis of a dominant narrative regarding the events of World War II in Bulgaria after 1944. Nonetheless, we must think of this path as a ragged one, frayed, like those fractal objects that, viewed from up close, lay bare their irregularities—and that only distance can smooth.

For those with a taste for paradox, one might add that Wolf's work was the only film on anti-Jewish persecutions (co)directed under Bulgarian socialism, precisely because it was not conceived as such by Bulgaria's cultural officials. For Bulgarian artists, defending the work also enabled a call for greater autonomy for the artistic field following the ideological crackdown of 1958. After the Cannes Festival, another film was proposed to the sight and memory of spectators—notable because it had offered Bulgarian Cinematography its highest mark of international recognition.

After 1959, far from being forgotten, as Bulgarian screenwriter Wagenstein has suggested,[140] *Zvezdi/Sterne* would go on to lead multiple lives. In 1979, for instance, the coproduction was projected in the presence of Wolf and Wagenstein at the General Assembly of the United Nations.[141] After the fall of communism, the drama would become the quintessential film released at the annual commemorations of the events of March 1943 in Bulgaria and abroad, though it was not always possible to determine which part of the past was being recalled to collective memory. Wagenstein's commitment to the recognition of Bulgarian responsibility for the deportations nonetheless allowed these reels to be associated, gradually, to the memory of Jewish destructions.

---

140 Vagenštajn, *Predi kraja na sveta*, 261.
141 Vagenštajn, *Tri scenarija*, 11.

With *Zvezdi/Sterne*, we have captured a moment in time, gleaning a few months from the more obvious interest of the 1960s in the events relating to the destruction of the European Jews. In the following chapter, rather than isolating a slice of time and space, we will embark on the traces of a strange visual object—its tribulations, its successive reshapings, the various identities to which it was assigned. These will dictate the extent of the territories to cross and the temporal coordinates of the inquiry. What kind of material is under our purview? A film reel, its editing process unfinished. What did it record? The deportations from the Greek territories under Bulgarian occupation.

Chapter 3

The Deportation of Jews from Northern Greece

The Mysterious Journeys of a Film from 1943

The deportations of March 1943 left a furtive visual trace: a few minutes of a silent film with strangely edited rushes.[1] Columns of exhausted people, bodies stooped under heavy bundles, sealed rail cars from which emerge faces set behind bars, the boarding of a steamboat: the narrative framework of this unique pictorial source on the roundups in occupied territories presents a deceptive familiarity. However, at the beginning of our investigation, everything about these reels resisted deciphering: the identity of those who commissioned them as well as their intended audience, the camera operator(s), the locations and dates of the shooting, and even the very purpose of the filming. Rarely has an archive been defined by what it lacks, what is missing; by its blanks and absences. The exceptionality of this footage that was subjected to an early "archivization"[2] and the enigmas surrounding its making most probably illuminate the obstinacy with which, since the end of World War II, political and cultural actors, and professional and lay historians, have tried to make it "speak." Silent, these images were smothered with an added soundtrack; mobile, they were fixed in photographic snapshots. Some frames

1   This research was supported by the WW2CRIMESONTRIAL1943–1991 project, ANR-16-CE27–0001–01, as well as by the encouragement and precious help of Alexander Friedmann, Paul Gradvohl, Tony Koleva, Éric Le Bourhis, Maël Le Noc, Mélisande Leventopoulos, Piotr Malachinski, Juliana Metodieva, Caroline Moine, Nurie Muratova, Catherine Perron, Marijana Piskova, Valérie Pozner, Sophie Reiter, Ida Richter, Éric Sangar, Andrea Simon, Jasmin Söhner, Katharina Stengel, Ania Szczepanska, Vanessa Voisin, Annette Weinke, Lindsay Zarwell, and Alexander Zöller. The author wishes to thank them warmly.
2   The expression is borrowed from Maeck and Steinle, *L'image d'archives*.

were even transformed into actual objects by the hands of a carpenter. Quoted and truncated, appropriated and diverted, put back on the editing table, these rushes traveled beyond the physical borders of Eastern Europe and the temporal watershed of 1989, while the spectrum of interpretations of the images kept on widening.

In this chapter, the exploration into the practices of documentation and representation of the Holocaust ventures into a new medium. *Zvezdi/Sterne* led us to explore cultural policies, one of the sectors of public action that— or so I contend—has shaped the intelligence and the publicly sanctioned remembrance of anti-Jewish violence. Following this venue reminds us that, in the discussions about the figuration of the Jewish raids, issues external to them had also been at stake, chief among them the search for autonomy by the art worlds and the negotiation of relations between two Eastern European allies. In this feature film, moreover, the power of conviction of the images was increased by the liberties taken in relation to factuality. Reality seemed all the more "real" as one stepped back from it. The rushes that we are dealing with now are of a different nature: they allow us to hope for a more precise documentation of *wie es eigentlich gewesen* (how it really was).

There is also a difference in the rules that governed the public exhibition of these visual sources. Whatever the limits imposed by the Bulgarian censorship on the cinematographic or televisual reruns of *Zvezdi/Sterne*, the Bulgarian–Eastern German film was designed to be shown. There is no evidence to date that the 1943 footage was intended, by those who commissioned it, to be shown beyond the decision-making circles associated with the implementation of anti-Jewish policies. In fact, invisible for more than twenty years, these shots only reappeared in the mid-1960s on the occasion of a lawsuit brought in West Germany against the former Nazi minister plenipotentiary in Sofia Adolf-Heinz Beckerle (June 28, 1941–September 9, 1944).

Exploring their manifold documentary or fictional uses in no way engages the production of a heroic narrative in which the visual archive would have been saved from oblivion, if not from destruction, by remarkable individualities and brought to the knowledge of an ever-widening public, as if a relationship of metonymy could be established between the "rescue" of the photographs and that of the Jews of Bulgarian citizenship. More trivially, the accessibility of the film footage followed the fluctuations of public management and private investment of the past in Bulgaria and beyond. Far from any reassuring linearity, the analysis will therefore delve into the power configurations that have underpinned the shifts in scopic regimes.

The question that serves as a guideline concerns the relationship between movement and the evolving meaning of images. Historians of science have recounted the way in which, at the turn of the seventeenth century—under the combined effects of the novel relationship to experimentation, optical knowledge, and visual regimes—images were constructed as instruments of elucidation, proof, and persuasion. Rejecting an exclusively illustrative use of visual items, the scientists living in those times conferred upon them a power to establish and disseminate scientific knowledge.[3] Questioning the capacity of visual artifacts to authenticate facts is one of the aims of the investigation carried out here. However, instead of looking at a specific place and time, as was the case with the 1945 trial and the 1959 film, we have chosen to trace the "social lives" of a protean object successively invested with the quality of factual document, court evidence, and testimony with memorial significance.

Such an approach was suggested as early as 1986 by Arjun Appadurai in his *Social Life of Things: Commodities in Cultural Perspective.* The anthropologist had the intuition that digging into the furrows of objects and the multiple recompositions they underwent would allow him to take a fresh look at the social phenomena he studied, revealing actors and mechanisms that were otherwise indiscernible.[4] In 1998, the historian Annette Wieviorka called for tracing the "migration of testimonies" of Holocaust survivors between documentary, judicial, and television uses.[5] It is the "migration of images" that will be discussed here.[6] This endeavor is not unknown to historians: several recent works have followed the travails of "trophy archives" and shown that the spoliations and restitutions of such documents shed light on the political and geopolitical confrontations of the Cold War.[7] In a similar way, we will here see that the viewings, citations, and circulations of the 1943 film fragment were the object of requests, personalized mediations, and value politics with unmistakable Cold War overtones.

Let us note as preface that the story we are reconstructing in what follows is one of a spectacular reversal of meaning. It concerns the way in which sequences probably filmed at the request of Bulgarian officials in charge of anti-Jewish policies—with the assent, if not a commissioning, by their German allies—showing convoys of deportees escorted mainly by Bulgarians, came to support a narrative of events centered on those (Bulgarian) Jews who were not deported and to buttress a vision of the role of the Bulgarian state articulated around the notion of "rescue." To this interpretive work, myriad actors (archivists, film professionals, journalists, intelligence agents, diplomats, historians) made unexpected contributions. Meanwhile, the images were envisaged in turn as a documentary record of

<hr />

3   Schaffer, "Natural Philosophy," 1–43.

4   Appadurai, *Social Life of Things.*

5   Wieviorka, *Era of the Witness,* 110.

6   See "La migration des images en Europe," a workshop organized by Valérie Pozner, Mélisande Leventopoulos, and Laurent Guido, November 28–29, 2016, at the Institut national d'histoire de l'art (INHA), Paris, http://www. airsc.org/wp-content/uploads/2016/11/La-Migration-des-images-en-Europe.pdf.

7   Sumpf and Laniol, with Rolland, *Saisies, spoliations et restitutions.*

the facts, pieces of evidence used in a legal arena, and testimonies at the service of public memory policies.

The investigation unfolds in three stages, each moment dealing with distinct processes of signification, veridiction, and conviction—mixing images, texts and sounds, documentary, and fiction, as well as unstable patterns of invisibilization of film sequences. The first moment, which parallels the events themselves, is outlined in dotted lines at the intersection between the writing of the images offered by three museum institutions, Bulgarian, American, and German. A consideration of their archive inventories, understood as instruments guiding the gaze, will show how poorly legible most film shots are, unless they are instantiated with wordy captions. Examining archivists' attempt to reconstitute the biography of the reels will also bring into relief the dispersion of the extant sources on the origins and content of the film footage, the autonomous lives experienced by film photograms, and the persistence of discrepancies between museum interpretations of this visual document.

The second moment coincides with the restart of trials for Nazi crimes in the FRG at the turn of the 1960s. As an object of transactions between East and West, the Bulgarian film footage was then called upon to support the accusation against the former Nazi minister plenipotentiary Adolf-Heinz Beckerle, who had negotiated with the Bulgarian authorities the deportation of the Jews. Even more than in the previous chapter, this case study will show the extent to which the nationalization of the past involves a plurality of spatial scales—national, regional, and international. As a junction between Bulgaria, West Germany, Israel, and the United States, the 1943 rushes will disclose the existence, during the Cold War, of a network of connections transcending the East-West divide.

Finally, the last moment is situated on the threshold of the fall of communism. The formulation by the Bulgarian authorities of a cultural diplomacy of "rescue of the Bulgarian Jews" intersects with the entry into a new era of knowledge and remembrance of the Holocaust. In those years set in documentary and fictional settings, the 1943 film footage offers a window onto the promotion of museums as key actors in the shaping and territorialization of Holocaust memory. In a counterintuitive way, the screening of these shots then takes part in making the immortalization of the faces of Jewish deportees a tool for valorizing the exceptionality of the nondeportation of Bulgarian Jews.

Archival Inventories as Texts and Gaze

In order to reduce the indeterminacy surrounding the production of the filmed sequences from 1943, we will proceed here in reverse, by exploring two techniques for verbalizing images, drawing on the assumption that looking at images usually amounts to writing the visual in an attempt to make it "speak." The iconographic document will first be approached *via* the rendering offered by the inventory catalogs. We will then return to the film shots themselves in order to establish a dialogue between the seen and the read, and to propose an outline of the events that the camera has captured.

Why start the investigation with the descriptive notes of the visual archives? Because they are the first interpretive glasses that the historian puts on and they shape his gaze into a rarely questioned contribution. As writings of parsimony, pedagogies of vision that aspire to scientific accuracy, the inventories are both precious sources on visual materials and objects of research in their own right, the writing of which results from the aggregation of composite elements with different historicities—animated and still images, oral testimonies, scientific works, exhibition catalogs. In many ways, these mosaic texts recall the complex arrangements of oral and written knowledge, experiences, and judgments at the basis of the production of maps in the time of empires.[8] In this case, the confrontation between writings that discern in these images different sites and protagonists allows us to begin a questioning of the role of museums in the production of knowledge about the past. Through this examination, the changing lights that labile presents have cast on pasts that are constantly reshaped through borrowings, citations, and confrontations between sources also become apparent. Thus, our investigation will progress toward its own disarmament, and it is at the end of this exercise in disorientation that we will look at these frames anew.

The 1943 palimpsest film footage features in at least three museum institution catalogs: that of the Bulgarian National Film Library (*Bălgarska nacionalna filmoteka*, BNF) in Sofia, that of the Film Department of the German Federal Archives in Berlin (Bundesarchiv-Filmarchiv), and that of the United States Holocaust Memorial Museum (USHMM) in Washington, DC. The titles of the reels and the notes that accompany them, true identity cards of the archived images, remind us that seeing presupposes knowledge. However, the superimposition of these inventories gives free play to the narrative and tends to destabilize its frames. By far the most enigmatic source comes from the Bulgarian National Film Archive's inventory of documentaries and newsreels in its possession. The existence of not one but two visual archives is mentioned. From the outset, the object bursts forth. The first mention is expeditious, undated, and devoid of any description of the pictorial contents (box 1).

---

8   Blais, "Les enquêtes des cartographes," 70–85.

> ## Box 1. "Izselvane na evrei." Archive inventory, Bulgarian National Film Archive (first reference)
>
> *Deportation of Jews, No. 12002.* One reel, 300 meters, positive
>
> Source: Bălgarska Nacionalna Filmoteka, *Filmografija na Bălgarskite Kino-pregledi, 1921–1944*, 13.[9]

The second entry is less allusive, but its title is all the more surprising since there were no deportations of Jews from Bulgaria in 1940 (box 2).

> ## Box 2. "Izselvane na evrei, 1940." Archive inventory, Bulgarian National Film Archive (second reference)
>
> *Deportation of Jews, 1940.*
> First part, 184 meters, silent, double negative.
> Second part, silent, working copy.[10]
>
> Note: the second part reproduces the first part almost identically.
>
> First part
>
> People carrying luggage walk in the streets. They climb up into trucks, trains, steamships. An inhabited place—laundry hanging on ropes. A row of wagons, a steamboat. People behind bars in trains (some images are repeated).[11]
>
> Second part
>
> Jews behind bars in a freight train. Inside the train car. Stepping out of the train car. Jews walking through streets. Boarding the steamer. Police officers beat people who have fallen to the ground.
>
> Source: Bălgarska Nacionalna Filmoteka, *Filmografija na Bălgarskite Kino-pregledi, 1921–1944*, 15–16.

The subject matter is sparse, to say the least: no location of the shots is listed. The Jewish identity of the people filmed is only made explicit in the

---

9   The date of this inventory is unknown. At the time of the field survey, it was impossible to consult the reels, officially owing to a breakdown of the Moviola.

10   This is a mounted positive.

11   The wording of the paragraph suggests that we are dealing with edited shots; "double negative" refers to what could be a second negative produced from the working copy mentioned in the second part of the entry.

second part, although strong similarities are noted with the first. Nothing is said about the political and temporal context of the convoys, nor about the destination of the people in transit. The nationality of the Jews is not mentioned, nor is that of the civilians and police officers escorting them. The date of the shooting, the identity of the operator(s), as well as that of the film commissioner(s) are elided.

The inventory of the United States Holocaust Memorial Museum in Washington, DC, is noticeably more detailed (box 3). The 6:32-minute, 190-meter-long rushes in the museum's possession were acquired from the Bulgarian National Film Library, by way of a private production company, Concordia, in February 1992.

Box 3. "Deportation of Jews from Thrace." Inventory of the USHMM Film Collections

Original notes indicate that this footage depicts the deportation of the Jewish communities of Kavála, Serres, and Drama in what is now Northern Greece. The deportation began on March 4, 1943, and included 3,000 people. They were taken by truck to the Drama train station, placed without food or water onto trains, and taken to Gorna Džumaja where they lived in a temporary internment camp until March 18, 1943. On that date, they were put in railway cars and taken to Lom on the Danube. At the port of Lom, four ships left for Vienna with 4,000 "passengers" on board on March 20 and 21, 1943. Their next stop was Treblinka.
Source: USHMM, RG-60.0466, film ID: 246, online.[12]

This sheet would have been written on the basis of data transmitted by the Bulgarian side at the time of the transaction—that is, in the period of political openness that followed the fall of communism and the election to parliament of an anti-communist majority (in October 1991). The Bulgarian writer and film director Bojan Papazov,[13] then cultural attaché at the

---

12   On February 4, 2020, the record was modified and completed. The new inventory takes a careful descriptive approach and suggests the filming occurred in Gorna Džumaja, Dupnica, and Lom. https://collections.ushmm.org/search/catalog/irn1002157.

13   Papazov, the Bulgarian screenwriter, is said to have had access to the holdings of the Bulgarian Film Archives holdings in the early 1990s and to have made a personal copy of a visual archive about one hour in length. Communication from a respondent who wishes to remain anonymous. Bojan Papazov did not wish to comment on the archives he was said to hold, nor on the transaction

Bulgarian Embassy in the United States, would have offered the USHMM the film object that came into his possession.[14]

The description of the rushes belongs to a different narrative genre. The writing oscillates between the adoption of an informative tone detached from the sequence of images it is supposed to put into context and an assignment of pieces of information to specific frames, referring to "original notes" of unspecified provenance. Are we suggesting here, by following the order of the film sequences, that the images were shot in Kavála, Serres, or Drama (the column of Jews crossing the city), in Drama (the alignment of the wagons), in Gorna Džumaja (the open-air internment camps), and in Lom (the boarding of the steamer)? Or only providing a framework that leaves the viewer free to interpret and situate the shots? If the second option is chosen, how can one explain the omission of other towns in Northern Greece (Komotini/Gjumjurdžina, Xánthi/Ksanti, Alexandroúpoli/Dede Agač, Eleftheroupoli/Pravište, Chrysoupoli/Sar Šaban, the island of Thásos/Tasos, Nea Zichni/Ziljahovo, Samotraki/Samothraki) where the Bulgarian police carried out roundups? And how can one understand the estimate of the number of deportees—3,000—when the arrests affected between 4,026 and 4,102 Jews?[15] According to the head of the USHMM's international archive acquisition policy at the time, historian Radu Ioanid, Romanian ambassador to the State of Israel from February 2020 onward, the topography of the shooting was established by the museum's archivists by cross-checking against contemporaneous photographs.[16] However, other identifications of locations continue to circulate (see map 2).

A third source, the Film Department of the Federal Archives of Germany, depicts a 177-meter visual document entitled "Die Deportation des Juden

---

with the USHMM. Email correspondence with Bojan Papazov, August 22, 2022.

14   Interview with Radu Ioanid, then head of international archival acquisition policy at the USHMM, June 20, 2017. The purchase reportedly followed a request by historian Sybil Milton relayed by archivist Henry Mayer to the Bulgarian cultural attaché in 1991, as evidenced by a letter preserved in the USHMM archives.

15   Danova and Avramov, *Deportiraneto*, 1:856–58.

16   Interview with Ioanid, June 20, 2017. The USHMM has a rich collection of photographs from the Central Zionist Archives, the Beit Lohamei HaGetaot, the Auschwitz-Birkenau Museum, the Jewish Historical Museum in Belgrade, Yad Vashem, and the Societal Educational-Cultural Organization of the Jews of Bulgaria. Some of the images are stills from the 1943 rushes. The author thanks Judith Cohen and the USHMM Photographic Archives for making these documents available.

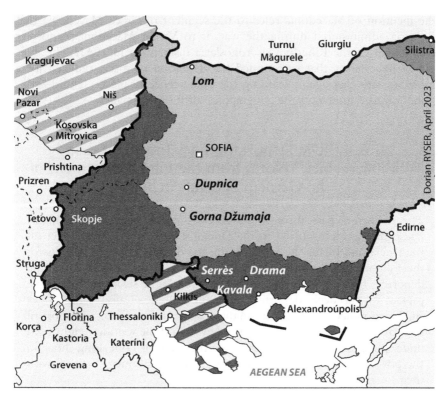

Map 2. Multiple locations of the Jewish deportees' journey filmed in March 1943. *Note:* The names of the cities mentioned in the inventories of the Film Department of the German Federal Archives and the USHMM are indicated in italics. Some of these locations are, understandably, mutually exclusive. *Source:* Centre de recherches internationales de Sciences Po (CERI).

aus dem Weißmeergebiet" (box 4)[17] The term *Weißmeergebiet* (literally, region on the White Sea) corresponds to the Bulgarian name *Belomorie*, an area in Northern Greece. However, the subtitle immediately introduces confusion: "Ungeschnittenes Material über die Deportation von 12 000 Juden aus dem Weißmeergebiet und Mazedonien vom 4 March–22 March 1943." The estimated number of deportees provided here concerns the whole of the Yugoslav and Greek territories occupied by Bulgaria. Moreover, does

---

17   Bundesarchiv-Filmarchiv, catalog: "Judisches Leben und Holocaust 1930–
     1945 im Filmdokument," film reference: BSN 26 108, 14. 1943, https://
     www.bundesarchiv.de/findbuecher/Filmarchiv/Holocaust/index.htm.

the mention of Macedonia refer to the segment of Greek Macedonia that Bulgaria administered during the war or to Vardar Macedonia, a former component of the Kingdom of Yugoslavia dismantled in 1941? The margin of uncertainty that surrounded the definition of space, reduced for a moment, stretches again, accusing the evanescence of places. The description, however, interrupts the geographical drift of the images.

> ## Box 4. "Die Deportation des Juden aus dem Weißmeergebiet." Notes from the Film Department of the German Federal Archives
>
> The deportees pass through Kavála with their luggage; they board trucks and are transported to the Drama station; the deportees get off the trucks and board the freight train; the doors of the cars are closed; the freight train departs and arrives in Lom; in the port of Lom, the deportees board the Danube steamer "Saturn"; the steamer departs; the captain on the deck; deportees from the Dupnica transit camp under Bulgarian police surveillance; buildings around the square; transport of deportees by truck to a train station; Jews board the waiting freight train under police surveillance; departure of the train for Lom (long shot); in the port of Lom, deportees board the Danube steamer "Saturn" with their luggage.
>
> *Source:* Bundesarchiv-Filmarchiv, BSN 26 108, 14. 1943.

Let us recapitulate the findings: the crossing of the city would have been filmed in Kavála, the trains at the Drama station; the port on the Danube would have been Lom. The camp scenes here are set in Dupnica, a town near the border with Vardar Macedonia, where a transit camp for Jews from Northern Greece was established. The presence of Bulgarian police officers is mentioned. The citizenship of the civilians and the captain of the ship is not provided. On what documents did the authors of this note base their deciphering of the images? The brief notice does not provide sources. In an extended note, however, mention is made of the catalog of an exhibition held at the Staatliche Kunsthalle in West Berlin in the spring of 1984.[18] Let's keep this fact in mind; it will be precious to us at a later stage of the investigation.

While there seems to be a consensus that the roundups recorded on camera are indeed those of Northern Greece, the plot thickens again when one considers two other sources, Macedonian and Bulgarian, respectively. The first comes from the *Memorialen centar na holokaustot na Evreite od*

---

18   Ruckhaberle and Ziesecke, *Rettung*, 109.

Makedonija (Memorial Center for the Holocaust of the Jews of Macedonia), which opened in Skopje in March 2011. Before its 2018 remodeling, on the second floor of the permanent exhibition the viewer was greeted by a montage of images including a photogram of the column of deportees, captioned in Vardar Macedonia.[19] The same location appears on the dust jacket of the book *Macedonian Chronicle: The Story of Sephardic Jews in the Balkans*, published in conjunction with the exhibition.[20] Could such an attribution come from the Jewish Historical Museum in Belgrade (*Jevrejski istorijski musej Belgrad*), which placed the scene in Skopje?[21] The second source is the catalog of the exhibition prepared by the Bulgarian Central State Archives on the occasion of the seventieth anniversary of the "rescue of the Bulgarian Jews" in 2013. A photograph showing the crossing of a street lined with buildings is captioned: "Deportation of Jews from Skopje. March 1943" (*Izselvane na evrei ot Skopie. Mart 1943 g.*).[22] The attribution is surprising to say the least: it is rare to see Bulgarian and Macedonian officials agree on any facet of the past.

A Film without an Author or Instructions?

Short of solving all these enigmas, can we at least identify the author(s) of the shots and their commissioners? What instructions presided over the making of the shots: were they intended to document the work of state bureaucracy in order to demonstrate its efficiency, to produce propaganda

---

19   Under the heading "Bulgaria's Participation in the Deportation of Jews from Macedonia," the image was formerly available online (accessed August 21, 2017; no longer active), but it is not found on the Fund's new website: https://holocaustfund.org.mk/. The Memorial Center's permanent exhibition was completely redesigned and partially opened in March 2018 (see also chapter 5). Excerpts from the 1943 dailies were still on display at a location in Macedonia on December 12, 2018 (per visit by the author).

20   Mais and Koska-Hot, *Macedonian Chronicle*; see also the photograms "Deportation of Macedonian Jews" and "Captured Jews" in Berenbaum, *Jews in Macedonia*, 42, 50. Another freeze-frame that, in the 1943 footage, precedes the photogram on page 42 by a fraction of a second is captioned "Deportation of Tracian [*sic*] Jews" (40).

21   See the notices of the pictures W/S #16,672 to W/S #16,676 from USHMM, from the Jewish Historical Museum in Belgrade.

22   Dăržavna Agencija Arhivi, *Truden izbor s goljamo značenie*, 56. This location was proposed as early as 1977 in the catalog of the permanent exhibition of the Jewish House of Sofia on the "rescue of Bulgarian Jews" inaugurated in 1963: Cohen and Assa, *Saving of the Jews*. It still appears on the website of the Bulgarian Central State Archives: https://jews.archives.bg/5-%D0%93%D0%90%D0%9B%D0%95%D0%A0%D0%98%D0%AF.

images intended for a wider public, or to capture the last moments of the deported populations?

A first clue is provided by the catalog of the German Federal Archives. Under the heading "Produktionsfirma," one can read "Bǎlgarsko selo, Sofia."[23] The copyist's hand, by making a mistake of one letter, dared an involuntary stroke of humor: "selo" means "village" in Bulgarian. The reference was probably intended as "Bǎlgarsko delo" (Bulgarian action), a foundation of private status established on March 31, 1941, to serve the National Propaganda Directorate of the Ministry of the Interior. With its publishing and film arms, the foundation was charged with "contributing to the propaganda of Bulgarian state and national actions and enterprises."[24] It was responsible for the production and distribution of newsreels and documentary films. At the end of 1943, the foundation numbered ninety-six employees and had branches in Skopje (Vardar Macedonia) and Xánthi (Greek Thrace).

That the shooting of these sequences was entrusted to the foundation is a plausible hypothesis, given the monopoly it held on the production of filmed images endorsed by the state. However, the footage does not appear in the activity report for the year 1943. The report lists the filming of 275 events and objects of "cultural and propaganda value." Sixty-two subjects are detailed, which do not include any "Jewish themes." In a country where the development of a film industry had remained embryonic between the two world wars, the number of experienced operators was modest: nine cameramen were identified among the foundation's employees in 1943.[25] Could the documentation of the raids have been offered to other hands deemed even more secure, possibly to German operators or to executives recently trained by them?[26]

In an interview conducted in 2016, Bulgarian scriptwriter and novelist Angel Wagenstein indicated that in Bulgarian film circles, Vasil Bakǎrdžiev, one of the pioneers of the Bulgarian ciné-actualités in 1935 and designers of the newsreels filmed after September 9, 1944,[27] was believed to be the

23 Bundesarchiv-Filmarchiv, BSN 26 108, 14. 1943.
24 CDA, F 15K, op. 3, ae. 2, l. 1–3, quoted in Piskova, "Iz dokumentalnoto nasledstvo na Fondacija 'Bǎlgarsko delo,'" 91, 101.
25 The report was written in 1947. Piskova, "Iz dokumentalnoto nasledstvo," 119–21.
26 In February 1943, a team of cameramen selected from Wehrmacht propaganda companies (*Propaganda Kompanien*) had been sent to Sofia to train Bulgarian operators for deployment in Bulgarian military units. The author thanks Alexander Zöller for sharing this information.
27 "Bakǎrdžiev, Vasil," in Janakiev, *Enciklopedija Bǎlgarsko kino*, 24.

author of the footage.[28] Yet his name does not appear among the operators of *Bălgarsko delo* in 1943. Could there be confusion with Vasil Holiolčev, a cameraman trained in France before the war who joined the foundation in 1942 and was much in demand in 1943?[29] The latter distinguished himself in filming the Allied bombing of Bulgaria in 1944 and acquired a certain renown by recording the epic of the 1944–45 "Liberation war." He was also a very active cinematographer between 1945 and 1957. For his part, Holiolčev attributed the shooting to Asen Čobanov, a colleague at the foundation to whom he reportedly gave advice on editing.[30]

What about the identity of those who commissioned the filming? Their names can be inferred, but not proven. In 1945, before the Seventh Chamber of the Bulgarian People's Court, the former head of the Administration Department of the Commissariat for Jewish Affairs, Jaroslav Kalicin, who was, together with Commissioner for Jewish Affairs Aleksandăr Belev and the German SS captain Theodor Dannecker, one of the pivotal organizers of the deportations, confirmed that he had demanded photographic capture of the May 1943 expulsion of Bulgarian Jews from specific provincial towns to other locations: "For these two actions [in Stara Zagora and Kazanlăk] I had given a deportation plan and instructions prepared by me. On my order, Jončev [a KEV official] had hired a photographer who shot the deportation from these two cities."[31] Before the Seventh Chamber of the People's Court, Pen̆co Lukov, another senior official in the Commissariat, similarly confirmed the taking of photographs in Skopje on March 29, 1945, during the departure of the last convoy from Vardar Macedonia, supervised by Dannecker and Belev.[32] If we are to believe the first commander of the Skopje camp, Pejo Draganov, these images were taken by a photographer from the Bulgarian police headquarters.[33]

Some additional cues are available: in the fall of 1944, Natan Grinberg was asked to seek incriminating evidence in the KEV archives and buttress thereby the preliminary investigation for anti-Jewish crimes. In his March 1945 deposition before the court, he too mentioned the existence of pictures shot in the Bulgarian transit camp of Dupnica, shortly before the

---

28   Interview with Angel Wagenstein, Sofia, December 12, 2016.

29   Piskova, "Iz dokumentalnoto nasledstvo," 96, 120–21, 203.

30   Testimony of Vasil Holiolčev at the Beckerle trial in Frankfurt, March 4, 1968, Hessisches Hauptstaatsarchiv [hereafter cited as HHStA], Abteilung (unit [Ab]) 631a, Band (volume [B]) 597, Blatt (sheet [Bl]) 223.

31   CDA, F 190K, op. 3, ae. 7, l. 15, quoted in Danova and Avramov, *Deportiraneto*, 566.

32   CDA, F 1449, op. 1, ae. 180, l. 34.

33   Ibid., l. 219.

transfer of Greek Jews to Lom: "One day before the Jews were sent to Lom, they were allegedly visited by Belev, etc., and a German, who ordered that a group of people presented separately, mainly with physical disabilities, be photographed; another group was allegedly expressly held back in order to be photographed as they left. The Commissariat also had similar photographs taken elsewhere, 400 according to the inventory, of which 330 were handed over to the Germans."[34]

However, during the trial before the Seventh Chamber of the People's Court in Sofia, there was no mention of motion pictures. In her biography of Dannecker, Claudia Steur reproduced four photographs showing the embarkation of deportees on trains and then on the steamer *Saturnus* at Lom. She indicated that these snapshots, found in the archives of the Beckerle trial in Frankfurt (1967–68), were taken at the request of Dannecker.[35] These are stills from the 1943 film footage. Underlining the role of Adolf Eichmann's envoy in the choice of transporting the Thracian Jews by boat rather than by train, she adds: "Dannecker had a film recording made of their shipment."[36] On March 28, 1943, Dannecker and Belev left Lom in a hurry to go to Skopje: "They wanted to supervise at least the departure of the last train again and have a film record made of it."[37]

On the basis of these data, we can hypothesize that the visual capture of the deportations was concerted between SS *Hauptsturmführer* Dannecker, no doubt anxious to prove his effectiveness to Adolf Eichmann, and Commissioner Belev. Such a decision was in line with the aspirations of other officials of the Commissariat, chiefly Kalicin. The inventory of the German Federal Archives in Berlin retains this option, which notes opposite "Sponsor": "Commissariat for Jewish Affairs."[38] A tenuous thread further attests to the relationship between "Bulgarian Action" and the KEV: on March 31, 1941, in accordance with the Law on Foundations, the registration of *Bălgarsko delo* took place in the presence of two witnesses; one of them was "Al. Belev," then a jurisconsult in the Ministry of the Interior.[39] There are no written records, however, that formally affirm the existence of a filming order addressed to the foundation by the Commissariat for Jewish Affairs.

---

34 Grinberg, *Dokumenti* (2015), 108.
35 Steur, *Theodor Dannecker*, 171–72.
36 Ibid., 105.
37 Ibid., 108.
38 Bundesarchiv-Filmarchiv, BSN 26 108, 14. 1943. The information was reportedly provided by Bulgarian archivists to their East German counterparts in 1983.
39 Piskova, "Iz dokumentalnoto nasledstvo," 91.

Scrutinizing Frames That Resist Analysis

Can we now look at these "frames that resist analysis"[40] while ignoring the corolla of words that were affixed to them, while also abandoning the illusion that today's researchers would be better able than their predecessors to make them speak? Gil Bartholeyns's warning against the reality effect of archives, this sensation of a past suddenly made tangible, comes to mind: "The notions of representation and of archival image have in common this presupposition of surface added to that of transparency. . . . Of a photographic or filmic nature, the archival image, considered as a document, brings to its height the presence of the referent and consequently the difficulty of stepping back to 'see' the image, to consider it as a visual object."[41] Should we then give up looking back at these silent images?

Two versions of the document have been consulted in the context of this research: the Berlin version and the Washington version. The film footage preserved in the Berlin archives is 14:50 minutes long and the Washington version is 6:32 minutes long.[42] The reels from the German archives, digitized, contain damaged frames whose luminosity extinguishes the viewer's gaze; they abound in repetitions; the pairing of shots filmed in distinct locations and the repetitions produce confusing effects.[43] However, the fact that the camera lingered on certain scenes makes it possible to note details that are elusive in the USHMM variant; tonal nuances are also introduced, particularly in the sequences shot in the internment camps. It is this version that will serve as the guideline for our analysis. The identification and localization of the images, the result of patient work rearranging the pieces of the puzzle and confronting them with topographical, archival, photographic, and testimonial sources, was carried out with Maël Le Noc as part of a research project completed in April 2020.[44]

The film opens with a twenty-second scene that follows a column of deportees crossing a street lined with turn-of-the-century buildings, two or

---

40   The expression is borrowed from Arasse, *On n'y voit rien*.

41   Gil Bartholeyns, "L'ordre des images," in Maeck and Steinle, *L'image d'archives*, 35.

42   In addition, there is a third film, *Die Deportation der Juden aus dem Weissmeergebiet*—with a title similar to the one in the German Federal Archives, although with different content—preserved in the holdings of the Bulgarian National Film Library but not included in its catalog, and lasting 10:14 minutes. We will return to this visual archive later.

43   The Bundesarchiv-Filmarchiv's digitized version, longer than the one mentioned in the inventory, consists of two reels—220 and 177 meters, respectively, for a total of 397 meters. We are dealing with several editing modules.

44   Ragaru and Le Noc, "Visual Clues," 376–403.

three stories high at most, and trees whose trunks have been stripped bare by winter. More than any other, this sequence has seen its attributed location travel among Northern Greece, Vardar Macedonia, and the "old" kingdom.

What elements do we possess to try to advance the investigation? If we gather the fragments scattered throughout the reel, three angles of view can be reconstructed: (1) upstream of the column, in a three-quarter position, at a man's height; (2) at a right angle to the flow of deportees marching in front of the lens—the camera went to the contact point, just a few meters away from the deportees; and (3) at the end of the procession, slightly over-hanging.[45] A brief shot, mixed with other scenes at the end of the film footage, immortalized the immobilized column waiting for the signal to leave. Could it be that the procedures for transporting the deportees were suspended in order to allow the scene to be captured on film?

In front of the camera, men, women, and young children pass by, wrapped up in makeshift clothing; the adults bend under bundles wrapped in blankets, a few suitcases, and the exceptional trunk. The youngest carry a profusion of bags and bundles. The outfits are dark, occasionally illuminated by white kerchiefs tied around the necks of women. The uninterrupted flow crosses the screen from right to left. This orientation and the slightly declining slope add—for eyes socialized to Christian imaginations of right/left, good/evil polarity—to the mute sadness with which the images are imbued. Some of the deportees turn their faces toward the camera; we read a hint of curiosity in the children's, veiled or worried looks in their parents'. This is followed by a close-up shot, as if the tripod had been placed at a distance of one meter, two meters at the most, from the deportees. The most common shot taken from these rushes was cut here, when a woman with her face wrapped in a white scarf approaches the camera with a bundle rolled up under her arm. At second 15, the camera closes on the procession. On the bent bodies, the luggage seems to take the place of huge heads. It is then that the eye catches sight of another broken line on the left, that of policemen in uniforms. A deportee turns around, caught by the camera, against the dozens of humans

---

45   A few additional street views were shot from above, presumably from the balcony of an apartment. In the digitized version in the Bundesarchiv-Filmarchiv, they are at minute 01:05:20 and show a slightly wider and more affluent section of street than the previous one. The inventory of the USHMM recently located this as a shot taken in Dupnica (https://collections.ushmm.org/search/catalog/irn1002157, min. 01:01:36); this hypothesis could not be confirmed by the author. The most one can note is that, in the film prepared in 1967 for the Beckerle trial, this same frame is commented on in voice-over as follows: "The town of Gorna Džumaja, today Blagoevgrad. Here the group [of deportees] was housed in a staging camp, where they remained until March 18."

stretched out in front. In 20 seconds, about 150 people have entered and exited the frame.

Is it possible to identify the location? The camera's side angle allows us to discern stalls with wood and glass fronts—on one we see the inscription *Sklad* in Cyrillic ("shed" in Bulgarian)—as well as piles of small cobblestones on the edge of the central bay. Some buildings have balconies with richly worked ironwork and distinctive moldings, which have survived to the present day. The professional Google Earth software used by Maël Le Noc confirmed that these buildings were located in Gorna Džumaja (now Blagoevgrad).[46] The Jewish deportees from Greece were filmed as they passed 19 and 21 Stambolijski Street, a north–south thoroughfare, parallel to the Bistrica River. Ironically, this street is located in the once multiethnic neighborhood of Varoša, where the small Jewish minority of this town of ten thousand inhabitants resided during the war. At the time of filming, the column was located a few meters from the municipal high school where one of the temporary detention camps was set up.[47] The column advanced north and was about to turn left, toward the camp. The arrangement of the shadows, stretching lengthwise to the right, tends to confirm the hypothesis of filming in the late afternoon, at the arrival of the deportees of the first convoy from Serres and Drama on March 6, or of the second convoy transported from Drama on March 7.[48]

Now comes the second sequence. Women and men, shackled with luggage, pull themselves into a truck. A stroller looks tiny next to the vehicle; braided with wicker, it seems to be waiting to get on board too. The presence of the camera is noted by everyone: a few women cast more or less furtive glances at it while helping passengers into the vehicle; in the middle of the screen, a man stares at the lens, a white bundle pressed against him, waiting for his turn; on the right of the shot, two young policemen look at the operator, wrapped up in their thick uniforms, hands in their pockets. One of them smiles, half-curious, half-intimidated. Then the truck pulls away, revealing a row of police officers and abandoned carts on the side of a narrow alley. It bears a license plate from the Sofia region (SF 319).[49] At the time, the towns of Dupnica and Gorna Džumaja were both attached

---

46 Ragaru and Le Noc, "Visual Clues."

47 The college has since given way to an interscholastic polytechnic vocational training center (*Mežduučilišten centăr za trudovo politehničesko obučenie*), in front of which a plaque in remembrance of deported Jews was affixed in 2008.

48 On this dating work, see Ragaru and Le Noc, "Visual Clues."

49 In a number of cases, trucks were used to ensure transfers of the sick and the elderly between temporary detention camps and railway stations in Northern Greece as well as in Bulgaria. The most singular case is that of the Jewish community of Kavála, which was transported in its entirety to Drama, some forty

to this district. For a moment, the camera changes its perspective, letting a little girl of no more than ten years enter the field, with a heavy white bundle tucked under her chin.[50] Behind her, one may discern a staircase down which deportees descend. The building has a regular architecture with rounded windows in the upper part and a slight overhang under the doorframe. It bears a high degree of resemblance to the Kartela tobacco shed at 64 Boris Street in Dupnica, where some of the Belomorie Jews were interned. Could this sequence have been shot in the Bulgarian city? Let's continue the investigation.

We are now in a train station. From the uncovered truck, about thirty passengers disembark. The wood of the uprights almost merges with that of the freight cars, accentuating the sense of intimate connection between the two stages of transport. There are no urban buildings in these bare images; the space is desolate, out of place, anonymous. The framing—an overall shot—adds to the silence of the images the muteness of its distance. There is no exercise in dramatization here, no scripting whose intentions could be easily reproduced. Nothing that could be used to celebrate the efficiency of the Bulgarians with their German allies; nothing that would establish a contemptuous distance, let alone a relationship of racial hierarchy, between the viewer and the Jews whose otherness would have been magnified. When the operator sketched a rapprochement, it is to capture the coming and going of Bulgarian sentries, the presence of civilians as well—men, always men. Stealthily, among them, the silhouette of someone who resembles Belev appears on screen (01:05:09:00). But was the commissioner for Jewish Affairs present on March 19 when the convoy of 1,422 deportees was sent from Dupnica? The examination of the 1945 trial archives offers contradictory clues. Grinberg, it will be remembered, mentioned a visit by Belev to Dupnica on the day before—not the day of—the deportations.[51] Lukov, the director of the Economic Department of the Commissariat, stated that Belev, Dannecker, and he had personally supervised the transports from Gorna Džumaja, Skopje, and Lom, but not from Dupnica.[52] Prosecutor Rahamimov, however, retained the hypothesis that the trio was present at

kilometers away, by fourteen military vehicles and a private truck on March 7 and 8, 1943. CDA, F 190K, op. 3, ae. 103, l. 2–12.

50 In the Bundesarchiv-Filmarchiv version of the film, this sequence appears at 01:03:11:00, dissociated from the first fragment of the scene (from 01:00:22:00 to 01:00:41:00).

51 Grinberg, *Dokumenti* (2015), 108.

52 CDA, F 190K, op. 3, ae. 33, l. 3v–10, quoted in Danova and Avramov, *Deportiraneto*, 583–85.

the departure of a transport organized, according to him, not on March 19, but on March 20.[53]

The wagons leave. The acronym "BDŽ" of the Bulgarian National Railways (*Bălgarska dăržavna železnica*) stands out clearly, as does the number 19 of a compartment. The camera films the convoy's bearing off in a curve that reveals the length of the transport. A squat building and square tower similar to those of the Dupnica train station emerge from the fog in the background. The lens lets a bridge appear, then recede; it lingers on a sentry in a deserted station whose layout, composition, and architecture evoke those of Dupnica. The cars are closed. In 1945, Kalicin, the man in charge of the deportations from Belomorie, stated before the judges: "I am not aware that the order to seal the cars [at Drama] was given, and most of the cars on the train that left in my presence were open. I assume that the order to seal the cars from the outside was given when the Jews entered the transit camps of Gorna Džumaja and Dupnica, and when they were transferred to Lom. The fact is that the trains that left these cities were sealed from the outside, as I was able to see later at the Sofia station."[54] This could confirm the hypothesis of filming on the outskirts of Dupnica.

The last railroad capture was made at the moment of the descent of a group of deportees: men first, luggage in front of them, then women and children. The presence in the footage of Lom's delegate for Jewish Affairs, Slavi Păntev (Belev's cousin), indicates that we are in the Danube city (02:01:26:18). Of the transports, the film has captured only one gesture of violence, the abrupt hand movement of a Bulgarian policeman disciplining a deportee. Was the brutality of the raids deliberately suppressed? Before it is possible to sketch out an answer, the viewer is confronted with a staggering shot: in a carefully composed image—probably filmed at another time—nine bright faces of youth and vitality, carefully framed in the opening of a wagon, present themselves to the spectator (02:05:24:15). There is little doubt that the scene has been staged: the well-fed young people have been asked to stare into the camera; the faces are smiling and confident. Suddenly, a young woman appears at the back of the group; her presence is so fleeting that she is barely noticeable; her face is radiant with *blondeur* and life.

On the banks of the Danube, the camera's eye becomes technical: a panning shot of a ship, the *Saturnus*; medium shots at the entrance and from the ship, close-ups of the personnel checking the deportees' identity documents. We notice Păntev, surrounded by Bulgarian policemen, German policemen,

---

53 CDA, F 1449, op. 1, ae. 185, l. 161.
54 Danova and Avramov, *Deportiraneto*, 633.

possibly from the *Wasserschutzpolizei*, and the captain of the ship.[55] The operator paid close attention to the actors of the macabre transfer and to their gestures (installation of a ramp, deposit of luggage, cover against bad weather, etc.). A high-ranking officer exits the screen from below. In 1945, Kalicin reported the following facts:

> The Jews rounded up in the Belomorie area, together with those from Pirot, arrived at the Lom station by two trains: the first on March 19 at 12:00 noon, and the second on March 20 at 10:30 a.m. The shipment of these Jews outside the borders of the Kingdom began immediately on four passenger steamers: (1) on March 20, at 2:00 p.m., 1,100 persons were shipped aboard the *Kara Georgi*; (2) on March 20, at 8:30 p.m., 877 persons left aboard the *Vojvoda Mišić*; (3) on March 21, at 8:00 p.m., 1,256 persons were shipped aboard the *Saturnus*; and (4) on March 21, at 8:00 p.m., 986 persons aboard the *Tsar Dušan*. In all, from the port of Lom 4,219 people of Jewish origin left the borders of the Kingdom.[56]

For the end—and at the cost of a reordering of the sequences—we have kept the most mysterious scenes of the footage, those that observe at length Jews gathered on the outskirts of transit camps. These images were filmed in at least two distinct locations. The first is a vast square surrounded by ramshackle little houses that can be reached by tiny sloping paths. The filming of open-air shots is so inconsistent with the testimonies of suffocating incarceration offered by the few survivors of the Bulgarian temporary internment camps that it creates an effect of cognitive dissonance.[57] The second location is also an exterior: in front of an internment center filmed in a wide-angle shot on a sunny day, a narrow river flows with dozens of Jewish internees just a few steps away.

---

55   A witness at the 1967–68 Beckerle trial in the FRG, Ernst Knapp, a former crew member of the steamer *Saturnus*, and Austrian by citizenship, recognized himself in the section of the film shot in Lom. HHSta, Ab 631a, B 597, Bl 220.

56   Grinberg, *Dokumenti* (2015), 116.

57   Most of these testimonies were given by doctors or pharmacists deployed in the "new" territories or responsible for ensuring rudimentary medical follow-up in Bulgaria's temporary detention camps. Of the testimonies of just the Bulgarian trials of 1945, see, on the Gorna Džumaja camp, those of physicians Iosif Konfino (CDA, F 1449, op. 1, ae. 181, l. 247–52) and Nisim Kjoso (CDA, F 1449, op. 1, ae. 182, l. 52–58); on Dupnica, those of physicians Persiado Rahamimov (CDA, F 1449, op. 1, ae. 193, l. 234–36) and Nisim Davidov (CDA, F 1449, op. 1, ae. 182, l. 133–37); and on the camp at Skopje, that of Berta Noah, a young woman whose marriage to a Spanish Jewish citizen saved her from deportation to Poland, and her husband, Miko Noah (CDA, F 1449, op. 1, ae. 190, l. 207–10).

The US and German inventories mentioned filming in the Bulgarian camps of Gorna Džumaja and Dupnica; the *Beit Lohamei HaGetaot* (House of ghetto fighters in Israel) noted filming in Kavála.[58] Is it possible to progress toward identification? Let us summarize the data at our disposal. First scene: in the background of the vast square, a mountain landscape dotted with houses stands out. Some internees are waiting, talking in small groups; others are busy with their luggage. From the heights of the staggered buildings, one can see the crisscrossing lines of drying cloths. It takes a few moments to realize that they are lying on barbed wire near a sentry whose bayonet draws a line parallel to that of a post.

Once again, one can only salute the resilience of the stone, of this building in the background with its characteristic tiny window and its architectural elements that the filmed faces could not entirely conceal: we are in the courtyard of the Gorna Džumaja secondary school. The second scene was recorded a few hundred meters away, in front of the Rajnov tobacco shed, which is betrayed by the structure of the relief and the landscape, as well as the white Hunting House (*Loven dom*) nestled on the green heights.[59]

In both internment camps, the tone of the filming is surprising. When it wanders through the schoolyard, the camera does not seem to be intrusive; it moves from one group to another. The camera lingers on the smiles of a group of young people and a woman with long curly hair whose joviality haloed the shots with a veil of unreality. Jewish stars have been sewn or pinned on their coats; one star is swinging at the end of a thin cord. Two young people are engaged in a discussion with an elderly man with a long white beard and a round hat; from time to time, he glances at the camera as if seeking its approval; behind them, the persistent smile of a teenager with short hair has crept in. The lens is close to the faces; the operator has abandoned the documentary style of the other shots of the camp. This is the second time that radiant images are offered. The same surprise recurs in front of the Rajnov tobacco shed when curiosity and life radiate from the footage: about twenty young people rush toward the camera; some greet the lens with their hands or caps.

How can we understand the coexistence of such dissimilar filming methods and atmospheres? In March 1968, before the Hessian regional court that was judging Adolf-Heinz Beckerle, the operator Vasil Holiolčev, who came to present the film as a witness for the prosecution, was questioned about these breaks in tone. From his deposition, the court notes preserved the following statement: "In the whole material, one can recognize three different moods,

---

58 See the descriptive notes of the photographs W/S #08 831 CD #0068, W/S #08 832 CD #0068, and W/S #08 834 CD #0068, USHMM.
59 Ragaru and Le Noc, "Visual Clues."

between frightened at the time of arrest, to laughing in the camp. Asked Chobanov (phon.) [Asen Čobanov] about this difference. C. answered me that the Jews had been told that they would remain within the boundaries of Bulgaria (in *Inneren Bulgariens*). After passing Sofia, the mood had deteriorated."[60]

The hypothesis is plausible; however, it omits the question of the staging of the images. Elsewhere in Nazi Europe, deportation operations were photographed (for example, in Würzburg, Bielefeld, Hanau, and Nuremberg)[61] and filmed (in Bruchsal, Dresden, Hildesheim, Prague, and Westerbork, among others)[62] by Nazi professionals and amateurs, and sometimes by unidentified photographers as well.[63] If perpetrators rarely hesitated to record scenes of violence, most of them also took care to give a bureaucratic rigor to their staging of the deportations.[64] Did the Bulgarian choices fit into this framework?

To whom were these images shown? Some contextual evidence suggests that the plans were not intended to be made public. In the fall of 1942, Interior Minister Petăr Gabrovski and Prime Minister Bogdan Filov had declined a German proposal for an anti-Jewish exhibition in Sofia, seeing it less as an instrument for reinforcing anti-Semitic sentiments among the population than as a possible hindrance to the implementation of state policies.[65] When it came to carrying out the deportations, the Bulgarian authorities favored discretion: unlike Nazi Germany, Bulgaria did not produce any fiction, documentaries, or newsreels with strong anti-Semitic content.

The preservation of the footage also remains mysterious. Standing before the judges, operator Holiolčev suggested that it had been found in the possession of Adolf-Heinz Beckerle at the time of his arrest in Svilengrad on September 18, 1944, and that the film was with the Jewish community of Bulgaria, which would have kept it until its rediscovery.[66] It is time to sketch out the story of this strange migration, which coincided with a reclassification of the images as trial exhibits.

---

60   HHStA, Ab 631a, B 597, Bl 226.

61   Milton, "Images of the Holocaust—Part I"; Levin and Uziel, "Ordinary Men, Extraordinary Photos," 265–93.

62   Ebbrecht-Hartmann, "Filmdokumente von Deportationen."

63   Ebbrecht-Hartmann, "Trophy, Evidence, Document," 509–28; Cole, *Traces of the Holocaust*, 85–118.

64   This point is highlighted in Milton, "Images of the Holocaust—Part I," 27.

65   On this proposition see Chary, *Bulgarian Jews*, 78. On the inauguration of an anti-communist exhibition as a substitute, see Filov, *Dnevnik*, 531–32.

66   HHStA, Ab 631a, B 597, Bl 226.

From Visual Document to Legal Evidence:
The Beckerle Case

As our investigation approaches the 1960s, it becomes hostage to the politi-cization of both the Cold War and the present day: one must come to terms with memories that fail and clues that are erased as the investigation pro-gresses. Around an investigation of a former Nazi diplomat posted in Sofia during the war, tenuous convergences between communist Bulgaria and capitalist West Germany are woven. In the FRG, in the late 1950s, a handful of jurists wished to prompt collective reflection on the workings of the Nazi system beyond the SS and the Wehrmacht. In Bulgaria, the publication of the memoirs of anti-communist exiles raised fears of a rehabilitation of King Boris III and the former monarchy. Any initiative that was seen as challeng-ing the image of a benevolent czar was welcomed. At the crossroads between these two sets of priorities, the 1943 footage was exhumed, placed on the editing table, juxtaposed with other frames, and sounded in German.

In 1956, Fritz Bauer, a forty-three-year-old lawyer, was appointed general attorney of the *Land* (federal state) of Hesse in Frankfurt (see figure 3.1). A survivor of the Holocaust who had found refuge in Denmark and Sweden during the war,[67] this Social Democrat close to Willy Brandt aimed to revive the prosecution of Nazi criminals at a time when the number of investi-gations was decreasing, and Chancellor Adenauer was pursuing a policy of reintegrating former high-ranking Nazi officials into the state apparatus.[68] In October 1958, the ministers of justice of the *Länder* decided to create a judi-cial investigative unit in Ludwigsburg, the Central Office of the State Justice Administrations for the Investigation of National Socialist Crimes (*Zentrale Stelle der Landesjustizverwaltungen zur Aufklärung nationalsozialistischer Verbrechen*, known widely simply as Zentrale Stelle), or Central Office, charged with carrying out preliminary investigations with a view to criminal indictments. The role the Central Office played in launching a new wave of criminal cases in the Federal Republic of Germany is well known.[69] Its foun-dation nevertheless rested on equivocal considerations, since the aim was to initiate proceedings before closing—or in order to close?—the books on the judicial phase, as the statute of limitations for the wartime crimes, initially set for May 8, 1965, approached.[70]

---

67 Wojak, *Fritz Bauer*; Meusch, *Von der Diktatur zur Demokratie*; Frei, "Fritz Bauer oder," 273–80.
68 Frei, *Adenauer's Germany*.
69 Weinke, *Eine Gesellschaft ermittelt gegen sich selbst*; Fleiter, "Die Ludwigsburger Zentrale Stelle," 253–72.
70 Wittmann, "Tainted Law," 211–29.

Figure 3.1. Attorney General Fritz Bauer on the television broadcast "Heute Abend Kellerclub," Sendereihe des Hessisches Rundfunks, December 8, 1964. *Source:* https://www.youtube.com/watch?v=72XO8-zrJe8, screen capture.

Convinced that he had to deal with—that is to say, against—the legal elites active under the Third Reich, Bauer was a proponent of a didactic vision of justice. The Auschwitz trial (1963–65), of which he was one of the main architects, is emblematic of his approach: in 183 days of proceedings, 360 witnesses from nineteen countries and several historians testified before the court, giving unprecedented resonance to the Nazi past in West Germany.[71] The examination of the role of the diplomatic corps under Nazism constituted another of his priority projects, the law on the civil service of 1951 having allowed many diplomats compromised under Nazism to be reintegrated into the Ministry of Foreign Affairs (*Auswärtiges Amt,* AA).[72] In 1956, the Frankfurt state prosecutor's office requested the personal files of several former diplomats from the ministry, including Adolf-Heinz Beckerle, minister plenipotentiary in Bulgaria, and Fritz Gebhardt von Hahn, who had worked as a deputy to Franz Rademacher, the head of

---

71   For a reconsideration of the trial, see Pendas, *Frankfurt Auschwitz Trial*; and Wittmann, *Beyond Justice*.

72   Döscher, *Seilschaften*. On the role of Reich diplomats in the Final Solution, see Browning, *Final Solution*; and one of the fullest recent accountings, Conze et al., *Das Amt und die Vergangenheit.*

D III, the section of the Department of German Internal Affairs (*Abteilung Deutschland*) of the AA in charge of Jewish Affairs.[73] Two years later, the return of a large body of trophy archives by the Allies—notably the surviving records of the Political Archives of the Foreign Ministry—provided investigators with a wealth of material. In September 1959, a preliminary investigation was opened against Beckerle, shortly before he was remanded to custody: the former minister plenipotentiary was charged as an accessory to the deportations of Jews from the Bulgarian-controlled territories. In 1963, a second investigation targeted Hahn, who was accused of complicity in the roundups carried out in these same territories as well as in Salonika, then in the German occupation zone. On December 23, 1965, a joint indictment was issued against the two defendants.[74]

Beckerle's trajectory has been thoroughly documented. Born in Frankfurt, the son of a postman, he owed his rise to an early Nazi commitment (see figure 3.2). At the age of twenty, he became a member of the National Socialist German Workers' Party (*Nationalsozialistische Deutsche Arbeiterpartei*, NSDAP, or Nazi Party), which he cautiously left after the abortive coup attempt in Munich in 1923. After some unfinished studies in economics and a brief expatriation to Latin America, he joined the party's *Sturmabteilung* (SA) in 1928 and became its director for Hesse state in 1931.[75] He was briefly elected to the Prussian Landstag in 1932, then to the Reichstag, and after Hitler's ascension to power, he was given the leadership of the Frankfurt police and managed to escape the purge of the SA in June 1934. The invasion of Poland in September 1939 propelled him to the head of the police in Łódź; a few months later, he was sent to the eastern front. It was on the strength of this experience that Beckerle was invited—though his social profile did not predispose him to such a career—to join the diplomatic corps. Appointed head of the German legation in Sofia in June 1941, he came from the cohort of "SA diplomats" deployed in the Reich's allied states (Hungary, Romania, and Bulgaria), where the Führer had deplored the ineffectiveness of German diplomatic action. They played an essential role in the implementation of the Final Solution.[76]

---

73   On Rademacher see Billig, "Le procès de Franz Rademacher," 27–36.

74   HHStA, Ab 631a, B 589.

75   HHStA, Ab 631a, B 597, Bl 2–4, for the restitution of Beckerle's personal and professional trajectory before the court, November 8, 1967.

76   The point was made by Christopher Browning: "Germany's client allies in southeastern Europe—Hungary, Romania and Bulgaria—likewise had embassies headed by SA-men. . . . Of these only Romania as yet had a complete adviser system, including the Jewish specialist Gustav Richter. Unlike the satellite states, these countries were not created by Germany, though the extent of their boundaries depended upon German generosity. Their slightly greater

Figure 3.2. Adolf-Heinz Beckerle, minister plenipotentiary of the Reich in Sofia (June 17, 1941–September 1944). *Source:* CDA, F 3K, op. 12, ae 1850, l. 2. Courtesy of the Bulgarian Central State Archives.

The indictment by the Hessian prosecutor's office was not Adolf-Heinz Beckerle's first encounter with the law. In September 1944, the diplomat had been intercepted by the Soviets while trying to reach Turkey with several other members of the German legation. He was tried by a Soviet military tribunal in 1951 and sentenced to twenty-five years in prison for his role in the repression of partisans on the eastern front. On March 22, 1950, as part of the policy of denazification, the court of the *Land* of Hesse (*Spruchkammer* Frankfurt-am-Main) classified him in absentia as a rank one

---

degree of independence from Germany made it more difficult to impose Nazi policies, including *Judenpolitik*, but at the same time this ensured a greater role for the Foreign Office." See Browning, *Final Solution*, 89.

criminal (*Hauptbelasteter*).[77] Five years later, Beckerle was released under the German-Soviet amnesty agreement of 1955. He was repatriated to West Germany, where he could have resumed his serene existence as an executive of the A. van Kaick Generatoren- und Motoren-Werke in Frankfurt, had it not been for the warm welcome he received from the mayor of Frankfurt on his return.

In July 1956, the Association of Victims of Nazism (*Vereinigung der Verfolgten des Naziregimes*, VVN)[78] filed a complaint for murder, manslaughter, grievous bodily harm resulting in death, arson, and crimes against humanity against Beckerle, acts he had allegedly committed while head of the Frankfurt police. The request of the VVN was rejected in April 1957.[79]

Learning from these experiences, Attorney General Bauer decided to approach the case from another angle, that of anti-Jewish persecutions in the Balkans.[80] Such countries as Bulgaria, Romania, and Hungary were allies of the Reich, not occupied states. Henceforth, exchanges regarding the implementation of the Final Solution transited through official diplomatic channels. The former SA officer turned minister plenipotentiary thus negotiated the deportations with the Bulgarian Foreign Ministry, the minister of the interior, Petăr Gabrovski, as well as the prime minister, Bogdan Filov. However, the Hessian state prosecutor's office, which was busy preparing for the Auschwitz trial and assisting the Israeli authorities in the Eichmann case, was severely understaffed. The transfer of the Beckerle case to the Zentrale Stelle, the director of which, Erwin Schüle, had been discussing it for some time, came to a standstill when the Hessian Ministry of Justice refused to finance the secondment of a staff member of the prosecutor's office to Ludwigsburg. The case began under uncertain omens, especially as evidence was scarce. It was the discovery of the diary of the former diplomat in the political archives of the West German Foreign Office at the end of 1964 that revived the investigation.[81]

At the time of the Auschwitz trial, Bauer had established relations with the Soviet General Prosecutor's Office, which he hoped to be able to put to good use: his early involvement in the antifascist struggle had enabled him to obtain documents from the Soviet War Crimes Investigation and Trial

---

77 HHStA, Ab 631a, B 571.

78 Reuter and Hansel, *Das kurze Leben der VVN von 1947 bis 1953*.

79 Wojak, *Fritz Bauer*, 384–86.

80 On the preliminary investigation, the trial, and Beckerle's defense, see Weinke, *Verfolgung*, 259–72.

81 HHStA, Ab 631a, B 618, Bl 86. On this discovery, see the letter by Prosecutor Richter to *Landgerichtsrat* Vollhardt, December 15, 1964: HHSta, Ab. 631a, B 570, Bl 2754.

Commission.[82] In the Beckerle case, however, the support of the USSR was slow in coming. In December 1965, the Soviets finally handed over a copy of the verdict from the 1951 trial to the German prosecutor's office. The case began to take shape. It remained to convince the Bulgarians to follow the path taken by the Soviets.

Judicial Cooperation between West Germany, the United States, Israel, and Bulgaria: A Tale of the Cold War

The Bulgarian trail followed two parallel paths—in Bulgaria and in Israel. Soliciting cooperation from Jerusalem was an intuitive choice. In 1959, Prosecutor Bauer was in contact with the Israeli authorities in connection with the Eichmann case; moreover, the scale of the Bulgarian aliyah in 1948–49 suggested that material evidence and testimonies of interest to the investigation could be found in the young State of Israel. The attention of the German investigators was first drawn to a Bulgarian immigrant, Benjamin Arditi, a former leader of the Revisionist Zionist movement in Sofia, who had been identified by the Institute of Jewish Studies of the Hebrew University in Jerusalem, and by Mordechai Shenshavi and David Remez, the initiators of the "Yad Vashem in Memory of the Jews of Europe Who Have Fallen" project, as a potential interlocutor as early as May 1947.[83] When he left Bulgaria, Arditi took with him a vast body of private and public archives. An amateur historian, he never ceased to offer a personal reading of World War II: in 1952, he published his first work, a situated piece of writing that credited King Boris with the nondeportation of Bulgarian Jews.[84] From this date on, Arditi became one of the privileged targets of Communist authors in charge of disseminating the Bulgarian-authorized interpretation of the past.

At the time when the Frankfurt state prosecutor's office began its investigations, the man who had in the meantime become a deputy of the conservative Herut Party in the Knesset was working on a second book, the manuscript of which had been sent to Yad Vashem in March 1959.[85] During

---

82 Söhner, "Der heiligen Rache darf nicht ein Auschwitz-Henker entgehen!," 157–72; Jasmin Söhner, "NS-Verbrechen ermitteln: Die Justizkooperation zwischen der Zentralen Stelle der Landesjustizverwaltungen zur Aufklärung nationalsozialistischer Verbrechen und der Sowjetunion (1955–1973)" (Philosophischen Fakultät der Ruprecht-Karls-Universität Heidelberg, 2023).
83 Yad Vashem, P. 37/17, Archive of Benjamin Arditti: Documentation Regarding the History of Bulgarian Jewry, 1850–1965, 1.
84 Arditi, *Roljata na Car Boris III pri izselvaneto na evreite ot Bălgarija*.
85 Yad Vashem, P. 37/17, 4–5.

the summer, on the recommendation of historian Josef Kermisz, the director of the memorial's archives, public prosecutor Wilhelm Wentzke (a key player in the first phase of the investigation) contacted Arditi with the aim of specifying "to which concentration or extermination camp the deportees were sent, and which Germans were involved in the arrests and deportations as perpetrators or accomplices."[86] Shortly afterward, the investigator addressed a similar request to the Bulgarian Olei Organization (*Hitachduth Olei Bulgaria*).[87] A ternary relationship between Yad Vashem, the German investigators, and the Bulgarian immigrant was then established.[88]

The reading of their letter exchanges allows one to follow the progress of the investigation through the increasing precision of the questions addressed. In the first phase, the Hesse state prosecutor's office took the initiative in the contacts; it was then briefly taken over by the Ludwigsburg office. At the end of March 1960, Prosecutor Wentzke had two main concerns: to determine whether, as Michael Molho had suggested,[89] some of the deportees from Greek Thrace had drowned in the Danube, and to locate the list of Greek Jewish deportees by name.[90] In the account of events given by Arditi in 1952, the German magistrate saw proof that in March 1943 no one in Bulgaria could have been unaware of the fate of the Jews sent to the eastern provinces of the Reich, especially not a member of the German diplomatic corps. The Israeli deputy was invited to make a statement in Frankfurt, and his help was sought in finding witnesses. The request was reiterated on August 30, 1960, by the investigating judge Heinz Düx, who had taken over the investigation.[91] On November 23, it was the turn of the journalist and former German resistance fighter Rudolf Küstermeier to ask Arditi to share his knowledge with the Hessian regional court. On December 28, the request became more pointed: General Attorney Bauer wished to speak with Arditi.[92] However, the Israeli parliamentarian did not appear as a witness for the prosecution at the trial.

In 1967–68, other Bulgarian Jews established in Israel took the stand. It may come as a surprise to find among them Natan Grinberg, the Communist

---

86 Ibid., 6–7.

87 Ibid., 8–9.

88 Ibid., 10. A copy of the indictment was informally provided by Prosecutor Wentzke to Joseph Karmisz in late 1959. On March 6, 1960, the latter provided the German investigators with a list of copies of the British archives available at Yad Vashem. Ibid., 12, 18.

89 Molho, *In Memoriam.*

90 Yad Vashem, P. 37/17, 14–15.

91 Arditi, *Yehudei Bulgariya bishnot hamishtar hanatzi.* This volume places greater emphasis on German responsibility for the deportations.

92 Yad Vashem, P. 37/203, 5.

activist born in 1903 in Sofia, a member of the party since 1925, who had played a pivotal role in the investigation phase of the trial for anti-Jewish crimes before the Seventh Chamber of the People's Court in the autumn of 1944, when he was assigned to explore the archives of the Commissariat for Jewish Affairs in Sofia. Although faithful to his Communist creed, Grinberg emigrated to Israel in 1953; there he resumed a career in import-export that had begun in Bulgaria after his return from political exile in France in 1935. In this professional capacity, he made several trips to Eastern Europe and to France, where his son, Jacques Grinberg, who became a famous neo-Expressionist painter, had settled.[93] In 1961, Grinberg, scribe of a history in which he was one of the actors, published a work seeking to shed light on the deportation from the occupied territories—and the nondeportation of Bulgarian Jews. Based on an extensive examination of German archives that were inaccessible in 1945, the volume offers a more nuanced view on the events than his earlier work: a new stress is brought to the pressures of the Third Reich on the Bulgarian state.[94]

In order to shed light on the decision of the West German prosecutors to solicit the testimony of Grinberg, one needs to bring into the story another key mediator in the conduct of the investigation, the Institute for Jewish Affairs (IJA) of the World Jewish Congress in New York, and more particularly its director, Nehemiah Robinson. Between the summer of 1959 and his death four and a half years later, Jacob Robinson's brother[95] constantly placed his contacts in the Western and Eastern European Jewish communities at the service of West German investigators—among others, the Union of Bulgarian, Yugoslav, and Greek *olim* in Israel; the chief rabbi of Bulgaria, Ašer Hananel (October 1959, March 1960); the Central Consistory of Bulgarian Jews (February 1960); and Bruno Fischer of the United Restitution Organization in the FRG.[96] In May 1960, the Consistory had given a disappointing response to Robinson's request for information,

---

93 The author thanks Ilya Grinberg, Natan Grinberg's grandson, for providing private archives of the Grinberg family. See also CDA, F 1B, op. 6, ae. 197, l. 6–8.

94 Grinberg, *Hitlerskijat natisk za uništožavaneto na evreite ot Bălgarija*. Some observers have seen this development as a reflection of intra-Jewish political disputes in Israel and of pressure exerted by the Bulgarian Communist Party on the author. See the Greek ed. of *Dokumenti*: Grínperg, *Dokouménta*, 16–35.

95 Jacob Robinson campaigned for Jewish voices to be heard at the Nuremberg trials: Cohen, "Doctor Jacob Robinson," 81–100.

96 MSS col. no. 361, C187/10, Bulgaria, correspondence, Deportation of Jews, 1960–68, World Jewish Congress (New York Office), Records at the American Jewish Archives, Cincinnati.

providing him with only two documents from the Nuremberg trial and the archive collection edited by Grinberg in 1945.

At the turn of the 1960s, the cooperation of Bulgarian authorities with Western judicial authorities could hardly be taken for granted. Following the lead of the Soviet Union, Bulgaria launched a media campaign calling for the nonapplicability of the statute of limitations to Nazi crimes.[97] The Auschwitz trial was the subject of extensive coverage,[98] in which the concern that the architects of Western justice wanted to conceal fragments of the past was forcefully expressed.[99] Media reports on the hearings were accompanied by the publication of papers denouncing the links between capitalist postwar West Germany and fascism, the controversial role of Hans Globke, the undersecretary of state and chief of staff of the German Chancellery (October 28, 1953–October 15, 1963),[100] and the multiple renunciations of justice in Europe.[101] As a counterpoint, some articles reminded readers that the Bulgarian People's Court had prosecuted authors of anti-Jewish crimes as early as 1945.[102]

The shift in the Bulgarian position occurred in 1966. On June 22, the Sofia prosecutor's office contacted its Hessian counterpart. Prosecutor Krăstev had reportedly been informed of the legal action against Beckerle and Hahn at a conference of the International Association of Democratic Lawyers (AIJD) in East Berlin. Welcoming "the noble procedure aimed at a severe judgment of Nazi crimes," he indicated that the Bulgarian procuracy would be willing to "point out new evidence" to the German jurists—granted they received a copy of the indictment.[103] Prosecutor Richter, who had taken over the Beckerle-Hahn case, seized the opportunity: the German

---

97   "Svetovnata obštestvenost e protiv sroka za davnost," *Evrejski Vesti*, November 9, 1964, 1. For an Eastern European comparative perspective, see Grosescu, "State Socialist Endeavours," 239–69.

98   *Evrejski Vesti*, April 17, 1964, 2; April 25, 1964, 2; May 11, 1964, 1.

99   "Strah ot istinata," *Evrejski Vesti*, October 26, 1964, 1–2.

100 Globke, a German lawyer and senior civil servant in the new Federal Republic, had been an early supporter of Nazi ideology and provided legal commentary that helped fashion the 1935 Nuremberg Laws against Jews. After the war, he had a brilliant career as chief of staff and then director of the Federal Chancellery, despite Bauer's efforts to bring him to justice. In 1963, he was tried in absentia in the GDR. Bevers, *Der Mann hinter Adenauer*.

101 "Ubiecăt na Ani Frank njama da băde săden," *Evrejski Vesti*, August 17, 1964, 2.

102 "Văzmezdieto," *Evrejski Vesti*, August 31, 1964, 2.

103 The Bulgarian prosecutor erroneously mentions the sending of "11,343 Jews to be exterminated" and "the preparation of 20,000 others from Bulgaria for the Treblinka concentration camps." HHStA, Ab 631a, B 612, Bl 12.

investigators needed a certified copy of the Dannecker-Belev agreement of February 22, 1943, concerning the deportation of 20,000 Jews from the "new territories," as well as witnesses who could attest to the authenticity of the document, and the originals of three reports mentioned in the indictment.[104] Above all, they sought to identify possible survivors among the 11,343 Jews deported to Poland.[105] The German side later added other exhibits to its desiderata, including a report by the commissioner for Jewish Affairs and statements by defendants before the Seventh Chamber of the People's Court in 1945.[106]

How can this reversal be explained? Did the cooperation of the Soviets with Attorney General Bauer encourage the Bulgarian to follow suit? Should their decision be attributed to the lobbying work carried out by several members of the Bulgarian Jewish community with the public authorities? Or was it due to the warming of Bulgarian–West German relations at a time when Bulgaria, closely linked by trade to the FRG, was considering the establishment of diplomatic ties?[107] Several hypotheses may be advanced, and one fact ascertained. Let us start with the hypotheses: first, by establishing Germany as the center of gravity of anti-Jewish persecution, the Beckerle trial was likely to strengthen the Bulgarian reading of wartime events. Far from aiming to highlight the diligent assistance of the Bulgarian state to German extermination projects, the investigation sought to confirm the accusations made against the German defendants. Second, the courtroom offered Bulgaria an international platform from which it could hope to give greater visibility to the thesis of King Boris's guilt in the Holocaust. Finally, the so-called Zionist Jews in Israel would likely lose their claim to a monopoly on Jewish writing of the history of the war. The fact is this: on September 30, 1965, representatives of the Soviet General Procuracy, the Polish Main Commission for Investigation of German Crimes in Poland (*Główna Komisja Badania Zbrodni Niemieckich w Polsce*), and the Bulgarian military procuracy met to discuss the case against Beckerle and possible legal assistance to the West German investigators and to decide which country should take the lead in this collaborative effort—given the fact that Beckerle had committed

---

104 The certified copy was delivered; however, the public prosecutor's office of Sofia did not provide the German investigators with the original kept in the archives.

105 HHStA, Ab 631a, B 612, Bl 1129–30.

106 HHStA, Ab 631a, B 598, Bl 400.

107 Baev, "Bulgarian–West German Diplomatic Relations," 158–80.

crimes in all three countries (in Łodz in 1939, in the USSR in 1941, and in Bulgaria after his June 1941 appointment as minister plenipotentiary).[108] Interestingly, the Soviet invitation to an East-West discussion of judicial collaboration across the Cold War divide did not provoke much enthusiasm on the Bulgarian side. In March 1966, the Bulgarian military procuracy addressed its Polish interlocutors by a letter in which they offered a one-page depiction of wartime events. However, they stated that no original archival documents bearing witness to these facts could be found in their possession. The original records, they argued, were located in Yad Vashem (an inaccurate statement, to say the least). By contrast, in June 1966, the Polish Main Commission forwarded to the Bulgarian military procuracy several precious documents, including records of train transports from Skopje, as well as from Bulgaria to Treblinka, unearthed at the time of the Ludwig Fischer trial. Strikingly, these data were delivered to Bulgarian scriptwriter Haim Oliver, whose name we shall encounter shortly.

As early as the 1950s, in Bulgaria, Israel, and beyond, disputes regarding the interpretation of the past had crystallized around two cleavages: the first saw a confrontation between Bulgarian Communist historians and the Bulgarian exiles who had fled Communist repression after 1944; the second took the form of a face-off between the Jews who had remained in Bulgaria and those who had begun a new life in Israel. Rehabilitating the figure of King Boris and the legacy of the monarchy was the major cause non-Jewish and Jewish exiles fought for. In the mid-1960s, the conflict hardened: former Queen Giovanna (Joanna), who had taken refuge in Spain, published her memoirs in Milan.[109] Shortly afterward, the Bulgarian authorities decided to launch an academic journal of Jewish studies, with multilingual summaries. The first two issues included articles denouncing the malignant role of the king and another hailing the fraternal bonds between Jews and non-Jews in Bulgaria.[110] The terms of the ideological engagement were clearly set out.

---

108 The document pinpoints the fact that Beckerle had ordered the murder of three Poles and, through the military command, the execution of twenty-five other Poles. The notes on the meeting do not shy away from referring to his role in anti-Semitic policies and the organization of the deportation of 20,000 "Bulgarian Jews" (according to the document). The Bulgarian participant was Maj. Gen. D. Kapinov, assistant to the general prosecutor and the prosecutor of the Bulgarian armed forces. Instytut Pamięci Narodowej w Warszawie, IPN BU 3058/84. The author wishes to thank Ania Szszcepanska for sharing these documents, as well as Paul Gradvohl and Piotr Malachinski for their insights on these files.

109 Giovanna di Bulgaria, *Memorie*.

110 The publication of a journal had been part of the Consistory's plans since the late 1950s. *Evrejski Vesti*, January 23, 1958, 1.

The cooperation between the Bulgarian and West German judiciaries did not follow any less bumpy a course. After the indictment was sent by Prosecutor Bauer on July 12, 1966, the Bulgarian response was unhurried. Seven months went by, at the end of which the 1943 film footage reappeared obscurely. On February 3, 1967, regretting having failed to locate possible survivors, the Sofia prosecutor wrote to his German counterpart: "However, we have found a short documentary film" that shows the "transport of a group of Jews through the territory of Bulgaria to Poland." He added: "I have personally viewed the film and I think it is of significance for the criminal proceeding. Unfortunately, the operator who shot the film passed away a few years ago, but there are witnesses who can confirm the authenticity of the footage. If you were interested, I could send you a copy."[111] In March 1967, Dimităr Dimitrov, the head of the Bulgarian commercial legation to Hesse— in the absence of Bulgarian diplomatic representation in Frankfurt, bilateral contacts were mediated by the legation—arranged a meeting between Attorney General Bauer and the Bulgarian journalist Isodor Solomonov,[112] head of the economics section at the newspaper *Otečestven front* (Fatherland Front) and editor in chief of the weekly *Evrejski Vesti*—an influential figure in the Jewish community.[113] The Bulgarian side undertook to provide documents and testimony on the condition that the East German lawyer Friedrich Karl Kaul, who had distinguished himself during the Auschwitz trial, would be allowed to represent the Bulgarian Jews who wished to bring a civil action. The Bulgarians also asked about the possibility of sending journalists to cover and photograph the trial.[114] Through Dimitrov, two photographs of Dannecker and two certified copies of reports (one by Beckerle, dated August 18, 1943, and a report from August 31, 1943, that bore the signature of SS-*Obergruppenführer* Ernst Kaltenbrunner, chief of the SS's central security apparatus, RSHA), were sent to the Frankfurt prosecutor's office.[115] However, there was no further news of the mysterious film.

Then comes one of those rare, fortuitous, moments when, plunged into the archives, one catches sight of an unexpected document slipped

111 HHStA, Ab 631a, B 612, Bl 1256.

112 Solomonov covered the trial for *Otečestven front* and later published "Procesăt Adolf-Heinz Beckerle i njakoi izvodi ot nego," *Godišnik na OKPOE* 15 (1980): 159–94.

113 HHStA, Ab 631a, B 618, Bl 166f.

114 On the role Friedrich Karl Kaul is said to have played in East Germany's decision to make the trials an arena for ideological struggle with West Germany, see Weinke, *Verfolgung*, 345–56. The East German lawyer was admitted to the West German bar to represent Solomon A. Levi on March 27, 1968. On Kaul's complex trajectory, see Rosskopf, *Friedrich Karl Kaul*.

115 HHStA, Ab 631a, B 612, Bl 1261.

between two sheets of paper: on May 31, 1967, the Sofia public prosecutor announced the dispatch of "a documentary film on the deportation of the Jewish population of Thrace in 1943 to the port of Lom on the Danube," for which three former colleagues of the deceased operator would provide testimony to authenticate the images. Two versions of this letter have been preserved in the German archives.[116] In the Bulgarian version, the prosecutor apologizes as follows: "The dispatch of the film was delayed because it had to be voiced over in German (*se naloži toj da băde ozvučen na nemski ezik*)." The German translator split this process into two steps—"translated into German and synchronized" (*ins Deutsch übersetzt und sinchronisiert*)— reducing the ambiguity of a Bulgarian statement from which it is difficult to determine whether a German voice was affixed to silent images or whether the film, already sounded, had its commentary translated into German. On July 12, 1967, the Hesse state prosecutor's office confirmed that it was considering using the document as evidence, but that it was imperative to have supporting witnesses available as soon as possible, since the opening date of the hearings had been set for November 8, 1967. It was up to the Bulgarian commercial legation to obtain visas for them.[117] After a few setbacks, the film was indeed accepted as evidence and screened in Frankfurt on March 3, 1968, with sound and image once again separated (see figures 3.3 and 3.4). But let us not hasten the course of the story.[118]

What, exactly, did the source material submitted to the state prosecutor consist of? Of that film reel, the archives of Beckerle's trial in Hesse state seem to have kept no trace. Three sources, however, allow us to infer the content of the document: the testimony of two operators, an album of photograms kept in the prosecution's files (figure 3.3), and handwritten notes taken by East German archivists—some fifteen years after the trial. Let us first examine the record of Vasil Holiolčev's testimony of March 4, 1968:

32. Witness Wassil Holioltschew—59 years old—cameraman, Sofia.

Between 1942 and September 9, 1944, I worked for the Bulgarian Weekly Newsreels. In March 1943, my colleague Tschobanov (phon.) [Asen Čobanov] was commissioned to make a secret film. T. returned toward the

---

116 Ibid., Bl 1308 (in German) and Bl 1309 (in Bulgarian).

117 Ibid., Bl 1319–20.

118 In April and May 1968, judge Helmut Bauer, prosecutor Ernst-Dieter Pischel, and the defense attorneys Egon Geis and Hans Schalast traveled to Israel to collect further witness testimonies. One of the witnesses, Dr. Leon Alfandari, a Bulgarian Jewish physician who had participated in the disinfection of the convoys in Lom and had witnessed the deportees' embarkation onto four ships, was asked whether he had noticed the filming of the process. He said no. HHSta, Ab 631a, B 615, Bl 32.

Alle Aufnahmen dieses Films sind autentisch. Sie wurden 1943 von Kameramännern der damaligen Filmgesellschaft „Bulgarsko Delo" — der erste Teil zur Dokumentierung, auf Wunsch des Kommissariates für Judenfragen, und der zweite Teil - für die Wochenschau gemacht. Sie wurden in dem Bulgarischen Filmarchiv aufbewahrt.

Figure 3.3. First plate of the photo album created, at the prosecution's request, from the 1943 rushes for the Beckerle trial in Frankfurt, 1967–68. *Source:* HHStA, Ab 631a, B 651a, Bl 71.

end of March 1943. At the beginning of April 1943, I saw the film. T. had shown it to me so that I could examine and evaluate it because I was one of the best operators. The film was not made public. It shows the deportation of Jews from the Belomorie region—Kavalla [*sic*], Skopje, Drama. One copy was intended for the German legation; two copies for the Commissariat for Jewish Affairs.

In response to the prosecutor's question:

T. died a year and a half ago. He must have worked for the German Legation for money. T. was blacklisted (*zwangsverschuckt*) after September 9, 1944, for 7–8 months for working with the German legation. T. had also received money from the German legation for the film.[119]

The geographical confusion about the location of the filming, which has accompanied us since the beginning of the chapter, reappears here: Jews from Vardar Macedonia or from Northern Greece? Even more fascinating are the testimonies of Ivan Makedonski and the reaction of Adolf-Heinz Beckerle to the announcement of the viewing of the film in court:

33. Witness Iwan Makedonski—49 years old—film employee (*Kinoarbeiter*).

Tschobanov (phon.) was in 1943 operator for the Bulgarian Newsreels, he had received an order from the management of the Bulgarian Newsreels to film secret objects. After the change of 9.9.1944 a new management took over the Bulgarian Newsreels following the arrest of its former director. We found a negative of the film and established that it represented the deportation of Jews from Drama, Seres, Kavalla, and Macedonia.

To the prosecutor's question:

The film was handed over at the request of the Jewish community.

Asked about the content of the film:

It shows the transport [of Jews] in freight trains to Gorna Džumaja, the trans-shipment to other trains, and the convoy to Lom. Beleff, Beckerle, Boris, and Filoff are shown. The first part of the film is original, the second part comes from the Film Newsreals.

Beckerle here:

He objects to the screening of the *entire* film.[120]

---

119 HHStA, Ab 631a, B 597, Bl 223.
120 Ibid., Bl 224 (emphasis added).

This statement leaves no room for doubt: excerpts from newsreels were added to the original film footage. Which frames were interspersed into the visual archive, and with what intent? Was retouching work done on the visual archive through the addition of frames featuring King Boris, Prime Minister Filov, Commissioner for Jewish Affairs Belev, and the German diplomat? The criminal investigative file Ks 2/67 GStA Beckerle "Fotographien aus bulgarischen Film," which contains fifteen photograms, can be used to identify the newsreels filmed.[121] The first ten photograms come from the 1943 rushes; from the eleventh to the thirteenth shot, King Boris was immortalized alongside Nazi hosts (figure 3.4); in the last shot Beckerle initials an agreement. It remains to be seen where this footage came from.

We are entering the realm of conjecture here; the investigation requires a spatiotemporal shift to the year 1983, and East-East cooperation. On the occasion of a meeting between archivists of the East German and Bulgarian film archives, Berlin archivists in Sofia were shown deportation footage with a German voice-over. They carefully noted the content; the audiovisual archive—a positive—consisted of three segments:

1. Deportation of Jews from Kavala, etc. (Thrace, Macedonia), their being loaded into trucks, transport by rail (also by steamer on the Danube), march through a Bulgarian town, interim internment camp, further transport by train, Bulgarian guards, takeover by German officers.
2. King Boris III received by Beckerle to visit a German exhibition in Sofia.
3. Beckerle and Prime Minister Dobri Boschilow [Bozhilov] sign an agreement.[122]

Could this be the visual document handed over to the Hessian state prosecutor in 1967? The hypothesis is tempting, although Prime Minister Filov has disappeared from the list of protagonists.[123] After the 1983 screening, the East German State Film Archive requested a copy of the film footage from its Bulgarian hosts; their request was not fulfilled until six years later, in January 1989. Under the title "Deportation of Jews" (*Izselvane na evrei*), they received the negative of a film presented as a production of "Bǎlgarsko Delo/Studio für Wochenschau und Dokumentarfilme." The reel, however, is not the one seen in 1983: silent, the document has been intercut using elements from sequences 2 and 3 described above. This version of the 1943 footage is the copy now held by the Film Department of the German Federal Archives.

---

121 HHStA, Ab 631a, B 651a, Bl 71.
122 These notes were provided to the author on condition of anonymity.
123 I confirmed this point by viewing the film *Die Deportation der Juden aus dem Weissmeergebiet*, which is preserved in the Bulgarian National Film Archive.

Figure 3.4. Seventh plate of the album created from the 1943 rushes for the Beckerle trial in Frankfurt, 1967–68. *Source:* HHStA, Ab 631a, B 651a, Bl 78.

In order to move forward in our investigation, a new detour through the catalog of the Bulgarian National Film Archive is warranted. The inventory of the newsreels shot in 1942 includes the following note: "Tsar Boris visits the German exhibition on land and sea transport. The German minister plenipotentiary Beckerle welcomes him. Present is the engineer Vasilev."[124] This may be sequence 2. The third segment, however, does not appear in the Sofia inventory. One final venue is worth exploring: it is known that Nazi Germany provided its allies with images from its film newsreels: *Die deutsche Wochenschau* or *Descheg-Monatsschau*. The digitized catalog of the latter refers to a film recording of a trade agreement between Bulgaria and the Reich signed by Prime Minister Dobri Božilov in the presence of Beckerle in Sofia on December 18, 1943.[125] Sequence 3 of the film was probably composed from newsreel shots, possibly filmed by *Bălgarsko delo* for *Descheg-Monatsschau*.

Ultimately, the photographic file and the testimonies converge to suggest that the film screened by the West German court in 1968 resulted from the addition to the 1943 footage of shots filmed in other circumstances. The presence of Beckerle on the screen tends to create, if not the impression of his physical presence at the time of the Jewish raids, at least that of a narrative continuity involving him in the preparation of the deportations. To have included images of King Boris shaking hands with Nazi leaders had little chance of influencing the course of the judicial proceedings. But the choice is consistent with the Bulgarian Communist political line aimed at denouncing the misdeeds of the monarchy.[126]

---

124 *Actualités* 54, 1942, Catalogue des actualités, Bibliothèque nationale de France, Paris, 23.

125 *Descheg-Monatsschau*, 23, 1944: "Erlängerung des zwischen Deutschland und Bulgarien bestehenden Wirtschaftsabkommens; Unterzeichnung des Vertrages am 18.12.1943 in Sofia durch den bulgarischen Ministerpräsidenten Dobri Bjiloff, den deutschen Gesandten Adolf-Heinz Beckerle und dem Präsidenten der deutschen Abordnung Dr. Landwehr," http://www.filmarchives-online. eu/viewDetailForm?FilmworkID=59411ac985c0350ad8bace86d075d1ec&content_tab=deu. This monthly edition of filmed news was produced by Descheg (Deutsche Schmalfilm-Vertrieb GmbH), a component of the UFA. The author thanks Alexander Zöller for his insights into *Descheg-Monatsschau*.

126 My viewing of *Die Deportation der Juden aus dem Weissmeergebiet* confirms this analysis: it opens with photographs by Theodor Dannecker, Adolf-Heinz Beckerle, and Belev, with the voice-over reconstruction of the chain of command: "The agreement [of February 22, 1943] was signed . . . for the Germans, by the special representative of Eichmann, the adjunct police attaché of the German legation in Sofia, SS *Hauptsturmführer* Theodor Dannecker, who was directly subordinate to the envoy Adolf Beckerle [*der unmittelbar dem Gesandten Adolf Beckerle unterstand*]." The shots filmed in Lom are vocally illustrated by excerpts from a report by Beckerle sent to

One might well imagine that this setup did not escape either the accused or his lawyers. The notes of the hearings are remarkable here; they suggest that someone creatively toyed with the image by adding a modulation of the sound:

At 17:00 the hearing continues in Landesbildstelle Hessen, Ffm., Gutleut-strasse 8–10.

The court announces its decision:

The film is to be constituted as the main object of the visual examination of the trial.

During the projection of the film with sound [the commentary], defense lawyer Geis protests vehemently, gesticulating so much that the state prosecution finally gives up.

Defense attorney Schalast [who represented defendant Hahn, judged alongside Beckerle] joins this objection, because the performance with sound goes far beyond visual inspection [*Augenscheinseinnahme*].

The screening was interrupted, and a recess was called. Both sides discussed the matter until it was finally determined that the entire film should be screened but without sound.[127]

One might think oneself thrust into a scene from Brian De Palma's *Blow Out* (1981), were it not for the dramatically nonfictional character of the superimpositions between sound and image in the courtroom. The scene continued after the film's screening on March 6. Here is a description by the German historian Annette Weinke, one of the first researchers to have examined the trial archives:

When Beckerle learned that these images were going to be shown during the trial, he reacted with extreme alarm because, unlike the written documents from the Bulgarian archives whose authenticity was not in doubt, the film was a propaganda product made by a Bulgarian Communist television station. The film sought to give the impression that Beckerle, Dannecker, Filov, Belev, and Boris were personally present at the port of Lom to supervise the embarkation of the Jews from Thrace. Beckerle described the film as a "sophisticated trick" designed to influence the impartial viewer. He once again claimed to have spoken out against the deportation of the Thracian Jews and stated that he was only be sent to Macedonia on the orders of the

---

the *Auswärtiges Amt* on March 26, 1943, and a report by the police attaché, Adolf Hoffmann, dated April 5, 1943. The involvement of the king is suggested as follows: "Tsar Boris III, one of those responsible for the deportation of the Jews from the occupied territories, visits a German exhibition in Sofia."

127   HHStA, Ab 631a, B 597, Bl 225.

tsar. Moreover, of this action he had thought nothing special, since in the pictures of the steamer the Jews were waving white handkerchiefs.[128]

The courtroom session notes provided some additional details:

Beckerle at the request of the prosecutor:

Any participation of the German legation in the film is totally excluded.

I have often been filmed for the *Newsreels.*

I strongly oppose my accuser [Prosecutor Wentzke].

That Hoffmann or Dannecker showed photographs, I do not deny. Those were individual photographs or photographs in an album.

I know that I have seen pictures in which Jews were waving handkerchiefs on a steamer.[129]

On June 28, 1968, the German prosecution decided to separate the Beckerle and Hahn cases so that Beckerle's health problems would not jeopardize the proceedings against the former referent for Jewish Affairs. Three days later, Fritz Bauer died suddenly.[130] On August 19, the trial against Beckerle was suspended; it was never to resume.[131] The accused died in his bed on April 3, 1976, in the city of Frankfurt to which his name was so inextricably linked.

When Art Meets the Intelligence Community

The story of the footage's brushes with the law does not end here. In Bulgarian Jewish circles, disappointment at the failure of the trial was immense; a fraction of the country's intelligence services seemed to have shared their frustration. From this crossroads, a film initiative was born, whose linchpin was Wagenstein. At the end of August 1968, from East Berlin, where he was working on a Bulgarian-German-Soviet project dedicated to Francisco de Goya, the screenwriter of *Zvezdi/Sterne* submitted to the script commission of the Sofia film studio SIF Bojana a proposal for a "documentary fiction" provisionally entitled "The Beckerle Affair." His letter, a virtuoso exercise, deserves to be quoted at length:

---

128 Weinke, *Verfolgung*, 269.
129 HHStA, Ab 631a, B 597, Bl 227.
130 On the unresolved conditions of this death, see Ziok, *Fritz Bauer.*
131 Fritz Gebhardt von Hahn was sentenced to eight years in prison for complicity in the murder of Jews deported from Bulgarian-occupied Yugoslavia and Greece, as well as from Salonika.

You are aware that an agreement was signed between our two studios in view of the deepening of bilateral contacts and the increase of coproductions between Bojana and the DEFA. . . . Their central editorial office asked me to submit some proposals. Which I did.

Here is the idea:

Before my departure, [Kostadin] Kjuljumov came to me with an interesting proposal for a film, which by its character is already a coproduction. In West Germany, for a long time, a slow, laborious and wordy trial has been going on against Hitler's ambassador to Bulgaria, Beckerle, a trial whose end is not yet in sight, and which will probably end in a "draw" "for lack of evidence." We think of the role that Beckerle played in the deportation of Greek Jews (about them we made "Zvezdi" at the time). . . .

The materials of the German embassy, including Beckerle's diary, have remained in our hands and Kjuljumov has access to them. The threads extend significantly beyond that time to the present day. This makes the subject even more topical. The DEFA is ready to start working together on this film without delay and has in fact proposed the name of the director, Yakim Hassler, and also—in case this proves to be necessary, but I do not think so—a cowriter for Kjuljumov. As we see it, the film would be made in the criminal genre with filmed documentary material from that time, many written documents, documentary film material from the current trial; thus, something sharper and more modern would be proposed, something like a fictional documentary, a genre not very developed in our countries. . . .

Kjuljumov asked that the initiative come from our editorial office, because he—for professional reasons—does not want to be the first to say "A" [give the green light]. And since I am not in Sofia, I would have liked to ask you, if you ever see any bread in this proposal, to simply call him and propose that he get to work—with, to begin with, something on the order of a simple systematization of the material. If you agree to the director coming from the German side, I could easily arrange a preliminary meeting where the contours of the future film would be defined. On the German side, Willi Brückner, the deputy chief dramaturge of the DEFA, has expressed a wish to take over the editing. If you do not mind, I will shake the carpet on the Bulgarian side.

And the carpet, according to the representatives of the DEFA, must be shaken without delay if the film is to enter the program for 1969. They are ready to take the initiative on their own and right away (they know our working rhythm!), but I think that it would be good in this case that the business stays with us. This would relieve Kjuljumov in his initial work phase. In any case, if necessary, he could come and make a jump here where they have perfectly systematized materials and documents of the period (with which they provoke the permanent concern of Messrs. Globke, Kiesinger,[132] and co.) and we could draw a first outline.

So, I would be grateful if you would immediately consider the proposal I am making, in order to simplify the channels, with the agreement of the general editorial staff of the DEFA.

In a few days I will take off for Moscow, I will return in October. . . .

Greetings from the bottom of my heart to all my colleagues in the script editorial office.

Signed: Angel[133]

In addition to the rhetorical art of the screenwriter, who oscillates between soliciting support and stating a decision already matured, between deference and authority, the letter delivers several valuable pieces of information. Wagenstein evokes the reluctance of the scriptwriter and writer Kostadin Kjuljumov to carry the project in his own name "for professional reasons." After the declassification of the Bulgarian State Security archives in 2007, former intelligence colonel Kjuljumov was identified as one of the founders and the first deputy director of the powerful Sixth Department of the political police, in charge of "ideological diversion."[134] Was this information known in Bulgarian artistic circles in the 1960s? Equally admirable is the suggestion that Bulgaria seized the archives of the diplomatic representation of the Third Reich after the war and held a copy of Beckerle's diary.

The reasons why the documentary was never made remain unclear. Was that the consequence of some internal dynamic at play within the artistic milieu, an effect of the party's reassertion of control over Bulgarian Cinematography after the crushing of the Prague Spring, or merely a loss of interest in the trial following its suspension?[135] Should this decision

---

132 At the time Wagenstein wrote these lines, Kurt Georg Kiesinger was German chancellor (December 1966–October 1969). The fact that a former member of the Nazi Party, who had been deputy director of the Reich's external radio propaganda, held such a position in postwar Germany caused great controversy in the FRG and internationally.

133 CDA, F 404, op. 3, ae. 21, l. 12–14 (emphasis added).

134 Metodiev and Dermendžieva, *Dăržavna sigurnost—predimstvo po nasledstvo*, 428–56.

135 In late 2016, Wagenstein, whose memory was otherwise dazzling, refuted the existence of such a project. The interview ended with an invitation from the artist "to never believe anything but the archives." Interview with Wagenstein, December 12, 2016.

be linked to the break in diplomatic relations with Israel, decided by the Eastern bloc in the aftermath of the Six-Day War? Although the anti-Jewish measures introduced in Bulgaria never reached the magnitude of the anti-Semitic campaigns initiated in the USSR and Poland in 1968, the calls for a demonstration of political loyalty were probably unfavorable to the making of films dealing, directly or not, with "Jewish themes."[136]

Disappearing rushes that reappear opportunely; a dream documentary that never sees the light of day: the 1960s were definitely a decade in which creative, politicized energies willingly instrumentalized moving images. Following their tracks has so far delivered three findings. First, the reclassification of the shots from the register of documentation of anti-Jewish activities to that of judicial evidence had as its counterpart a new designation of the authors of the acts listed: responsibility shifted from the figures present on the screen (mostly Bulgarian civilians and policemen, as well as German police at the port of Lom) to the "absent" (from the footage) Beckerle, the symbol of German guilt who can only be visually attested to at the price of reassembling the shots. The evocative power and dramatic intensity of the images pointed to the search for those responsible by name.

Second, in the Cold War years, following the trail of the visual archive sheds light on the existence and workings of transbloc judicial cooperation: specifically, a fairly dense web of contacts was woven despite the fact that the FRG and Bulgaria did not maintain diplomatic relations. These links were deployed in the personalized mode of exchanging favors. Even when experienced by their protagonists as the fruit of a circumvention of political and institutional blockages, they could only take place with the consent of the state bureaucracies of the two countries and the Bulgarian party leadership.

Finally, the 1960s saw the crystallization of the theme of the "rescue of Bulgarian Jews" as a weapon in the interpretive struggles over the political legacy of King Boris. This motif will only acquire an autonomous dynamic at the turn of the 1970s–80s. To approach its transformation into a pillar of Bulgarian cultural diplomacy requires a new expansion of the field of investigation: a few stops on the shores of memory and a renewed attention to the transactions between documentary and fiction.

---

136 Marinova-Christidi, "From Salvation to Alya," 235. The development of a rhetoric equating Zionism with imperialism, the struggle against the influence of Israel, and the ideological surveillance of Bulgarian Jews—all were documented in Comdos, *Dăržavna sigurnost i evrejskata obštnost v Bălgarija*.

Cultural Diplomacy and the "Rescue of the Bulgarian Jews"

At a time when knowledge and memory of the Holocaust were increasingly being institutionalized in universities and museums in the West, the 1943 filmic record of the deportations resumed their peregrinations, crossing paths with engaged artists in West Germany and memory entrepreneurs in the United States. Once a judicial exhibit, the filming of the deportations acquired a new testimonial quality. This transformation came at the cost of a reversal of meaning: the shots of the roundups, which until then had served to found interpretive regimes of anti-Jewish violence and to designate the guilty, started to be used as well to signify an innocence—that of the "Bulgarian people," authors of the "rescue of the Bulgarian Jews." The victims present in the image served to evoke the crime, of course, but also and above all the survivors, and to honor the memory of those who had contributed to their exceptional survival.

To tell the story of this metamorphosis, a few elements of context are needed. During the era of détente and under the leadership of Ljudmila Zhivkova, the daughter of dictator Todor Zhivkov (1954–89), who chaired the Committee on Culture between 1975 and her untimely death in 1980, international cultural exchanges received a new impetus from the Bulgarian authorities, whether toward the "Third World"[137] or the United States.[138] Similar to other Eastern European states, Bulgaria undertook to strengthen the legitimacy of a socialist regime that was already thirty years old through an appeal to patriotism and an international opening that met with strong support in cultural circles.[139] Turned into an object of patrimony and pride, the past was exported, while national grandeur was magnified through an ever deeper digging into the entrails of time, medieval and even ancient.[140] The cultural calendar, conventionally ordered around the celebration of selected episodes of Bulgarian socialism, started to herald the names of heroes of the precommunist national epic. This exaltation of national greatness by socialist rulers reached its peak on the occasion of the ceremonies of the 1,300th anniversary of the founding of the first Bulgarian state in 681.[141] In a Balkan region where identities are labile and intertwined, the Bulgarian policy of nationalizing the past soon gave rise to historiographical

---

137 Dragostinova, "Natural Ally," 661–84.
138 Dragostinova, "East in the West," 212–39.
139 Gigova, "Feeble Charm," 151–80.
140 Marinov, *Nos Ancêtres les Thraces*.
141 Elenkov, *Kulturnijat front*; Kalinova, *Bălgarskata kultura i političeskijat imperativ*.

and memorial controversies, in particular with the Socialist Republic of Macedonia in Yugoslavia.[142] Peripheral to our subject during this period, they would become an essential component of it in the years 1990–2000.

Gradually, the destiny of the Bulgarian Jews became one of the key themes in this writing of Bulgarian exceptionalism. To determine to what extent this choice was influenced by—and in turn informed—diplomatic relations with the State of Israel is a challenge in the current state of the scholarly literature. Rumjana Marinova-Hristidi recently emphasized that Bulgarian-Israeli relations should be thought of as a ternary relationship, mediated by the USSR, and dependent on the tectonic events in the Middle East. She recalled the pro-Arab commitment of Bulgarian diplomacy, its role as a relay for the Soviet Union in the region, as well as its decision-making autonomy when it came to relations with the Jewish state.[143] This tangle of priorities leaves unresolved the question of whether the valorization of the theme of "rescue" in the late 1970s was envisaged, at least in certain segments of the Bulgarian state apparatus, as a possible vehicle for closer ties with Israel.[144]

In 1977–78, the preparation of the thirty-fifth anniversary of the events of 1943 gave rise to a wide array of documentary, museum, and scientific initiatives: at the House of Jewish Culture (*Evrejski kulturen dom*), the permanent exhibition on the "Rescue of the Jews of Bulgaria" marked the culmination of several decades of production of a textual and visual narrative, with a catalog published in 1977 in several languages.[145] Meanwhile, the Bulgarian Academy of Sciences (*Bălgarska akademija na naukite*) was preparing an edited volume intended to substantiate the veracity and accuracy of the museum's displays with archival evidence.[146] The commissioning of a documentary film concluded this commemorative program. The project manager was Haim Oliver, a former partisan and close friend of Wagenstein.

According to the recollections of his son, screenwriter and writer Oliver developed an interest in the Holocaust in 1958 when he was invited to participate in the design of the first exhibition on the "rescue of the Bulgarian Jews" at the House of Jewish Culture.[147] From that time on, he hoarded secondary literature and archives. In 1967, he made a name for himself

---

142 Troebst, *Die bulgarisch-jugoslawische Kontroverse*.

143 Marinova-Christidi, "From Salvation to Alya."

144 Behind the valorization of the "rescue of Bulgarian Jews," Marinova-Christidi sees Todor Zhivkov's aspiration to distance himself from the anti-Semitism prevalent in the USSR at the end of the 1970s. Ibid., 235.

145 Cohen and Assa, *Saving of the Jews*.

146 Koen, Dobrianov, and Manafova, *Borbata na bălgarskija narod za zaštita i spasjavane na evreite v Bălgarija prez Vtorata svetovna vojna*.

147 Interview with Dik Oliver, Sofia, December 13, 2016.

by publishing *We Were Saved: How the Jews in Bulgaria Were Kept from the Death Camps*, a work that would provide the framework for all subsequent state-sanctioned writings.[148] The choice of the publishing house, the influential Sofia Press; the recourse to the "official and patrimonial export circuit";[149] and the simultaneous distribution in four languages (Bulgarian, English, German, and French) sufficiently indicate the attachment of the authorities to a project presented by its author as a refutation of the "erroneous" vision of history offered by Queen Giovanna, living in exile in Spain, and by conservative Knesset member Benjamin Arditi in Israel.

Ten years later, Oliver was commissioned to make a documentary re-creation of his 1967 opus, namely *Transportite na smărtta ne trăgnaha* (The death convoys did not leave, 1977, 38 min.). Entrusted to cinematographers Baruh Lazarov and Sami Bidžeranov, the work was "dedicated to all those who, during those tragic years, reached out to their fellow Jews," and was intended to be screened during the commemoration of the thirty-fifth anniversary of the "rescue of the Bulgarian Jews." The heart of the matter is made clear in minute 3:

> Outside the list [of countries that deported their Jewish population] remains one and only one country, Bulgaria, the country where there was never a ghetto. In truth, many Jews died during those years, but none were exterminated as Jews. All the Jews fell with their arms in the fight against fascism, as Bulgarian citizens. Bulgarian Jews were not affected by the death camps. Such a unique historical fact borders on a miracle. During those years, the Hitlerites ruled the country. In Sofia, Adolf Beckerle, the Nazi ambassador, dictated and the minister-president, Bogdan Filov, slavishly carried out his will; the monarcho-fascism led by Boris III was as fierce and cruel as elsewhere. In spite of this, the death convoys did not leave. How was such a miracle achieved? The answer is complex. Many different factors were involved in the rescue of the Bulgarian Jews. *But in the end, they can be summed up in one—the struggle of the Bulgarian people led by the Communists.*[150]

The filmic narrative follows a three-step progression: the Nazi persecution of European Jews and its legislative transposition in Bulgaria in the winter of 1940–41, the roundups of March 1943 and the failed deportations of Bulgarian Jews, and the protests of May 1943 against the Jewish expulsions from Sofia and other Bulgarian cities. A triple sound device supports this argument: first, a male voice-over comments on the facts, whose precise

---

148 Oliver, *Nie, Spasenite*.

149 This phrase is borrowed from Ioana Popa, *Traduire sous contraintes: Littérature et communisme (1947–1989)* (Paris: CNRS Éditions, 2010).

150 Oliver, *Transportite na smărtta ne trăgnaha* (emphasis added).

prosody and sober tone aim to accredit the documentary truth of the images. Oliver then inserted excerpts from interviews with prominent figures in the Jewish community and non-Jewish personalities who denounced the persecutions. On the screen, the spontaneity of their words is somewhat tempered by the reading of testimonies cautiously put down on paper. Finally, musical interludes give unity to the narrative. The opening of the film is based on a game of contrast, of questionable taste, between a young singer in a turtleneck sweater and bell-bottoms who, guitar in hand, is humming a ritornello, and the immense photograph on the wall behind him where the remains of a young man's face caught between barbed wire, barely covered by a cap, are exposed.

In this tailor-made product, the alert viewer may be stunned to see two excerpts from the visual archive of 1943, which appear toward the middle of the narrative.[151] The first depicts the waiting in the camps—the washing hung along the barbed wire, the close-up shots of young girls with broad smiles. The second was cut from the sequence of the embarkation at Lom. This represents a major break in Bulgarian state policy: until then, the 1943 rushes had been kept off-limits and away from public view. What is the rationale behind their presentation? Let us look and listen more carefully.

The images of the deportations were encrusted on a chiseled visual and narrative box. Their distribution follows the evocation, in voice-over, of the signing of the agreement of February 22, 1943, between Eichmann's special envoy, Dannecker, and the commissioner for Jewish Affairs, Belev:

Thanks to the Tsar, the agreement was implemented. First, the deportation of the Jews from Greece, from Drama, Seres, Ksanti, where

[*Here, in the middle of the sentence, precisely at this point, the first shots of the temporary internment camp of 1943 appear.*]

the Germans reigned supreme.

[*In the background, an elderly woman's voice[152] begins a melody whose volume gradually asserts itself until it replaces the male commentary; one then discerns that she is singing a mourning song in Judeo-Spanish (Ladino).*]

The trains passed through Bulgaria.

---

151 Precisely at minute 18:25. In addition, a few furtive shots were scattered throughout the documentary: they capture the curve of the train leaving the station, here, the column of deportees crossing a street, there.

152 This voice is that of Wagenstein's mother: see Rumjana Uzunova, "Razgovor s Anžel Vagenštajn," roll 262, Radio Free Europe/Radio Liberty, November 20–24, 1989.

The superimposition between text and images acts as a powerful resigni-
fier of the action: the destruction of the Jews is imputed to the Germans,
locally relayed by the king; the use of the passive voice conceals the precise identity of those individuals who took part in the arrests; we learn only
that there was transit through Bulgaria. A few moments later, the voice-over
depicts the horror of the deportations, "this unprecedented crime," and the
appalling conditions of the journey: "Seeing them in such a state, the entire
population of Lom stood up and managed to help with warm food and
clothing." Finally, the mournful melody returns, illustrated by frames borrowed from the history of Jewish persecution in Europe: a female with a terrified look in her eyes and a photograph of a column of naked women from
the Mizocz (Mizoch) ghetto, probably taken by a member of the Ukrainian
police before their execution in Rovno on October 13–14, 1942.[153]

Although the persecution of Jews was not omitted,[154] in the general
economy of the film the struggle against anti-Jewish measures takes center stage according to the principle that the very accentuation of violence
magnifies the audacity and courage of those—non-Jews and Jews alike—who
rose up against persecution.[155] Beyond intellectual circles and the Orthodox
Church, which became one of the pillars of the national patrimonialization
of the Communist regime in the 1970s, the celebration of popular unanimity in support of the Jews led to the reincorporation into the narrative of
Bulgarian integrity of two politicians, both of whom had been condemned
by the People's Court in 1945: Dimitar Pešev, vice president of the so-
called fascist National Assembly; and the former minister of justice Nikola
Mušanov, an opponent of the wartime Filov government who had consistently denounced anti-Jewish policies and died in prison at the height of
Communist repression in 1951. Guilt is now concentrated in the figures of
King Boris and his obedient shadows, Prime Minister Filov and Minister of
the Interior Gabrovski.[156] As in the Beckerle trial, the use of words is called
for to make those missing faces appear on screen—yesterday the diplomat,

---

153 Frequently reproduced during the Cold War, this scene was long misidentified
as showing a column of women and children sent to the gas chambers. About
and Chéroux, "L'histoire par la photographie," 8–33.

154 Forced labor in particular is not shown. In the exposition of the exclusionary
measures applied from January 1941 onward, no mention is made of professional prohibitions, taxation of Jewish assets, and Aryanization policy.

155 This emphasis on the Jewish contribution is rare. It was entrusted to the
president of the Societal Educational-Cultural Organization of the Jews of the
People's Republic of Bulgaria (*Obštestvena kulturno-prosvetna organizacija na
evreite v Narodna Republika Bălgarija*, OKPOE), Josif Astrukov, who, meanwhile, denounced the passivity of the Jewish bourgeoisie.

156 However, there was a shift toward attributing the crimes to all the ministers
and deputies in power between 1941 and 1944.

today the king and the prime minister—as if words could act like chemical color developers.

One innovation, however, is noteworthy: in the 1977 documentary, the use of the 1943 rushes goes beyond the designation of those responsible; it also goes past the lionization of a society united in the fight for the Jews. The presence of the deportees in the footage serves to give relief to those, the Bulgarian Jews, whose absence means that they remained alive. The singer's voice amplifies this effect, as it calls out to the viewer like a leitmotif:

> You who are alive,
> You who, at this moment,
> Take a look at the screen
> Or clutch the darkness in your hands,
> Since you are alive (*poneže ste živi*)
> Listen to this story
> It ends well. . . .

> [*The camera, which was previously in a wide shot, moves closer to the singer at midbust.*]

> It begins with this, that
> The Third Reich in Nuremberg decided by a majority
> Until the end of time to turn the earth into a paradise
> For one and only one race
> One race only
> With only one racist party
> Everything else is racial waste,
> All the rest must be killed
> But all the rest is you

> [*The singer points the index finger of his right hand at the spectator.*]

> Picture the map with its two hemispheres

> [*The camera pulls back slightly, the shot hardly breathes.*]

> Imagine on it the country Bulgaria
> Imagine on it the country Bulgaria

> [*The operator begins a close-up that ends on the singer's face.*]

> There they did not leave
> No, they did not leave
> Over there, they did not leave
> To death—the convoys.[157]

---

157 At minute 16, just before the mention of the deportations, these words are repeated in full, from "One race only / With only one racist party." A third iteration is offered at minute 26:44, as a transition to the events of May 1943.

The narrative is indeed edifying. The viewer may be tempted to see, behind the insertion of images of the deportations, a subtle attempt to make accessible to a wider audience shots that had remained confidential and, thereby, to trespass the boundaries of the state-sanctioned narration of the past. Archives, however, remain silent on the origins, the commissioning, and the making of this documentary film. Sketching connections between sources—as in a Mnemosyne album—will help to thwart this silence. Consider the catalog of the permanent exhibition at the House of Jewish Culture. Its luxurious English version, *Saving of the Jews in Bulgaria, 1941–1944*, opens with the following preface:

> The exhibition is unique because of the historical fact—unique and exceptional—to which it is dedicated: the rescue of Bulgarian Jews from extermination by Hitler's agents during the years of the Second World War.
>
> It is hardly necessary to recall that wherever Hitler's boot landed during those years, an identical fate awaited the Jewish population—annihilation, total physical extermination, foreseen by the sinister Nazi concept of the "radical solution of the Jewish problem" in Europe. From the occupied European countries to the fascist camps and death factories, convoys began transporting millions of Jews, while others transported millions of anti-fascists of other nationalities to the same destinations. . . .
>
> The only Jewish population in occupied Europe that survived in its entirety, and that on the territory of its own country, was the Jewish population of Bulgaria. A miracle? Without a doubt! But a miracle that has nothing supernatural about it because it is the result of a human struggle: the struggle of the Bulgarian people against fascism that lasted no less than 21 years under the leadership of the heroic Bulgarian Communist Party. . . . (By the way, for the same reason, Bulgaria was also the only satellite country of Hitler not to have sent any soldiers to the Eastern Front against the Soviet army.) . . .
>
> This is the historical truth!
>
> The exhibition "The Rescue of the Bulgarian Jews" is a gesture of gratitude of the Jewish population for the anti-fascist and humane achievement of the Bulgarian people and their Communist Party: a proof of their dedication to their native land—Bulgaria—and to the cause of building socialism in the renewed Bulgarian land. At the same time, it is a unique monument of gratitude to the thousands of anti-fascist supporters, including those from the Jewish population, who gave their lives for the triumph of freedom and socialism.
>
> For all these reasons, and rightly so, the exhibition bears as its motto the words of the unforgettable leader and teacher of the Bulgarian people, the great anti-fascist fighter Georgi Dimitrov:
>
> > During the dark and infamous fascist regime, our people did not allow the extermination of their fellow citizens—the Jews. As is universally acknowl-

edged, Bulgaria was the only country where, under the fascist regime, the lives of the Jews were saved from the brutal hands of Hitler's butchers and cannibals. This binds our Jewish brothers in a bond of eternal gratitude to the noble and democratic Bulgarian people and their Homeland Front.[158]

For good measure, a quote from dictator Zhivkov follows the reference to the founding father of Bulgarian communism. Beyond the familiar motifs—the exceptionality of the Bulgarian trajectory, the virtues of the people guided by the party—it is worth noting the accentuation in the 1977 retelling of the protests against anti-Jewish policies of a date that would gain prominence during the 1980s: the demonstration of May 24, 1943, against the expulsions of the Jews from Sofia.[159] To the Bulgarian Communist authorities, the episode (the history of which remains to be written in a dispassionate way) presented two virtues. First, at the cost of factual accuracy, it insisted on the leading role of the Communist Party in the organization of the demonstration by offering the opportunity to weave the figure of Zhivkov into a heroic framework from which he had been absent until then. Second, the singularization of the collective action of May 24 wove together the socialist motifs of solidarity between Jews and non-Jews and of Jewish resistance. Let us read the Bulgarian Communist leader in this same preface: "One of the stormiest anti-fascist demonstrations in which Jews from Sofia massively participated was organized in the capital. It was a great honor for me to be entrusted with the organization and guidance of this demonstration of the Central Committee of the party, and I can personally testify to the feelings of internationalism of our people, to their humanism. It is true that many Bulgarian Jews perished, but none solely because they were Jews."[160]

We may be reassured: in this paper re-creation of the permanent exhibition of the House of Jewish Culture, the 1943 deportation rushes have not been forgotten. On the left-hand page, an image looks at us with its cold immobility: it is the shot of the column of deported Jews walking down a street. At the point where the march has been captured by the camera, a woman in a white kerchief calls out to the lens. The caption indicates that the snapshot was taken "in Macedonia and Thrace," a strange formulation unless the operator had the gift of ubiquity. In the end, the confrontation

---

158 Cohen and Assa, *Saving of the Jews*, n.p. (emphasis added).

159 The history of this event remains to be written; that is, the documenting of the scale of the mobilization (estimates range from a few hundred to several thousand participants), the role of the Communists in its preparation, the presence of non-Jews alongside Jewish demonstrators, as well as the assessments of the resort to this particular mode of public protest by Jews of various political persuasions.

160 Cohen and Assa, *Saving of the Jews*, n.p. (emphasis added).

between Oliver's documentary and the exhibition catalog suggests that by
the late 1970s, the 1943 footage had ventured on a new phase in its journeys, one in which it was reclassified as visual evidence of the extraordinary
"rescue of the Bulgarian Jews."

From this date on, public uses of the footage multiplied, benefiting from
the constant shifts between the filmic image and the photographic medium.
The most emblematic episode took place in 1984 in West Berlin, where the
law took a back seat to art, to which it nevertheless provided indispensable
material.

The "Rescue" Goes West: Managing Scarcity and Acquisition Competitions

Born in Stuttgart, Dieter Ruckhaberle (1938–2018) belonged to a generation of artists whose entire work was underpinned by the urgency of understanding past popular support for Nazism in Germany. Early in his career, as
director of the cultural service of the Kreuzberg district in West Berlin, he
discovered socialist realism and worked to give this Eastern European definition of aesthetics expert validation and acceptance. In 1978, he became the
director of the Staatliche Kunsthalle in West Berlin, which was created on the
initiative of Berlin state. The Kunsthalle soon established itself as an avant-
garde scene with left-wing convictions. Ruckhaberle took advantage of the
window of opportunity opened by Chancellor Willy Brandt's *Ostpolitik* to
establish relations with Eastern European artists.[161] In 1983, the Kunsthalle
devoted a large exhibition to the rise of Nazism; Bulgarian scriptwriter
Wagenstein attended the opening and informed Ruckhaberle that Bulgaria
might wish to host the exhibition in Sofia.[162] This was a first in the history
of the Berlin institution. The offer was accepted. *Antifascismus 1933–1983*
(Antifascism 1933–1983) was honored a few months later in the brand-
new National Palace of Culture, a building dedicated to the memory of the
recently deceased daughter of the dictator, Ljudmila Zhivkova. Christiane
Zieseke, who then worked with Ruckhaberle, retained vivid memories of
this episode: "The exhibition was one of the most complex I have ever had
to put together. We spent three weeks in Sofia without Dieter Ruckhaberle
being able to join us. He was employed by a government agency; I was a
freelancer. We called the German embassy every day; West Berlin was an
enclave in the heart of Eastern Europe, and the Federal Republic of Germany

161 Interview with Dieter Ruckhaberle, June 24, 2017.
162 Ruckhaberle, *Wege zur Diktatur, Ausstellung, Staatliche Kunsthalle Berlin und Neue Gesellschaft für bildende Kunst.*

insisted that the city be presented as part of the German state. Impossible to get a visa."[163]

In the course of their exchanges, Wagenstein confided to the director of the Kunsthalle the secret of the "rescue of the Bulgarian Jews," which was "good news for Bulgaria and very bad news for Germany," Ruckhaberle recalled in an interview, "since she had done everything in her power to deport these 48,000 Jews."[164] This revelation had a staggering effect on the artist: "I went to Bulgaria at my own expense. I had to see this with my own eyes."[165] In the wake of this trip, Ruckhaberle threw himself into an exhibition project titled *1943—Die Rettung der bulgarischen Juden* (1943: The rescue of the Bulgarian Jews), which opened in 1984. Despite its extreme rich and diverse sources, the exhibition paradoxically ended up accrediting the theses of Bulgarian Communist historiography. How this result was achieved is a story worth telling.

Of the textual and visual narrative that the exhibition at the Kunsthalle in Berlin offered to the spectator, only the catalog remains today, a catalog remarkable in many ways.[166] A timeline of rarely equaled precision followed the course of the war, the adoption of anti-Jewish measures, and the planning of the Final Solution; it refined in particular the knowledge of the preparations for the deportations from the summer of 1942 on. Most importantly, thanks to the availability of German documents, the events were situated within the wider context of anti-Jewish persecution in Europe. In the end, however, the "rescue of the Bulgarian Jews" once again projects its legibility onto the mosaic of clues about the historical events. How did this happen to be? The answer is depressingly simple. This outcome stemmed prosaically from the choice of sources: these were German when it comes to establishing guilt and Bulgarian when establishing innocence.

Prior to the exhibition, Wagenstein told his German interlocutors about the Beckerle trial in 1967–68.[167] Ruckhaberle's assistant Zieseke then obtained permission from the Hessian state prosecutor's office to consult the archives of the proceedings. In the case records, the art curator unearthed damning data on the role of the Third Reich and, more specifically, its diplomats in the preparation of the Final Solution.[168] In Bulgaria,

---

163 Interview with Christiane Zieseke, June 21, 2017.

164 Interview with Ruckhaberle, June 24, 2017.

165 Ibid.

166 Ruckhaberle and Ziesecke, *Rettung*. The spelling mistake in Christiane Zieseke's patronymic features in the original publication.

167 Interview with Zieseke, June 21, 2017.

168 It cannot be ruled out that Wagenstein's mention of the trial was guided by the hope of gaining access to West German judicial sources that remained closed

by contrast, the curators of the exhibition, escorted by Wagenstein, worked closely with Interfilm, the branch of Sofia Press responsible for providing visual material to its foreign partners. They were given the documents usually cited in Bulgarian writings, supplemented by the 1978 volume edited by the Bulgarian Academy of Sciences (Koen et al.) and Oliver's 1967 *Nie, Spasenite*—that is, the documents relating to the rise of "fascism," the dynamism of "progressive" Jewish cultural life, and the expressions of solidarity with the Jews, on three occasions: at the time of the adoption of anti-Jewish legislation (December 1940), the preparation of the roundups (March 1943), and the relegation to the province (May 1943). Although the petition of the deputy speaker of the National Assembly, Pešev, against the government's anti-Jewish policy was not elided, it was the antifascist struggle that took center stage in the story, which ended with the acclamation of the Red Army.

The concluding sentence of the catalog repeats almost verbatim Zhivkov's statement quoted in Cohen and Assa's *Saving of the Jews*: "Many Jews perished in Bulgaria between 1941 and 1943 as fighters in the anti-fascist resistance, as partisans, and as political prisoners, but none had to die just because they were Jews."[169] No wonder the Bulgarian authorities welcomed the Kunsthalle's initiative with enthusiasm: "The project received very clear support from the authorities," Zieseke noted in an interview. "The Bulgarian government was very interested; it was the first time an exhibition of this kind was held in the West. I had talks with the Committee for Culture; they helped us as much as they could. As soon as we applied for permission to go somewhere, it was granted."[170]

Undoubtedly, the reproduction of certain German documents could have aroused the reservations of the Bulgarian authorities—namely, archives suggesting that the Nazis had adopted a more reactive than proactive attitude in the face of their Bulgarian ally's anti-Jewish initiatives.[171] However, the thematic breakdowns, the arrangement of iconographic sources, and the

---

to the Bulgarians. In an interview, the scriptwriter lamented the failure of the Bulgarian authorities to repatriate to Sofia the significant amount of archives obtained by the West German commissioners. Neither Ruckhaberle nor Zieseke remembered this episode.

169 Ruckhaberle and Ziesecke, *Rettung*, 109.

170 Interview with Zieseke, June 21, 2017.

171 The Nazi diplomat emphasized that the text opened the way to the adoption of more radical measures and asked whether he should reopen bilateral discussions on the future of the anti-Jewish program. Following the adoption on August 26, 1942, of the decree establishing a Commissariat for Jewish Affairs and envisaging the possibility of deportations, Martin Luther, *Unterstaatssekretär* at the German Ministry of Foreign Affairs and liaison

choice of titles contributed to reassuring them, since they closely espoused a Bulgarian reading of the past. The description of the preparations for the roundups in the occupied territories is thus offered under the title *1943— Die Rettung der bulgarischen Juden*. At no time does the effect of framing shine through as strongly as in the use of visual archives of the deportations. This is due in part to the insertion of clips from the 1943 film footage. They are included on page 77 of the catalog where, in the upper half of a sheet devoted to "Die Deportation der Juden aus Mazedonien und Trakien," a picture shows an elderly man in a light-colored scarf, a wide-brimmed hat, and a Star of David on his coat, handing his identity documents to a policeman. The still was taken from the sequence filmed in front of the steamer *Saturnus* in Lom.[172]

Yet the astonishment here arises from another graphic choice, that of the photograph reproduced on the cover of the catalog. Men with luggage get off a wagon. In the foreground on the left, a young Bulgarian policeman in a double-breasted uniform stares at the camera. His face is beautiful, hairless; the lips are tight. A little farther back, to his right, a Jewish deportee exchanges with the lens a look of painful anxiety. The scene is easily recognizable: it was shot at the arrival at Lom, on the banks of the Danube, of a deportation convoy from Northern Greece. The page has been divided into two sections linked by a yellow border, a color long associated with infamy and that, more than any other, symbolized the stigmatization of the Jews. The title of the book was composed in what initially seems an ordinary design, black letters on a white background, with a more surprising yellow frame: *Rettung der bulgarischen Juden—1943: Eine Dokumentation* (figure 3.5). It is necessary to pause for a moment to consider what is being shown: on the cover of an exhibition catalog, which is intended to publicize the exceptionality of the "rescue of the Bulgarian Jews," a picture has been chosen of the Jews who were rounded up and *not* rescued. Here, the images of the arrests no longer serve primarily to document the deportations; they are intended to invite the viewer to imagine their converse: the nondeportation of the Bulgarian Jews.

What do we know about the reception of the Kunsthalle exhibition in West Germany? In an interview, Ruckhaberle spoke of his disappointment at the lukewarm reception: "Angel Wagenstein brought in Bulgarian journalists, to whom I gave interviews. But on the German side, the press was

---

officer with the SS, also asked the minister whether he should offer the Bulgarians German assistance in organizing the deportations.

172 Ruckhaberle and Ziesecke, *Rettung*, 77. Zieseke did not recall the existence of such a film being mentioned in Frankfurt or Bulgaria.

Figure 3.5. Front page of the exhibition catalog *Rettung der bulgarischen Juden—1943: Eine Dokumentation*, Berlin, Staatliche Kunsthalle, 1984.

almost silent despite the enormous work we had done."[173] One may presume that the exposure of documents from Communist Bulgaria, a country whose image had been tarnished by its alleged involvement in the attempted assassination of Pope John Paul II on May 13, 1981, were viewed with perplexity by a Western audience. These were times when cultural policies had highly political overtones: "The visitors were mainly people interested in the theme of antifascist resistance," Zieseke recounted. "Those who shared this orientation came."[174] Left-wing sympathizers, then. Yet the paths of poster-

---

173 Interview with Ruckhaberle, June 24, 2017.
174 Interview with Zieseke, June 21, 2016.

ity are mysterious: the 1984 German catalog now features in the collections of the New York Public Library. Moreover, this same work is referred to as a source for the description of the 1943 rushes in the inventory of the Film Department of the German Federal Archives.[175]

Shall we cease to encounter these mutually reinforcing entanglements between archival, historical, artistic, and political writings? The story of one more journey of the 1943 film footage—to the United States, a few months before the fall of communism—is unlikely to dissuade us that it could be so. This time, the main protagonists include archivists and historians, diplomats as well as members of the intelligence community.

A Late Socialist Intrigue: Sofia-Washington-Jerusalem and the Politics of Culture

In 1988, while Bulgarian communism was slowly cracking and an aging Zhivkov was reluctantly initiating a pale imitation of Mikhail Gorbachev's perestroika, the commemoration of the forty-fifth anniversary of the "rescue of the Bulgarian Jews" was offered flamboyant celebrations by the People's Republic. On November 16 and 17, an international conference was organized in the Palace of Culture, whose three-thousand-seat auditorium had hosted the previous year a film festival teeming with Western guests. Under white lights whose elegant geometric composition overhung a vast rectangular room, about eighty participants (political figures; members of charitable, community, or memorial institutions; historians, etc.) had been invited for the occasion.[176] The list of guests, which provides a detailed map of the individuals and institutions Bulgaria had managed to rally to its cause, comprised representatives from Israel, including Shulamit Shamir, the wife of Prime Minister Yitzhak Shamir; the president of the Bulgarian *olim* association, Leon Semov; and members of the Israel-Bulgaria Association and the Doron Foundation. Representatives from the United States (B'nai B'rith International and the United Jewish Appeal), France (the Paris branch of the World Jewish Congress, among others), the UK, Denmark, Italy, Austria, and Mexico, as well as two Eastern bloc countries, Hungary and the GDR, also attended. Without doubt, the preeminent participant was Shulamit Shamir. Born Sarika Levi in 1923 in Bulgaria, she emigrated to Palestine at the age of seventeen, Shamir never ceased to show her attachment to the land of her birth and to work for Israeli-Bulgarian rapprochement. At the

---

175 Ruckhaberle and Ziesecke, *Rettung*, 102.

176 The OKPOE Almanac published a list of forty-nine participants by name: "Učastnici v "Krăglata masa," *Godišnik na OKPOE* 23 (1988): 292–93.

invitation of dictator Zhivkov, she had already visited Bulgaria in 1986; this time she returned in an official capacity.

From the guest list one more name stands out, that of the American historian Frederick Chary, author of a monograph, *The Bulgarian Jews and the Final Solution, 1940–1944*, published in 1972.[177] While conducting his doctoral research in the late 1960s, Chary had been able to access archives in Israel, Macedonia, and Bulgaria, notably copies of the protocols of the Bulgarian People's Courts stored in Yad Vashem. Despite the fact that he had dedicated an entire chapter to the deportations from Greek and Yugoslav territories under Bulgarian control,[178] he recalled:

> My book was received very well in Bulgaria although there was some official criticism because I did not say the Communist Party saved the Jews, but I also did not credit the king. I went to Bulgaria almost every year from 1966 to 1989 and gave a number of papers on the Jews as well as other topics. Especially after Vicki Tamir published her book[179] (partially plagiarized from mine) claiming Bulgaria was the most anti-Semitic country in Europe they elevated me to the highest circles of academia. Ivan Ilchev[180] wrote that I was a leading worldwide Bulgarian specialist.[181]

At the November 1988 conference, the presence of an American historian represented a welcome scholarly endorsement.

The Bulgarian interpretation of wartime events was entrusted to the young Ilčo Dimitrov, then minister of education and culture, representative of a generation of historians who had undertaken to emancipate the writing of history from Soviet shackles. In honor of the distinguished Western guests, the minister amended the official rhetoric somewhat and praised the contribution of British and American pressure to King Boris's decision not to deport the Jews from the "old" kingdom.[182]

This exercise in public diplomacy and soft power would not have reached completion were it not for the screening of filmic images whose documentary, testimonial, and commemorative values converged to herald Bulgarian "exceptionalism." This time, Oliver had been commissioned to write the

---

177 Chary, *Bulgarian Jews*.
178 Ibid., 101–28.
179 Tamir, *Bulgaria and Her Jews*. The book, by a nonprofessional historian, offers a very critical reading of the history of relations between Jews and non-Jews in Bulgaria, as well as of Bulgarian politics during World War II.
180 Son of the Communist historian and minister of education and culture Ilčo Dimitrov, Ivan Ilčev is a specialist in Balkan history.
181 Email correspondence with Frederick Chary, October 1, 2016.
182 "Predotvratjavane deportacijata na bălgarskite evrei v nacistkite konclageri," 8 546, November 16, 1988, and 8 588, November 17, 1988, Arhiv na Bălgarsko nacionalno radio.

screenplay of a feature film, *Ešelonite na smărtta* (The transports of death; Borislav Punčev, 1986, 118 min.), a piece whose stretching of historical factuality went so far as to lead even those figures most closely associated with the dissemination of the socialist narrative about the war to disavow the film.[183] "Working on this script was a nightmare for my father," reported Dik Oliver. "I do not remember how many drafts were written. They kept coming back with new requests for modifications. He was literally exhausted from the writing. He died just before the film was released."[184] Indeed, to the usual pictorialization of the rescue, this fiction added a glorification of Zhivkov and his supposed talents as the organizer of the May 24, 1943, demonstration. This was the supreme stage of socialist modeling of the past. It stands as no surprise, therefore, that excerpts from the 1943 rushes were once again woven into the plot of the movie, as if it had become impossible to discuss the "rescue" without incorporating shots of the "unrescued" (those deported).

A few months prior to this international commemoration in Sofia, the Bulgarian production had crossed the ocean, trespassed the boundaries of the Cold War, and been screened in the West before a chosen audience of American diplomats, members of Congress, and leaders of Jewish organizations in Washington, DC. In an article coupled with a photogram from the movie that showed demonstrators being dispersed by Bulgarian police on May 24, 1943, the *New York Times* reported on the event in minute detail:

> WASHINGTON, April 15—An invited audience of members of the diplomatic corps, Congress and the Jewish community saw the American premiere of a movie Thursday night *that depicted events few knew anything about: how Bulgaria became the only Nazi-allied country in World War II to protect its entire Jewish population from the death camps.*
>
> *The audience was impressed.*
>
> "It's fair to point out that I'm not the greatest fan of Bulgaria, but we should give credit where credit is due," said Senator Larry Pressler, Republican of South Dakota. "It's a unique bit of history."
>
> The Bulgarian film, "Transports of Death," was shown at the Kennedy Center for the Performing Arts by the American Film Institute as part of a series of foreign films not in general release. It will be made available to a wider audience only if a demand for it arises.
>
> Wider demand is merited, said Ina Ginsburg, a trustee of the Film Institute, who noted that Shulamit Shamir, wife of Israeli Prime Minister

---

183 Uzunova, "Razgovor s Anžel Vagenštajn."
184 Interview with Oliver, December 13, 2016.

Yitzhak Shamir, had placed a print of the film at Yad Vashem, the Holocaust memorial in Jerusalem.

"If people have compassion and courage, they can succeed where others
fail," Ginsburg said of the depiction of the Bulgarian action protecting its
50,000 Jews from the Nazis.

The film was produced last year by Bulgaria's state-run movie agency. It is
a drama, filmed in color but with captured black-and-white documentary
footage spliced in. The plot concerns efforts by the Communists-led anti-
Nazi underground to thwart the deportation of the Jews, and deals with
the anguish of the Jews who at first hesitated to act against the Government and then did so only out of desperation. At one point, they march to
the palace of King Boris 3rd, but are beaten by soldiers on horseback. The
film shows a troubled monarch, caught between the demands of the Nazi
overlords and, on the other hand, the appeals of the Jews, the Bulgarian
Orthodox Church, and intellectuals that no Jews be transported from the
country. The Communists, who were to take control of the Government
in 1944 in a coalition with three other parties, are shown as the leaders of
the armed resistance.

Although one scene shows Greek Jews being transported through Bulgaria
on the way to death camps in Poland, that aspect does not receive full
treatment in the movie. During the war, Bulgarian forces occupied much
of Macedonia in present-day Yugoslavia and much of Thrace in Greece.
From these regions, 11,000 Jews were arrested by police under Bulgarian
authority and transferred to German SS units who then sent them to the
camps.

More than Denmark

But it is the treatment of Bulgarian Jews with which the movie is concerned, and it moved Representative Tom Lantos, Democrat of California,
to say, "It is remarkable that Denmark gets so much credit for saving its
Jews, while Bulgaria did even more."

Mr. Lantos fought as a teenager in the resistance against the Nazis in his
native Hungary. "I am deeply moved by what the Bulgarians did," he said,
adding that "the film was powerful and gripping."

The Bulgarian ambassador to the United States, Stoyan I. Zhulev, said that
although it is difficult to explain how Bulgaria was able to save its entire
Jewish community, one possible reason might be that "My country's long
history of suffering under the Ottoman Empire made Bulgarians sympa-
thetic to others who are oppressed."[185]

---

185 Irvin Molotsky, "Film Tells How Nazi Ally Saved Its 50,000 Jews," *New York
Times*, April 17, 1988 (emphasis added). A caption in the article reads: "A

This journalistic account is astounding in several respects. First, one may remember that praise of Bulgarian Communist initiatives was a rare occurrence in the United States at the time.[186] Second, the article is fascinating in that it reveals several mechanisms through which, on that occasion, images were granted the power to authenticate truth. Although the author cautiously distanced himself from the collective enthusiasm aroused by the screening, and chose to offer instead a detailed depiction of the 1943 film footage, the title and the content of the story nonetheless espoused the topoi of the revelation of an "exceptional historical fact," elevating fiction to the rank of a source for history. How can one account for such an outcome? Was the insertion of visual archives sufficient to modify the regime of truthfulness of the fictional plot? Or could this metempsychosis have resulted from the respectability of the audience thus converted to the Bulgarian reading of the past?

No less disturbing was the contribution of competing acquisition endeavors to the valorization of this iconographic product. As the *New York Times* article notes, Ina Ginsburg of the American Film Institute, an offshoot of the National Endowment for the Arts created in 1967 to preserve America's filmic heritage, reported that the wife of the Israeli prime minister had deposited a copy of the film at Yad Vashem. In other words, the factual documentation value of a work initially commissioned by the Bulgarian Communist state would be accredited by the reputation of its purchasers, in this case the most renowned Holocaust museum. The day after the event at the Kennedy Center for the Performing Arts, historian and archivist Sybil Milton, a leading figure in the development of the visual history of the Holocaust and former director of the archives department at the Leo Baeck Institute in New York (1974–84), requested a copy of the movie from the cultural attaché of the Bulgarian Embassy in Washington, Čavdar Popov.[187] The Bulgarian diplomat promptly obliged and was thanked by mail on June 3, 1988. No doubt, the presence of archival material Western scholars knew precious little about at the time had not been lost on the visual expert. In retrospect, however, one cannot fail to note the element of irony in this exchange: Americans sought to obtain, through personalized mediations closely followed by members of the intelligence community, a fiction placed at the service of a Communist campaign to publicize the "rescue of Bulgarian Jews."

---

scene from the film 'Transports of Death,' which tells how Bulgaria saved its entire Jewish population from Nazi death camps during World War II."

186 Enjoying the unflattering reputation of being the "most faithful satellite" of the Soviet Union, Bulgaria appeared, at the time of Gorbachev's reforms, as a state resistant to political opening.

187 Milton, "Images of the Holocaust—Part I," 27–61; Milton, "Images of the Holocaust—Part II," 193–216.

The context of the late 1980s sheds light on these Cold War transactions: as the past of anti-Jewish persecutions acquired increasing significance in public life and collective memories in the United States, Israel, and Western Europe from the late 1970s onward, the Holocaust was transformed into an arena where East-West confrontations were fought by proxy. In a pioneering study, French historian Annette Wieviorka has described the dawn of "the era of the witness"; that is, the transformation in memory regimes, which occurred at the junction of an emerging a social demand for testimony, the valorization of the figure of the survivor, and the redefinition of the foundations of Jewish and Israeli identities.[188] Incrementally, a wide array of political and social actors engaged in the commemoration of the destruction of the European Jews, a role that until then had been mainly confined to Jewish organizations. In response to the public impact of the television series *Holocaust* (1978) in the United States, President Jimmy Carter decided in 1980 to create a presidential commission on the Holocaust. In October of the same year, the Senate approved the formation of a Holocaust Memorial Council chaired by Elie Wiesel, the future Nobel Peace Prize winner, to formulate an American project for the remembrance of the genocide of European Jews.[189] Chancellor Helmut Kohl was quick to express alarm at the risk of "reducing German history to a Holocaust history sanctioned by the United States."[190]

By the time the Kennedy Center for the Performing Arts organized the viewing of *Transports of Death*, the future United States Holocaust Memorial Museum (USHMM) had already defined a policy for the acquisition of documentary sources on the Holocaust. Milton was one of the prime movers of this policy. However, when it came to documenting the fate of Jews in Southeast Europe, her efforts were hampered by the scarcity of sources on the Sephardic Jewish world, which was largely exterminated during World War II.

Having learned of the existence of Oliver's 1977 documentary film during an evening at the Bulgarian Embassy in Washington, Milton, Michael Berenbaum, and Sara Bloomfield, who were in charge of developing the museum project, expressed the wish to obtain a copy of the documentary. Their wish was only fulfilled in 1992, three years after the fall of communism.[191] Meanwhile, in 1996, the USHMM launched a second acquisi-

---

188 Wieviorka, *Era of the Witness*, 96–144.
189 Young, "America's Holocaust," 68–82.
190 Eder, *Holocaust Angst*, 84.
191 The February 1992 transaction was mediated by the cultural attaché of the Bulgarian Embassy, Bojan Papazov, a screenwriter and movie director by trade. A government official in Washington, he also ran the private production

tion process for three documents: *Die Deportation der Juden aus dem Weissmeergebiet*, the feature film *Zvezdi/Sterne*, and three newsreels from 1946–47 with a total length of 2,673 meters.[192] Reference to the financial transaction has been preserved in the archives of the USHMM, but of the documents themselves, no trace is to be found.

What findings have these last journeys of the 1943 film footage delivered? First, following the convoluted uses of these visual archives has opened a window on broader historical processes, in this case the partial shift of the places where knowledge and representations of the Holocaust are produced—from the courts of justice to museums. Moreover, their path has crossed the Americanization of the memory of anti-Jewish persecutions, a phenomenon that was in no way circumscribed to East-West dynamics, but did come to bear upon them.[193] Second, at the turn of the 1970s–80s, the Bulgarian socialist narrative of the events of March 1943 acquired its definite form. Interestingly, this narrative presents affinities with the reading of the war produced by the People's Court in 1945. The March "trial of the anti-Semites" had outlined the guilt of a handful of pro-Nazi leaders and collaborators, spotlighted solidarity in combat and sorrow between Jews and non-Jews, as well as the valor of the innocent Bulgarian people. Three decades later, something akin to an engraver's artful transposition took place: tiny shifts had occurred, infinitely fine tonal nuances have been added, and color values modified.

In the commission of the facts, guilt was narrowed down. Around a central protagonist, the Nazis, the range of Bulgarian fascist "henchmen" refocused on the figure of King Boris, the embodiment of a fascist era whose starting point was set in 1923. Likewise, the image of the crimes has been blurred: the variety of anti-Jewish measures (discriminatory taxation, professional exclusions, Aryanization of property, housing segregation) in the "old" kingdom has been reduced to the Law for the Defense of the Nation and the expulsions of May 1943. The rendering of the deportations from the territories under Bulgarian occupation had also lost precision. Meanwhile,

---

company Concordia, through which the USHMM acquired a public archive from the Bulgarian Film Library, in this case 190 meters of 35 mm reel for $371. The description of the archive by Papazov is partly based on the record of the Film Library. However, this cryptic note was added: "As for the other 7,000 Jews, Bekerle [*sic*] indicates that it is not known how they were transported." This number corresponds approximately to that for the Jews deported from Vardar Macedonia; henceforth, one may hypothesize that the audiovisual archive concerns the roundups in Greece.

192 *Kino Pregled* 44/47; *Kino Pregled* 89/46; *Kino Pregled* 163/47.

193 Novick, *Holocaust in American Life*; Flanzbaum, *Americanization of the Holocaust*.

the antifascist struggle and the mobilizations in favor of the Jews carried out under the enlightened leadership of the Communist Party were drawn in stark graphite, while a cult of personality developed late by Zhivkov, now the chief "rescuer," favored a reweighting of the May 24, 1943, demonstration. At the center of the picture, there remained, however, the innocent Bulgarian people and Bulgaria's exceptional historical trajectory.

In this etching, one final trait deserves note: the "national tolerance" of the Bulgarian people as the driving force behind their compassion for the Jews gained in emphasis. This would surely come as a surprise to those who remember that, in the second half of the 1980s, Bulgaria launched a forced assimilation campaign of a magnitude and violence unmatched in Europe during that period. Denying the existence of a Turkish minority in the country, the authorities—the police and the army—forced some 800,000 Turks[194] to Bulgarize their names at gunpoint, prohibited any expression of a Turkish cultural identity, including the use of Turkish in the public square, and imprisoned those who protested against the denial of their identities, while proclaiming the total unification of the nation.[195] The Communist

---

194 Despite the absence of official statistical data on Muslims in mid-1980s Bulgaria, archival records are available: in June 1985, a report from the Ministry of the Interior claimed that 822,588 name changes had taken place from 1984 to 1985; in May 1989, a military source indicated a total of 1,306,000 name changes. These sources do not include the Bulgarian-speaking Muslims whose names were changed in 1972–74, nor the Muslim Roma subjected to renaming in 1958–59. In December 1985, Bulgaria's population was 8,948,649. See census results, https://www.nsi.bg/Census/SrTables. htm, and AMVR [Archives of the Ministry of the Interior], F 1, op. 12, ae. 661, l. 35; and AMVR, F 1, op. 12, ae. 940, l. 32, in Avramov, *Ikonomika na "văzroditelnija proces,"* 110.

195 Since the end of socialism, the forced assimilation campaign has been significantly documented through the publication of archival collections, academic writings, and testimonies. Several pieces of scholarship have also set it against the background of nation-state-building processes in post-Ottoman Bulgaria, and of recurring efforts to forcibly assimilate Bulgarian-speaking Muslims. See, among others, Gruev and Kaljonski, *Văzroditelnijat proces*; Avramov, *Ikonomika na "văzroditelnija proces"*; Ivanov, *Kato na praznik*; Jalămov, *Istorija na turskata obštnost v Bălgarija*; Ivanova, *Othvărlenite "priobšteni" ili procesa*; Pašova and Vodeničarov, *Văzroditelnijat proces i religionznata kriptoidentičnost*; Ragaru, "Symbolic Time(s) of Violence"; Ragaru, *Assignés à identités*, 45–72; Neuburger, *Orient Within*. For archival collections, see Baeva and Kalinova, *"Văzroditelnijat proces"*; and Angelov, *Strogo poveritelno!* On memorial issues, see Evgenia Kalinova, "Remembering the 'Revival Process' in Post-1989 Bulgaria," in Todorova, Dimou, and Troebst, *Remembering Communism*, 567–94.

rulers claimed that all the Turks who had until then lived in the country had arrived in Turkey between 1968 and 1978, following the conclusion of a bilateral agreement on migration. Those Muslims who remained in Bulgaria, they further contended, were not Turks; they were Bulgarians. In official discourse, the renaming campaign was depicted as a "revival process," through which descendants of Bulgarians who had been forcibly converted to Islam during Ottoman times were voluntarily reclaiming a Bulgarian national identity. The peak of the dissemination of data relating to the "rescue of Bulgarian Jews" thus coincided with an exercise in ethnic engineering that could also be claimed as "exceptional."

Epilogue

In March 2011, a permanent exhibition opened to the public at the *Memorialen centar na holokaustot na Evreite od Makedonija* (Memorial Center for the Holocaust of the Jews of Macedonia), located in Skopje (Republic of Macedonia, today the Republic of North Macedonia). The exhibit was only sparsely populated with artifacts, written archives, and other original documents. In order to re-create a sense of the past, its designers turned to the world of things and materiality, reproducing a wooden wagon bearing the acronym BDŽ (*Bălgarska dăržavna železnica*, Bulgarian State Railway Company), which was similar to the vehicle filmed in March 1943. The image itself was no longer enough; a three-dimensional object created an immersive environment and brought those dramatic historical moments to life.[196] Eleven years later, the wagon remains on display in the permanent exhibition, which was completely redesigned in 2018. A notice now indicates that the wagon was donated by the Macedonian railway company (*Podarok od Makedonski železnici A.D., Makedonija*), after undergoing restoration.[197]

Writing this chapter, more than any other, has been an exercise in humility. It was necessary to grapple with missing archives and ebbing memories, to accept that certain questions may be left unanswered, and to deal with unresolved enigmas even while remaining committed to the pursuit of knowledge about the events of 1943 and their discontinuous presence in distinct public spaces. One main thread persisted throughout the research process: refuting any opposition between reconstituting the facts and interrogating narratives

---

196 A photograph of this re-creation was reproduced in Berenbaum, *Jews in Macedonia*, 51, with a legend reading: "Carriage od [*sic*] Bulgaria State Railways, that was used for transpot [*sic*] of Jews" that might have suggested that the artifact was of the period.

197 Per visit to the exhibition by the author, December 12, 2018.

of the past. Between these non-coextensive spaces, there do exist links and pathways that we can follow in order to elucidate historical moments, as well as the production of knowledge representations of that which is no more.

In various fields, scholars have shown how images emerge from the shifting frames and mediations through which sight is rendered possible. But the human eye is calibrated. In order for visual sources to speak, one must loosen one's fascination with recorded scenes, in order to explore how such scenes were made legible. Considered in these terms, reconstituting the social lives of the 1943 film fragment enables us to see how images can acquire changing definitions, along with shifts in value.

More specifically, in analyzing the evolving interpretations of the 1943 film footage, we have zoomed in on three techniques for creating meaning. First, vision was transcribed into language through ekphrastic practices within archival collections, exhibition catalogs, as well as notices for documents donated or sold. Second, the interpretation of the original frames evolved through the accretion of additional shots, which had been made elsewhere and in distinct circumstances. Third, the seen subsequently came to be heard, as images were edited through voice-overs, musical framing, or song. In turn, a diversity of factors—from archival tracing and the search for eyewitnesses to the documentary value conferred on the images through the reputation of the acquiring institutions—conspired to grant credibility to the film fragment.

Ultimately, the story told in this chapter is one of dramatic meaning-making activities. Once endowed with documentary qualities, a film fragment took on the power to serve justice, before (eventually) being assigned the status of testimony in the service of memory politics. Meanwhile, as it migrated from historical document to fiction, from cinematographic mobility to the fixity of glossy paper, a 1943 visual source that had most likely been produced for the Bulgarian Commissariat for Jewish Affairs—and that had immortalized the faces of Jewish victims of genocide—was used for the purpose of designating the perpetrators of German war crimes in the 1960s. Later, in the 1970s and 1980s, it would serve to herald the "rescue of the Bulgarian Jews." In shifting the public's attention from the absences immortalized on film to the Jewish presences that remained off-screen, Bulgaria's publicly sanctioned readings of the past changed focus as well: from guilt on the part high-level Nazi and Bulgarian officials to the innocence of an undivided Bulgarian people.

At the same time, tracing these visual migrations can unveil several insights into the periodization of communism and the study of the Cold War. Our journey through the socialist era via the 1943 film footage has opened a window into the heterogeneous temporalities often gathered under the single notion of "socialism." Toward the end of World War II, sanctioning crimes against the Jews had served an internal political agenda—to demonstrate the extent of fascist crimes in order to legitimize the new regime. But it also constituted a diplomatic move—authorizing Bulgaria's existence as a nation that had resisted Nazism, and thus eliciting clemency from the victorious powers. As elsewhere in Eastern Europe, the onset of the Cold War, the suppression of political opponents in the late 1940s, and late Stalinism's anti-Semitic campaign all led to the silencing of references to wartime violence against Jews. Then came a change in atmosphere in the 1960s that paved the way for (timid) cooperation across the East-West divide, especially with those West German prosecutors who wanted to reckon with the Holocaust. Such a collaboration offered the Bulgarian authorities a stage on which they could put forth their own reading of the war—an alternative to the narrative of anti-communist exiles who had sought refuge in the West, or the non-communist Bulgarian *olim* who had settled in Israel. In the 1970s through the 1980s, finally, Jewish experiences during World War II were selectively rediscovered, as they were invested with the capacity to underpin dictator Zhivkov's project of national renewal and self-celebration, both at home as well as abroad.

Late socialism in Bulgaria should thus be differentiated from that of the Soviet Union: as late Brezhnevism stifled dissent and the expression of Jewish identities, an estimated 150,000 Jews emigrated to Israel in the 1970s.[198] Meanwhile, Soviet trials for war crimes were not entirely discontinued.[199] This background reminds us that the historical and memory policies of the Eastern bloc could never be reduced to directives from Moscow. The existence (indeed the broad extent) of East-West circulations undercuts a vision of two autarkic blocs. To grasp these circulations requires abandoning any assumption of systemic East-East solidarity and broadening the focus of analysis beyond the European continent into Israel and the United States, as well as paying close attention to the familial and other affective ties that united—and divided—the descendants of Jews born in Bulgaria.

In particular, the case study of the legal proceedings against the former Nazi minister plenipotentiary Beckerle underlines the utility of overcoming a binary choice between a reading of East-West relations centered on confrontation and closure and an analysis of interactions under a model of

---

198 Kostyrchenko, "Politika sovetskogo rukovodstva v otnoshenii yevreyskoy emigratsii posle XX s"ezda KPSS," 202–19.

199 A case in point is that of former Soviet Nazi collaborator Feodor Fedorenko, who served at Treblinka extermination camp. Fedorenko, who had immigrated to the United States after the war, was apprehended there in 1978 and deported to the USSR in 1984. Judged in the Crimean regional court in 1986, he was sentenced to death and executed on July 28, 1987. See Bazyler and Tuerkheimer, *Forgotten Trials*, 247–73.

rapprochement, or even convergence, during the period of détente. In contrast to these approaches, we have uncovered a configuration of fragile and discontinuous exchanges that can only be deciphered through close attention to the social characteristics of the actors involved, as well as the diversity of their professional worlds (artistic, diplomatic, security, etc.). This Bulgarian-German episode, above all, does not discount discordant interpretations of World War II or the prosecution of war criminals after 1945. If certain individuals—Fritz Bauer, in particular—shared biographical features with their Eastern European interlocutors, and a common wish to prevent the return of Third Reich cadres to power, such collaboration did not lead to an ensuing convergence of their legal or political agendas. On the contrary, it might be argued that Cold War collaborations like this one provided a means (if not a condition of possibility) for continued competition between East and West. After all, it was through the public arena of the Frankfurt trial that Bulgarian leaders' interpretation of the events could resonate in the West. Similarly, they redoubled their denunciation of the imperialism of Western justice after the prosecution of Beckerle was dropped.

In no other chapter thus far has there been such talk of intrigue: a chapter whose topic did not exactly lend itself to fictional games—Cold War intrigues, one might say, and with good reason. In shifting to the historiographical and memorial controversies of postcommunism in the next two chapters, however, I would like to leave us with two links to the Communist era. The first concerns the various mediators who served the politics of the past on behalf of states and/or private actors. World War II survivors, museum curators, operators and filmmakers, journalists, (script)writers, intelligence agents, magistrates, and diplomats will all play a part in the postcommunist era, as they did toward the end of the war. Given such a proliferation of individuals vying to offer their own interpretation of the facts, we should be skeptical of any model by which historians would hold a monopoly, or at the very least a preeminent authority, over authorizing and legitimizing certain retellings of the past.

The second connection between communism and postcommunism lies in the structuring role played by internal Jewish divisions in knowledge production as well as in representations of anti-Jewish violence—in Bulgaria as in the rest of Europe; in Israel as in the United States. In chapter 1, the 1945 trial before the Seventh Chamber of the People's Court illuminated the depth of political and social cleavages within the Bulgarian community. Examining the post-1989 memorial controversies will lend new prominence to these cleavages, all while restoring the contributions of survivors and descendants of Balkan Jews to the production of knowledge concerning Jewish experiences of the war.

Chapter 4

Accounts of "Rescue" and Deportation in Dialogue

Memory Controversies after 1989

March 2018. We now return to the scene with which this book opened: the commemoration of the seventy-fifth anniversary of the "rescue of the Bulgarian Jews" and the deportation of Jews from the occupied territories. In the process, we catch a fleeting glimpse of Bulgarian prime minister Bojko Borisov standing before the former internment camp for the Macedonian Jews. The ceremony emerges in dramatic relief, sculpted from a profusion of memorial initiatives, their complexity defying comprehension. In the pages that follow, we will depict these initiatives in a telegraphic manner, as concise vignettes, gradually broadening the spatiotemporal frame. The desired effect is not to saturate, but rather to progressively enrich and refine our understanding of the images in view. Personal histories, professional identities, and the operating logics underpinning these commemorative sites will come into sharper focus. In this way, we shall delve into the central subject matter of this chapter: the examination of post-1989 memorial controversies surrounding the events of the Holocaust.

Let us begin by considering the handful of days leading up to and following March 10, the day on which the minister of the interior, Gabrovski, rescinded orders to arrest the Bulgarian Jews. On February 19, 2003, the Bulgarian Council of Ministers declared March 10 to be the "Day of the Rescue of the Bulgarian Jews, of the Victims of the Holocaust and the Crimes against Humanity."[1] In the Republic of North Macedonia, the

---

1 Decision no. 105 of the Council of Ministers, February 19, 2003. In March 2009, on the occasion of the sixty-sixth anniversary, the website of the Bulgarian National Assembly suggested a different designation: "Day of the Holocaust and the Crimes against Humanity." http://www.parliament.bg/

commemoration of the early-morning roundups of Jews that occurred in Skopje, Bitola, and Štip typically falls on the following day.[2] This interval, albeit a single day, marks the stark contrast in the fates of these two Jewish communities. In 2018, the temporal gap was further highlighted—the commemoration took place on March 9 in Bulgaria, and on March 12 in Macedonia—in a move that paradoxically symbolized the beginnings of a rapprochement, as the scheduling enabled the Bulgarian and Macedonian delegations to attend each other's ceremonies on both sides of the border.

Sofia, Bulgaria: March 9, 2018, 10:30 a.m. In front of the monument to the rescue located next to the Bulgarian parliament, a minute of silence opens the ceremony organized by the municipality of Sofia and by the Šalom Organization of the Bulgarian Jews, "in memory of the Jewish deportees and in tribute to the rescue of Bulgarian Jews." The participants include the head of parliament, several parliamentarians, two vice ministers of foreign affairs, the Israeli and American ambassadors to Bulgaria, the deputy mayor of Sofia, the director of the Auschwitz-Birkenau Foundation, officials from the World Jewish Congress (WJC), the American Jewish Joint Distribution Committee (JDC), and the American Jewish Committee (AJC); the chairman of the Israel-Bulgaria Parliamentary Friendship Group, a delegation of Jews of Bulgarian origin now living in Israel; representatives from Jewish communities in Greece and Turkey; as well as the president of Šalom. For the first time, Goran Sadikarijo is attending the ceremony in his official capacity as the president of the Holocaust Memorial Center for the Jews of Macedonia; as is Ambassador Jovan Tegovski, the head of the Macedonian delegation to the International Holocaust Remembrance Alliance (IHRA). The Bulgarian president, Rumen Radev, was meant to be present, but his schedule changed

---

bg/news/ID/1721. In Bulgaria, March 10 is more commonly referred to as the "Day of the Rescue of the Bulgarian Jews." In their recent public speeches, up until 2023, the heads of Jewish community institutions and Bulgarian state officials had spoken of "the rescue of Bulgarian Jews and tribute to the 11,343 Jews from Macedonia, Greece, and the Pirot region." In March 2023, the frequent, if not exclusive, resort by state-sponsored media and public authorities to the notion of the "rescue" was one of the factors in a particularly bitter commemoration of the eightieth anniversary of the nondeportation of the Bulgarian Jews and the deportation of the Jews from the Bulgarian-held territories. Other factors included the attribution of the "rescue" to the *entirety* of Bulgarian society and to the *Bulgarian state*, alongside an attempt at rehabilitating the role of King Boris in the spring of 1943.

2   In North Macedonia, March 11 is the official remembrance "Day of Deportation of 7,144 Jews to the Death Camp Treblinka in 1943."

at the last minute.[3] In her speech, National Assembly Speaker Cveta Karajančeva celebrates "the politicians, the Orthodox Church, and the entire Bulgarian society, which all stood up as one to defend their fellow citizens." Aleksandăr Oskar, the president of Šalom, reminds the audience, "Our duty is to remember and not to forget all those worthy Bulgarians who made the right choice, who chose life."[4]

March 9, 2018. Several hours later, the Bulgarian parliament hosts the launch of the book *75 Years: The Unforgettable Figures of the Rescue*, published under the editorial coordination of Maksim Benvenisti, former head of Šalom.[5] "We hope that this publication will turn all of you into intellectual partners in the research and the identification of the individuals [who participated] in the Rescue," Benvenisti declares, before he invites his guests to visit an exhibition dedicated to the members of the Twenty-Fifth National Assembly who fought against the anti-Jewish policies.[6]

March 9, 2018. At the Sofia synagogue, a magnificent early-twentieth-century building, a commemorative event has been arranged with Prime Minister Borisov, WJC president Ronald S. Lauder,[7] Central Israelite Spiritual Council president Sofia Koen, and the president of Šalom. The latter presents Jordanka Făndakova, mayor of Sofia, with the Šofar Award in recognition of the efforts to combat anti-Semitism and incitement to racial hatred. The significance of this moment is amplified by the "Lukov march" taking place in Sofia on February 13, 2018. This annual gathering of radical nationalists and neo-Nazis commemorates the execution of General Hristo Lukov, leader of the Bulgarian National Legions, by a member of the Jewish Communist resistance in 1943.[8]

What elements, then, are at our disposal?

Stages: monument, parliament, synagogue.

---

3   Juliana Metodieva, "Gorčivijat vkus ot zabraven pametnik na bălgarskata gordost," *Marginalia.bg*, March 27, 2018.

4   "Predsedateljat na parlamenta Cveta Karajančeva i narodni predstaviteli učastvaha văv văzpomenatelnoto čestvane na 75-ta godišnina ot spasjavaneto na bălgarskite evrei," *Novini*, March 9, 2018.

5   Organizacija na evreite v Bălgarija Šalom, *75 godini*.

6   https://www.facebook.com/ŠalomBulgariaOrganization/.

7   Imanuel Marcus, "Ronald S. Lauder: 'The Jews Will Never Forget the Bravery of the Bulgarians,'" *Magazine 79*, March 10, 2018.

8   "World Jewish Congress Marks 75 Years since Rescue of 48,000 Bulgarian Jews from Nazi Deportation," March 10, 2018, https://www.worldjewish-congress.org/en/news/world-jewish-congress-marks-75-years-since-rescue-of-48000-bulgarian-jews-from-nazi-deportation-3-6-2018.

> **Actors:** elected representatives, officials from community organizations, members of the diplomatic corps, an Israeli Jewish delegation, representatives of museums and international bodies committed to recognizing and remembering anti-Jewish persecutions during the war.

Focusing exclusively on March 9, 2018, is nonetheless too narrow a time frame to take into account other institutionalized forms of collective memory. To adequately address these, the temporal scope must be extended by ten days, at least.

March 5, 2018. The "Istorija" broadcast of the first channel of Bulgarian national television is devoted to the theme "Who saved the Bulgarian Jews—and how?" While seated in front of the screens that continuously display images of the Holocaust, scholars as well as a representative from Šalom are invited to debate. On-screen, the aforementioned question remains imposing in a visually striking manner; in contrast, the discussions confront both the Bulgarian state's anti-Jewish measures and the deportations.

March 6, 2018, 5:30 p.m. In Stara Zagora, on account of a partnership between Šalom, the regional directorates of the archives, and the historical museums of Stara Zagora and Šumen, the exhibition "Rescue: March 10, 1943" is inaugurated on the occasion of the "Day of the Rescue of the Bulgarian Jews."[9] The accompanying text pays tribute to politicians, the Orthodox Church, and ordinary citizens. It refers to the duty of remembering the victims of the Holocaust in Europe and in the occupied territories. In 2012, the European Parliament declared March 6 to be the "Day of the Righteous."

March 8, 2018. Šalom opens its commemorative program with a concert held at the National Academy of Music of Pančo Vladigerov, named after the Bulgarian Jewish composer born in 1899, deceased in 1978—which is attended by, among others, a delegation of Israeli Jews of Bulgarian descent. The musical performance follows the bestowal of a "Certificate of Non-Forgetting" to the president of the Bulgarian Doctors Union, Vencislav Grozev, in memory of the organization's denunciation of anti-Jewish legislation in the fall of 1940. The document was jointly issued by Šalom and the Union of Bulgarian Jews in Israel (*Yehud Olej Bulgaria*). An independent honors policy separate from those of the Bulgarian state and Yad Vashem is thus formulated and defines the actors deemed to have been pivotal in a righteous struggle.

---

9   https://bg.facebook.com/BulgarianArchives/ (accessed February 14, 2020; no longer active).

March 8, 2018, 6:00 p.m. "Rescue of the Bulgarian Jews" is the title given to an exhibition opening in the lobby of Sofia's municipal library. Engineer Georgi Măndev, an amateur historian with fierce patriotic convictions, and the secretary of a Bulgarian and Jewish Friends Club,[10] has contributed his own private archives. In attendance is Samuil Arditi,[11] the son of Benjamin Arditi, an Israeli politician and amateur historian who wrote on the fate of the Jews in Bulgarian-held territories. The king's contribution to the rescue lies at the heart of a ceremony filmed by the nationalist television channel Skat. The turnout, however, is sparse.

March 15, 2018. Bulgaria's Central State Archives inaugurates its own exhibition. Several weeks earlier, the director of the archives, historian Mihail Gruev, had given an interview to the popular newspaper *24 Hours* (*24 časa*), to launch a series of articles on "The Rescue of the Jews and the Bulgarian Righteous." There, Gruev notes that the exhibition will aim to document the trajectory of the lesser-known Righteous Among the Nations. Their descendants were invited to make themselves known through a press call. The final outcome, however, diverges from that which was proposed. Under a title that situates the persecutions at the forefront ("1943: Persecution and Defense: The Fate of the Bulgarian Jews"), the exhibit displays documentation that for the most part was already published in 2013.[12]

March 20–22, 2018. Bulgaria's President Radev makes an official visit to Israel on the occasion of the seventieth anniversary of the establishment of the State of Israel, as well as the seventy-fifth anniversary of the "rescue of the Bulgarian Jews." In Jerusalem, the president pauses for a moment of reflection before the eternal flame in memory of the victims of the Holocaust. He reminds those present of the exceptional status of the "rescue of the Bulgarian Jews." In so doing, he notes, "[we have] written the most glorious chapter not only in Bulgarian history but in the history of the world," recalling also the 11,343 Jews who were not saved "because, unfortunately, they were not Bulgarian citizens."[13] His visit coincides with the Sixth Global Forum for Combating Anti-Semitism.

---

10   See the engineer's Facebook page: https://www.facebook.com/mandevgeorgi.
11   The author of several brochures on Jewish fates during the war, Samuil Arditi was awarded a medal by the Bulgarian Foreign Ministry in 2010 for his contribution to the development of Bulgarian-Israeli relations.
12   Dăržavna Agencija Arhivi, *Truden izbor s goljamo značenie.*
13   Greer Fay Cashman, "Visiting Bulgarian President Says Proud of His Country's Holocaust Rescues," *Jerusalem Post*, March 20, 2018. The unveiling in Tel Aviv of a replica of the Sofia monument to the rescue had to be postponed due to the poor state of conservation of the monument, which was commissioned in 2013. Metodieva, "Gorčivijat vkus."

We have barely extended the spatial and temporal gamut, and already the narrative plot has thickened. Professional and lay historians, journalists, representatives from the State Archives and from the various libraries—all have joined the cohort of actors identified above. The State of Israel and references to the "rescue" in Bulgarian-Israeli relations have entered our field of view. Finally, the example of Stara Zagora suggests how commemorative practices are diffused on a regional scale: we ought also to mention the ceremonies held in the Danube port of Lom—from where the maritime convoys departed in March 1943, and where a commemorative plaque was placed in 2008; in Plovdiv—the city of Metropolitan Kiril, future patriarch of the Bulgarian Orthodox Church, who took on the cause of the Bulgarian Jews in wartime; and in several former centers of Jewish life such as Varna and Vidin, among others.

In Macedonia, the commemorative rituals also combine wreath-laying with reflection, exhibitions with "academic" publications, appeals for testimony, and entreaties to remember.

Skopje, Macedonia: March 12, 2018. The ceremonies open with a procession, the "March of the Living," which departs from the old clock tower of the Skopje train station—the time of which was forever frozen by the 1963 earthquake, and whose building now houses the Museum of Skopje—and culminates at the former Monopol Tobacco Company warehouse, which was converted into a transit camp during the war. The prime minister of Macedonia, Zoran Zaev, embraces his Bulgarian counterpart, Borisov, in a gesture repeatedly broadcast in the Macedonian news. Simultaneously, a second march takes place in Bitola, historically the seat of the largest Sephardic Jewish community in Macedonia. Both are placed under the banner of "Never Again" (*Da ne se povtori*).[14]

March 12, 2018. The Bulgarian and Macedonian heads of government convene at the Monopol site. The commemorative plaque, which had first been inaugurated in the 1980s, has had its inscription edited: the crime is now without an author. The Macedonian prime minister delivers a speech that looks to the future: "Today, we return to the lessons of the past in order to shine a stronger light onto the future path that we have chosen together."[15] At no point is Bulgaria mentioned by name.

March 12, 2018. In the evening, the new permanent exhibition of the Holocaust Memorial Center for the Jews of Macedonia is presented to a chosen audience of guests by American consultant Michael Berenbaum. Berenbaum was one of the key figures in the establishment of the USHMM,

---

14   Ljubčo Popovski, "Makedonskiot signal," *Deutsche Welle*, March 17, 2018.
15   "'Marš na živite' vo Skopje: Da učime od minatoto za da ne se povtori," *Deutsche Welle*, March 12, 2018.

where he served as director from 1993 to 1997, before assuming the role of executive director of the Survivors of the Shoah Visual History Foundation (today, the USC Shoah Foundation), founded by filmmaker Steven Spielberg. Although a public opening had initially been scheduled, delays in completing the final section of the exhibition—one devoted to memories of the war—caused the event to be postponed. The Bulgarian prime minister is not in attendance. The exhibition tells the story of the Sephardic Jews in Macedonia and the Balkans before, during, and after the Holocaust. Its account of anti-Jewish persecutions highlights the links between local history and the European dimensions of the destruction of the Jews.

The identities of the guests are familiar to us, as the same names circulate from one country to another; the distribution of key terms equally remains unchanged. Only the tone is modulated, shifting from a major key lauding the rescue into a minor tone of mourning. How could one not think here of the curve of political discourse (*la courbure de la parole politique*), in which French philosopher Bruno Latour (1947–2022) saw not a sign of duplicity, but the result(s) of adjusting to flexible circumstances?[16] Could there be moments, nonetheless, when these curves do begin to align?

As we near the conclusion of our journey through knowledge and representations of anti-Jewish persecutions occurring in the Bulgarian-controlled regions during World War II, we can contemplate how each chapter has acted as a stop along the path, investigating the construction of legal, fictional, and historical knowledge. In each chapter, we have encountered one and the same enigma: how and why, from the polyphonic representation of the past, did the nondeportation of Bulgaria's Jewish citizens become the main focus of narration, commemoration, and transmission in the Bulgarian public sphere—and even beyond it? At every turn, we have continuously stumbled upon the same juxtaposition: the overpublicized "rescue of the Bulgarian Jews" and the obscured realities of deportation working in tandem to obfuscate the retelling of the actual events. Through this practice, the fate of the Jews of Yugoslavia and Greece under Bulgarian occupation was relegated to the sidelines; so was any examination of the "old" regime's anti-Jewish policies.

In the ways in which the string of 2018 ceremonies have reconstituted the past, chosen participants, and propagated discourses of legitimation, these ceremonies provide, however, a more nuanced reading of the competing narratives. They also shed light on the tentative emergence of spaces of codified dissent. One might inquire whether the explanation for this emergence lies in the fact that, thus far in the story, we have traversed Communist countries where historical accounts were routinely subjected to public

---

16   Latour, "Si l'on parlait un peu politique?," 143–65.

intervention. With the socialist system in ruins, could the disputes over the Holocaust, while not being overcome, have been institutionalized?

To address these questions, let us turn to the public controversies that have garnered increasing attention in Bulgaria and other Balkan states, as well as in countries where Jews from Southeast Europe settled, since the demise of socialism. The notion of controversy is understood here as a catalyst for contention over interpretation and, therefore, can become an "instrument for exploration and learning."[17] New ideas are generated as opposing positions clash.

One question, in particular, serves as the chapter's cornerstone, one that involves reflecting on ruptures and wondering about the continuities through which discontinuities are crafted. In academic writings on Eastern Europe, two positions have been championed in turn. The first, in the 1990s, stemmed from a hope that the fall of communism might open the door to a writing of the past emancipated from ideological control. The second, more commonly found in recent scholarship, tends to identify a number of previously overlooked continuities behind the political rupture at the end of the Cold War. Correspondingly, interpretations of 1989 have evolved. In the wake of the collapse of the Berlin Wall, many accounts were informed by a teleological vision of the expected democratic outcome. In recent years, the increasing involvement of public authorities in the writing of history in countries such as Poland[18] and Hungary,[19] the passing of laws that circumscribed invocations of the Holocaust, and the resurgence in nationalist sentiments, have prompted a renewed cultural opposition between central Europe—said to have long harbored xenophobic temptations—and a supposedly flawlessly democratic "old Europe."[20] Beyond these exoticizing effects, such readings fail to restore the diversity of historical moments of the last three decades. Today, the sweeping notion of "postcommunism" can no longer provide us with a pass for not having a more finely textured periodization of the aftermath of the fall of the Iron Curtain.

The twin theses of tabula rasa and historical determinism additionally neglect how similitude can be constituted out of difference. The challenge is to identify the continuities that effect change, as well as the structuring (dis)continuities that give each configuration its unique features. Rather

---

17 Barthe, Callon, and Lascoumes, *Agir dans un monde incertain*, 64.

18 Behr, "Genèse et usages d'une politique publique de l'histoire," 21–48; Koposov, "Populism and Memory."

19 Gradvohl, "Orban et le souverainisme obsidional," 35–45.

20 Witness Philipp Dodd's introduction to a BBC *Arts and Ideas* program devoted to "Michael Ignatieff and Central Europe," February 13, 2018, https://www.bbc.co.uk/programmes/b09rm9qq.

than abiding by a linear conception of temporality, we will embrace Michel Serres's invitation to think about the simultaneous coexistence, at any given point in time, of social sectors whose rhythms, measures, and breaking points differ.[21] The historian's pace of time does not match the rhythm of commemorative initiatives or the temporality of political decisions. Unanticipated reconfigurations occur precisely as a result of the friction between these temporal tectonic plates.

Two case studies will illustrate this proposition with regard to the postsocialist knowledge and remembrance of the Holocaust and its periodization: the first is the instance of 1989–90, which will be approached via the internal debates within the Bulgarian Jewish community. The second is situated at the turn of the twenty-first century. We shall examine the reverberations of the past through Bulgaria's National Assembly and several other European parliamentary bodies. In both scenarios, the "hierarchy of merits" in the "rescue of the Bulgarian Jews" remains the key entry point through which new ways of considering historical facts are apprehended. Additionally, in the present chapter, the stress will be on the agency of the Jewish communities of the Balkans, Israel, and the United States as crucial actors in competing memory initiatives.

Bringing Back the Polyphony of the Past: (In)divisible Truths

With each new present a new past emerges: in Bulgaria, as with many other Eastern European countries, the fall of communism prompted a reassessment of decades of dictatorship, and by extension, a reevaluation of the orders from the precommunist era. Two questions supersede all others: First, had Bulgaria experienced fascism? And second, how should we interpret the coming to power of the predominantly Communist Fatherland Front on September 9, 1944—as a coup d'état backed by the Red Army or as the result of a popular uprising? No less poignant is the question of which voices are authorized to narrate Bulgaria's national history and, furthermore, to embody its historical continuity. In the immediate postwar period, the left-wing's power had claimed that it had embodied during World War II "another Bulgaria," one foreign to the "fascist government." After 1989, the introduction of political pluralism and the reopening of the borders made room for the voices of Bulgarian anti-communist émigrés, who, while living in exile during socialism, had sought to perpetuate an alternative reading of the communist historical canon abroad. Their return to Bulgaria raises novel

21 Serres, *Éclaircissements*, 89–92.

issues regarding the writing of history. A new restitution of the Jewish past emerges at the intersection of these political and spatial fault lines.

It is undoubtedly difficult, thirty-three years after the end of the "actually existing socialism," to resurrect the atmosphere of elation and anxiety that followed the November 10, 1989, overthrow of the person who had ruled Bulgaria for thirty-five years. In the latter half of the 1950s, Todor Zhivkov, a former printworker, had built his political career on the basis of an unwavering loyalty to the Soviet Union. Sustained rates of industrialization within a rural country, the advent of a consumer society with low levels of inequality, the adoption of bourgeois values among the socialist elites, and the skilled co-optation of the intelligentsia—these developments had spared the Zhivkov regime the political upheavals of Czechoslovakia (1968) and Poland (1980–81). Bulgaria seemed to age alongside its ruler. By the fall of 1989, the cascading collapse of the Eastern European regimes had saddled Bulgarian society with doubts: elsewhere, change was possible . . . but in Bulgaria?

Few anticipated the "Palace Revolution" that brought to power polyglot members of the former nomenklatura, provoking astonishment within the Jewish community as well. Following the closure of the Jewish Scientific Institute—whereby it was transformed into a section of the Historical Institute of the Bulgarian Academy of Sciences in October 1951—and the marginalization of the Jewish Consistory, it was the Social, Cultural, and Educational Organization of Jews in Bulgaria (*Obštestvena kulturno-prosvetna organizacija na evreite v Narodna Republika Bălgarija*, OKPOE), established in 1959, that had become the key actor for a Jewish community that was by then called upon ad nauseam to proclaim its loyalty to the Communist Party as well as its gratitude for the "rescue." Presided over since 1963 by Josif Hananel Astrukov (Herc), successor of the faithful Communist lawyer Isak Frances, whose alleged pro-Zionist orientation had earned him an abrupt dismissal, OKPOE slowly declined alongside the regime it served. One might scrutinize its annual reports to no end without finding any cultural initiatives likely to be suspected of undermining "national unity" (to use the terminology of the time). In early 1990, in a tone not devoid of sarcasm, Communist lawyer Vitali Tadžer summed up the rules that had governed the chronicle of Jewish life in OKPOE's periodical, *Evrejski Vesti*, for several decades:

> I used to read over the "old" EV [*Evrejski Vesti*] in a matter of minutes. It was incredibly monotonous and boring. In its content, style, and language, it reproduced its elder sibling *Rabotničesko delo* [The Worker's Cause, the organ of the Communist Party]. On the first page, it informed us of the decisions of party congresses, plenums, and other political or national events. . . . The second page was packed with manifestations of

anti-Semitism—but only in nonsocialist countries; information about the fascists that had been found and prosecuted—but only in nonsocialist countries; and then sinister, dark descriptions of Israel, too. The third page had a commemorative character and offered several columns. . . . I would carefully read the fourth page. That was the most "Jewish" one: it gave an account of the culture of the Jewish street.[22]

On January 13, 1990, OKPOE acquired interim leadership, led by the film director Edi Švarc, age fifty-two; two months later, at the close of a heated congress, it was rechristened Šalom, the Organization of the Jews in Bulgaria (*Organizacija na evreite v Bălgarija*). The status of the organization adopted on March 27 rejected any political subordination and promised to the regional subdivisions of Šalom the level of autonomy state socialism had deprived them of. In a spirit of synthesis—which reminds us that change owes more to the recombination of words and priorities than to their actual replacement with novel ideas—Šalom defined its mission as "fight[ing] against all forms and expressions of fascism, national chauvinism, and anti-Semitism," as well as "defend[ing] and strengthen[ing] Jewish ethnocultural traditions and values."[23] This formulation rests on an implicit critique leveled at the former leadership. They had failed to defend Jewish interests;[24] to denounce expressions of anti-Semitism in a society supposedly unable to tolerate any such manifestation on two counts—as Bulgarian *and* socialist; and to cultivate a commitment to Jewish historical and cultural heritage among the youth.[25]

Gradually, the silence over the repression suffered by Jews under socialism began to break. In mid-1989, this had already begun with the launch of a newspaper column entitled "The Truths That Return." Articles were published uncovering the Stalinist purges of Bulgarian Communists: the three thousand party activists who had fled Bulgarian "fascist" repression and settled in the USSR in the interwar period, six hundred of whom were said to have died there. Haim Juda Pizanti, a Communist Jew from Vidin, was among them.[26] After November 9, 1989, the memory of Communist

---

22   Vitali Tadžer, "Kakăv da băde 'Evrejski vestnik,'" *Evrejski Vesti*, August 14, 1990, 2.

23   "Deklaracija na Organizacijata na evreite v Bălgarija 'Šalom,'" *Evrejski Vesti*, March 27, 1990, 1.

24   Josif Belo, "Gorčivi razmisli," *Evrejski Vesti*, January 8, 1990, 2.

25   "Otkrit plenum na obštestvenata kulturno-prosvetna organizacija na evreite v Bălgarija," *Evrejski Vesti*, January 22, 1990, 2.

26   Penčo Kovačev, "Iz arhivite. Istinite se zavrăštat," *Evrejski Vesti*, October 23, 1989, 1–2. *Evrejski Vesti* refers to a list of 416 names published in *Rabotničesko delo* on September 11, 1989.

violence extended to include the anti-Semitic campaign orchestrated at the turn of the 1950s—a slavish, yet timid, imitation of Stalinism.[27] A trickier question was the line adopted by OKPOE during the forced assimilation campaign carried out against the Turkish minority in the 1980s. Between 1984 and 1989, the Communist Party authorities had forcibly changed the names of over 800,000 Turks to Bulgarian patronyms, while prohibiting expressions of Turkish linguistic, cultural, or religious identities. Those who opposed the so-called revival process—a supposed voluntary return of the Turks to their "true" Bulgarian identity—faced repression, including expulsion and imprisonment at the reactivated camp of Belene, where opponents to the Communist regime had been detained in the 1950s. Confronted with a wave of protests in the spring of 1989, the ruling elite decided to deport the protesters. It ended up organizing the largest population transfer that Europe had experienced since the end of World War II—the expulsion of around 340,000 Bulgarian Turks to Turkey.

In the midst of the massive displacement of Turks, OKPOE had issued a statement claiming that minority rights were fully respected in Bulgaria:

> The central leadership of OKPOE in the NRB [People's Republic of Bulgaria] expresses its full support for the statement made by Comrade Todor Zhivkov on May 29 on Bulgarian radio and television. We, the Bulgarian Jews, more than anyone else, can claim that genocide, racial prejudice, and persecution on account of religious beliefs have not existed and do not exist in our country. . . . OKPOE in the NRB considers that it is its civic and patriotic duty to express the most determined protest against the inventions of the Republic of Turkey regarding the persecution and the killings in our country. . . . The Bulgarian people are peaceful and tolerant, and have always sought peace in their homes as well as in our common European home.[28]

Soon after, *Evrejski Vesti* portrayed the forced population transfer as an indolent movement, "as if people had taken narcotics," disoriented by a Turkish mirage.[29] In December 1989, Wagenstein claimed his distance from this shameful episode;[30] *Evrejski Vesti* relayed his position.[31] In March

27   *Evrejski Vesti*, October 17, 1989, 2.
28   "Deklaracija," *Evrejski Vesti*, June 12, 1989, 1.
29   "Pătjat kăm bezrazsădstvoto," *Evrejski Vesti*, July 24, 1989, 1.
30   "If the expression of solidarity with the Jews in 1943 had been akin to our wholehearted and immoral compassion [toward the expelled Bulgarian Turks]," writes Wagenstein, "we would have turned into smoke in the chimneys of Auschwitz to the last one; today, we would be feeding the clouds of the endless blue meadows of Yehova, blessed be its name." Anžel Vagenštajn, "Evrejski hohmi," *Evrejski Vesti*, December 11, 1989, 2.
31   Samuel Franses, "'V poriva kăm demokracija,' and Remark on the Repeal of the Decisions Regarding the Assimilation," *Evrejski Vesti*, January 8, 1990, 2.

1990, when nationalist protesters opposed the restoration of Turkish rights decided upon by the Communist Party in late December 1989, Šalom professed a timid mea culpa: in a press release, the organization wished to "react strongly to perversions of the totalitarian regime with its administrative command system and mistaken policy on the national question, with its setbacks and errors arising from the forced and rapid assimilation of nationalities and religious minorities."[32]

Once a show of self-criticism had been accomplished, it was time to build a new future. But which position to take up on the partisan chessboard? In the late 1940s, the Jews who had remained in Bulgaria had made a double choice—identity-based and political. For four decades, a relationship of synonymy had been established between "adopting" a homeland *and* a political cause. How could they be "Jews of Bulgaria" in a state that had renounced socialism? How could Jewish and Bulgarian identities, cultural and religious affiliations be reconciled? What international prospects could exist for such a community, when its ties with Israel had suffered from the diplomatic fallout of the Six-Day War in 1967, and when its relations with major Western Jewish organizations had been frozen by the Cold War? As a debate on the reasons for and dynamics behind the massive Jewish emigration to Israel in 1948–49 took shape, fissures appeared within the community.[33] In the winter of 1989–90, the Bulgarian political sphere became polarized between the "reds" of the former Communist Party (BKP)—renamed the Bulgarian Socialist Party in February 1990 (*Bălgarska socialističeska partija*, BSP)—and the "blue" members of the new Union of Democratic Forces (*Săjuz na demokratičnite sili*, SDS), an anti-communist alliance that encompassed a broad spectrum from social democrats to right-wing nationalists.

The Šalom leadership adopted a reformist socialist line; the new editor of *Evrejski Vesti*, Eliezer Alfandari, repeated ad infinitum that "the newspaper is not 'blue,' but it is no longer 'red.'"[34] These divisions were extended during the first multiparty elections in June 1990, which, unlike the elections in Poland, Hungary, and Czechoslovakia, saw the former Communist Party win the majority of seats. On the benches of the newly elected assembly there were those faithful to the party (e.g., Wagenstein), former Communists who opted for the Union of Democratic Forces (e.g., musicologist Lea Koen), and representatives of a new generation with resolutely North American leanings (e.g., Solomon Passy and Ilko Eškenazi).

Against all odds, one of the points of contention crystallized around the legacy of the "rescue of the Bulgarian Jews." Those who distanced themselves

---

32 "Deklaracija na Organizacijata na evreite v Bălgarija 'Šalom,'" *Evrejski Vesti*, March 27, 1990, 1.
33 Emil Aladžem, "Dimitrov i preselvaneto," *Evrejski Vesti*, August 25, 1990, 3.
34 Eliezer Alfandari, *Evrejski Vesti*, August 25, 1990, 3.

from the BKP accused their former allies of having failed to confer sufficient international recognition to this historic achievement. Kalo, a longtime
member of the OKPOE Executive Committee, offered an eloquent reply:

> In his article "Joys and Disappointments," published in issue 24 of the
> journal *Evrejski Vesti*, the writer Viktor Baruh . . . contends that the orga-
> nization "lulled" the Jews "to sleep" for years, erecting a wall between
> them and democratic Jewish communities across the world that had none-
> theless remained interested in the lives of the Bulgarian Jews and in their
> rescue during World War II. According to the author, to this day many of
> them know nothing about this phenomenon. Even the Sofia Roundtable[35]
> bore witness to this, etc. . . . We are not trying to shy away from criticism,
> but how true is all of this?
>
> *For if there is one thing we have accomplished during these long years as mem-*
> *bers of the Executive Committee, it is mostly the propagation of the unique*
> *fact of the rescue of the Bulgarian Jews. Everywhere and by any means.*
> *Including on the occasion of Jewish congresses, conferences, celebrations.* . . .
> Not to mention the role of our "Almanac" whose English edition was dis-
> tributed worldwide. From Argentina and Japan, to Israel, Spain, and other
> Western countries, we received letters of commendation for the original
> insights we offered.
>
> Despite the imposed limitations, many foreign guests from Western coun-
> tries including the United States have visited the organization and have ex-
> amined with interest the exhibition on the rescue of the Bulgarian Jews.[36]

To those who might have doubted that the initiatives on the "rescue" of
Jewish institutions were closely coordinated with the Communist state, this
statement offers an unequivocal confirmation. There was one point, however, where all members of the Jewish community were on the same page:
attributing credit for the rescue to dictator Zhivkov would not stand up
to an examination of the facts. Beginning in 1990, the OKPOE Executive
Committee admitted as much in a tone reminiscent of the earlier demonstrations of self-criticism:

> Under intense pressure on us, and especially on certain members of the
> Executive Committee, by the chancellery of the former secretary-general
> and the leadership of the Institute of History of the BKP, we were forced
> to magnify the myth of Todor Zhivkov's participation in the protest of May
> 24, 1943. As illegal secretary of the illegal Third district committee of the
> BKP, he would not have been able to participate in a public demonstration.
> This same misrepresentation was imposed in the film "Ešelonite" and in

---

35   The November 1988 international conference.

36   Avram Kalo, "Taka li e?," *Evrejski Vesti*, January 8, 1990, 2 (emphasis added).

some literary writings. Unfortunately, with the help of our Almanac, this version (of the past) spread all around the world; and the [1988] Roundtable marked its acme. Under the directive of the Institute of History of the BKP, this interpretation was also imposed in the exhibition devoted to the rescue of the Bulgarian Jews. . . .

Now, the organization will take responsibility for disclosing to the Bulgarian people as well as the global community the truth [*istinata*] about the distortions of the historical truth [*pravda*].[37]

These debates threatened to shatter the socialist historical edifice, which rested on the pillars of the existence of fascism and resistance to it in wartime Bulgaria. Thereby, they ran the risk of simultaneously destroying the only figure of Jewish heroism allowed under socialism—that of the Jewish partisan.

When History Takes Center Stage

Under socialism, the writing of history was entrusted to institutions directly subordinated to the party (the most prominent being the Institute of History of the Communist Party, linked to the Central Committee[38]), integrated into the Bulgarian Academy of Sciences (the Historical Institute and the Institute for Balkan Studies[39]), or the University of Sofia (the faculty of Philosophy and History; after 1972, the faculty of History). In a country that only gained independence belatedly—in 1878 de facto and in 1908 de jure—the establishment of communism may have played a more pivotal role in fostering the development of history as a central discipline, with the objective of consolidating the new nation-state, more so than elsewhere in Central Europe. Following the regime change of September 9, 1944, an initial stage of repression[40] was succeeded by a notable rise in the number of historians, along with the institutionalization and professionalization of the historical discipline.[41] Throughout the years, the epicenter of historical scholarship shifted from the University of Sofia to the research institutes

---

37 "Doklad na Izpălnitelnija komitet," *Evrejski Vesti*, January 22, 1990, 1.

38 In Bulgarian: *Institut po istorija na BKP*. In 1969, the Institute of History of the Communist Party was integrated into the Academy for Social Sciences and Social Government (*Akademija za obštestveni nauki i socialno upravlenie*, AONSU), formerly the High Party School.

39 In Bulgarian, respectively: *Institut po istorija* and *Institut za balkanistika*.

40 Mutafčieva et al., *Sădăt nad istoricite*.

41 Including via the creation of journals: *Istoričeski pregled*, at the Institute of History of the Academy of Sciences, in 1945; the *Bulgarian Historical Review*,

of the Academy of Sciences; however, neither this evolution nor the social capital of historians affiliated with the Institute of History of the Communist Party subdued the prestige of the University of Sofia.

Questions concerning fascism and the antifascist struggle exerted a profound influence in establishing the legitimacy of history as a scientific discipline.[42] Marxist-Leninist principles and the adherence to a positivist epistemology, in part derived from academia prior to the Communist era, molded the contours of historiography across differing historical moments to varying extents. Until the close of the 1960s, a narrative of historical continuity was woven between the fateful year of 1923 (the assassination of Agrarian leader Stefan Stambolijski in June; a failed Communist uprising in September) and 1944 (the September 9 "revolution"). During these two decades, Bulgaria was said to have been continuously governed by fascist governments. With marked persistence, historical writing aimed to support this thesis of continuity, while also striving to identify the unique traits of Bulgarian fascism.

From the end of the 1960s onward, the historical continuum spanning 1923–44 was marred by intermittent disruptions: certain bourgeois governments had shed their "fascist" label following a careful evaluation of their stance toward the USSR and the Communists, as well as the choices made by their members in September 1944.[43] The catalogue of those deemed fascist withered, while the introduction of the notion of gradual or "creeping fascism" (*fašizacija*) enabled the discernment of several political junctures within the interwar period. During the 1970s, a new generation of historians aspiring to wrest the writing of history from the grips of the Soviet canon revisited the heroic motifs of a precommunist era. The struggles for social *and* national emancipation were juxtaposed, when not held to be synonymous.[44] Ascribing to this articulation, a profusion of academic publications emerged, in which the German presence in Bulgaria during World War II was no longer portrayed as an occupation.

Three months after Zhivkov's downfall, the debate regarding fascism had undergone a reframing, predominantly driven by commentators outside the realm of academia. Rather than scrutinizing the continuity of the 1923–44 timeline, or singling out its protagonists, the focus had shifted toward refuting the very existence of fascism in precommunist Bulgaria. These debates took place within the pages of daily newspapers (*Demokracija*, the organ of

---

available in English, French, German, and Russian, in 1973; and *Vekove*, in 1972. See Elenkov, "Science of History."

42   Koleva and Elenkov, "Did 'the Change' Happen?," 94–127.

43   Daskalov, *Ot Stambolov do Živkov*, 187–226.

44   Marinov, "Ancient Thrace," 3:10–117.

the Union of Democratic Forces; and *Duma*, the daily of the Socialist Party), as well as cultural weeklies (e.g., *Literaturen forum*, *Kultura*). These print materials soon reached the Jewish press. A musical composer by trade, Milčo Spasov initiated the offensive by penning an article in *Demokracija* provocatively entitled "Was There Fascism in Bulgaria?" The author professed an inability to identify in the pre-1944 era the three characteristics of fascism—a revolutionary party, radicalized youth organizations, and the state's obsessive interference in the economy and daily life.[45] Then, in January 1991, geophysicist Dimităr Zidarov raised the voice of the noncommunist left that had long been silent. With an article published in *Evrejski Vesti*, he drew attention to the responsibility of the Communists in the triumph of fascism in Europe, attributing this outcome to their relentless efforts to undermine the bourgeois order and their ominous silence in the face of the first Nazi atrocities.[46]

The article was published on the fiftieth anniversary of the enactment of the first Bulgarian anti-Jewish law (January 23, 1941). *Evrejski Vesti* placed it alongside a text by Leon Mitrani, a nuclear physicist, on anti-Jewish persecutions. At no prior moment had the acceleration of time appeared so dizzying: the era when depictions of the "rescue of the Bulgarian Jews" reduced the account of anti-Jewish policies to a mere footnote now receded into a distant past. The revised histories of the Jews in Bulgaria encompassed even the post-1878 construction of the nation-state, with expressions of anti-Semitism and the professional restrictions imposed upon Jews embedded in state-building processes now taking a prominent place:

> When we speak of the Bulgarian Jews' rescue from the gas chambers, one should not forget that during World War II, here, Jews were the subject of cruel and inhumane persecution; that there were expressions of gross anti-Semitism; that the tide was turning toward the establishment of the most barbaric Nazi-style fascism; and that only the reversal of the course of the war, and a few other factors, interrupted this process.
>
> Germs of anti-Semitism had been with us for a long time; they were already present at the time of liberation from the Turkish yoke. They were mainly manifest in cities wherein Bulgaria Jews were concentrated. Most of the population lived in rural areas, and anti-Semitism was absent there. Thus, it is possible to claim that anti-Semitism in this country, unlike in Poland, for example, was not a national phenomenon [*obštonacionalen*], but rather was evident only in specific, limited urban circles. Nonetheless,

---

45 Milčo Spasov, "Imalo li e fašizăm v Bălgarija?," *Demokracija*, February 28, 1990, 2.

46 Dimităr Zidarov, "I fašizăm, i bolševizăm—rožba na krizi," *Evrejski Vesti*, January 21, 1991, 2.

there were limitations that, albeit not established by law, were respected, and considered natural. For instance, Jews did not have access to state administrative or executive positions. They could not own land or work in agriculture. Their access to army leadership posts was also limited, although during the wars the Jews lost many victims, a number of whom stood out in their bravery. Though there was no explicit ban, Jews could not teach in Bulgarian schools; they were not allowed in the courts except as lawyers. It was impossible to imagine a Jewish policeman, and truly inconceivable that a Jew should be mayor or prefect of a district. All this was considered perfectly normal, and the Jews themselves did not express a wish to change the order of things.[47]

Likewise, Mitrani's depiction of the adoption of anti-Jewish legislation during World War II deviated sharply from the socialist narrative. Instead of focusing his account on those public figures and professional corporations that opposed the adoption of a discriminatory text in the fall of 1940—as was customary in socialist writings—the author recalled that this piece of legislation was discussed publicly, and that it held a certain level of popular support:

> It would be simplest to explain things away with the pressures of Hitler's Germany, to insist that no one here wanted to harm the Jews, that "such were the times." However, we should not forget that the Law for the Defense of the Nation was not simply adopted by the rulers in haste, as a decree (as would later be the case), but that it was passed by the acting parliament after heated debate and in full public view. The newspapers reported on all the phases of the process, and publicists from every political leaning (parties were banned) spoke out in favor or against the law. Many people supported the need to adopt measures against the Jews and to limit their "destructive activity." Others were occupied with the purity of the Bulgarian nation and found it necessary to stave off the possible infiltration of impure Bulgarian Jewish blood into the Bulgarian race. Alongside those who shouted "Death to the Jews" and "Jews, Get Out of Bulgaria," other more "moderate" voices were also heard, those who wanted "only" to limit "Jewish influence."[48]

The volte-face was no less spectacular in the treatment of the inevitable theme of the "rescue of the Bulgarian Jews." Here the author expanded the spectrum of the defenders and weighed their role in relation to German military setbacks:

---

47 Leon Mitrani, "Izvestija za naroda a ne za partija (nejuridičeska studija)," *Evrejski Vesti*, January 9, 1991, 2.
48 Ibid.

Amid this complex situation, the rescue of the Bulgarian Jews was the result of many factors, and it is difficult to identify just one that can be described as decisive or essential. Perhaps, the traditional tolerance of the Bulgarian people, despite isolated expressions of anti-Semitism, played a decisive role. Sympathizers of the banned parties—Communists, social democrats, radicals, democrats, and others—also contributed to the rescue of the Jews. The Church and the artistic unions played a very important role; and, in all likelihood, the king also made a significant contribution. *Obviously, if not for the heavy losses suffered by the Germans on the front, there would have been no question of saving the Jews in Bulgaria.*[49]

Mitrani concluded with a stunning explanation of the potential monetization of the diplomatic advantages of the "rescue":

In any case, this rescue, unique among the countries occupied by or allied to Germany, is an immense source of capital for our country—one that until now our incompetent leaders have not taken advantage of. Instead of broadly, consistently, and unendingly promoting the Bulgarian people as saviors of the Jews, our pitiful politicians have tried to pose as saviors themselves and to draw personal and partisan benefits from doing so. . . . It is hardly possible to imagine the potential aid, investments, and credit from the most developed countries that we lost in trying to make Todor Zhivkov the savior of the Jews. *Hopefully the current and future leaders of our country understand what a good investment the Bulgarian people made almost half a century ago in saving tens of thousands of Jews.*[50]

At least, the argument is clear as day. Yet, how to interpret such an astonishing rediscovery of anti-Jewish crimes? The answer is disconcertingly simple: were the thesis of a Bulgaria without fascism to be proven, the antifascist past would lose its future—and with it, erase the only Jewish presence in the Communist narrative: that of the partisans. Zidarov was well aware of these stakes, as he underlined the aporias of socialist discourse: "With us there were antifascists, a resistance, and resistance heroes; therefore fascism existed!"[51] In the public discourse about history, the contribution of the partisan movement to the "rescue of the Jews of Bulgaria" and, more broadly, to the outcome of the war quickly crumbled; the noncommunist component of the resistance units resurfaced; the interdependence of the partisans with the Soviet Union was underlined; the 1923–44 periodization was replaced with a logical and chronological congruence between the Communist resistance and the postwar establishment of a dictatorship. Soon, academic research would question the tactical choices made by the

---

49   Ibid. (emphasis added).
50   Ibid. (emphasis added).
51   Zidarov, "I fašizăm, i bolševizăm," 2.

partisans during the war: prioritizing sabotage of the Bulgarian economic infrastructure (with the idea that it served the German war economy), they argued, mainly weakened the nation's production apparatus and led to deteriorating local living conditions.[52]

With the erosion of the legacy of the partisan movement, it became crucial for the Left to recall the cruelty of anti-communist repression *and* anti-Jewish violence. In 1993, *Duma* took up the topic of the persecution of Jews.[53] Meanwhile, the rehabilitation of the precommunist era by right-leaning intellectuals turned into idealization of the interwar period as an era adorned with the charms of civility, prosperity, and European democracy. The responsibility for the "rescue of the Jews" was now to be attributed to the bourgeois elite, whose decapitation by the justice of the People's Courts in 1945, seen in this light, seemed even more of a disgrace.[54] The return of exiles who had fled Bulgaria after September 9, 1944, contributed decisively to this reshuffling of historical virtues. In this myriad of novel historical accounts, the ties that bound the story of the Holocaust and the making of the nation were not undone. They were refastened otherwise.

Renegotiating the Territorial Span of Bulgaria's Historical Narrative

The act of fine-tuning the narrative around anti-Jewish policies to further elevate national accomplishments was not unprecedented; the practice was reconfigured, nonetheless, with a distinct set of conditions. The establishment of socialism had convinced many elite officials to go into exile, among them Crown Prince Simeon Saxe-Coburg-Gotha, who fled to Spain with his mother, Queen Giovanna, and her sister Marija Luiza; as well as members of the diplomatic corps who, prudently, chose not to return to Bulgaria after the war. Beginning in the latter half of the 1940s, Bulgarian émigrés who had settled in Europe, the United States, and Latin America attempted to forge a resistance against the Communist regime, by utilizing the personal connections established prior to the war, the bonds of which were reinforced not only by political affinities and common social and professional paths, but also by the shared experience of exile.[55] The opening of the studios of Radio

---

52   Koleva and Elenkov, "Did 'the Change' Happen?," 115–21.

53   Deyanova, *Očertanija na mălčanieto*, 152–69.

54   Benatov, "Debating the Fate," 108–30.

55   Groueff, *My Odyssey*. Son of Pavel Gruev, personal secretary and chief of cabinet to King Boris and a childhood friend of Christo Boyadjieff, Stephane Groueff worked briefly at the French weekly *Paris Match* alongside former

Free Europe (RFE) in Munich in 1951 served as a rallying point. However, the ideological divisions from the precommunist era were not dissolved by the shared experience of exile. Bulgarian émigrés in the United States, for instance, were divided among the Bulgarian National Committee "Free and Democratic Bulgaria," led by former Agrarian leader G. M. Dimitrov; an American branch of the conservative "Foyer bulgare," established in Paris at the end of the 1940s; and a staunchly nationalist "National Front."[56] As hopes of rapidly overthrowing the dictatorship faded, efforts refocused on promoting an alternative to the historical consciousness championed by the Communist regime.

In the 1960s, Christo Boyadjieff launched an English-language journal, the *Bulgarian Review*, that toed a similar political line to that of the "Foyer bulgare" in Paris. Boyadjieff, who once served as the wartime secretary of the Bulgarian legation in Bucharest, made a new chapter in his life as the representative of a Scandinavian paper-import company in Rio de Janeiro. While he enjoyed the support of other diplomats-turned-journalists in Paris and Washington,[57] East-West détente and the routinization of Communist orders limited the impact of their endeavors until the accession of Gorbachev to power in the USSR in 1985. It was at that point that the "Foyer bulgare" adopted the name "The Free Bulgarians" and resolved to underwrite two book-length studies. In the first, Boyadjieff would counter the perceived Communist offensive on the "Jewish question" by dedicating a volume to his own interpretation of the "rescue of the Bulgarian Jews," to be financed by a sponsor;[58] in the second, the journalist Stephane Groueff, son of the former head of the king's cabinet, would compose a testimonial-style biography devoted to Boris III.[59] Published in May 1987 under the title *Crown of Thorns*, the latter had a notable launch, with Saxe-Coburg-Gotha. The Bulgarian branch of RFE/Radio Liberty then devoted to it fifty episodes; its recital even managed to traverse the Berlin Wall.[60] In light of this success, on September 10, 1989, the confidence of Free Bulgarians in the political efficacy of publishing historical works had been reinstated:[61] the

---

Bulgarian diplomat Evgeni Siljanov. He then moved to the United States, where he pursued a successful career in journalism.

56   *Drugata Bălgarija.*
57   For example, the ex-diplomat Evgeni Siljanov, a journalist at *Paris Match* and cofounder of the Bulgarian branch of RFE in Munich, and John Dimitri Panitza, a journalist at *Reader's Digest*. See Nedeva, *Misija Pariž.*
58   Groueff, *My Odyssey*, 644–60.
59   Groueff, *Crown of Thorns.*
60   Ibid., 642–43.
61   *Drugata Bălgarija*, 266–67. The resolution of September 10, 1989, was also meant to fight against "Bulgarian national nihilism," thus

release of Boyadjieff's opus *Saving the Bulgarian Jews in World War II* followed several months later.[62]

To these men and to their books, Zhivkov's fall gave a new lease on life. Their ambition was to regain a place, commensurate with their former standing, within Bulgarian society *and* within the historical narrative, from which they believe themselves to have been unjustly written out. Cognizant of the prestige typically bestowed upon external observers in a long-isolated country, those once exiled composed a melody that proves captivating: under their pen, the interwar period becomes ever more illustrious, and the lauded figure of the king comes to symbolize an auspicious era when Bulgaria was said to have held its own place in the concert of European nations.

In September 1990, Boyadjieff was in Sofia. The Sofia University Press was considering publishing his tome on the "rescue" in Bulgarian. He gave an interview to the press, which is reprinted in *Evrejski Vesti*:

– Mr. Boyadjieff, what prompted you to study the colossal mass of documents related to the "Bulgarian Jewish question" and to write this book?

– Two motivations guided me. The first was the magnitude of the event. Can you imagine: in all the civilized world, only little Bulgaria managed to save all its Jewish brothers from Hitler? I juxtaposed this Bulgarian expression of humanity with another event that also perpetuated the name of the Bulgarian community (*pleme*): the spread of Christianity and the culture of Old Bulgaria throughout Eastern Europe, including also in Russia. . . . And the rescue of the Bulgarian Jews during World War II must be connected to and placed alongside these spiritual expressions. . . . The rescue of the Bulgarian Jews is recognized worldwide as a major act of humanity, which neither aimed at, nor counted on any extrinsic reward.

My second motivation was to respond polemically to the claims of a party that has incapacitated all cultural and state institutions—the claims that it was precisely this party that played the decisive role in the rescue of the Bulgarian Jews. I wanted to refute all the propagandistic nontruths that historians had written under orders, especially the thesis according to which Todor Zhivkov had organized the May [1943] action, and taken part in it. In my book, everything is based on historical documents.

- Do you think that the rescue of the Bulgarian Jews represents a contribution to democracy?

---

reprising—unwittingly?—a formula used by the Communist Party authorities since the early 1970s. There was no mention of the forced exodus of 340,000 Turks of Bulgaria in the spring and summer of 1989 and no more than a cryptic allusion to Turkey.

62 Boyadjieff, *Saving the Bulgarian Jews.*

– Of course. I want to stress in particular the role of the people. Tsar Boris III needed the support of the parties and of the Bulgarian Orthodox Church. But this is really the whole epic of the Bulgarian people, an epic that differs radically from the permanent wars, revolutions, and political struggles [depicted in Communist historiography].

– *Have the Bulgarian Jews themselves contributed to illuminate the questions relating to their rescue?*

– Without a doubt. First Benjamin Arditi. His book *The Role of Tsar Boris III in Saving the Bulgarian Jews*, albeit short, is a classic study. In 1968, I met some influential Bulgarian Jews in Israel, including Arditi. I told him, "We are grateful to you for defending the compromised name of Tsar Boris." To which he replied, "I have written a book in defense of the truth, not of Tsar Boris."

– *What remains to be done to reveal the whole truth?*

– All the archives must be released to historians: those of General Lukov, St. Mošanov,[63] B. Filov. It will be necessary to examine the archives of the Commissariat for Jewish Affairs, but also those of the Church, as well as many private archives in Bulgaria and Israel.

– *Had you hoped that one day your book would be published in Bulgarian?*

– The invitation from the University Press Sv. Kliment Ohridski was a pleasant surprise for me. I have always wanted for my book to be published in Bulgarian, and so I immediately translated it into Bulgarian and sent it to the publishing house. I think that its release will help to clarify facts that have been presented in a distorted way by your historians.

(*Sofijsko utro*, no. 15/1990, interview by Albert Benbasat)[64]

The mention of General Lukov in a discussion of the "rescue of the Bulgarian Jews" may come as a surprise. As minister of war (1935–38), Lukov had worked toward Bulgaria's military rapprochement with Nazi Germany. In 1942, he took on the leadership of the Union of Bulgarian National Legions (*Sǎjuz na bǎlgarskite nacionalni Legioni*),[65] an anti-Semitic and pro-Nazi organization. In February 1943, the general was killed by two members of the resistance, in all likelihood much to the relief of

---

63 Nephew of the Democratic Party leader Nikola Mušanov, Stojčo Mošanov was a conservative and Anglophile political figure who rallied the legal opposition to the Bulgarian governments during World War II. After September 9, 1944, he fell victim to the Communist repression and spent long years in prison.

64 "Epopeja na bǎlgarskija narod," *Evrejski Vesti*, October 23, 1990, 3 (italics added).

65 Poppetrov, *Socialno naljavo*, 379–482.

King Boris III, who suspected him of entertaining too-close relations with Minister Plenipotentiary Beckerle and feared that he might hold political ambitions.[66]

With a creation of a new roster of "saviors," the prime objective of the former exilés was to produce a counterhistory—one that would subvert the Communist master narrative with a portrayal of Orthodox and conservative heroism. In this endeavor, the rehabilitation of the king was essential. On April 10, 1990, Groueff gave an interview to the magazines *Kultura* and *Septemvri*, which appeared in September and was excerpted in *Evrejski Vesti*. The title of the article—"Tsar Boris, Who Said 'No' to Hitler"—is suggestive:

> – *I would like us to turn to the Bulgarian Jews, because it is often said that the tsar saved the Bulgarian Jews, whereas there was a time in Sofia when some claimed that it was not him, but the Communists who had saved the Jews. Could you shed some light on this question?*

> – Yes, I took care to be fully objective in this research, and I came to the conclusion (to me, an indisputable one) that the Bulgarian people are not racist. As Bulgarians, we at least have this virtue: we have always regarded all minorities, whether Armenian or Jewish, as our compatriots. . . . That is precisely what enabled the rescue, and I would not ascribe such an immense contribution to one man—the Tsar. He did not act alone. It was the Bulgarian people who really saved them. Starting with those very courageous members of parliament—a little over forty people, beginning with Deputy Speaker Pešev—to the Bulgarian writers who signed official petitions and [letters of] protest. At the time, this was a risk. The Holy Synod—another major factor—and all the opposition groups, including, obviously, the Communists, were against it, but Aleksandăr Cankov—extreme right, a staunch pro-German, and a man of great courage—he too signed it in protest. However, I must underline one fact: beyond the sympathies and antipathies of the people as a whole, there was all the same a single man who, in those years, could say "yes" or "no." . . . This man was Tsar Boris. And it turned out that he said "no"—a very difficult choice. The archives bear witness to this. There are documents from the German Embassy in Sofia; there are intelligence reports. On this issue, a great patriot abroad, Hristo Bojadžiev, a former diplomat, has just published a book on the rescue of the Bulgarian Jews.[67] In the book (which I hope will soon be available in Bulgaria), Bojadžiev provides facsimiles of German and Bulgarian documents where we see that *the Bulgarian people as a whole—from the extreme*

---

66   Miller, *Bulgaria during the War*, 72–74.
67   Boyadjieff, *Saving the Bulgarian Jews*.

right to the far left—were in opposition, and the decision was ultimately made by Tsar Boris, who said "no" to Hitler.[68]

Three aspects of the argument are worth noting. First, Groueff emphatically claims a Bulgarian "we," the ownership over which was at the time the subject of much debate; second, the category of the "Bulgarian people" is here reimagined in sharp contrast to the socialist "progressive masses"; and finally, all political factions are now being showered with praise—including even the "extreme right."

What does this examination of the early stages of postcommunism suggest? Within a mere matter of months, the questions fervently debated within the Jewish community assumed a central place in the Bulgarian public sphere. This was primarily due to their alignment with the political and historical issues that transcend them. The framing of these discussions of the Jewish past was not entirely novel, hinting at the filtration into the post-1989 period of dynamics from prior to the collapse of communism. At the same time, the leaders of the Bulgarian Jewish community were divided on the extent to which they could relinquish aspects of the Communist political legacy without undermining the Bulgarian Jewish identity, the construction of which had been so intimately tied to the fulfillment of the Communist project. At the intersection of these processes, the past was rewritten as palimpsest: borrowing from communism the "rescue of the Bulgarian Jews" framing, and from the anti-communist discourse a novel distribution of heroic roles. King Boris succeeded Zhivkov as the embodiment of the "virtuous Bulgarian people."[69] As for the (individual and sector-specific) efforts that ensured the preservation of Jewish lives—these continued to be credited to collective entities.

The second moment of our investigation takes place in a significantly updated political scene: on the threshold of the millennium, the cleavage between "reds" and "blues" acquired an exceptional intensity, prefiguring its obsolescence. At times, the line separating professional and lay historiography has became obscure. While still vivid, the debates relating to the king's role in the "rescue" paved the way for a broader reevaluation of all the parliamentary, intellectual, and religious elites once repressed under communism. As Katherine Verdery has shown, postcommunism has set dead bodies in motion, resurrecting bygone statues of the past and turning the tributes to former "heroes" into on the loci of political competition.[70] One figure in

---

68   ". . . Car Boris, kojto kaza 'ne' na Hitler," *Evrejski Vesti*, October 9, 1990, 3 (emphasis added).
69   Nojkov and Radev, *Tsar Boris III*.
70   Verdery, *Political Lives*.

particular embodied the reordering of honored figures: D. Pešev, the former deputy speaker of the National Assembly (1940–43), advocate of a technocratic government seduced by Hitler's "new order" (*Neuordnung*), who took up the cause of the Jews of Bulgaria in March 1943. The newfound visibility that was conferred on his actions, emerging on the Bulgarian, Italian, Israeli, and European stages, constitutes a prime vantage point for observing political conflicts, as well as an apt mechanism for revising historical representations. Finally, the onset of Bulgaria's accession talks to the European Union (EU), effective on March 28, 2000, on the one hand, and the renewed involvement of Balkan-origin Jews in writing and remembering the history of World War II, on the other, together contributed to the exacerbation of debates surrounding the past. In dialogue with both the movement on account of which the Holocaust itself became a cornerstone of Israeli identity[71] and representatives of the "second" and "third" generations embarking on a search for roots,[72] numerous descendants of Bulgarian and Macedonian Jews who had settled in the United States and Israel, returned to Southeast Europe, bringing expectations, as well as questions, with them.

Words and Walls of Conflict in Balkan Jewish Communities

In many ways, the Balkan configuration can be situated within a global phenomenon in which the words of survivors and their descendants were gradually invested with a unique experiential and historical quality. In Bulgaria, testimonies began to be solicited prior to the end of communism: in the second half of the 1980s, a section of the OKPOE Almanac was devoted to Jewish autobiographical narratives. However, at the time, these efforts to remember were intended to serve the regime; the authorities had insisted that those Jews who had stayed in Bulgaria adhere unequivocally to publicly sanctioned interpretations of the war. References to suffering at the hands of the fascists found a counterpart in praise for the antifascist struggle and solidarity between Jews and non-Jews. The lifting of censorship in the 1990s injected the decade with an intoxicating fervor for speech, and the telling of life stories—big and small—now made possible.[73] Self-published memoirs flooded the market, while professional and lay historians, political

---

71 Yael Zerubavel, *Recovered Roots*.

72 Jurgenson and Prstojevic, *Des témoins aux héritiers*.

73 Mutafčieva, *Istorija naselena s hora*; Koleva, *Bălgarija – Izrael*.

figures, and ordinary citizens all threw themselves into the "battlefield" of the past.[74] The new times liberated memories and subsequently reshaped them.

Contributing to these transformations were the vast initiatives for collecting testimonies that had originated in the United States and now extended to Eastern Europe:[75] the Fortunoff Video Archive for Holocaust Testimonies; the USHMM "oral history" project; and the Shoah Visual History Foundation, brainchild of director Steven Spielberg, all reached Bulgaria. Some 757 Bulgarian Jews took part in the Spielberg project, laying bare gestures of solidarity, as well as intimate wounds, before the camera. Appeals to memory and collections of witness accounts adhered to formal configurations different from those that prevailed during the socialist era. Strikingly, the recordings expose a diversity of social divisions (between bourgeois elites, the worlds of artisans and small shopkeepers, working-class milieus) and political ones (bourgeois parties, right- and left-wing Zionists, social democrats, Communists) that Communist discourse had coerced into a binary: Jewish "Zionists" who had settled in Israel versus "progressive" Jews who had remained in Bulgaria.[76] Above all, for the participants in these projects, recording of oral history induced a temporal contraction, as if the sharing of war memories and the emotional intensity now attributed to experiences that had long been sidelined, if not silenced, worked to minimize the decades spent under communism. The past was more present than ever. The very fact that the interviewees were given a videotape on which their voices were etched further magnified the symbolic value accorded to the individual memories they had shared with their interviewers.[77]

Tensions between familial networks of transmission, attachment to the land of origin, and community building on a national and political level were just as evident among Jewish emigrants in Israel and the United States. The opening of the Communist bloc stimulated memory tourism; in turn, the search for family roots, longings for lost identities, and pilgrimages of cultural significance became intertwined. Personal journeys to the Balkans undertaken after 1989 were often prompted by family bereavements, the occasional discovery of fragmented archives, or the opening of legal proceedings for the restitution of property nationalized by the Communist states. During these sojourns, the presence of descendants confronted the

74 Traverso, *L'Histoire comme champ de bataille.*
75 Byford, "Remembering Jasenovac," 58–84.
76 USC Shoah Foundation, The Institute for Visual History and Education, http://sfi.usc.edu/; Byford, "Remembering Jasenovac," 78.
77 The author wishes to thank Emil Benbassat for sharing his recollections of participating in the Spielberg project.

sparseness, if not the absence, of traces of the defunct world. Such travels were integral, implicitly, to the movement that established the memory of the Holocaust as one of the central components of Jewish and Israeli identities. Beginning in the 1960s, the State of Israel had, for instance, started to organize visits by Israeli youth to the former death camps in Poland, revisiting the markers of collective suffering in order to reinforce attachments to the Israeli state.[78] Those who undertook these trips often bore hopes of bridging genealogical gaps. Ultimately, memories were shaped at the intersection of local identity dynamics and the changing expressions of a contemporary "long distance nationalism."[79]

This post-1989 rediscovery of the lands of origin afforded unprecedented visibility to the painful contrast between the fates of those Jewish citizens of Bulgaria who survived and descendants from the Kingdoms of Yugoslavia and Greece, where almost all families had been exterminated. A reanchoring into these contrasting pasts resulted, in turn, in harshly divided memorial initiatives.

From this point of view, the so-called Bulgarian forest affair is a particularly noteworthy case. In 1993, descendants of Bulgarian Jews living in Los Angeles launched a "project to commemorate the rescue" through the inauguration of a "Bulgarian forest," to be planted not far from Jerusalem. King Boris was among the historical figures to whom they wished to pay homage. The initiative sparked a countermovement by families of Jews stemming from Vardar Macedonia and Aegean Thrace, in particular through the Association of the First Generation of Macedonian Immigrants in Israel (*Dor hemshech shel joztej Makedonia beIsrael*), then led by the former diplomat Nissim Yosha, whose family was from Bitola and had settled in Israel in 1933.[80] A flurry of protests followed, from Israel, Macedonia, the United States, Italy, and Bulgaria, led by politicians, journalists, public intellectuals, and Holocaust survivors and their descendants. The mounting waves of controversy dictated the rhythm with which essays with broad public reach were published: one was authored by the Bulgarian-born Israeli politician and essayist Michael Bar-Zohar, who, in 1998, rendered in expressive terms the entangled array of actions that had allowed the Bulgarian Jews to escape extermination—all while highlighting the contributions of

78   Feldman, "Marking the Boundaries," 84–114.
79   Glick Schiller and Fouron, *Georges Woke Up Laughing*.
80   Nissim Yosha denounces this as "Holocaust denial" and characterized King Boris as a "war criminal." Association of Jews from Macedonia in Israel and Nissim Yosha, "The Active Role of Bulgaria in the Holocaust against the Thrace and Macedonian Jews," *Rehovot*, August 7, 2001.

the king and of Liljana Panica, personal secretary of Belev, the commissioner on Jewish Affairs.[81]

In 1996, an initial compromise had seemingly been found, with the joint inauguration of three monuments: the first to commemorate King Boris and Queen Giovanna; the second, Metropolitan Stefan and National Assembly Deputy Speaker Pešev; and the third, the deportation of the Jews from the occupied territories. The decision nonetheless failed to halt the tide of litigation. As the state organ in charge of commemorating the genocide of the Jews in Israel, the Yad Vashem Institute formed an ad hoc commission to be led by Supreme Court Justice Moshe Bejski, a Holocaust survivor himself.[82] After a number of hearings with groups of survivors, historians, and memorial institutions, the commission proposed, in July 2000, replacing this trifecta with one sole monument commemorating the victims of the extermination *and* those responsible for the "rescue of the Bulgarian Jews." In Bulgaria, the decision generated virulent responses, all the more so in the lead-up to the 2001 parliamentary and presidential elections.

In the pages that follow, we will address this controversy and illuminate its stakes via the parliamentary debate of July 27, 2000, a defining moment in the composition of the Bulgarian political chessboard, with the Holocaust as proxy. At stake is a motion of censure, laid down by conservatives against the National Assembly chairperson Blagovest Sendov (a left-wing politician), who had taken a stance in the affair of the "Bulgarian forest." The legislative space is especially enlightening, insofar as it was established as a pillar of "democratic consolidation" in the 1990s; it also provides an insight into the beginning of Bulgaria's integration into the EU. Stepping away from the challenges facing the Bulgarian parliament, we will address the role of the National Assembly and the European Parliament in the shaping of public discourse and historiographical reflections on the past. This, in turn, will allow us to examine how and in what manner the circulation of a new iteration of the "rescue" narrative came to pass.

The "Blagovest Sendov" Affair: A Bulgarian Forest in the (Domestic) Political Arena

In July 2000, the Bejski Commission's announcement that the three monuments would be removed from the "Bulgarian forest" stirred the Bulgarian parliament—about to break for vacation—out of its summertime stupor. The revelation that several Bulgarian public figures had written Israeli head

---

81   Bar-Zohar, *Beyond Hitler's Grasp*.
82   Ofer, "Tormented Memories," 137–56.

of state Ezer Weizman a letter expressing support for the position of the descendants of Macedonian and Greek Jews who had objected to Boris III being credited with the "rescue of the Bulgarian Jews" and cleared of responsibility for the raids in the occupied territories set off a remarkable chain of events. The initiative stemmed from Nir Baruh, a former Israeli diplomat born in the Bulgarian city of Kjustendil, author of a critical study of the actions of the monarch and a member of the Bejski Commission.[83] The initiative had then been furthered in Bulgaria by scriptwriter Angel Wagenstein. Signatories included socialist historian Ilčo Dimitrov, who had delivered a speech on the rescue at the international conference in Sofia in November 1988; several members of Šalom; as well as Speaker of the National Assembly Sendov.[84] The latter, a mathematician by profession who held the positions of vice chair of the Bulgarian Academy of Sciences and rector of Sofia University, was an experienced politician; despite not being a member of the Communist Party, he was an MP during the socialist era and proceeded to become vice president of the Council of Ministers for Spiritual Development. Acting as chairman and deputy speaker of the Socialist-majority National Assembly between 1995 and 1997, he maintained his position even with the coming to power of an anti-communist majority in April 1997. In July 2000, deputies of the ruling anti-communist coalition, United Democratic Forces (*Obedineni demokratični sili*, ODS), passed a motion calling for Sendov's resignation on the grounds of misusing the authority of a Bulgarian institution, which he had used to cast a personal judgment on history and memory policies, without an official mandate. In doing so, the motion alleged that he had brought the country's standing into disrepute on the international stage and threatened Bulgaria's integration process into the EU and NATO.

The scandalized reaction to Sendov's public remarks must be taken in its proper context: governed by a young socialist prime minister, Žan Videnov—a dogmatic economist devoid of government experience—between January 1995 and February 1997, Bulgaria was in the throes of a dire financial and social crisis, witnessing predatory incursions on public

---

83   Baruh, *Otkupăt na Car Boris.*

84   "Blagovest Sendov: Zašto da ima ploča na car Boris III, s kojato da se gavrjat neprekăsnato?," *Sega*, July 19, 2000. In an interview, Sendov had noted, "The dispute concerns the question of knowing whether this can be attributed to Tsar Boris III or not. Insofar as two groups of Bulgarian Jews are present— some, wealthier, who emigrated from Bulgaria before the start of the repressions, and others who remained here and fell under the Law of Defense of the State [*sic*], which was far from light for those Jews who remained here. And yet this law was signed by Boris III."

assets that mutated into hyperinflation by the end of winter 1997.[85] After five weeks of sustained public protests, the executive branch was finally compelled to set a date for elections: April 17, 1997. The "blue coalition" of the ODS emerged victorious and subsequently negotiated a stabilization agreement with the International Monetary Fund, restarted the privatization process, and addressed Bulgaria's delayed progress toward its EU accession. The strategy proved a success: having been excluded from the "first wave" at the Luxembourg European Council (December 12–13, 1997), Bulgaria was invited to initiate discussions on EU membership at the Helsinki Summit (December 10–11, 1999). Given the unpopularity of the reforms and owing to accusations of corruption within ruling circles, the majority nonetheless remained divided. As the legislative (June 2001) and presidential (November 2001) elections approached, the priority objective was to revive the militant supporter networks, which provided fertile ground for a new round of condemnation of the "crimes of communism."

From 1999 onward, the government of the economist Ivan Kostov saw to a proliferation of memorial initiatives, even one ordering the destruction of a mausoleum in August of the same year—a mausoleum that had been built in the capital city of Sofia in 1949 in memory of the first leader of Communist Bulgaria, Georgi Dimitrov.[86] One of the government's most emblematic actions, however, was the passing of a law that qualified the Communist regime as "criminal."[87] Approved on April 26, 2000, in Article 4, the text stipulated that "all actions by those who, during the period indicated, aimed to resist and overthrow the Communist regime and its ideology, are righteous, morally just, and worthy of tribute."[88] The document denounced a system that had been established with a foreign power's backing, had abdicated national sovereignty, had suppressed human rights, and had led the country to "national disaster"; it further criticized the "deliberate and intentional destruction of traditional values of European civilization" and "the manipulation of education, culture, and science to political goals and ideological ends" (Article 2, paragraphs 1 and 9). Invoking the letter of the law rather than a parliamentary resolution to circulate this political message, the majority was attempting to lend credence to an otherwise symbolic measure: the characterization of the regime as "liable to prosecution" was

---

85 Avramov and Sgard, "Bulgaria."

86 Todorova, "Mausoleum of Georgi Dimitrov," 377–411.

87 Deyanova, "Des condamnations locales du communisme à la condamnation internationale de janvier 2006," 193–213.

88 *Zakon za objavjavane na komunističeskija režim v Bălgarija za prestăpen*, D.V., no. 37, May 5, 2000, https://www.lex.bg/laws/ldoc/2134920192.

omitted in the final version of the text, and no compensation was anticipated for the "victims of communism."

The recollection of the passage of a law criminalizing the former Communist regime was still vivid at the opening of the plenary session on July 27, 2000. The sparring sessions that ensued were remarkably intense; these confrontations—surprisingly animated—that took shape over the course of the session conferred a startling materiality to political speech. Reading the retranscription of the plenary session transports one to a vibrant soundscape, where the murmur of onomatopoeia and rhythm of scattered applause adorn the exchanged words. The interactions strictly adhered to a codified ritual: the impromptu speeches brimming with uncontrolled emotion, a staple in the National Assembly in the early 1990s when the benches were filled with novice politicians, had now become a rarity. On this theatrical stage, as the discussions were transmitted by radio in real time, the actors were fully immersed in their performance—they trialed their arguments and sharpened their rhetorical skills. Had an observer been exposed only to brief excerpts of this parliamentary session, she would have failed to grasp what made these speeches so compelling—not only were these interactions verbal; they were physical too, with power relations gauged quite literally by the acoustic prowess of each parliamentary faction.

A few introductory remarks will facilitate a close reading of the debate. In the National Assembly formed following the April 19, 1997, elections, five parliamentary groups came to share the auditorium: the ODS, with the Union of Democratic Forces (*Săjuz na demokratičnite sili*, SDS) at its core and obtaining a majority of 137 seats out of 240, was opposed by the Democratic Left (*Demokratična levica*, DL), which was centered around the Bulgarian Socialist Party (BSP), and held 52 seats. Several parties operated on the margins: aligned with the ODS, a coalition representing the interests of the Turkish and other Muslim minorities (Union for National Rescue, *Obedinenie za nacionalno Spasenie*, ONS); and on the socialist side, the Euro-Left (*Evrolevica*, EL), which had emerged following a split within the Socialist Party. The Euro-Left faced an acute dilemma with the call for Sendov's resignation: should they distance themselves from their socialist counterparts to consolidate their social democratic identity—even if it meant endorsing a right-wing proposal—or should they vote against this resolution, and risk being seen as nothing more than a splinter group of the former Communists?

The proposal for sanctions was defended by Djanko Markov, a member of the SDS and highly controversial individual. As a World War II legionnaire, he had been present among the ranks of the SDS, which often served to discredit the anti-communist coalition because it hinted at a link to the pre-communist pro-Nazi movement. Indeed, one particular phrase uttered by

Markov at the July 27, 2000, meeting (not featured in the excerpts presented here) has lingered in collective memory: "The deportation of an enemy population is not a war crime."[89] It will help to keep it in mind as we proceed with our discussion. A second nationalist voice invited to portray the position of the United Democratic Forces was that of Krasimir Karakačanov, a historian at the helm of the Internal Macedonian Revolutionary Organization (*Vătrešna Makedonska revoljucionna organizacija*, VMRO), a small group that positioned itself in line with the powerful eponymous structure, the historical VMRO created in 1894 to oppose subjection to the Ottoman Empire that had spearheaded the insurrection against the Ottoman Empire at the turn of the twentieth century.[90] One may note the unique alliance of a professional nearing the end of his career and an ambitious newcomer, neither of whom, at that point, held a prominent role within the ODS. Consideration of their standing in these circles sheds light on the probable reason behind their dedication to memorial causes, which served as a source of political visibility at that point in time.

On the socialist side, the distribution of roles followed a different logic. Georgi Părvanov, the president of the Socialist Party and its parliamentary group, a historian by training, was assigned to deliver the response. His university degree was of less import than the authority he claimed after many years as a politician, one who aspired to the highest office. Fifteen months later, he would be elected president of the republic. In this capacity, he

---

89 The phrase is from the following paragraph: "Tsar Boris did not have the possibility of saving the Jews of Belomorie. The deportation of an enemy population is not a war crime (*deportacijata na vraždebno naselenie ne e voenno prestăplenie*). The United States deported the population of Japanese descent of the Pacific Coast during World War II. And nobody sued them for it. The Bulgarian people could not oppose (this measure) when the Germans commanding the Balkans decided that this enemy population should be deported." http://www.parliament.bg/bg/plenaryst/ns/6/ID/2170.

90 Krasimir Karakačanov was cofounder of the United Patriots (*Obedineni patrioti*) coalition, allied to the party of Prime Minister Borisov, Citizens for the European Development of Bulgaria (*Graždani za evropejsko razvitie na Bălgarija*, GERB). In addition to the VMRO-BND (*Vătrešna makedonska revoljucionna organizacija—Bălgarsko nacionalno dviženie*), the coalition included the xenophobic organization *Ataka* and a group resulting from a split within *Ataka*, the National Front for the Defense of Bulgaria (*Nacionalen front za spasenie na Bălgarija*, NFSB). In May 2017, Karakačanov was appointed deputy prime minister and minister of defense. In March 2018, he was part of the delegation present at the commemorations in Skopje. In 2011, it was revealed that he had collaborated with the former Communist State Security on the "Macedonian question." See https://desebg.com/prezident/443-2011-10-20-15-26-05.

would work together with the son of King Boris, Simeon Saxe-Coburg-Gotha, who had taken up the role of prime minister.[91] Let us now turn to the parliamentary debate:

National Assembly, 417th plenary meeting, July 27, 2000

Speaker Jordan Sokolov (ODS): Would anyone who took part in introducing the proposal wish to speak? Mr. Djanko Markov has the floor.

Djanko Markov (ODS): Mr. Speaker, ladies and gentlemen, my fellow deputies, I have voted in favor of broadcasting this session on television, for I believe in the importance of this act. This is not only about judging the actions of Professor Sendov and determining whether these were right or wrong. Through this act the National Assembly, for the first time, at least since I have been present in this space—has been asked to rule on the actions of a man who occupies the highest position in the State of Bulgaria.

Reply from the DL: For the second time![92]

Markov: This act deserves our serious attention and our assessment of its potential impact. It is not a question of whether Professor Sendov expressed a personal opinion on the issue of who did or did not contribute to the rescue of the Bulgarian Jews, on who bears blame. In that area, no one can argue that Professor Sendov does not have the right to express his personal opinion. But Professor Sendov is also deputy speaker of the Bulgarian parliament—the most eminent institution of the Bulgarian nation. And it was precisely in this capacity that he acted against Bulgaria's national interests. [Exclamations from the DL: "Eeee!" Applause from the ODS bloc.]

Speaker Sokolov: Silence, please.

Markov: And I will substantiate these remarks, dear ladies and gentlemen! . . . This is not about whether the State of Israel and the Jewish people should dismantle one [commemorative] plaque or another. It is their sovereign right to judge [on whom to confer] the credit and responsibility for the fate of their compatriots during World War II and to act accordingly. . . . But we have a priority over other European nations that were under the auspices of Germany during World War II. This advantage of

---

91 The former monarch announced his entry into politics on April 6, 2001. In June 2001, the National Simeon II Movement (*Nacionalno Dviženie Simeon Vtori*, NDSV) won 42.73 percent of the vote in the legislative elections.

92 This statement refers to the March 25, 1943, sanction against Deputy Speaker of the National Assembly Pešev, in reprisal for the petition he had circulated against anti-Jewish policies.

ours is specifically expressed on this map that I present as documentation, a map that the American historian Raul Hilberg reproduced in his book *The Destruction of the European Jews*. It is used in that book, but I have it in a German translation from a study by the historian Heinz Höhne, published in Hamburg in 1966 and entitled *History of the SS: The Order of the Skull*.[93] On this map, ladies and gentlemen, are shown. . . . [murmurs and retorts]

Speaker Sokolov: Please, silence in the chamber.

Markov: In Poland, 90 percent of Jews were exterminated; in Germany, Austria, and Czechoslovakia, 50 percent; in Romania, 28 percent; in Slovakia, Belgium, and Luxemburg, 56 percent; in Denmark, 1.5 percent (seventy people were killed). All the others were saved by boat. In Bulgaria, it says—zero! In Bulgaria, ladies and gentlemen, zero! [sustained applause and a chorus of "bravos" from the ODS bloc] This is the plaque commemorating the saviors of the Bulgarian Jews. This zero gives me great pride—as a Bulgarian, as a citizen, and as a man! [applause from the ODS bloc] But when Professor Sendov looked at this zero, he said, "Tsar Boris sent 12,000 or 11,343 [Jews], whatever their exact number, to their death in the Treblinka camp and other camps in Poland." Tsar Boris sent them off!

Here is another map! Please, Mr. Speaker, the map. Here is another map published in Goebbels's newspaper *Das Reich*, on which the Belomorie and Macedonia are marked as belonging to the Bulgarian government—unlike the Dobrudža, which is included in the state of Bulgaria. Here is Hungary; Transylvania is within the borders of the Hungarian state, but Vojvodina is indicated as being under Hungarian government. In that sense, I won't linger over the details of historical facts, because that is another task; that project falls to another institution. But I do want to establish an immediate parallel between the Bulgarian parliament of 1943, when forty-two people signed a petition to the national government and intervened in favor of the Bulgarian Jews, and the present moment! These people all belonged to the majority. Pešev had not wanted the members of the opposition to sign. [murmurs and retorts from the DL bloc] The opposition!

Speaker Sokolov: Please! [inaudible murmurs and retorts from the DL bloc] There were, there were.

Markov: I beg your pardon! I cannot speak in such conditions! Please be silent if you wish to hear!

Reply from the DL: We do not wish to hear!

---

93   This is a book by journalist Heinz Höhne, *Der Orden unter dem Totenkopf: Die Geschischte der SS* (Gütersloh, Ger.: Mohn, 1967).

Speaker Sokolov: Silence, Ms. [Stanka] Veličkova [DL deputy]!

Markov: Does what I am saying need to be heard? What is not true? [inaudible murmurs and retorts from the DL bloc]

Speaker Sokolov: Silence, please.

Markov: These forty-two people, as I was saying, belonged to the majority, the government majority. And these people placed humanity above politics. They were in favor of that policy—the alliance with Germany. How and why is another question. . . . [murmurs and rejoinders from the DL bloc] But when it came to the fate of these people [the Jews], they placed humanity above politics! [Long and fervent applause from the ODS bloc] Such was the courage of the National Assembly. And among these people, dear colleagues, more than half were killed by the rulings of the People's Court. [booing from the DL bloc] . . .

Today, *when the efforts of an entire people, the efforts of each Bulgarian citizen, are directed toward raising the prestige of our country, not the standing of one kind of government over another, but our country and our people, Professor Sendov is spreading overwhelmingly false information, information that harms the interests of the Bulgarian people and nation. That is why Professor Sendov has no place as deputy speaker in the Bulgarian National Assembly.*[94] [sustained and prolonged applause from the ODS bloc] . . .

Speaker Sokolov: Thank you, Mr. Markov. Please! When I look left, the shouting needs to stop! [Calm, if you will, so that] we do not end up reduced in number today. Mr. Georgi Părvanov has the floor.

Georgi Părvanov (DL): Mr. Speaker, ladies and gentlemen, my fellow deputies: this current campaign is part of an initiative, an attack against a decision that does not come from Bulgaria. This decision was taken without regard for the positions for or against it, that were adopted by parties and individuals within our country. The essence of this decision was to express a great esteem for the Bulgarian people, for all the courageous men and women who contributed to the rescue of the Bulgarian Jews. *The attack from the Union of Democratic Forces reveals spotty historical knowledge, ignorance, and misunderstanding of the facts.* It is an attack by which those in power have used Boris III and the dynasty to try to prop up their own declining popularity.

What about what was heard in the debate up until now? A serious debate requires going beyond the scope of discussions on the fate of the 50,000 rescued, and that of the 11,000 Jews who perished. [retorts from the majority] *Historical truth, Mr. Petrov, requires us to say that Boris III was*

---

94 All italics added.

the leader of an anti-Semitic regime. [murmurs and retorts from the SDS] *This is known throughout Europe.* [applause from the DL] You are the only ones who have not grasped this. The anti-Semitic state policy was juridically founded on the Law for the Defense of the Nation, itself based on the Nazi model, and on the application decree, both of which were approved by the king himself, Mr. Petrov. [retorts from the SDS]

This anti-Semitic policy had also been formed by other normative and legislative acts; for instance, the Law on the Ad Hoc Imposition of the Property of Jewish Persons, from February 1941, which also received the blessing of Boris III. [response from the SDS: "Tsar Boris III!"]

How, gentlemen on the right, will you, as the inheritors of this regime, explain the policy restricting [the rights of] Jews during this era? Are you familiar with the concept? How will you approve of the fact that these restrictions, in practice, signified the deprivation of all Jewish political and civil rights, their de facto placement outside the law, the dispossession of their property and the right to exercise their professions and crafts, forced taxation, internment, their recruitment into special Jewish labor units, their expulsion (*izselvaneto*), [from Sofia and other cities to the countryside in May 1943], and even the ban on freely circulating in the streets? How will you explain and justify this? [energetic DL applause, SDS retorts]

I ask you, dear ladies and gentlemen, is this the policy that you wish to commemorate with monuments? [SDS murmurs and retorts, DL applause]

We cannot comment on whether Boris III instigated the anti-Jewish policies, or if he was forced to undertake these repressive acts, under the effect of external pressure—or under a so-called groupthink effect, as some writers have suggested. *In this case, what is significant and undeniable is that Boris III personified the anti-Semitic regime, that he personified the Bulgarian Holocaust* . . .

Asen Agov [SDS, from his seat]: *This debate is about Sendov.*

Pǎrvanov: This, Mr. Agov, was the regulatory basis for deporting those 11,000 Jews from the newly liberated Bulgarian lands of Thrace and Macedonia. During that same year, 1942, they were deprived of Bulgarian citizenship—unlike, we may note, the Greek and Yugoslav population. With this document, they had already been condemned in practice . . .

Ekaterina Mihajlova [SDS, from her seat]: *We are talking about Sendov, not Boris III.*

Pǎrvanov: *The behavior of the Bulgarian people during the war was not a historical exception. It corresponded to a religious and ethnic tolerance formed over centuries.* It speaks of the humanism and democratic spirit that developed throughout the complex and contradictory history of our nation.

Voices in favor of the rescue of the Jews were raised in every democratic society—from the legal opposition, as in Professor Stajnov and Nikola Mušanov;[95] from representatives of the Union of writers, lawyers, painters, other prominent figures, and politicians. It is particularly important to emphasize the role of the Bulgarian Orthodox Church. Once more, let's bow to their achievement! *But if you are paying attention, if you are underlining their names, then I ask of you, as you call upon them, why those thousands of fallen, murdered antifascists, who gave their lives to the rescue of the Jews—why do these people remain anonymous?* [heckling from the SDS]

Hristo Tarakčiev [SDS, from his seat]: Scoundrels!

Speaker Sokolov: Silence in the chamber, please!

Părvanov: Each time that the SDS descends into political and legal crisis, it relies on political provocations relating to the national past. This was the case in 1992, and it is the same in the fall of 1999. Finally, and this is my last point, *the whole campaign is really aimed at rehabilitating the pro-Hitler regime that ruled Bulgaria during World War II.* [bravos and roaring applause from the DL] Such rehabilitation involves several stages: from restitution [of property nationalized by the Communist regime] to the decision of the Constitutional Court to exonerate those who were deemed to have led the country into war and anti-Semitic policies. A decision that, I recall, provoked the protest of the Speaker of the Knesset, Dan Tikhon.

Since the beginning of the year, the SDS has made constant, stubborn efforts to burnish its political image. By playing this card, you did not manage to resolve the issue, but by its latest actions the SDS has officially identified itself with the pro-Nazi regime, *proving that it is the moral and political heir of those who led us into war alongside Nazi Germany.* [bravos and roaring applause from the DL] We support a new reading of history, ladies and gentlemen: a perpetual reexamination of history, of the past.

Agov: What about the People's Court?

Părvanov: National healing and agreement on reforms are unthinkable in the absence of such a relationship to historical events and processes. A mature, a wise relationship to history requires that we refuse to fetishize it, that we refuse the strategy of constantly, unendingly weaving our history with a complex and contradictory legacy, and with the work of parliament.

---

95 In the National Assembly, both members consistently objected with much courage, acumen, and eloquence to the anti-Jewish measures imposed in Bulgaria and the occupied territories during World War II. After September 9, Petko Stajnov became foreign minister (September 9, 1944–March 31, 1946); Mušanov, a major figure of the Democratic Party, fell victim to Communist repression.

Bulgarian people's ethnic tolerance, the same way that the act of 1984 to 1989 was an act forged by the Bulgarian Communist Party, led by a man whose name I do not wish to speak, with the support of the Bulgarian special services—the State Security.

And when, Mr. Părvanov, you speak of dismantled commemorative plaques, could you, Mr. Părvanov, enumerate the monuments in the cemeteries of Bulgarian villages and hamlets that you have destroyed so that Turkish names do not appear there? Do you remember the shots that were fired? Do you recall the stream of 300,000 people who left Bulgaria as a result of this act of the Communist Party? *Is it ethnic peace that the BSP is speaking of, as heir to the BKP?* No, it is something else. At some point Mr. Sendov compared himself to Mr. Dimităr Pešev. I will say this: Mr. Sendov, you were a deputy in the Eighth, Ninth, and Tenth National Assemblies of the People's Republic of Bulgaria. Did you, then, accomplish what Mr. Dimităr Pešev did? Did you prepare a statement? Did you find forty-two people to support and contact Todor Zhivkov? [SDS applause] Among those who were elected by 99.99 percent of voters, did other deputies intervene to defend the Bulgarian people as an ethnically tolerant European community? No. But Dimităr Pešev and forty-two members of the Twenty-Fifth National Assembly did so, and we must honor them for it. In conjunction with this, the decision not to deport the Bulgarian Jews was taken by the head of state of the time; in this case, Tsar Boris III. . . .

Speaker Sokolov: Thank you, Mr. Ivanov. . . . Does someone else wish to speak? Mr. Blagovest Sendov has the floor.

Blagovest Sendov (DL): Ladies and gentlemen, my fellow deputies! Today you are taking part in a convincing demonstration of the Kostov regime's attempt to rehabilitate the personal regime of the monarch, which bound Bulgaria to the Tripartite Pact during World War II and turned it against the Western democracies. . . . *The Kostov regime has declared its desire to join the European Union, but it wants to enter as a proud heir to the state leaders who were allies of Hitler.* The democratic Europe of today has developed out of a common struggle and victory against Hitlerism. There is something unsavory in Mr. Kostov's logic, something that our friends in Europe and the United States will surely see, those who fought together against Hitlerism and lost dear victims in this fight.[97]

---

97   Stenogrami ot plenarni zasedanija: Četiristotin I sedemnadeseto zasedanie, Sofija, July 27, 2000, otkrito v 9.05, https://www.parliament.bg/bg/plenaryst/ns/6/ID/2170.

A few minutes after debate ended, the National Assembly proceeded to its vote: 130 deputies approved the motion, 80 opposed it, and 16 abstained.[98] What a spectacle of bravado! Let us review a few of the implicit conventions adhered to in this verbal sparring. The first convention, of feigning to leave the terrain of the past to the historians while surreptitiously claiming it for oneself, is a rhetorical tool shared by deputies of all political leanings. More intriguing yet is the panoply of evidence that the deputies instrumentalize to wage their battles; this included display of maps published in scholarly works; citation of books by both professional and lay historians, mostly of foreign origin; reading of excerpts from archives; references to external sources of validation (foundations, associations, state parliaments), as well as recall of personal memories (some elements are missing from the excerpts chosen). In other words, the legal, scientific, and testimonial evidence, on the one hand, and that which spans both domestic and international scales, on the other, become enmeshed, woven into a complex lyrical tapestry.

A second observation: power obeys rules of precedence with clockwork precision. The most prominent figures made sweeping contributions, which served as markers of their authority and/or legitimacy; to round out their arguments, they delegated particular aspects to their coalition partners or lower-ranking officials. Reading the minutes of the session prompts not so much a sense of tedium at the repetition of rhetorical motifs and techniques, but a feeling of wonder at seeing how, with each speech, a compounded yet coherent puzzle gradually unfolds.

The underlying mechanisms behind these interactions can be readily discerned. For the Socialists, it was paramount to downplay the significance of Deputy Speaker Sendov's statement and pretend that the judgment issued by the Bejski Commission was solely pertinent to Jews in the context of intra- and interstate (dis)agreements. Conversely, the ODS sought to magnify the importance of this gesture that, by implicating Bulgaria, would have been detrimental to the national interest. Molding the fabric of time to reaffirm partisan identities was our political protagonists' second objective. During the 1990s, on account of market reforms and the inherent uncertainty of their outcomes, the past was given more weight in the definition of party identities: by reviving long-standing historical conflicts, political actors could mitigate the difficulties of anticipating future social stratification and identifying segments of the electorate to target. Finally, as a minor side note, it is not evident that strict temporal delineations were at play in the aforementioned remarks. During the debate, the "red" and "blue" deputies were determined to keep the discussion firmly rooted in the present

---

98 The decision to remove Speaker Sokolov from his post was published in DV, August 1, 2000.

whenever any mention of the past was to their disadvantage, insofar as severing ties between "then" and "now" was advantageous—as evidenced by Deputies Mihailova (SDS) and Agov (SDS), who, aggravated by the socialist leader's critical remarks regarding the king, invited Părvanov to circle back to the actions of the deputy speaker of the Assembly. The rhythmic oscillation between temporal passages, configured at different intervals and scales, served to sharpen their proverbial barbs.

Here, two distinct uses of the past are evidenced: the first involves consigning one's opponents to the past, entrapping them in a straitjacket that would permit no escape; the second rests on implicating one's adversary with a tainted legacy. Regardless of the prevailing method, the political constructions of Jewish fates characteristically passed through a wrinkle in time, drawing certain aspects of the past into the purview of the present day while relegating others to oblivion. The socialist approach rested upon the drawing of historical continuity between the ODS and the pro-Nazi wartime regime. This stance undermined the Kostov government's professed modernity and European orientation, concomitantly displacing its geographical anchoring toward a mooring in the Third Reich.

For Părvanov, an avowed Socialist, to level accusations of historical ignorance toward the representatives of SDS was a deliberate and intentional act, not a chance occurrence. Since its reestablishment in 1990,[99] the leaders of the Socialist Party sought to discredit their opponents by categorizing them into two distinct societal universes: on the one hand, the *restitutki*, those benefiting from the restitution of property that had been nationalized by the Communist state in 1947; and on the other, the *lumpenproletariat*, whose overstated rhetoric was described as indicating their marginal social status. In stark contrast, the Socialists emphasized their own rational approach to governance, one shaped by four decades of state service. By insisting on their long expertise and implying the use of time as a measure of judgment, the Socialists' strategy mirrored that of the "blues," who incessantly mocked the "red" elite that had been hastily trained in the schools of the Communist Party in Bulgaria and Moscow. The "reds" were characterized as perpetuating, under the guise of apparatchiks, an impersonation of a peasant ethos and uncivilized ways. The "blues" also advanced the argument of continuity, alleging that the Socialists were willing hostages of the Communist model of power, and therefore incapable of reinventing themselves. During January–February 1997, protesters portrayed in the symbolic register of decay and decrepitude the party's "centenary"—*stoletnicata*, a phrase referring to a successor party—to the point of staging its funeral.[100]

99   Touykova, "Conversion partisane et usages politiques du passé," 67–96.
100 Ragaru, "Bulgarie, 1989," 172–202.

Ensnared by their affiliation to communism, which they themselves did not disown, the representatives of the Socialist Party were subjected to further censure by their "blue" opponents, who cast them back into another temporal realm—that of the forced assimilation of the Bulgarian Turks. This reminder held the former Communists, who had endorsed the use of violence against minorities, to account, with a scathing critique of their lack of moral backbone. In turn, this underlined the ODS's commitment to defending human rights, a priority concern for the European Commission in evaluating candidate countries for the EU as outlined in the 1993 Copenhagen criteria. In essence, while the Socialists held that any unbroken ties between the SDS and the "fascist" era would disqualify that party from fulfilling the promise of a European future, from the perspective of the anti-communist rulers, it was the legacy of the brutal treatment of minorities during the 1980s that excluded the Socialists from a future that both parties sought to shape, using the past as proxy.

In concluding this reflection on the uses of history, we would be remiss not to highlight the discourse that surfaced over the course of the debate, concerning the personification of historical facts and the significance of heroes within national storytelling. This conversation was initiated by Junišev, a lawyer and radical democrat, who pointed out that failing to acknowledge those who were instrumental in the "rescue of the Bulgarian Jews" may result in the dilution of individual virtues into anonymous glory and, thereby, in a blurring of Bulgarian greatness altogether. Would it not be more advantageous to highlight unique personalities who would act as effigies of collective virtue, thereby allowing the latter to be elevated through the very representation of illustrious figures? His plea was not devoid of ulterior motives: by espousing King Boris as a paramount hero, the argument challenged the allusion made by the Socialist leader to antifascist partisans, whose collective *and* anonymous contribution had been omitted from the postcommunist national narrative. The discourse is thought-provoking for two reasons. First, it interrogates one of the central tenets of political (re) presentation: the continuous making of the absent present. Second, in his speech, Junišev raised the issue of the counterheroic aspects in the historical narrative, brought about by questioning—after 1989—the idea of the nation as a crucible of history. In doing so, he hinted at one of the possible prerequisite conditions for reaching the consensus, which crystallized in the late 2000s around a cross-partisan objection to the disappearance of heroes.[101]

To address this precise point, we must direct our attention to the figure of Pešev, despite this shift at first appearing as counterintuitive. On July 27, 2000, when the Bulgarian Left invoked 1943, the Right immediately

101 Dejanova, "Non-Saved Jews," 162–72.

retorted with its own comparative parallel, denouncing the contrast between Pešev's bravery in March 1943 and Sendov's utter lack of action in the face of the oppression of the Turkish minority in the latter half of the 1980s. At the turn of the millennium, Pešev remained a polarizing figure: he had been sentenced by the People's Court in 1945, and his role in the "rescue of the Bulgarian Jews" was largely downplayed throughout the Communist regime. Yet the tale of his gradual rehabilitation—a process characterized by multiple iterations and on various scales—sheds light on the convergence of the "blue" and "red" interpretations of the "rescue."

Dimităr Pešev: A New Topography of Memory

Dimităr Pešev's trajectory, like that of many others who intervened on behalf of persecuted Jews, is far from linear. Born in 1894 in the city of Kjustendil in western Bulgaria, Pešev first embarked on a career as a judge and prosecutor, before helping to engineer the emerging authoritarian technocracy in the 1930s.[102] His detachment from partisan struggles and reputation for efficiency and discretion resulted in his appointment as the minister of justice in 1935, shortly after King Boris established his personal rule. Representing the Kjustendil constituency, Pešev ascended to the position of deputy speaker in the Twenty-Fourth (1938–39) and Twenty-Fifth (1940–44) National Assemblies, serving as the voice of executive power in the chamber. He defended Bulgaria's entry into the Tripartite Pact on March 1, 1941, and cast his vote in favor of the Law for the Defense of the Nation. In June 1942, he approved the government's full control over the "Jewish question"; and on November 11 of that same year, he delivered a speech that indicated he was still impressed by the Reich's "new order."[103]

In early 1943, a pivotal turning point occurred for Pešev, when he became aware of the preparations to deport the Jews from both the "old" and the "new" Bulgarian kingdoms. Multiple narratives surrounding these events have been offered, each providing a distinct perspective on the role played by both Jews and non-Jews in resisting deportation, as well as denoting their varied political leanings. We will examine a few pivotal moments. Prior to the outbreak of World War II, the town of Kjustendil was host to a

---

102 See the introduction by Nikolaj Poppetrov to Pešev, *Spomeni*, 7–32. This contrasts with Tsvetan Todorov's depiction of the representative, which insists on his "stinging defense of democracy, parliamentary principles, and personal freedoms." Todorov, *Fragility of Goodness*, 26.

103 *Stenografski Dnevnici na XXV ONS, 9-to zasedanie*, Sofia, November 11, 1942.

prominent Jewish community of approximately 980 individuals. This community grew in number during the war, as Jews from the city of Sofia sought refuge in Kjustendil, hoping to find a less repressive environment in the provincial town. During the final week of February 1943, the Commissariat for Jewish Affairs requested that its regional delegates draw up lists of Jews deemed "undesirable," with a specific focus on Communist and public figures, in anticipation of forthcoming raids. In regions adjacent to the border of Vardar Macedonia to the west and Greek Thrace to the south, the prospect of detaining the Jewish community in its entirety was being considered. On February 26, an emissary from the Commissariat was dispatched to Kjustendil, tasked with identifying a suitable facility to serve as a temporary detention center and commandeering the necessary equipment. The request made to the local Jewish municipality (*evrejska obština*) to provide tools and cooking utensils raised alarm within the community.

Through his network of contacts, as well as by receiving individual appeals, the news of the impending deportations had reached Pešev. In his memoirs, penned between 1968 and 1970,[104] the politician predominantly recalls a conversation with Dimităr Ikonomov, the deputy from Dupnica, a city where a temporary internment camp had been established:

> As I was trying to understand what was happening and why, I received a visit from Dimitar [Dimităr] Ikonomov, the deputy to the National Assembly from the town of Doupnitsa [Dupnica]. He and I had had our differences on certain issues that had come up in the Assembly, and our relations had grown so strained that we were no longer on speaking terms. I was therefore surprised to see him. . . . He told me that he had just returned from a visit there and was extremely depressed from what he had witnessed taking place in the street. He described a distressing scene—Thracian Jews, old people, men, women, and children, carrying their belongings, defeated, desperate, powerless people, begging for help as they crossed the town on foot, dragging themselves towards some unknown destination.[105]

Historian Frederick Chary has suggested the plausible hypothesis that the targeted communities of Kjustendil and Sofia likely first sought support from those who had previously expressed favorable sentiments toward the Jews, before considering the prospect of appealing to members of the majority as

---

104 In 1968, at the request of the Bulgarian State Archives, Pešev began writing his memoirs. When he died, the archives received part of the manuscript; his family kept the other half, which recounted his experience of the People's Court and prison, until 2002.

105 Excerpt from Pešev's diary in English translation, reproduced in Todorov, *Fragility of Goodness*, 158.

the more effective means of influencing the government.[106] On the evening of March 9, a delegation composed of four elected officials and prominent figures from Kjustendil traveled to the capital. The following morning, Pešev received them at his residence; a meeting at the parliament was scheduled for the same afternoon. Accompanied by several deputies, the deputy speaker of the National Assembly secured an audience with the minister of the interior, Petăr Gabrovski, and eventually succeeded in persuading him to halt the ongoing arrests of Bulgarian Jews.[107] A week later, when the Jews from the Greek occupied territories still remained in Bulgarian provisional camps, Pešev presented a petition to the prime minister condemning the anti-Jewish policies. Only signatures of majority deputies were solicited, to prevent the action from being interpreted as a hostile gesture toward Germany, while at the same time still demonstrating the extent of internal opposition to the deportations. The outcome was as anticipated: Prime Minister Bogdan Filov took the opportunity to reassert his authority. After exerting pressure on several deputies to retract their signatures from the petition initiated by Pešev, he turned to the National Assembly. On March 24, sixty-six representatives voted in favor of condemning Pešev, while thirty-three opposed, and eleven abstained. The following day, Pešev was relieved of his duties as deputy speaker; however, he retained his parliamentary mandate.[108]

In the wake of the events of September 9, 1944, Pešev was arrested and brought before the Second Chamber of the People's Court. In his oral argument, defense counsel Nisim Jašarov focused less on Pešev's advocacy for the Bulgarian and foreign Jews and instead accentuated the defendant's refusal, as justice minister, to sanction the execution of Damjan Velčev—a member of the then very influential organization of Bulgarian military officers, the Military League who had received a death sentence in 1936 for his involvement in a failed coup d'état the preceding year. Velčev had assumed the office of minister of defense on September 9, 1944. Regrettably, Jašarov's approach was not very effective, as Pešev was eventually sentenced to fifteen years of imprisonment and confiscation of property. By the close of 1945, Pešev obtained an early release but thereafter led a secluded existence until

106 Chary, *Bulgarian Jews*, 90–100.
107 There are many gray areas here: were there one or two interviews with the minister of the interior? Did Gabrovski seek the approval of the prime minister before suspending the arrests? Who gave this instruction "from above," mentioned in a report of the German police attaché Adolf Hoffmann? The king himself? See Bericht der Polizei-Attaché Hoffmann an das Reichssicherheitshauptamt (RSHA) – Attachégruppe, April 5, 1943, PAAA (*Politisches Archiv des Auswärtigen Amtes*), R 100 863, Bl 178–83.
108 Todorov, *Fragility of Goodness*, 25–26; Chary, *Bulgarian Jews*, 96–99; Filov, *Dnevnik*, 561–64.

his passing in 1973. In the months preceding his death, the Yad Vashem Institute honored him, along with two other members of the Kjustendil delegation—Deputy Petăr Mihalev and businessman Asen Sjučmezov[109]—with the esteemed title of "Righteous Among the Nations."

The growing national and international recognition of Pešev took place across multiple channels, spanning Israel, Bulgaria, and Italy. The first indication of his rediscovery emerged in 1996, when Pešev became one of the beneficiaries of the "Bulgarian forest" tribute. A year later, on the sixty-fourth anniversary of the "rescue of the Bulgarian Jews," President Petăr Stojanov (SDS) awarded him, along with the other members of the Kjustendil delegation, the Stara Planina Order of Merit.[110] According to the 1991 Bulgarian Constitution, the privilege of bestowing such distinctions is one of the few sovereign functions of the head of state. Elected in November 1996 and inaugurated in January 1997, Stojanov embodied the aspirations of a "blue" wave in Bulgaria. In the run-up to the anticipated April elections, any initiative that served to remind the citizens of the ills of communism was most welcome.

It was, however, the September 1998 publication of a book authored by Gabriele Nissim, a Milanese journalist of Bulgarian-Jewish descent, that gave Pešev's actions their international visibility. The idea is said to have come to Nissim as he was finalizing a draft of a separate book, at Yad Vashem, on the contribution of Eastern European Jews to the establishment of socialism.[111] Three years of research followed, punctuated by encounters with Pešev's nieces and Norbert Yasharoff, the son of the lawyer who had defended Pešev in 1945. *The Man Who Stopped Hitler*, as the book came to be titled, became the focus of a meticulously crafted media campaign.[112] Following the book's launch at Milan's Teatro Franco Parenti on September 24, 1998, a flurry of accolades ensued in the halls of the parliaments of Rome, Sofia,[113] and Strasbourg, as if the recognition accorded to the parliamentarian of yesteryear would bolster, by association, the authority of the assemblies where his name was being invoked. The United States was not exempt from this sequence of events: Nissim presented his book to the USHMM on March

---

109 The two other members of the delegation, lawyer Ivan Momčilov and teacher Vladimir Kurtev, a VMRO activist, were granted the title of "Righteous" on September 4, 1991, and May 3, 2010, respectively.
110 http://paper./standartnews.com/archive/2002/07/20/thecountry/ s3430-8.htm (accessed February 17, 2020; no longer active).
111 Nissim and Eshkenazi, *Ebrei invisibili.*
112 Nissim, *L'Uomo che fermò Hitler.*
113 On November 6, 1998, the Bulgarian parliament hosted a commemorative ceremony in the presence of Nissim, recently awarded the Order of the Madara Horseman by President Stojanov. http://www.peshev.org/gn-sofii.htm.

20, 1999.[114] Two months after its publication, the translation of the book into Bulgarian[115] provided an occasion for a new round of celebrations at the Bulgarian National Assembly. The Anti-Defamation League (ADL) agreed to procure 30,000 copies in an effort to "help Bulgarians to get to know their own history."[116] On March 21, 2000, the German edition of the book[117] and its author finally made its way to the Bundestag.

Let us pause briefly to consider one of these legislative episodes, specifically at the Italian parliament, where, on October 16, 1998, a special session was held in the presence of the Bulgarian ambassador to Italy, Dimităr Lazarov; the Israeli ambassador, Yehuda Millo; the president of the Italian Jewish Community, Amos Luzzatto; the former Israeli diplomat N. Baruh; and two of Pešev's nieces. Ivan Kurtev (SDS), the deputy speaker of the

114 Let us note that one more protagonist contributed to the rediscovery of Dimităr Pešev—the Bulgarian-born French philosopher Tsvetan Todorov. In 1999, his collection of archival records and memoirs was released in French in a book series *Histoire à deux voix* (Albin Michel) headed by archivist and historian Sonia Combe. A specialist on East Germany who was familiar with the Bulgarian context, Combe told the author she was behind the idea for the book. However, she thought it best to ask Todorov to pen the introduction in order to help ensure a wide audience for the book. In Bulgaria, Combe met Pešev's nieces, who entrusted her with parts of Pešev's memoirs. Most of the remaining documents come from archival collections edited by David Koen (1995) and Vitka Toškova (1992). In Bulgaria, Todorov had earlier made a name for himself with a volume of testimonies of former detainees at the Belene Communist camp. In 1999, his influence over the discussion of the "rescue of the Bulgarian Jews" remained limited to the small French-speaking community. *La fragilité du bien* was not translated into Bulgarian; the introduction to the book circulated in 2013, however, on *Librev.com*, an authoritative website with several pieces on the deportation of Jews from the occupied territories. In 2015, it also appeared as "The Rescue of the Bulgarian Jews" ("Spasjavaneto na bălgarskite evrei") in a volume of essays by Todorov titled *The Totalitarian Experience* (*Totalitarnijat opit* [Sofia: Iztok-Zapad, 2015]), 213–46, https://www.ozone.bg/media/pdfs/556467669df7b. pdf. Sociologist Liliana Deyanova recalls that excerpts from the introduction had earlier circulated in the anti-communist daily *Demokracija*, and in the right-wing publication *Anti*, which was committed to the denunciation of the "crimes of communism." Communications from Sonia Combe (Paris, May 2013), Stilijan Jotov (by email, December 5, 2022), Aleksandăr Vezenkov (by email, December 9, 2022), and Liliana Deyanova (by email, November 30 and December 4, 2022).

115 Nissim, *Čovekăt kojto sprja Hitler.*

116 "The Story of The Bulgarian Jews," *Ivansk Project e-Newsletter* 41 (March–April 2010): 2.

117 Nissim, *Der Mann, der Hitler stoppte.*

Bulgarian Assembly, delivered a flamboyant speech, centered on the denunciation of the crimes of communism and an effort to tie postcommunist Bulgaria's democratic aspirations to the purported parliamentary vitality of the interwar period:

> Honorable Speaker, Members of Parliament, Ladies and Gentlemen,
>
> The Bulgarian Parliament has been in existence for one hundred and twenty years. During difficult times and fateful moments in our nation, there have always been members who, regardless of their political loyalties, have demonstrated their value as citizens, showing that they were willing to sacrifice their own serenity and their well-being to defend the constitutional rights of their fellow Bulgarians. . . .
>
> In 1943, Bulgaria was allied to the Rome-Berlin Axis. One had to be a great man, and a politician with strong democratic principles, like Dimităr Pešev, to take such a courageous and determined position against the annihilation of the Jews in Bulgaria. But his commitment did not end there: he also convinced forty-three [*sic*] deputies, members of the government majority, to add their signatures to the letter that he wrote in order to save the Jews. . . .
>
> During the long forty-five years of Communist dictatorship in Bulgaria, it was forbidden to speak of Dimităr Pešev and his fellow deputies of the 25th National Assembly.
>
> The Communist leaders showed no greater leniency towards the deputies whose courageous gesture contributed so much to our nation's prestige and status. In 1945, twenty of them were sentenced to death. Dimităr Pešev himself was sentenced to fifteen years' imprisonment; he ended his days in poverty and oblivion. Dimităr Pešev, the Deputy Speaker of the Bulgarian National Assembly, left an edifying example of loyalty to democratic principles, respect for humanity, and Christian love towards his neighbor.[118]

Democracy, humanism, and Christian roots: these are the three connotations associated with the signifier "Pešev"—albeit a minor bending of the facts, given that the Bulgarian politician in question did not always exemplify a steadfast commitment to the principles of democracy.

The same rereading of both the past *and* present characterized all Bulgarian memorial initiatives during a period when the country sought to position itself as a credible partner in the eyes of the EU. These initiatives capitalized on the preoccupation of the Council of Europe and the European Community institutions about the risk of a new "Berlin Wall of

---

118 http://www.peshev.org/kurtev.htm. Original speech in English.

memory," succeeding that of the Cold War era.[119] In 1992, Bulgaria's entry into the Council of Europe conferred upon its delegation a coveted seat at the Parliamentary Assembly of the Council of Europe (PACE), an arena prized for cultivating transnational memory initiatives.

Lăčezar Tošev (SDS), a scientist-turned-politician, who rose to prominence through his environmental activism during the fall of the Communist regime, was among the Bulgarian officials on the Council who worked not only toward a "denunciation of the crimes of communism," but also to publicly commemorate the Holocaust—namely, the "rescue of the Bulgarian Jews."[120] Under his leadership, in 1999, the Bulgarian parliament presented the Council of Europe with a bust of Pešev, sculpted by Ivan Minekov.

Following its session on September 20, 1999, the Committee on Works of Art within the Council accepted the gesture, responding with the recommendation that the statue include no other inscription than the name of the artist, the creator of the monument, and the date."[121] The inauguration on January 25, 2000, was attended by the president of PACE and the Speaker of the Bulgarian National Assembly. Concurrently, the ceremony provided Tošev the opportunity to promote the king's cause: "Under the erstwhile Bulgarian Constitution the final decision had to be taken by the monarch. His refusal to deport the Jews would result in a direct confrontation with Hitler which certainly was not riskless back then. It must be said, to his credit, that Tsar Boris III decided to disallow the deportation. Consequently, the entire Jewish community, numbering then 50,000 people, was rescued and never deported to the death camps. The petition did attain its objective."[122] The association between the conservative politician and the monarch is not immediately apparent. In 1936, Pešev's refusal to endorse Velčev's death sentence had offended the king—and by including the monarch among the addressees of his March 1943 letter, the deputy speaker effectively compelled Boris III to take a public position on the "Jewish question," discussion of which had previously been confined to committee meetings of a select few.

In Nissim's book, as well as in his subsequent contributions, no connection is drawn between the deputy speaker and a hypothetical Bulgarian democracy, on the one hand, or between his merits and those of the king,

119 The expression is borrowed from Droit, "Le Goulag contre la Shoah," 101–20.

120 http://toshev.blogspot.com/2009/12/mr-latchezar-toshevs-speech.html.

121 Ministers' Deputies, *CM Documents, 685 Meeting, 20[–21] October 1999, 13.1 Committee on Works of Art, Report of the Meeting* (Strasbourg, September 20, 1999), CM (99), 143, October 18, 1999.

122 *Reči na ceremonijata po darjavane na bjusta na Dimităr Pešev na Săveta na Evropa, Strasburg, 25 januari 2000 g.*, http://toshev.blogspot.com/2009/12/mr-latchezar-toshevs-speech.html. Original speech in English.

on the other. To the Milanese journalist, Pešev—once a supporter of the Third Reich—was an extraordinary figure precisely because he went through a moral conversion, which Nissim conveyed to the Bulgarian deputies in November 1998:

> Honorable Speaker Sokolov,
>
> Honorable Members of Parliament,
>
> . . . Pešev was not a "good man" acting on society in order to oppose the forces of evil. He was, to the contrary, a man who occupied a position at the highest level of government and who used every ounce of his power to accomplish what no other politician in the Axis dared to do.
>
> The deputy speaker of parliament . . . converted important politicians who, until that point, had looked away or had let themselves be influenced by the Germans, into men endowed with conscience and conviction. As incredible as it may seem, he even managed to convince the minister of the interior—the man who had meticulously organized the secret deportation plan—to telephone all the local police headquarters and revoke that order. . . .
>
> At that time, the sentiment that philosopher Hannah Arendt has described as "the banality of evil" was triumphant. . . . Even King Boris, who had authorized the deportations of the Jews from Thrace and Macedonia and who had, by his silence, approved the Belev-Dannecker Plan, emerged from inertia and, shortly before dying, spurned Hitler's pressing demands. . . .
>
> The extraordinary story of your deputy speaker could have been known across the globe; Pešev's name might have become as familiar to students across the world as that of the young girl from Amsterdam, Anne Frank. . . . The new totalitarianism could not let the truth be told about such men who had been courageous enough to stand against evil. Their story would have become a dangerous example, a subversive influence in a Gulag regime.[123]

The recounting of these three political interpretations of the heroic figure of Pešev illuminates the malleability of his trajectory, susceptible as it is to variant readings. Within the Bulgarian political sphere, sentenced by the People's Court in 1945, the conservative politician embodied the historical narrative that anti-communist politicians and intellectuals sought to propagate. For certain political actors and memory entrepreneurs, the invocation of his name, additionally, provided a means to differentiate between the king, the prime minister, and the "bourgeois" political elite. Pešev's actions stood out in contrast to those of the former head of the Council of Ministers and,

---

123 http://www.peshev.org/gn-sofia.htm.

perhaps, the monarch. Almost imperceptibly, there developed the possibility of transcending the dispute that divided the "reds" and "blues"; virtue was being reallocated at two distinct levels—parliamentary and individual.

Concurrently, Pešev's standing as a senior official of an institution that had been established as the very expression of democracy in the 1990s facilitated a broad reappropriation of his actions beyond the limited purview of Bulgaria. Indeed, both members of parliamentary assemblies and voters could readily align with this memorial cause. The resonance of Pešev's role in the "rescue of the Bulgarian Jews" within the PACE and the European Parliament can be most accurately understood by taking into account that both assemblies were at the time motivated to bolster their centrality within the European institutional framework.[124] Pešev, by extension, personified the virtues of the parliamentary assemblies per se. Moreover, marked by the decline of the utopian vision of the "transition to democracy," together with a disillusioned outlook on the present, the turn of the millennium yearned for narratives of personal integrity that transcended partisan affiliations. In Europe, citizens were increasingly disenchanted with ideologies and sought stories of individual exceptionalism. In this regard, the trajectory of the "Bulgarian Schindler"[125] held great public appeal. This global shift toward individualism and an apolitical definition of virtue would paradoxically pave the way for the reintroduction of an earlier concept—that of the exceptionally tolerant Bulgarian society—by adding a reference to the role of individuals and their unique virtues.

What lasting imprints shall we carry forward from this pivotal moment at the dawn of the new century? First, as in the early 1990s, we observe the use of savior figures as synecdoche: in a volatile present, they offer a sense of certainty derived from a morally righteous past. In 2002, the former residence of Pešev in Kjustendil was restored with the support of the Organization of Bulgarian Jews in Israel, the municipality of Kjustendil, and the Israeli ambassador to Bulgaria, Emanuel Zisman, himself a native of Plovdiv. In 2003, the property was transformed into a museum, inaugurated on the occasion of the sixtieth anniversary of the "rescue of the Bulgarian Jews." A decade later, a replica of the bust donated to the Council of Europe in 2000 was installed in Sofia Park, as if to symbolically reaffirm Bulgaria's affiliation with and anchoring in Europe. On January 27, 2014—International

---

124 On the empowering of the European Parliament, see Costa and Magnette, "Idéologies et changement institutionnel dans l'Union européenne," 49–75; and Hix and Høyland, "Empowerment of the European Parliament," 171–89. Regarding the commitment of PACE and the European Parliament to history and memory, see Perchoc, "Un passé, deux assemblées," 205–35.

125 Arrigo Levi, "Il nazionalista che salvò gli ebrei: La lista di Peshev; Uno Schindler bulgaro," *Corriere della Sera*, September 24, 1998.

Holocaust Remembrance Day since 2005—it was at this statue that the extermination of the European Jews was commemorated. The association between the commemoration of Jewish suffering in Europe and the "rescue" in Bulgaria began to crystallize in time.[126] Two years later, the celebration of March 10 took place first at the Monument to the Rescue and, subsequently, at the stone image of Pešev.[127]

Second, the episode relating to the Council of Europe underscored a critical aspect—namely, that Bulgarian memorial activism is distinct compared to other Central and Southeast European trajectories, a fact deserving of consideration. In Bulgaria, the memory of communism and that of the Holocaust were not perceived as opposed, but rather as juxtaposed. On the right of the political spectrum, it is often the same elected officials who have sought to legislate on the history of communism *and* Nazism, who simultaneously advocate for the acknowledgment of Communist crimes *and* for the remembrance of the Holocaust—precisely since they understand the latter to be a commemoration of the "rescue of the Bulgarian Jews." As the next chapter will demonstrate, this unique characteristic became increasingly pronounced as Bulgaria approached its EU accession date. Over time, Bulgarian elites began to view European institutions as the ideal arenas for a diplomatic positioning of the "rescue" of the Jews.

---

126 https://offnews.bg/obshtestvo/74-g-ot-spasiavaneto-na-balgarskite-evrei-649382.html.

127 http://www.bta.bg/bg/live/show/id/0_oxz39wvp (accessed February 19, 2020; no longer active).

Chapter 5

Fruitful Disputes?

Transnational Mobilizations and the Institutionalization of a Space of Dissensus

The fact that 1989 was not a watershed in all areas of social life in Bulgaria and that the notion of "postsocialism"—stretched out over decades with contrary undulations—ended up obscuring the changes it was supposed to shed light on are among the lessons learned in chapter 4. Between the implementation of institutional reforms, the emergence of new spaces for expressing disagreements, and the moment when historical discussions acquired rekindled visibility, a temporal gap was observed. It feels appropriate to account for this time lag by suspending the narrative. In the present chapter, the analysis resumes in the early 2000s, its object unchanged to the study of interpretive disputes around the facts of World War II. In order to elucidate controversies whose new acrimony prefigures their partial overcoming, however, attention is geared toward the pluralization of theaters and scales of interaction. Two countries stand at the core of the investigation—Bulgaria and the Republic of Northern Macedonia, whose Jewish population was almost completely exterminated during the war. At the time when the subject of the Holocaust entered into their bilateral relations, Bulgaria was a member state of the European Union (EU), aware of the resources of this membership, while North Macedonia aspired to start accession talks. A corolla of protagonists came to surround this duo as the field of discussion stretched across Europe and the Atlantic.

As in earlier chapters, the search for clues traverses a diversity of objects (films, documentaries, exhibitions), places (museums, commemorative scenes, parliaments), and repertoires of action (letters, petitions, public hearings, resolutions). The diplomacy of private actors—museums and Jewish community organizations, in particular—takes center stage, as does the circulation of people and ideas between national, regional, European, and international arenas. The chapter's key aim is to demonstrate the instituting force of these debates. No matter how bitter the discussions were, I argue that they encouraged a more precise documentation of the facts, as new stakeholders, issues, interests, and alliances came to the fore. In the last resort, these controversies helped to redefine the ways of formulating discussions of the Holocaust in Bulgaria and beyond.

To conduct this ultimate phase of the research, what time frame do we need to carve out? A decade, more or less—namely, the years 2007–19. The earlier years encompass three pivotal moments in the academic, political, and European arenas. First, by the mid-2000s, the organizational and generational transformations driven by the fall of communism within the historical profession had indeed corroded the boundaries between academic, expert, and advocacy knowledge, on the one hand, while fostering a strong internal differentiation within the academy itself, on the other. Largely absent from disputes about the Holocaust until then, Bulgarian scholars finally stepped in. The temporal distance between public debates and historiographical renewal is no less remarkable in the newly independent state of Macedonia (then recognized as the Former Yugoslav Republic of Macedonia, FYROM, by the United Nations): in that country, the nation-building process had been so deeply entangled with the Yugoslav experience (1944–91) that following the violent collapse of Yugoslavia the Macedonian political elites were initially reluctant to encourage a reconsideration of the Communist historical canon for fear of weakening the very foundation of the young state. The barely avoided Macedonian civil war in 2001 and the persistence of disputes with Serbia, Greece, and Bulgaria additionally favored a cautious evolution of the politics of history and historical writing.

Second, this historical conjecture would come to an end with the ascent to power in July 2006 of Nikola Gruevski, the leader of the Internal Macedonian Revolutionary Organization–Democratic Party for Macedonian National Unity (*Vnatrešna makedonska revolucionerna organizacija–Demokratska partija za makedonsko nacionalno edinstvo*, VMRO-DPMNE), a right-wing nationalist party that favored an authoritarian style of governing. The new head of the executive invested the historical repertoire with a fervor unknown to his predecessors. In his endeavor to imbue the Macedonian people with a sense of historical greatness, he decided to resort to an inspirational past. For a decade, the past was simultaneously dug up—in the archaeological soil of a nation endowed with a new yet older pre-Slavic ethnogenesis—and elevated through the frantic erection of statues and monuments throughout the urban space of the capital, Skopje. Two temporal orders were held together, whose elasticity was carried to the point of tearing: one, an age-old past that the accelerated engraving in stone made spectacular, and two, the sluggish pathway of Macedonia's progress toward EU accession. It is at their intersection that the history of anti-Jewish persecutions acquired an unprecedented acuity: in a context when Macedonian grandeur and its historical predicament came to occupy the pedestal of national discourse, Jewish suffering gradually assumed the status of a synecdoche for Macedonian national suffering; previously marginal in the quarrels between Bulgaria and Macedonia about the past, it became one of their cardinal points of reference at the turn of the 2010s. More broadly, in the insecure environment created by the end of the Cold War, the design of competitive memorial geographies was used to cement rival senses of community and to achieve political recognition.

Third, the EU enlargements of 2004 and 2007 constitute the last pivotal moment in the transformation of the topicality conferred on the Holocaust. Even prior to the accession of new central European members, the engagement of the Council of Europe and the European Union with history and remembrance policies had turned the European institutions into arenas where historical disputes were exposed and amplified. In choosing to oscillate between a logic of enlargement by wave versus a case-by-case basis, the EU also became a major stakeholder in the painful redefinition of symbolic hierarchies between postcommunist states whose history has, since the retreat of the Habsburg and Ottoman Empires, all too often been influenced by external arbitrations. Meanwhile, the evolving relations among the European Parliament, Commission, and Council that occurred concurrently with enlargement further increased the resonance conferred on battles over the telling of Europe's past.

Were one to present, in the mode of the philosophical tales of the eighteenth century, the lessons that the investigation carried out in this chapter hopes to deliver, the reader would be invited to pass impartial judgment along the following lines:

Wherein one will discover how the community and global arenas were invested by Bulgarian and Macedonian memory entrepreneurs, and how, weakened on a European scene of which Macedonia is not yet a member, those actors advocating the recognition of a Bulgarian coresponsibility in the deportations from the occupied territories invested museum spaces in order to publicize the contradictions of Bulgarian public discourse.

Wherein one shall reflect on the interactions between memorial initiatives and scholarly research that have enriched historical knowledge, as well as the virtues of living on the margins of academia.

Wherein one shall observe how an insensitive shift in the framing of controversies took place at the dawn of the 'teens of the twenty-first century, removing from the themes of the "rescue of the Bulgarian Jews" and the hierarchy of merit their exclusive capacity to structure debates, and allowing for a resurgence of questions about the destiny of the Jews who did not survive.

Wherein the role of coupling between the calls for a remembrance of the Holocaust and the denunciation of contemporary anti-Semitism will radiate in the appreciation of the historical quarrel by the leaders of American Jewish organizations, the leaders of the Bulgarian Jewish community, and the Bulgarian government.

Wherein a narrowing of the statements likely to lend themselves to collective validation will be observed—a narrowing that does not prohibit the reconduction, in some social worlds, of readings of Jewish destinies in terms of "rescue."

Charting a New Historiography

In the works devoted to the production of historical knowledge in Europe, three lines of demarcation are usually drawn.[1] The first opposes a model of state interference in the writing of history to a model of autonomy of the historical discipline—the latter being held to be the only way to ensure an effective scientific confrontation between divergent interpretations of the past. The second draws a line between professional historians active exclusively in academic circles and lay commentators whose contribution to historical knowledge is deemed negligible but who, as memory activists present in the public sphere, wish to confer the value of established facts on individual experiences and recollections of the past. Finally, a third division opposes a golden age in which historians would have enjoyed a monopoly on the narration of the past to a contemporary era that would disperse their authority among essayists, memory entrepreneurs, and public actors.

In many respects, the Bulgarian postcommunist trajectory invites nuances to these divisions. The post-1989 period was indeed accompanied by contradictory changes in the demography of historians, in the institutions and financing of research, as well as in "social demand."[2] Of the institutional landscape of the Communist era that had been underpinned by three buttresses—Sofia University, the institutes of the Bulgarian Academy of Sciences, and the institutions under the tutelage of the Communist Party—only the last one collapsed. The former High Party School, renamed the Academy for Social Sciences and Social Government (AONSU) in 1969, closed its doors in 1990, while the Institute for the History of the Communist Party under the Central Committee disappeared entirely. In academia, the shift to a market economy, the reduction of public funding, and the quest for a better future led to a massive brain drain. Between 1988 and 1993, social sciences

---

1   As pointed out in Behr, "Science du passé and politique du présent en Pologne."
2   Koleva and Elenkov, "Did 'the Change' Happen?," 94–127.

and hard sciences institutes lost 31 percent of their staff and 18.9 percent of their scholars. Some six hundred such individuals left for the United States, Germany, Canada, and Great Britain, relying on their multiple linguistic skills, international experience acquired prior to the fall of communism, or involvement in internationalized research networks.[3]

The social sciences were less affected by this brain drain because of the new careers that sprang up in the political and bureaucratic fields, thanks to the regime change. Polyglot researchers in their thirties reoriented themselves toward the nongovernmental sector, which blossomed in a matter of years as a result of Western funding. Those were times when an irenic vision of "civil society" prevailed—one that drew on twofold intellectual baggage: that of Anglo-American and European foundations that viewed the poorly reformed postcommunist states with mistrust;[4] and that of Eastern European dissidents, whose opposition to Communist regimes in the 1970s–1980s had relied on an individual ethic based on "antipolitics."[5] In Bulgaria, the fact that former Communists remained in power until 1997 (with the exception of the 1991–92 parenthesis) confirmed the preference of the major donors—the United States Agency for International Development (USAID), the Soros Foundation, the Open Society Institute, the German Friedrich Naumann, the Friedrich Ebert and Konrad Adenauer Foundations, the EU's PHARE[6] and Democracy programs[7]—for cooperation with private actors.[8]

Thus, in 1990, with the support of representatives of the midlevel nomenklatura, the Center for the Study of Democracy (*Centăr za izsledvane na*

---

3   Nationally, the migration of graduates is estimated at 87,895 in 1990, 46,496 in 1991, 69,348 in 1992, and 66,426 in 1993. Cited in Bobeva, Chalakov, and Markov, *Migracijata—evropejskata integracija i izticaneto na mozăci ot Bălgarija*, 15–16.

4   This line of argument is built on an analogy between NGOs and "civil society" with little explanatory power; see Leca, "De la lumière sur la société civile," 62–72.

5   Konrad, *Antipolitics*.

6   Created in 1989 as the Poland-Hungary Economic Reconstruction Assistance (program—*Pologne Hongrie Aide à la reconstruction économique*, PHARE), then renamed the Community Assistance Program for Central and Eastern European Countries, the program was originally intended to support the transition to a market economy and democracy. From 1997 onward, its priorities were reoriented toward the EU preaccession process.

7   Originally with a budget of ecu 5 million, this program was launched after the European Parliament adopted a European Democracy Initiative in 1992 calling for support to Eastern European nongovernmental sectors.

8   Genov and Becker, *Social Sciences*, 34–62.

demokracijata, CID) was born, a think tank that would serve as a model followed by many private expert institutes. One of them, the Center for Liberal Strategies (*Centăr za liberalni strategi*, CLS), launched in 1994, welcomed the economist and historian Roumen Avramov, who would become one of the key players in the renewal of studies on anti-Jewish policies. In the first half of the 1990s, the private-sector knowledge scene acquired two other institutions of interest to our discussion: the International Center on Minority Problems and Intercultural Relations (*Meždunaroden centăr po problemite na malcinstvata i kulturnite vzaimodejstvija*, IMIR) and the Bulgarian Helsinki Committee (*Bălgarski Helzinski Komitet*, BHK). Their founders, Ottoman historian Antonina Željazkova and philosopher Krasimir Kănev, had both joined the team of advisers on ethnocultural affairs formed by philosopher and former dissident Želju Želev (SDS) after his election to the presidency in August 1990. In a context overshadowed by social mobilizations hostile to the restoration of the rights of Bulgarian Turks announced by the leaders of the Communist Party in December 1989 and by the proximity of the Yugoslav armed conflict, minority issues occupied a nodal place in the strategy of international aid donors. Founded in April 1992 in partnership with Birmingham and Warwick Universities, IMIR aimed to encourage research and expertise on minority issues.[9] The BHK was created at the same time and quickly established itself as one of the main protagonists in the field of human and minority rights.[10] Prompted to adjust to the changing preferences of the donors, these institutions engaged in cause lawyering and/or the publication of scholarly pieces whose rigor had nothing to envy compared to the output of universities.[11]

What about the academic world? There a certain amount of continuity was observed in the definition of missions, methods, and research objects against a background of institutional pauperization, erosion of salaries, nonrenewal of positions, and disaffection of students for a specialization that offered limited professional prospects. Above all, the historical discipline found itself orphaned from a Communist historical policy that, under Todor Zhivkov, had set up historians as the spearhead of an all-conquering rediscovery of the past. Although deeply divided over its appreciation of the defunct regime, historians struggled to reinvent their social role.[12] In

---

9   In 2002, IMIR published a remarkable annotated bibliography on Jewish history in Bulgaria: Eškenazi and Krispin, *Evreite po bălgarskite zemi*.

10   A joint initiative of the BHK, Šalom, and the Open Society Institute conducted a pioneering study on anti-Semitism in the Bulgarian media in 2003–4: Krispin, *Antisemitizăm v Bălgarija dnes*.

11   IMIR has published several PhD dissertations, including that of Ulrih Bjuksenšjutc: *Malcintsvenata politika v Bălgarija*.

12   Daskalov, *Ot Stambolov do Živkov*, 187–295, 296–446.

1993, Georgi Markov, a specialist in diplomatic and military history, became director of the Bulgarian Academy of Sciences' Institute of History, going on to serve a ten-year tenure. There he defended the national canon while climbing the academic hierarchy until he received the honorary title of academician in 2008.[13] At Sveti Kliment Ohridski University in Sofia, a brief hope for renewal was held out by Balkan history scholar Ivan Ilčev—the son of Communist historian and former minister of education Ilčo Dimitrov—before he took over as rector in 2008 and the hopes for change faded away.

The 1990s saw the emergence of private universities, some of which had ephemeral futures. The New Bulgarian University (*Nov bălgarski universitet*) was established on the premises of the former AONSU and included a few specialists in the history of communism and teachers known for their anticommunist commitment. In 1991, on the borders of Greece and Macedonia, the Soros Foundation, USAID, and representatives of Bulgaria's anticommunist emigré community founded an American University in Bulgaria (AUBG), which was intended to be a relay point for the democratization process in the Balkans. The dynamism of AUBG's student recruitment rendered it an essential step on the road to internationalization and expatriation of generations of graduates, rather than a player in the Bulgarian research landscape.

A second wave of reforms accompanied the preparation of Bulgaria's accession to the EU. As the major private aid providers redirected their programs to the Caucasus and Central Asia, a new European knowledge economy started taking shape. No more bypassing the states: from the late 1990s onward, the EU elites determined to strengthen public institutions now seen as privileged partners. At the Bulgarian Ministry of Higher Education and Research, a Scientific Research Fund was created, which was endowed with a generous budget. In the solicitation of new public funds, the experience acquired in the service of private foundations paradoxically provided a comparative advantage to those NGOs that had made the demarcation from the state a component of their institutional identity. While the professionalization of the field of expertise favored a clearer separation between scientific knowledge and advocacy, two new private research centers were making their mark on Sofia's intellectual scene.

The Institute for Study of the Recent Past (*Institut za izsledvane na blizkoto minalo*) was born in 2005 on the initiative of former minister of culture Ivajlo Znepolski (1993–95), an ex-member of the Institute of Contemporary Social Theories (*Institut za săvremenni socialni teorii*, IIBM) of the defunct High Party School, who became, after 1989, a pivotal actor in critical

---

13   In 2010, Georgi Markov's former affiliation with the Communist intelligence services was made public. Comdos, *Rešenie*, 110 (February 9, 2010).

historiography of socialism.[14] With the help of solid international funding and a partnership with the Siela publishing house, the IIBM attracted the collaboration of renowned academics while offering young researchers lacking a permanent position contracts on deliverables. Although the history of communism was the main focus of the research conducted under its aegis, the promotion of oral history by the institute extended to the collection of Jewish life stories.[15] The second actor on the Sofia-based private research scene, the Center for Advanced Study Sofia (CAS), the Bulgarian branch of the Network of European Institutes for Advanced Study, has advocated a multiperspectivist and transnational writing of Balkan history since its creation in 2001.[16] Today, the worlds of history in Bulgaria are thus not primarily organized around an opposition between public and private research, nor even between historians who produce knowledge and private foundations that privilege advocacy initiatives. The essential divide separates academics with access to national, European, or international funding from those without; the possibility for scholars to undertake innovative work therefore depends on their ability to occupy positions at the confluence of the academic and private sectors.

In the intellectual landscape that has just been sketched out, how is the history of Jewish destiny written? The former quasi monopoly held by the Communist organization of the Bulgarian Jews (OKPOE) has disappeared. Beyond the publication in 1995 under the direction of David Koen—an authorized pen of the Communist era—of a collection of archive documents whose main innovation lay in the title, *Survival 1940–1944* (*Oceljavaneto 1940–1944*),[17] the publishing activity of Šalom, its successor, has been confined to works of historical popularization and to the perpetuation of the narrative of the "rescue of Bulgarian Jews."[18]

Renewal came from elsewhere. The transfer to the Bulgarian Central State Archives of funds from the Ministries of the Interior and Foreign Affairs, the slightly relaxed access to military archives, as well as the establishment in 2007 of a Commission for the Disclosure of Documents and Identification of Bulgarian Citizens Affiliated with the State Security and Intelligence Services of the Bulgarian National Army (*Komisija za razkrivane na dokumentite i za objavjavane na prinadležnost na bălgarski graždani kăm Dăržavna sigurnost i razuznavatelnite službi na Bălgarskata narodna armija*, or Comdos) made exceptionally rich material available to scholars. The digitization of the

---

14   http://minaloto.bg/.
15   Koleva, *Bălgarija – Izrael.*
16   https://www.cas.bg/en.
17   Koen, *Oceljavaneto;* Koen, *Evreite v Bălgarija.*
18   Organizacija na evreite v Bălgarija Šalom, *75 godini.*

funds and the intense editorial activity deployed by the CDA and Comdos also placed important archival materials within the reach of a wider public. In 2012, Comdos delivered a volume devoted to the Communist-era surveillance of Jewish communities by the intelligence services that also shed new light on anti-Jewish policies during wartime.[19] A few months before the celebrations of the seventieth anniversary of the "rescue of the Bulgarian Jews" in 2013, the CDA undertook the monumental work of digitization of the *funds* relating to the history of the Jews of Bulgaria.[20] In parallel, the upload of the protocols of the chambers of the People's Court (1944–45) began.[21] Finally, the archive-sharing partnerships sealed with major international institutions such as the USHMM and Yad Vashem have expanded the territories for consulting copies of Bulgarian documents.[22] If one adds to these developments the adoption of liberal legal rules concerning the reproduction and publication of archival documents, one can better understand the profusion of archival collections published in recent years. In 2007, the German Federal Archives (Bundesarchiv), the Institut für Zeitgeschichte in Munich, and the Department of Modern and Contemporary History at the University of Freiburg launched a large-scale project, *The Persecution and Murder of European Jews by National Socialist Germany 1933–1945* (*Die Verfolgung und Ermordung der europäischen Juden durch das nationalsozialistische Deutschland 1933–1945*), which aims to provide a comprehensive view of the Holocaust in Europe. Drawing extensively on documents preserved in the CDA, the volume dedicated to the Bulgarian case (associated with Slovakia and Romania) benefited from this liberalization.[23]

In Bulgaria, the movement to publish primary sources has continued to grow since the late 1990s. In the course of the editions, the portrait of the legal framework of anti-Jewish persecutions acquired a pointillist precision.[24] A wealth of reports from the police, intelligence services, agents of the Commissariat for Jewish Affairs, bureaucrats, and diplomats now make it possible to follow, step by step, the conception and application of anti-Jewish

---

19 Comdos, *Dăržavna sigurnost i evrejskata obštnost v Bălgarija.*

20 Dăržavna Agencija Arhivi, *Evrejskata obštnost v Bălgarija*, http://archives.bg/jews/.

21 Dăržavna Agencija Arhivi, *Naroden săd*, http://archives.bg/narodensud/.

22 Communication with Anžel Čorapčiev, archivist at Yad Vashem, Sofia, June 14, 2016.

23 Hutzelmann, Hausleitner, and Hazan, *Die Verfolgung und Ermordung der europäischen Juden durch das nationalsozialistische Deutschland.*

24 Koen, *Oceljavaneto*; Paunovski and Iliel, *Evreite v Bălgarija meždu uništoženieto i spasenieto*; Institut po istorija na BAN, *Obrečeni i spaseni*; Dobčev, *Antievrejskoto zakonodatelstvo i negovoto preodoljavane*; Cekov and Taneva, *Antievrejskoto zakonodatelstvo v Evropa i Bălgarija.*

measures.[25] This chain of publications has also renewed our knowledge of the relationship between Bulgaria and Nazi Germany and, incidentally, of Bulgarian decision-making autonomy.[26] At the same time, the publication of the minutes of the meetings of the Holy Synod has offered a detailed vision of the response of the Bulgarian Orthodox Church to the persecution of the Jews.[27] The publication of the diaries of high-ranking German[28] and Bulgarian officials,[29] as well as of members of the opposition[30] has broadened the range of points of view captured in the course of events or in retrospect.[31]

Documentation of the deportations from the occupied territories has followed, albeit at a slower pace. In 2004, Ivan Hadžijski offered a lengthy introduction to a collection of archives centered on this topic, a rare occurrence at the time.[32] The most important initiative to date remains the two-volume edition coordinated by Nadja Danova and Roumen Avramov.[33] With exceptional thoroughness, the two Bulgarian historians inventoried all the previous publications of the documents they reprinted, opening the way to a study of the policies of publicization or eclipse of specific archival records. Their editorial choice of materials also shed light on lesser-known facets of Bulgarian policies, such as the differential treatment of Jews with and without Bulgarian citizenship. Furthermore, they drew up a list of the names of Jews rounded up from the Yugoslav and Greek territories under Bulgarian control. Two introductory texts completed this masterly work: a review of the literature by Nadja Danova; and a reflection by Roumen Avramov that places the deportations from the occupied territories in the economy of World War II and of Bulgarian state anti-Semitism.

Not without surprise, this renewal came from the margins of institutionalized history of the war. The documentation of the facts has benefited from

25 Gezenko, "Zakonodatelnata i izpălnitelnata vlast v izgraždaneto na anti-evrejskoto zakonodatelstvo," 162–76.
26 Toškova, *Bălgarija, svoenravnijat săjuznik na Tretija rajh;* Biljarski and Gezenko, *Diplomatičeski dokumenti po učastieto na Bălgarija v Vtorata svetovna vojna.*
27 Taneva and Gezenko, *Glasove v zaštita na graždansko obštestvo.*
28 Toškova, *Iz dnevnika na Bekerle – pălnomošten ministăr na Tretija Rajh v Bălgarija.*
29 Filov, *Dnevnik;* Lulčev, *Tajnite na dvorcovija život;* Mitakov, *Dnevnik na Pravosădnija ministăr v pravitelstvata na Georgi Kjosejivanov i Bogdan Filov.*
30 Niselkova and Hazan, *Nikola Mušanov.*
31 Pešev, *Spomeni.*
32 Hadžijski, *Sădbata na evrejskoto naselenie v Belomorska Trakija, Vardarska Makedonija i Jugozapadna Bălgarija prez.*
33 Danova and Avramov, *Deportiraneto.*

the contribution of archivists—Ivanka Gezenko and Vărban Todorov, in particular.[34] The seizure of Jewish themes by jurists also delivered some remarkable insights: in 2015, Zdravka Krăsteva, an associate professor of law at Sofia University, penned an outstanding contribution on the issue of Bulgarian sovereignty over the occupied territories and the legal responsibility of the Bulgarian state for the deportations.[35] Among political scientists, Albena Taneva was a research assistant to the Israeli politician and lay historian committed to the cause of "rescue" Michael Bar-Zohar,[36] before devoting a doctoral dissertation to the study of public discourse on this theme.[37] She also established a small Center for Jewish Studies (*Centăr za evrejski izsledvanija*) at the Faculty of Philosophy at Sofia University.

Within the historical discipline, the impetus was given either by scholars whose expertise was neither in World War II nor in Jewish studies, or by brilliant young polyglot scholars, critics of the national canon, who were recognized abroad but lacked strong institutional positions in Bulgaria.[38] Nadja Danova, a historian and senior researcher at the Institute of Balkan Studies of the Bulgarian Academy of Sciences, had previously risen to prominence with her work on Bulgaria's cultural renaissance in the nineteenth century. Roumen Avramov, an economic historian who held senior positions at the Bulgarian Central Bank, was a researcher at the private Center for Advanced Studies, when he began a pioneering investigation into the expropriation of Jewish property in Bulgaria during the war.[39] It was through oral history research that the Jewish experiences of forced labor were addressed by the ethnologists Evgenija Troeva and Ana Luleva.[40] Some historians such as assistant professor of contemporary history at the South-West University of Blagoevgrad, Stefan Dečev, have devoted much acumen to the popularization of scientific knowledge in the media (Deutsche Welle, Svobodna Evropa, among others). A voice from the field of history of philosophy, that

---

34   See Železčeva, "Novi strihi kăm săzdavaneto i dejnostta na Komisarstvoto po evrejskite văprosi," 20–37.

35   Krăsteva, "Pravni aspekti na dăržavnata antievrejska politika," 77–192.

36   Taneva has also translated into Bulgarian Bar-Zohar's *Beyond Hitler's Grasp*.

37   Albena Taneva, "Liderskijat obštestven model: Spasjavaneto na evreite v Bălgarija v političeskija diskurs," PhD diss., Universitet Sv. Kliment Ohridski, 2007.

38   One thinks in particular of the remarkable work of Aleksandăr Vezenkov: "Spasjavaneto na bălgarskite evrei: Unikalno li e naistina?," *Kultura*, October 18 and November 1, 2013.

39   Avramov, *"Spasenie" i padenie*; Ragaru, "La spoliation des biens juifs en Bulgarie pendant la Seconde Guerre mondiale," 176–218.

40   Troeva-Grigorova, "Prinuditelnijat trud prez Vtorata svetovna vojna v spomenite na bălgarskite evrei," 39–54.

of professor Stilijan Jotov from Sofia University, took an active part in the discussion of historical controversies over the wartime fate of Jews in Bulgaria.[41]

These contributions, it should be recalled, were delivered in close dialogue with the initiatives of memory entrepreneurs and human rights activists. Predictably, the public calls for clarification of the facts have followed the rhythm of commemorations of the "rescue of the Bulgarian Jews," moments of high media and editorial visibility. It is enough to recall the celebration of the seventieth anniversary in 2013 to be convinced: exhibition catalogs,[42] symposium proceedings,[43] and archival collections[44] were published alongside pamphlets betraying the bitterness of intra-Jewish disagreements about the war.[45] On October 5–7, 2012, Juliana Metodieva, editor in chief of the Helsinki Committee's monthly *Obektiv*, organized an international symposium, "Fully Knowing Your Past" (*Da opoznaem minaloto si*).[46] In the wake of this international conference, the director of the BHK, Krasimir Kănev, denounced Bulgarian "complicity in genocide" and called on the Bulgarian state to acknowledge its responsibilities in the historical events.[47] The public response was immediate: on January 17, 2013, several Bulgarian intellectuals, historians, and elected officials sent an open letter to the head of state, the prime minister, and the parliament denouncing the "political instrumentalization" of history. This was a reminder, if one were needed, that a fringe of the historical profession acquiesces in, and even actively supports, the

---

41   Stilijan Jotov, "70 godini vojna na interpretaciite," *Librev.com*, May 17, 2023, https://librev.com/index.php/discussion-bulgaria-publisher/2058-70. One may additionally showcase the contribution of other disciplines, namely sociology, to the examination of public discourse. See, for instance, the writings of Prof. Liliana Deyanova, from the Sofia University Sveti Kliment Ohridski: Dejanova, "Non-Saved Jews," 162–72.

42   Dăržavna Agencija Arhivi, *Truden izbor s goljamo značenie*.

43   Grozev and Marinova-Hristidi, *Evreite v iztočna Evropa i Săvetski săjuz v godinite na Vtorata svetovna vojna i studenata vojna*.

44   Todorov and Poppetrov, *VII săstav na Narodnija săd*.

45   Samuil Arditi, *Čovekăt, kojto izigra Hitler: Car Boris III—gonitel ili prijatel na bălgarskite evrei* (Ruse, Bul.: n.p., 2013); Spas Tašev, *Deportacijata na evreite ot Vardarska Makedonija i Belomorieto: Fakti i mitove* (Sofia: Makedonski naučen institut, 2012).

46   Juliana Metodieva, ed., "Da opoznaem minaloto si," *Obektiv* 209, October 2012, https://www.bghelsinki.org/bg/magazines/broj-209; Juliana Metodieva, "Otzvuci ot konferencijata 'Da opoznaem minaloto si,'" *Librev.com*, October 2012, https://www.librev.com/index.php/discussion/bulgaria/1799-2012-10-10-10-11-08.

47   Krasimir Kănev, "Zašto deportiraneto na evreite ot Makedonija i Trakija prez Vtorata svetovna vojna e săučastie v genocid," *Obektiv* 210, October 2012.

Bulgarian state's policy toward history. The letter ended with an interpellation of the institutions representing the Jews of Bulgaria:

[During the war] Bulgaria was an ally of Nazi Germany, but against the will of the latter, it *saved* several tens of thousands of human lives. . . . In this situation, the same Bulgarian state did *not* save tens of thousands of human lives on the territory of Yugoslavia and Greece. On this basis, certain personalities and circles in Bulgaria and abroad call its behavior criminal. They keep trying to shift the historical guilt and, incidentally, Bulgaria's debt to the Jewish community. . . . We declare that this accusation against Bulgarian society is hypocritical and unfair, and that it is the application of a moral double standard. . . . We would appreciate that the leadership of the Organization of Jews Šalom clarify the political language in which they interpret the events related to the rescue/nonrescue of the Jews from our homeland—Bulgaria—having in view the new evidence and the acknowledgment by renowned Holocaust expert Šlomo Šealtiel[48] on November 3, 2012, on national television (BNT) of the fact that Bulgaria was unable to stand up to Hitler's Reich.[49]

Shortly thereafter, the adoption of a declaration by the Bulgarian National Assembly on March 8, 2013, deploring the powerlessness of the Bulgarian authorities in preventing the deportation of Jews from the occupied territories suggested that a cross-party consensus with strong patriotic content had been consolidated.[50] Meanwhile, in the daily press (e.g., *Dnevnik*), the intellectual weekly *Kultura*,[51] and the monthly *Obektiv*,[52] discussions on the political uses of history were nonetheless taking place among sociologists,[53] philosophers,[54] and historians who aspired to emancipate history from its

---

48   An Israeli historian, from a Jewish line of Bulgarian descent, Šlomo Šealtiel is the author of several books on the history of Bulgarian Jews and Zionism.

49   *Otkrito pismo: Bălgarija meždu osanna i razpni ja; Za imeto Bălgarija i negovata upotreba v konteksta na Holokosta* (Sofia: January 17, 2013).

50   Deklaracija na Četirideset i părvoto Narodno săbranie na Republika Bălgarija po povod godišninata ot spasjavaneto na bălgarskite evrei o počitane pametta na žertvite na Holokosta, https://www.parliament.bg/bg/declaration/ID/14359.

51   Roumen Avramov, "Za čoveškata cena na nacionalnija ideal: Razgovor s Koprinka Červenkova," *Kultura*, April 19, 2013.

52   "Dăržavnijat antisemitizăm 1940–1944," *Obektiv* 202, September 2012, https://www.bghelsinki.org/bg/publication/drzhavniyat-antisemitizm-1940-1944-g.

53   Liliana Deyanova, "Mălčănija v istorijata: Istorija i istoričeska sociologija na kolektivnata pamet," *Marginalia.bg*, July 6, 2015.

54   Jotov, "Spasenieto na bălgarskite evrei."

ancillary function in service to the nation.[55] To this day, however, these debates have not migrated into the writing of historical monographs or a new generation of school textbooks.

Having sketched this overview of the positions and entanglements among academic, expert, and activist spaces in Bulgaria, it is now possible to widen the focus to the second actor in the controversies: the Republic of North Macedonia. The late appearance of North Macedonia in the narrative is owing to the mid-2000s change of government there that placed Jewish destinies in orbit around memorial disputes relating to Macedonian history and identity.

Bulgarian-Macedonian Holocaust Controversies

Until the breakup of Yugoslavia and the proclamation of an independent state of Macedonia in 1991, the history of the Jewish community of Macedonia had remained on the margins of a topography of the Holocaust written on the scale of the Yugoslav Federation; in Yugoslavia, the bulk of the work had focused on Croatia, Serbia, and Bosnia-Herzegovina.[56] In 1952, the Federation of Jewish Communities in Yugoslavia (*Savez jevrejskih opština Jugoslavije*) supervised the construction of monuments in Belgrade, Zagreb, Sarajevo, Novi Sad, and Ðakovo.[57] It would take another six years before a seven-branched candelabra would become part of the urban landscape of Bitola, in the south of the Socialist Federal Republic of Macedonia, to commemorate the extermination. The memorial reads:

March 11, 1943

To the 3,013 Jews, our fellow citizens, victims of fascist terror

The citizens of Bitola, March 11, 1958

The words on the monument thus subscribed to socialist ideological imperatives (figure 5.1). On this occasion, a booklet was published under the auspices of the local union of partisans that explicitly referred to the "Jewish genocide."[58]

---

55 Vezenkov, "Spasjavaneto."
56 Džulibrk, *Istoriografija Holokausta u Jugoslaviji.*
57 Kerenji, "Jewish Citizens of Socialist Yugoslavia," 179–236.
58 *11 Mart 1943–1958 Bitola.* At the same time, Jakov Aroesti and the ethnographers Duško Konstantinov and Miloš Konstantinov dedicated an 804-page typescript to the 3,013 Jews of Bitola on the model of the books of remembrance: Aroesti, Konstantinov, and Konstantinov, "Bitoljski jevreji, Bitola."

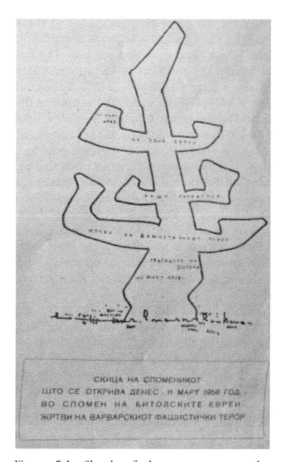

Figure 5.1. Sketch of the monument to the "victims of fascist terror" inaugurated in Bitola, Socialist Federal Republic of Macedonia, March 11, 1958. *Source: 11 Mart 1943–1958 Bitola: Na 3 013 Bitolski evrei—žrtvi na fašizma* (Skopje: Opštinski odbor na Sojuzot na borcite od NOB Bitola, 1958), 2.

How can this low level of interest be understood? At the end of World War II, in which the violence of the German, Hungarian, Italian, and Bulgarian occupations had been redoubled by intercommunal and ideological confrontations of rare virulence, Tito had built the Yugoslav Federation on an obliteration of the recent rifts. Yugoslav historians were invited to produce a historical narrative exalting the brotherhood between peoples; in ways reminiscent of the Bulgarian configuration, and although the Jewish survivors had sought to invent their own ways of remembering,[59] a desingularization of the Jewish experience had resulted. The strong representation of partisans among the survivors of Macedonia had also favored the heralding of only one figure of Jewishness—that of the antifascist fighter.[60] The theme of anti-Jewish persecution was the subject of the isolated attention of Aleksandar Matkovski, an Ottoman historian, at the turn of the 1950s–1960s.[61] In 1986, an anthology of archives completed this sparse editorial landscape: for the first time, Jewish testimonies collected by the State Commission for the Establishment of Crimes Committed by the Occupying Powers and Their Collaborators in 1944–1945 (*Državna komisija za utvrduenje prestaplenieto na okupatorite i nivnite pomagači*) were contained in a documentary collection that included archives of the Jewish community in Skopje and the list of deportees compiled in German at the temporary detention camp there. Although not silenced, the low solidarity of non-Jews with their Jewish fellow citizens was blamed on the speed of the Bulgarian arrests; the Jewish struggle against the fascist occupier was placed at the heart of the analysis.[62]

Such a configuration might obfuscate the fact that history had become one of the great public causes in Macedonia as early as 1944. In 1912, at the end of the First Balkan War, this multiethnic and multiconfessional Ottoman province, in which a national movement had crystallized at the turn of the twentieth century, had been incorporated into the Kingdom of Serbia as "Southern Serbia" (*Južna Srbija*).[63] Transformed into the Vardar Banovina (*Vardarska banovina*) with expanded borders within the Kingdom of Yugoslavia in 1929, Vardar Macedonia had to wait until 1944 to acquire the

---

59   Kerenji, *Jewish Citizens.*

60   Case, "Combined Legacies,'" 352–76; Troebst, "Macedonian Historiography," 107–14; Ragaru, "Bordering the Past," 1–32.

61   A first manuscript of ninety-one typescript pages was written in 1957 in Serbo-Croatian, before being published in Macedonian, Hebrew, and English. Matkovski, "Macedonian Jewry in 1943," 203–58; Matkovski, *Tragedijata na Evreite od Makedonija.* In the early 1980s, an expanded version appeared in: Matkovski, *Istorija na Evreite vo Makedonija.*

62   Kolonomos and Vesković-Vangeli, *Evreite vo Makedonija vo Vtorata svetska vojna.* This publication was intended to refute the suspicions, reactivated in the 1980s, of a Jewish reluctance to rejoin the ranks of the partisan movement. Case, "Combined Legacies," 363.

63   The two Balkan Wars (1912–13) saw Southeast European states that had gained independence during the nineteenth century join forces, and then clash, over the European territories still under the control of a weakened Ottoman Empire.

status of a constituent unit in the new Yugoslav Federation. A Macedonian nation was officially recognized for the first time and a process of literary standardization of the Macedonian language—a South Slavic language close to Bulgarian and Serbian—was undertaken. In 1948, the Scientific Institute for the National History of the Macedonian People (*Naučen institut za nacionalna istorija na makedonskiot narod*) was tasked with working toward the knowledge and consolidation of national identity.[64] In this endeavor, World War II was from the outset a key episode, placing Bulgarian and Macedonian historiography at odds: presented in Bulgarian writings as an emancipation from the "Serbian yoke," the Bulgarian occupation was portrayed by Macedonian historians as a negation of Macedonian national identity.[65] Denouncing the violent policy of Bulgarianization implemented during wartime by the occupiers had the additional virtue of silencing the uncertainties of identity—local, regional, or national Macedonian identity, Serbian identity, Bulgarian identity, or even Greek identity?—that had long prevailed among a Slavic population incorporated into the Ottoman Empire for five centuries.

However, it was during the 1970s and 1980s that Bulgarian-Macedonian disagreements became more bitter. In the Socialist Federal Republic of Macedonia, the quest for ever deeper national origins led local historians to claim as Macedonian several historical figures whom their colleagues considered Bulgarian. On both sides of the border, academics and intelligence services used archives, monographs, memoirs, and symposia to refute the theses of the other side. The anti-Jewish persecutions nevertheless remained on the periphery of the controversies concerning the ethnogenesis of the Macedonian people.[66]

One might have expected the collapse of Yugoslavia to prompt a radical departure in the writing of Macedonian history: overnight, Macedonia became the level from which "a chosen, inspiring past,"[67] emancipated from any external tutelage, could be narrated. The affirmation of Macedonian statehood intervened, however, under dark auspices: while civil war raged at its gates, the country had to face the disavowal of an Albanian minority,

---

64 Brunnbauer, "Historiography, Myths," 165–200.

65 Terzioski, *Denacionalizatorskata dejnost na bugarskite kulturno-prosvetni institucii vo Makedonija*; Mitrevski, *Skopje 1941 niz bugarskata upravno-policiska arhiva i ustaško-domobranskata dokumentacija*; Institut za nacionalna istorija, *Izvori za Osloboditelnata vojna i Revolucijata vo Makedonija*.

66 Troebst, *Die bulgarisch-jugoslawische Kontroverse*; Marinov, *La Question macédonienne de 1944 à nos jours*.

67 The expression is borrowed from Di Lellio and Schwander-Sievers, "Legendary Commander," 518.

which felt excluded from the nation-state project in the making.[68] The creation of an independent state also aroused the reservations of Greece, whose ruling elites worried about a possible Macedonian irredentism.[69] And although Bulgaria recognized Macedonian independence in January 1992, the Bulgarian authorities were suspected of denying the existence of a Macedonian language distinct from Bulgarian, if not of a Macedonian nation.

This climate of uncertainty encouraged a policy of "continuity by default."[70] The place of socialist Yugoslavia in the national historical narrative was gradually constricted[71] by historians close to the VMRO-DPMNE, the anti-communist nationalist formation that claimed the heritage of the anti-Ottoman struggle.[72] Under socialism, the left wing of VMRO had been credited with the creation of a Macedonian nation, Tito's partisan movement with a patriotic and Communist struggle against the Bulgarian occupiers, and the Communists with the institutionalization of the Macedonian republic, language, and people. Scholars affiliated with VMRO-DPMNE proceeded first to rehabilitate those socialists repressed after the war because of their supposedly autonomist views, then partisans who had belonged to the Bulgarian-led resistance fraction, and finally members of the right wing of the VMRO. Some formerly stigmatized pro-Bulgarian figures were adorned with patriotic colors in a move that aroused the ire of the ex-Communist Macedonian elites.[73]

During the first postcommunist decade, these modulations only marginally affected the deciphering of Jewish destinies: as in the past, relations between Jews and non-Jews were placed under the sign of solidarity. The contribution of the Jews to the struggles of the Macedonian people was hailed; anti-Jewish persecutions were imputed to the Bulgarian occupiers and their German protectors. The specificity of anti-Jewish crimes was silenced, whereas Jewish agency was confined to the partisan movement.[74] The calendar, the rituals, and the speeches accompanying the

---

68 Neofotistos, *Risk of War.*

69 Shea, *Macedonia and Greece.*

70 Marinov, "Historiographical Revisionism," 1–19 (here, 9).

71 Stefoska and Stojanov, "Remembering and Forgetting," 206–25.

72 In 1893, a political organization was created in Salonika, soon endowed with an armed branch, and engaged in a struggle against Ottoman rule. Its leaders defended political projects ranging from Macedonian autonomy within the empire to an attachment to Bulgaria. Perry, *Politics of Terror.*

73 Marinov, "Historiographical Revisionism," 9.

74 The few publications are local initiatives promoted by the Jewish Community of Macedonia (*Evrejska zaednica vo Makedonija*) and by amateur historians on the occasion of the five-hundredth anniversary of the expulsion of the Jews from Spain and Portugal, in 1992, and the fiftieth anniversary of the

annual commemoration of the roundups displayed a similar continuity. At best, the Jewish—that is, partisan—struggle was reclassified as a national—Macedonian—Jewish struggle.[75]

The first major shift occurred when VMRO-DPMNE won the July 5, 2006, parliamentary vote. The economist Nikola Gruevski was elected on a platform of reaffirming national pride in a country shaken by the Albanian insurgency of 2001,[76] and where measures to protect minority rights promoted by the international community were strongly resented by the majority. Prime Minister Gruevski decided to place historical policies at the heart of his legitimacy-building strategy: he sponsored a de-Yugoslavization of the historical narrative and aimed to anchor "Macedonianness" in a long pre-Slavic period. The experience of the Kingdom of Yugoslavia (1918–41) was reread in an unfavorable light; Macedonian emancipation was attributed not to the partisan movement (pro-Yugoslav and Macedonian), but to a Macedonian (and not Yugoslav) VMRO. In the same way, the adjective "social" disappeared from descriptions of the revolutionary struggle, while references to "the Macedonian people and the nationalities," inherited from the Yugoslav language, were refocused on the titular nation alone. At the same time, the origins of the Macedonian people were no longer sought between the two world wars, or even in the anti-Ottoman struggle of the nineteenth century, or in medieval times. The new ethnogenesis, achieved through a process of "antiquitization,"[77] traced the appearance of a Macedonian nation distinct from the Hellenic world back to antiquity. Thereby, the Macedonians ceased to be Slavic since the settlement of Slavs in the Balkans dated only to the sixth century CE.

Two facets of this reengineering of the past affected the comprehension of the Holocaust and, incidentally, the relationship with Bulgaria. First, the Macedonization of heroism had as its counterpart that of historical suffering. While the public discourse drew up a new cartography of

---

deportations, in 1993. Šarović et al., *Štipskite evrei*; Kitanoski and Loteska, *Skopskite evrei*; Dimovski-Colev, *Bitolskite evrei*. Among translations, see Assa, *Makedonija i Evrejskiot narod.*

75   Case, "Combined Legacies," 367.

76   In the winter of 2000–2001, armed clashes broke out between Albanian rebels and the Macedonian armed forces. Fueled by the frustrations of an Albanian minority that felt marginalized within the Macedonian nation-state project, this violence was defused by the conclusion, in August 2011, of the Ohrid Agreement under the close supervision of the international community. The agreement provided for a legal, institutional, and symbolic rebalancing of relations between the majority and minorities. Balalovska, Silj, and Zucconi, "Minority Politics."

77   Ulf Brunnbauer, "Serving the Nation," in Brunnbauer, *(Re)writing History.*

victimhood—victims of the Balkan Wars (1912–13), of international geopolitics, and of communism—analogies flourished between the Jewish and Macedonian experiences. The beginnings of such an evolution were already perceptible during the previous mandate of the VMRO-DPMNE, between 1998 and 2002.[78] In 2013, in his opening address at the symposium organized by the Macedonian Academy of Sciences and Arts (*Makedonska akademija na naukite i umetnostite*, MANU) on the occasion of the seventieth anniversary of the Jewish deportations of March 1943, the president of the academy, Vlado Kambovski, returned even more forcefully to the elective affinity between the two peoples: "The Macedonian people are the people who best understand the fate of the Jews because they have a similar historical experience, having been subjected to biological and national destruction."[79]

The encounter between the Macedonian and Jewish pasts also took a second path, this one of stone and bronze, with the launch of an ambitious urban project, *Skopje 2014*, at the end of which the capital was lined with statues intended to inscribe the national teleology on the cityscape.[80] In February 2010, a video simulation, posted on social networks by a communication agency working for the executive branch, proposed a stroll through the future city's monumental past: opposite the Museum of the Macedonian Struggle for Independence,[81] inaugurated on September 8, 2011, stood the future Holocaust Memorial Center for the Jews of Macedonia. Although the two initiatives had different origins, in Bulgaria the inclusion of the Memorial Center in the *Skopje 2014* initiative was held to be proof that the memorialization of the Holocaust, far from aiming at a better knowledge of the facts, served the historical politics of the ruling elites.

In this context, the shooting of *The Third Half* (*Treto poluvreme*, 2012), a feature film by Macedonian director Darko Mitrevski, confirmed

---

78   For the concluding remarks of Vladimir Naumovski, chairman of the Macedonian delegation to the Washington Conference, on the restitution of looted Jewish property in November 1998, see Bindenagel, *Washington Conference*, 110–13.

79   Speech of Vlado Kambovski on the occasion of the international symposium "The 70th Anniversary of the Deportation of the Jews of Macedonia," March 12, 2013 (author's audio archive).

80   Green, "Counterfeiting the Nation?," 161–79.

81   The museum was originally given a convoluted name Museum of the Macedonian Struggle for Statehood and Independence, Museum of VMRO, and Museum of the Victims of the Communist Regime (*Musej na makedonskata borba za državnost i samostojnost, Muzej na VMRO i Muzej na žrtvite ot komunističkiot režim*). With a change in government majority in 2017, it adopted the shorter designation of Museum of the Macedonian Struggle for Independence (*Muzej na makedonskata borba za samostojnost*).

the Bulgarian leaders in their conviction that the Macedonian authorities had decided to deploy an "anti-Bulgarian" campaign on the terrain of Holocaust history. Adapted from true events, the work told the story of the "Makedonija" soccer team and its coach, a German Jew, during World War II. The Bulgarian occupation and the deportation of Jews were explored through the love affair between a young Jewish girl (inspired by the life of Neta Koen, a Holocaust survivor) and a Macedonian soccer player. The feature received generous funding from the government and the Macedonian Film Fund (*Filmskiot Fund na Republika Makedonija*).[82] Macedonian media followed the progress of the project, covering the prime minister's visit to the set in October 2011.

In the fall of 2011, three Bulgarian MEPs—Andrej Kovačev of the European People's Party (EPP), Evgeni Kirilov of the Progressive Alliance of Socialists and Democrats (S&D), and Stanimir Ilčev of the Alliance of Liberals and Democrats for Europe (ALDE)—brought up with the European commissioner for enlargement, Štefan Füle, what they considered to be a "manipulation of history."[83] Interviewed in November, Kovačev stated:

> [*The Third Half*] has been decreed a national priority by Macedonia; in times of crisis, it has received subsidies of more than one million euros from the Macedonian state, and we are concerned that it presents the deportation of Jews from these territories in an essentially anti-Bulgarian light. We believe that this is not the right way to ease relations between the two countries. Obviously, not only should the tragedy of these people never be forgotten, but the full truth about this past should be told. Which states saved their Jewish citizens during the Second World War—Bulgaria and the Netherlands [*sic*]? To our regret, the Bulgarian state could not save this population as well. Our wish was not to focus on this particular aspect or on the film alone, but on the whole policy of the Republic of Macedonia. The latter, unfortunately, distorts history in order to build its national identity.[84]

---

82 Declared to be of national interest, the film is said to have received 1 million euros from the Macedonian state, 500,000 euros from the Macedonian National Film Fund, and additional support from the Jewish Holocaust Fund of Macedonia, the Jewish Community of Macedonia, and the Czech Film Fund (out of an estimated budget of 2.15 million euros). *The Third Half* was submitted to the Oscar committee for selection in the foreign film category, but without success. *Makedonija 24*, October 4, 2011.

83 "Macedonian Film Infuriates Bulgaria," *Euroactiv.com*, October 28, 2011.

84 *Agence Fokus*, December 2, 2011, http://andrey-kovatchev.eu/post/andrey-kovachev-provokaciite-spryamo-balgariya-ne-doprinasyat-za-evropeyskata-integra- ciya-na-makedoniya-5885 (accessed December 30, 2022; no longer active).

On November 27, 2012, the speech before the European Parliament by Macedonia's foreign minister Nikola Poposki (VMRO-DPMNE) provided the Bulgarian MEPs with a new opportunity to denounce Macedonia's alleged instrumentalization of history: "Bulgaria does not want to slow down the path of Macedonian citizens to the European Union," insisted Kovačev, but the key to this path lay in Skopje. It is not in Athens, Sofia, or Brussels. . . . You rightly said that history should be left to the historians, but you do not leave it; all of Skopje is girded with history."[85]

Three parameters illuminate the choice of Bulgarian MEPs to bring the bilateral discord into the EU arena: the involvement of EU policymakers in the historical policies of candidate member states, the EU's treatment of Bulgaria's past during accession talks, and the observation of the policy levers offered by membership. As the controversy moved to the European stage, it took on a new coloring, with discussions of the memories of communism and the Holocaust in Eastern and Western Europe reverberating in it. We need to change scale to follow these reconfigurations.

When European Institutions Discuss History and Memory

As early as the late 1980s, the Council of Europe was beginning to grapple with questions of history and memory[86] as part of its effort to address national minorities' rights.[87] Following the demise of socialism, the European Parliament[88] and the European Commission followed suit, as the commission was called upon to establish the conditions for Eastern European candidates hoping to join the European Union. The politics of history and remembrance featured among these conditions.[89] Moreover, the outbreak of a war in Yugoslavia created a context in which a European—that is, French-German—model of reconciliation rose to the rank of an instrument

---

85 Speech of November 28, 2012, https://www.youtube.com/watch?v=7XtLnJAwJQU.

86 Georges Mink and Laure Neumayer, eds., *History, Memory and Politics in Central and Eastern Europe: Memory Games* (Basingstoke, UK: Palgrave Macmillan, 2013).

87 Garcia, "Vers une politique mémorielle européenne?," 179–201.

88 Perchoc, "Un passé, deux assemblées," 205–35.

89 The conditions defined at the Copenhagen European Council in June 1993 included "that the candidate country has achieved stability of institutions guaranteeing democracy, the rule of law, human rights and respect for and protection of minorities." https://www.consilium.europa.eu/media/21225/72921.pdf.

of pacification.[90] This posture of exporter of norms was all the more easily endorsed by those who sought to promote the integration of new countries into the EU, as they wished to bolster the legitimacy of the European project by grounding it in a common historical narrative. In turn, this narrative would facilitate the identification by European citizens with the EU.

Although it was often presented as a form of historical reparation for the long decades of East-West separation, the enlargement process was not free of misunderstandings. Memory policies took their place among these painfully divisive topics. In retelling the history of the twentieth century, the former members of the Soviet bloc were said to give precedence to the crimes of communism, and ignore the Holocaust, which was considered to be better known and remembered in the West.[91] Conversely, the candidates for EU accession deplored what they saw as the insufficient sensitivity of EU member states to the specific Eastern European experiences of Communist repression. Faced with the threat of a new "iron curtain of memory,"[92] the European institutions urged candidate states to subject their interpretations of history to critical scrutiny.

The dilemma of reconciling divergent historical narratives was intensified following the EU's 2004 enlargement to ten new members, seven of which had been part of the former Soviet bloc. Several of these newcomers took advantage of the opportunity to make their vision of the past known and obtain the backing of EU institutions in the disputes that opposed them to their neighbors, first and foremost Russia. The European Parliament became a privileged stage for these combats,[93] as it lent itself more readily to the construction of historical causes than the European Council, where decisions are made unanimously.[94] The result was a profusion of written reports and oral questions, plenary sessions, and resolutions, over which the delegations of the Baltic countries, Poland, and Hungary worked assiduously. At stake in these struggles was nothing less than the granting of the same status to the denial of communism's crimes as to Holocaust denial. While the European Council and the European Commission were less receptive to these memorial undertakings, several statements acquired a certain legitimacy there too: specifically, that Europe had experienced two totalitarianisms in the course of the twentieth century—communism and Nazism—and that the European member states were responsible for publicizing these misdeeds. In June

---

90   Bessone, "La réconciliation par l'histoire en Bosnie-Herzégovine," 149–75.
91   Blaive, Gerbel, and Linderberger, *Clashes in European Memory.*
92   Droit, "Le Goulag contre la Shoah."
93   Beauwallet and Michon, "L'institutionnalisation inachevée du Parlement européen," 147–72.
94   Littoz-Monnet, "Explaining Policy Conflict," 489–504.

2011, the European Council thus encouraged "initiatives aimed at inform-
ing and educating the public about Europe's totalitarian past and at under-
taking research projects, including those with an international dimension,"
based on the belief that "there can be no reconciliation without truth and
remembrance."[95] In a twofold movement, the Holocaust came to lose part
of its uniqueness as communism was assumed to have been uniformly totalitarian throughout its existence.

It was amid this landscape that Bulgaria's EU accession talks took shape.
Surprisingly, neither the European Commission nor the members of the
European Parliament demanded that this candidate reevaluate its role in the
destruction of the European Jews, give greater visibility to the memory of
the victims, and "correctly" remember the Holocaust. No Bulgarian government was invited to set up an international commission of historians, unlike
the Baltic States[96] or Romania.[97] Until the 2010s, Bulgaria was not seen as
a country where the crimes of Nazism and communism could be set against
each other; nor was it perceived as a state where reevaluating the Stalinist
period threatened to rehabilitate pro-Nazi commitments in the name of
anti-Sovietism or to resurrect anti-Jewish feelings. This was all the more so
as Bulgarian diplomatic action, which aimed to have the "Bulgarian exception" acknowledged, had begun to bear fruit.

Ultimately, only one Bulgarian past seemed to fall under the "Copenhagen
mnemonic accession criterion": that of communism. On several occasions,
EU officials expressed the wish that the files of the former Bulgarian State
Security be opened in order to shed light on the Communist past and
the origins of postcommunist organized crime networks. The request was
granted by the Bulgarian authorities a few months prior to EU accession.[98]
In its resolution of November 30, 2006, the European Parliament welcomed
"the decision to provide access to the files of the secret service, a measure
that will help build public confidence and demonstrate a clear break with the
past, and recommends that such disclosures be controlled by a non-partisan
and respected commission."[99] End of discussion.

95 Council of the European Union, *Draft Council Conclusions on the Memory of
    the Crimes Committed by the Totalitarian Regimes in Europe*, Brussels, June 8,
    2011. See also *European Parliament Resolution of 2 April 2009 on European
    Conscience and Totalitarianism*, Brussels, April 2, 2009.
96 Onken, "Finding Historical Truth," 109–16.
97 Wiesel et al., *Comisiă internaţional pentru studierea Holocaustului în
    România*.
98 Ragaru, "Les dossiers de la Sûreté d'État bulgare," 205–27.
99 European Parliament Resolution on the Accession of Bulgaria to the European
    Union (2006/2114(INI)), Brussels, November 30, 2006, https://eur-lex.

Beyond the accession process, a third and final parameter encouraged Bulgaria's authorities to bring the dispute with Macedonia into European venues: the handling of contentious issues between member states and candidate countries by EU elites. As early as 1991, the past had interfered in Macedonia's Euro-Atlantic future. Dreading the prospect of being dragged into the Yugoslav wars, the former Socialist Republic of Macedonia declared independence in September 1991. An EU member since 1981, Greece feared that an independent state of Macedonia might harbor territorial ambitions on a northern Greek province that bears the name of Macedonia, or that it might claim a right to protect a "Macedonian minority" in Greece. At the extraordinary European summit dedicated to the situation in Yugoslavia, held in Brussels on December 16, 1991, Greece thus bargained for (and obtained) the insertion of the following statement into the final declaration: "The Community and its Member States also require a Yugoslav Republic to commit itself, prior to recognition, to adopt constitutional and political guarantees ensuring that it has no territorial claims towards a neighbouring Community State and that it will conduct no hostile propaganda activities versus a neighbouring Community State, including the use of a denomination which implies territorial claims."[100] This statement did not prevent the European arbitration commission on Yugoslavia (commonly known as the Badinter Arbitration Commission), which had been set up in August 1991 to establish the criteria for recognition of the states that emerged from the former Yugoslavia, to recommend that the European Community accept the Republic of Macedonia's request for recognition on January 11, 1992; the Macedonian Constitution had been amended a few days earlier to clarify that the new state did not harbor any irredentist claims on its neighbors.[101]

Nevertheless, in Greece these concessions were deemed insufficient: the very use of the word "Macedonia" in the country's name provoked intense fear and resentment. In the name of European solidarity, the European Community refrained from officially recognizing Macedonia's independence. In doing so, the EC sent a powerful signal to its member states: each one

---

europa.eu/legal-content/EN/TXT/PDF/?uri=CELEX:52006IP0511&from =FR.

100 See "Declaration on Yugoslavia (Extraordinary EPC Ministerial Meeting, Brussels, 16 December 1991)," https://www.dipublico.org/100637/ declaration-on-yugoslavia-extraordinary-epc-ministerial-meeting-brussels-16-december-1991/.

101 Maurizio Ragazzi, "Conference on Yugoslavia Arbitration Commission: Opinions on Questions Arising from the Dissolution of Yugoslavia," *International Legal Materials* 31, no. 6 (November 1992): 1488–1526.

of them had a de facto veto on the community's external actions.[102] Sixteen years later, the principle of European unanimity continued to paralyze the EU. While the European Commission recommended opening accession talks with Macedonia in December 2009, the recommendation was not followed by the European Council.[103] Meanwhile, the Greek veto also frustrated Macedonia's first attempt to join NATO in April 2008.[104] The unfolding of this bilateral controversy at the level of EU institutions was not lost on the Bulgarians.

Upon joining the EU in 2007, Bulgaria was entitled to eighteen MEPs, whose party affiliations reflected the structuring of the Bulgarian political spectrum around two poles. The populist right-wing Citizens for the European Development of Bulgaria (*Graždani za evropejsko razvitie na Bălgarija*, GERB) held five seats in the 2007–9 and 2009–14 European Parliaments. They were members of the European People's Party Group (EEP). The Bulgarian Socialist Party, with five and then four MEPs, caucused with the Party of European Socialists (PES). On their margins were the Movement for Rights and Freedoms (*Dviženie za prava i svobodi*, DPS), representing the interests of Turkish and Muslim minorities, with four and then three seats in the European Liberal Democrat and Reform (ELDR) Group; and the xenophobic *Ataka* (Attack), whose three MEPs sat in both parliaments among the unaffiliated members. Unlike their Polish, Hungarian, or Romanian colleagues, however, few members of the Bulgarian delegation took up the cause of the "crimes of communism."[105] Debating the Communist past on the European stage was unlikely to bring dividends in the domestic political arena: following the erosion of the divide between "reds" and "blues" in the early 2000s, putting communism on trial had ceased to figure high on the political agenda. The few prosecutions of Communist leaders that had begun after the downfall of the Communist regime were suspended in the mid-1990s, and there had been no serious talk of "lustration" measures after 1998. Although discussions about the future

---

102 Macedonia was recognized by the EU in 1993 under the name Former Yugoslav Republic of Macedonia (FYROM).

103 The observation of another dispute may have influenced the strategy of Bulgarian officials: the territorial controversy between Slovenia and Croatia over the Bay of Piran. At the end of 2008, the Slovenian leadership succeeded in getting the EU foreign ministers not to follow the recommendations of the European Commission to close the accession negotiations with Croatia by the end of 2009. Croatia finally joined the EU in July 2013, but not without agreeing to set up an arbitration commission.

104 Oana Lungescu, "Nato Macedonia Veto Stokes Tension," *BBC News*, April 4, 2008.

105 Neumayer, *Criminalisation of Communism*.

of the Communist monumental heritage periodically resurfaced, Sofia's urban landscape was transformed more through a commercial logic than an ideological logic. Bulgaria built no national Park of Dead Statues or House of Terror, unlike Hungary; nor was there an Institute of National Memory on the Polish model.

Apart from efforts by a handful of activists, journalists, and elected officials, the stigmatization of the Communist past had moved to the present, becoming an instrument for denouncing postcommunist collusion between political and economic circles. The creation of catchall parties with charismatic leaders—the National Movement Simeon II (*Nacionalno Dviženie Simeon Vtori*, NDSV) of the former king in 2001, the GERB formation of the former bodyguard Bojko Borisov after 2009—contributed to this flattening by offering "temporary partisan accommodation"[106] to those politicians who proved capable of ideological agility. The proportional representation system also favored the formation of surprisingly ecumenical government coalitions.

In the Parliamentary Assembly of the Council of Europe (PACE), then in the European Parliament, the names of a few individuals stand out, however. Their trajectory is notable in that it accompanies the entry of the rhetoric of the "rescue" and anti-Jewish persecution into European venues. We have already come across in chapter 4 the figure of Lačezar Tošev (SDS), a member of PACE, who worked toward denouncing the "crimes of communism"[107] and achieving recognition for the "rescue of Bulgarian Jews." This biologist by training, born in 1962, belonged to a generation whose entry into politics followed a commitment to the environmental dissidents' network *Ekoglasnost* formed at the end of the 1980s. Able to claim scientific and social legitimacy—as a descendant of a line of notable figures—Tošev gained a parliamentary seat after the first multiparty elections in June 1990. He continued to serve as a Bulgarian MP in the Bulgarian National Assembly until 2005, demonstrating a rare loyalty to the anti-communist Union of Democratic Forces (SDS). In 1992, he joined the Bulgarian delegation to PACE as a member of the European Democrats faction (1992–97), before becoming vice president of the EPP-ED group (1997–2005) and serving as deputy speaker (1998–2000). After 2005, Tošev remained in Bulgarian parliamentary circles as an expert to the deputy speaker of the Fortieth National Assembly, Filip Dimitrov (2005–9, SDS). He regained office in 2009 and

---

106 Ragaru, "En quête de notabilité," 71–99.

107 See his contribution to the adoption of the PACE *Resolution 1481 (2006): Need for International Condemnation of Crimes of Totalitarian Communist Regimes* (reporter: M. Lindblad) in Tošev, "Kratka hronika na priemaneto na rezolucija 1481 na PACE."

then brought his European experience to bear during the preparations for Bulgaria's rotating EU presidency in 2018. In this career, which combined the positions of activist, expert, and elected official, the cause is anti-communist, conservative, and patriotic. The crimes of communism and the "rescue of the Bulgarian Jews," defended together, are part and parcel of a heroic vision of history and an aspiration to consecrate in law the interpretation of the past on offer.

In the European Parliament, three other representatives made a name for themselves, as they took up historical advocacy. However, the 2011 episode in which European Commissioner for Enlargement Štefan Füle was called to account in relation to the Macedonian film *The Third Half*, however, reveals a complex configuration in terms of generation, party affiliation, and engagement. Kovačev, the youngest member of parliament in this team of three (born in 1967), was also the most influential (affiliated with the governing party, GERB, he chaired the Bulgarian delegation).[108] After the fall of socialism, he had obtained a doctorate in biology from Germany. His entry into politics in 2007, at the age of forty, was not the culmination of an activist career but rather drew on entrepreneurial success and a strategy of internationalization. Promoted to vice chairman of GERB's Foreign Affairs and European Affairs Committee in 2007, Kovačev became a member of the European Parliament without ever having held an elective office in Bulgaria. He joined the informal Reconciliation of European Histories group, which consisted of elected representatives with conservative leanings, most of them from the new member states. Regardless of their differences in age and career, Kovačev shared with Tošev an interest in questions related to communism, the former intelligence services, and Bulgarian minorities abroad, as well as an eagerness to defend the Bulgarian national epic. He was a member of the EU–Republic of Macedonia Joint Parliamentary Committee created on March 10, 2004, under the Stabilization and Association Agreement (SAA), and repeatedly spoke out against the abandonment of Bulgarian monuments in Macedonia and the alleged pressure exerted on Macedonian citizens who possessed a Bulgarian national consciousness.[109]

The professional and political profile of the second signatory of the letter, the socialist Evgeni Kirilov, stands in sharp contrast with that of Kovačev. Twenty years his senior, Kirilov was trained as an engineer in East Germany before pursuing studies in international law and international economics at the Faculty of International Economic Relations of the famous Moscow

---

108   Reelected in 2014, Andrej Kovačev consolidated his institutional positions by becoming a quaestor, vice chairman of the Committee on Foreign Affairs, and member of the delegation for ties with the United States.

109   See Kovačev's blog: https://andrey-kovatchev.eu/.

State Institute of International Relations (MGIMO). His career was spent at the United Nations Educational, Scientific and Cultural Organization (UNESCO), in the shadow of the foreign intelligence services.[110] Thanks to his unwavering loyalty to the Communist Party, he joined the Supreme Council of the successor party in 1997 and served four terms in the Bulgarian National Assembly (1995–2007), specializing in foreign affairs and security.

Finally, the political background of the third signatory, Stanimir Ilčev, born in 1953 in Burgas. He occupied a generational midpoint between his two colleagues. Here we leave the world of science for that of journalism. By virtue of his position at the American University in Bulgaria, a private university founded with the support of George Soros, Ilčev built international networks that led him to join the National Movement Simeon II in 2001, winning two terms in the Bulgarian parliament and chairing the Bulgarian delegation to the NATO Parliamentary Assembly between 2001 and 2005.

Divided in terms of party affiliation as well as geopolitical allegiances (pro-Western versus pro-Russian), the three elected officials did, in 2011, agree on one cardinal point: they considered that politicians were entitled to establish *the* truth about the past and to inscribe it in public remembrance. In the controversy with Macedonia, they needed to determine on what terms to frame the discord. Should the question of the Holocaust be met head-on? Should the quarrel be presented as a falsification of history, an attack on good neighborly relations, and a breach of democratic norms? With the support of the Bulgarian executive, the MEPs decided to bypass the sensitive issue of the Holocaust and opted for two tried and tested strategies at EU institutions: the defense of minority rights and good neighborly relations.

Their efforts were not without success. In the fall of 2012, the European Commission's annual report assessing Macedonia's progress toward integration paid unprecedented attention to the Bulgarian-Macedonian dispute.[111] A month later, Bulgaria joined the states reserved on the opening of accession talks for Macedonia—France and Greece—and the Council conclusions mentioned "the importance [for Macedonia] of maintaining good neighborly relations."[112] In an interview, the then president of Bulgaria, Rosen

---

110 Evgeni Kirilov's affiliation to the Communist state security service was disclosed in 2007. Comdos, *Rešenie* 1, April 24, 2007.

111 European Commission, *Report from the Commission to the European Parliament and the Council, The Former Yugoslav Republic of Macedonia: Implementation of Reforms within the Framework of the High Level Accession Dialogue and Promotion of Good Neighbourly Relations*, Strasbourg, April 16, 2013, COM (2013), 205 final, 18, https://eur-lex.europa.eu/legal-content/EN/TXT/?uri=CELEX%3A52013DC0205.

112 Gerald Knaus, "Macedonia and the EU Council Conclusions," *Balkan Insight*, December 13, 2012.

Plevneliev (GERB), confirmed the shift in his country's line in a sibylline manner: "Bulgaria is not a second Greece; we did not veto [the December European Council]; we listed the problems," before calling for the signing of a bilateral treaty of good neighborliness, a "standard European practice."[113] The head of state also claimed a role for Bulgaria in the EU's external action toward Southeast Europe: "What we have to understand is that Bulgaria is a member of the European Union, a member that is not expected to keep quiet, but to form the position of the European Commission and the European Union in the region where we live with the best intentions and in the name of European values."[114]

One of the Bulgarian proposals was the creation of a bilateral commission to organize joint celebrations of events and heroes that both countries considered to be in their national pantheons. The idea was timely: 2013 marked, in addition to the 70th anniversary of the 1943 (non)deportations, the centenary of the Balkan Wars and the 110th anniversary of the anti-Ottoman uprising of St. Elijah.[115]

One conclusion can be drawn from this episode: at a time when the European Commission was, with growing perplexity, noting the weakening of democratic commitments on the part of Macedonian leaders,[116] the EU did not provide the Macedonian side with an appropriate forum for debating then dominant representations of Jewish destiny in Bulgaria and beyond. Marginalized on this point, those who advocated for the Bulgarian state to recognize responsibility for the acts of war had to find alternative allies. It is

---

113 *Politika.net*, January 27, 2013, http://www.youtube.com/watch?v= 9Lqoef6_ UIE (accessed April 16, 2020; no longer active).

114 Ibid.

115 Also known as the Ilinden Uprising, this rebellion organized on August 2, 1903 (St. Elijah's Day), on the initiative of the VMRO aimed at emancipation from Ottoman rule. The Ottoman army crushed the short-lived Republic of Kruševo in November 1903. The extent of the physical and human destruction, as well as the migration resulting from the Ottoman repression have— together with the memory of the creation of an autonomous political entity and the valor of poorly armed fighters—conferred a central place to the memory of this uprising in the identity constructions of Macedonia, Bulgaria, and Yugoslavia. On the Macedonian case, see Brown, *Past in Question*.

116 European Commission, *Commission Staff Working Paper: The Former Yugoslav Republic of Macedonia 2011 Progress Report; Accompanying the Document Communication from the Commission to the European Parliament and the Council*, Brussels, October 12, 2011, SEC (2011) 1 203 final, 5–9; European Commission, *Commission Staff Working Paper: The Former Yugoslav Republic of Macedonia 2012 Progress Report; Accompanying the Document Communication from the Commission to the European Parliament and the Council*, Brussels, October 10, 2012, SEC (2012) 332 final, 6–13.

this shift, and the ensuing partial reformulation of the controversy, that we must now recount. It is time to leave the field of politics behind for that of museums and Jewish organizations, all while considering the global dimensions of this bilateral dispute.

Games of Scale: Debating Bulgaria's Memory Policies

A twin evolution has occurred in recent decades in the representation of the Holocaust and the war: the earlier stress on heroism has given place to an exposure of the suffering of the victims. A large body of works has addressed the challenges of the "museal inscription of erasure," especially as generations of witnesses gradually depart.[117] Where is remembrance of the Holocaust to be located? How can it be inscribed in urban spaces?[118] Today's scenographies are less concerned with describing collections of objects than with encouraging the immersion of visitors through interactive and digital devices.[119] Meanwhile, controversies over the rival memories of communism and the Holocaust have reached museums.[120] Last but not least, in the United States the museum treatment of the destruction of the European Jews has been the subject of a remarkable reflection considered from the point of view of German-American bilateral relations.[121]

The angle chosen here is somewhat different. The purpose is to identify, from the Balkan terrain, signs of the growing authority claimed by museums and memorials in the accreditation of the past, whether through diplomatic action, support for research (study centers, scholarships, symposiums, specialized journals, book series), or pedagogical activities. In order to account for the translation from a political field, where political beliefs and militant expertise are among the resources conventionally mobilized, to museums whose managers are more inclined to seek legitimacy in moral, historical, or intimate registers, the reflection here will draw on the case of the Memorial Center for the Holocaust of the Jews of Macedonia (*Memorijalen centar na holokaustot na Evreite od Makedonija*). From this institution, inaugurated in March 2011, the analysis of memory controversies will radiate toward the USHMM, Yad Vashem, the Treblinka Museum, and the Mémorial de la Shoah in Paris.

---

117 Delphine Bechtel and Luba Jurgenson, eds., *Muséographie des violences en Europe centrale et en ex-URSS* (Paris: Éditions Kimé, 2016).
118 Chevalier, "Musées and musées-mémoriaux urbains consacrés à la Shoah."
119 Young, *At Memory's Edge*.
120 Sarkisova and Apor, *Past for the Eyes*; Zubrzycki, *Crosses of Auschwitz*.
121 Eder, *Holocaust Angst*.

The genesis of the Jewish Holocaust Memorial Center in Macedonia ties together several threads. In the aftermath of World War II, compensation schemes for Jewish victims of the Holocaust were negotiated, particularly on the initiative of the Conference on Jewish Material Claims against Germany (or simply, the Claims Conference).[122] However, Jews under Soviet influence were mostly excluded from these measures.[123] As soon as communism fell, several Jewish organizations lobbied for extension of compensation to Jews in the East who were doubly victimized—by Nazism and communism. Their efforts were coupled with a broader questioning of the limits of the reparations negotiated at the end of the war.[124] At the crossroads between the mobilization of Jewish institutions, including the World Jewish Congress, law firms, and political actors, the questions of Jewish bank assets declared unclaimed,[125] forced labor,[126] and spoliated works of art acquired a novel visibility that was reinforced by contemporary sensitivity to the moral, symbolic, and psychological dimensions of reparation.

Against this background, the USHMM was invited by the US Department of State to coordinate the Washington Conference on Holocaust-Era Assets (November 30–December 3, 1998). Forty-four governments and thirteen nongovernmental organizations were represented. For the first time, a Macedonian delegation was invited to take part in the discussions. Its members did not fail to highlight Bulgaria's responsibility in the economic dispossession of the Jews of Macedonia.[127] Prior to the meeting, however, the leaders of the Union of Jews of Macedonia (*Evrejska zaednica vo Republika Makedonija*) asked their government about the Jewish assets held by the Macedonian Central Bank. A six-member commission was charged with estimating the value of Jewish property; two years later, the Macedonian parliament amended the Law on Denationalization passed in the context of the restitution of property nationalized under communism to take into account the situation of assets formerly held by Jews.[128] Treasury bonds would be issued for properties that could not be physically returned; the resources

122 Zweig, *German Reparations*.
123 Schraftstetter, "Diplomacy of *Wiedergutmachung*," 459–79.
124 Marrus, *Some Measure of Justice*; Dean, Goschler, and Ther, *Robbery and Restitution*.
125 Rickman, *Swiss Banks*.
126 In August 2000, the foundation Erinnerung, Verantwortung und Zukunft, cofinanced by the German state, was established to compensate Jewish victims of forced labor. Goschler, *Compensation in Practice*.
127 Bindenagel, *Washington Conference*.
128 Zakon za izmenuvanije i dopolnuvanje na zakonot za denacionalizacija, State Gazette of the Republic of Macedonia (*Služben vesnik na Republika Makedonija*), April 31, 2000.

would be allocated to the newly created Fund for the Holocaust of the Jews of Macedonia (*Fond na holokaustot na Evreite od Makedonija*), whose presidency was entrusted to Samuel Sadikario. Shortly thereafter, the fund undertook to give life to the project of the Memorial Center mentioned at the Washington Conference in 1998. The foundation stone was laid in September 2005 in the former Jewish quarter of Skopje.

The initiative took six years to complete, the fruit of two relational triangles: Macedonia, the United States, and Israel, on the one hand; and the Berenbaum Group, Edward Jacobs Design, and the USHMM, on the other. The director of the Los Angeles–based consulting firm of the same name, Berenbaum was commissioned to design the Skopje memorial by the Holocaust Fund in November 2009. From his vision of the project, the American consultant offered the following script:

> A word about Museums or at least the way in which my colleagues and I fashion historical museums: we believe that historical museums must be a storytelling Museum. Unlike most artifact-centered historical museums, which tell the stories of the artifacts they possess, we believe that this Museum—both in design and exhibition—must be driven by the story that is told. It is on the basis of the story that artifacts are collected and exhibited, that photographs are gathered and chosen, and the diverse media—film, video, narrative tale, text, design and atmosphere—should be shaped. So as we began our work, we asked: What is the story to be told?[129]

The architectural and graphic design was awarded to Edward Jacobs Design, formerly Mishkenot Ltd, based in Israel and the United States, a partner in the Berenbaum Group.[130] Journalist, photographer, and filmmaker Edward Serotta, who was also the founder of Centropa, an online Jewish survivor testimony initiative, and journalist and essayist Yitzchak Mais curated the permanent exhibition.

At the time of the anthracite building's opening in March 2011, the scenography was in its early stage.[131] Sparse in terms of display cases, the

---

129 Michael Berenbaum, "Preface Macedonian Chronicle," *Los Angeles: The Berenbaum Group*, March 10, 2010, http://berenbaumgroup.com/index. php?option=com_content&view=article&id=117:preface-macedonian-chronicle&catid=34:recent-publications&Itemid=48 (accessed January 31, 2023; no longer active).

130 https://www.edwardjacobsdesign.com.

131 Based on observations made by the author at the Memorial Center in September 2013, December 2014, November 2015, and October 2016. The list of international "authors of texts and consultants" associated with the project was then engraved on huge panels on the ground floor in the following manner: "Dr. Eliezer Papo, Israel; Dr. Jane S. Gerber, United States; Dr.

museum tour consisted mostly of photographs, maps, and texts printed on large panels. The accent was placed on the emotional investment of the visitors. From the entrance, a cascade of interlocking television screens framed with their smooth metal the faces of Macedonian Jews photographed at the request of the Bulgarian occupation authorities in 1941–42. Hanging in intertwined positions, the portraits with frightened looks and outfits betraying modest social conditions haunted visitors as they stopped in front of the three urns of remembrance (Skopje, Bitola, and Štip)[132] and walked along an artistic installation composed of 7,144 hanging threads—representing the Jewish lives taken. A few computers offered testimonies from the Shoah Visual History Foundation. To the refutation of a material reconstruction of the past, one object was an exception: it was the reproduction, mentioned in chapter 3, of a wagon similar to those that transported the deported Jews of Macedonia in March 1943.

Although the narrative of the Holocaust was intended to be inscribed in the centuries-old history of the Sephardim, the articulation between the long and short terms remained weakly conceptualized. In the evocation of the war, the links between the experience of Vardar Macedonia and that of the German, Croatian, Italian, and Hungarian zones of the dismembered Kingdom of Yugoslavia were summarily treated. The tragedy of the Jews of Salonika was mentioned, but the rest of Greece, including zones under Bulgarian occupation, remained out of focus. The visitor wishing to link Southeast Europe to the continent-wide destruction of the Jews was similarly left at a loss. The antifascist resistance and the liberation of Skopje were presented in terms that historians of the Yugoslav Communist period would not have rejected. Finally, the responsibility of the Bulgarian authorities in the anti-Jewish persecutions was asserted without ambiguity.[133]

Since March 2018, the museum has been completely redesigned and, as a consequence, remarkably enriched. The ground floor entrance still welcomes visitors with images, suspended from the ceiling, of lives that were shattered in 1943. Beginning at the first staircase, however, there is now an

---

Michal Held, Israel; Dr. Michael Berenbaum, United States; Dr. Steven S. Sage, United States; Dr. Yitzchak Kerem, Israel; Mr. Edward Serotta, Austria; Mr. Mark Cohen, USA; Mr. Yitzchak Mais, Israel. The director of the Institute of Macedonian National History (*Institut za nacionalna istorija*, INI), Prof. Dr. Todor Chepreganov, as well as research assistants are also involved."

132 The urns containing the ashes of Macedonian Jews exterminated in Treblinka were transferred to Macedonia in 1961; they were exhibited in Skopje, Bitola, and Štip before being handed over to the Memorial Center in 2011.

133 In 2012, Berenbaum authored a bilingual book largely inspired by the permanent exhibition: *The Jews in Macedonia during World War II / Evreite vo Makedonija za vreme na vtorata svetska vojna*.

extensive timeline that follows Jewish history from Abraham and Moses up to the post-Yugoslavian founding of the Republic of Macedonia in 1991. This broadened temporal outline reinforces significant links to the history of Judaism and Israel. Whenever narrower territorial approaches have been preserved, it is in the interest of better understanding each era; for instance, Constantinople and Sarajevo are mentioned in the context of Sephardic Jews in the Ottoman Empire. There is a didactic approach to the treatment of economic, social, cultural, and religious experiences, and the graphics seem to be directed toward a school-age audience. Distinct, immersive spaces have been created, each of which reconstitutes the successive stages of Sephardic Jewish history. Furniture and assorted objects, including private donations by members of the Macedonian Jewish community, are interspersed with music, excerpts from documentary films, photographs, and comic strips, as well as a collection of maps.

The transformations are no less apparent when it comes to tackling World War II. The curators have resituated the extermination of Macedonian Jews within the general framework of the war. An educational introduction to Nazism serves as a prelude to describing the "Bulgarian Occupation, 1941–1944" (the names of those occupied territories remain unspecified), along with a description of how the Treblinka death camp operated. Close attention has been paid to reconstructing the trajectory of the three main communities—Štip, Bitola/Monastir, and Skopje—that were deported in March 1943 from Vardar Macedonia. The Jews of Pirot in Serbia and those of Western Thrace in Greece, who met the same fate, have not been forgotten. Nor has the museum's narrative ignored the March 1943 Bulgarian social protests, which succeeded in postponing the deportations of those Jews who held Bulgarian citizenship from Bulgaria's "old" kingdom; here a particular emphasis has been placed on the role of Dimităr Pešev and the Bulgarian Orthodox Church. Continuities between the museum's representation of the past and a Yugoslavian narrative are more noteworthy when it comes to the Liberation and the resistance movement. As to individual survivors' trajectories, those who aided Jewish victims, as well as the citizens recognized as Righteous Among the Nations by Yad Vashem, have all been given an expanded overview. The museum's perspective on the role of Bulgaria now emphasizes that in November 1941, this country handed the Serbian Jews over to the Germans after the former had fled to Macedonia; that their fatal destiny could be traced to the Commissariat for Jewish Affairs, to Interior Minister Gabrovski, the Council of Ministers, and King Boris III. As already noted, a wooden wagon bearing the initials "BDŽ" still figures among the artifacts on display, but it is now presented as a donation from Macedonian Railways and has undergone restoration.

The Memorial Center quickly established itself as a notable destination for Jewish and non-Jewish tourists alike who aspire to learn about the region's history.[134] It is located at the entrance to the old city, adjacent to a fifteenth-century Ottoman bridge, the new Museum of the Macedonian Struggle for Independence, and one of Skopje's most picturesque neighborhoods of old Ottoman caravansaries, jewelers, and tailors. The museum has engaged in publishing activity and is actively collecting public and private archives.[135] This endeavor faces significant challenges. For a long time deprived of its own state, Macedonia has indeed seen large segments of its history administratively produced and archived outside its territory, whether in Serbia— notably for the antebellum period—in Bulgaria, in Israel, or in the United States. Natural disasters have additionally contributed to the dispersal of primary sources: in 1963, the city of Skopje was devastated by an earthquake; following that natural disaster, the archives of the Jewish communities of Macedonia were transferred to the Jewish Historical Museum in Belgrade, only to be returned to the Memorial Center in March 2011.[136]

Following their appointments, the director of the museum, Goran Sadikarijo, and the leaders of the Macedonian Jewish Holocaust Fund set out three priorities: to obtain full recognition of Jewish persecution locally and internationally, to affirm the Macedonian national identity of the exterminated Jews, and to publicize the role of the Bulgarian state in the destruction of Jewish lives. At that time, they did not call for a critical reconsideration of Macedonian public discourse on the historical events. The Macedonian public discourse indeed centered on the assertion of a collective Macedonian innocence in anti-Jewish persecution, solidarity between non-Jews and

---

134 The annual number of visitors, ranging from 30,000 to 40,000, comprised mostly Macedonians until 2017. In 2018, the distribution between Macedonian and foreign citizens was reversed for the first time. Special attention was at the time paid to school visits. Communication from Goran Sadikarijo, director of the Memorial Center, December 11, 2018.

135 The Fund has, among other efforts, supported the publication of books designed for a broad audience—for example, Lea Cohen's *You Believe: Eight Views on the Holocaust in the Balkans*—as well as the dissemination of the writings of renowned former partisan Žamila-Andžela Kolonomos: *Dviženjieto na otporot i evreite od Makedonija*. Moreover, it worked to publicize books by lay historians and precious testimonial writings published earlier in Israel: Shlomo Alboher, *The Jews of Monastir, Macedonia*; and Gitta Kalderon, *Mishloach Manot: A Life Story*.

136 Communication with Vojislava Radovanović, director of the Museum of Jewish History, Belgrade, October 1, 2014.

Jews,[137] as well as unanimous Jewish adherence to the Macedonian national project at the turn of the twentieth century.[138]

Advocating for the incorporation of the history of the Holocaust into Macedonian school textbooks, the museum, in partnership with the Mémorial de la Shoah in Paris, proposed training courses initially intended for Macedonian teachers only (Paris 2014; Skopje 2015; Skopje 2016), then extended to Bulgarian (Skopje 2017; Sofia 2018), and Greek (Thessaloníki 2017; Skopje 2018; Skopje, 2019; online 2020) pedagogues. Several sessions also brought together North Macedonia, Bulgaria, and Greece (online 2021; Kavála 2022; Sofia 2023), thanks to a dialogue with the Ministries of Education and the Jewish communities of the three countries.[139] Equally central has been the development of links with major Holocaust museums and Balkan and American Jewish organizations.

In 2008, a first symbolic victory was achieved with the installation, at the Treblinka Holocaust Memorial, of a stele engraved with the name "Macedonia."[140] "For sixty-five years, the Jews of Macedonia did not have their own monument," rejoiced the deputy foreign minister, Zoran Petrov,

---

137 Several recent pieces of scholarship suggest that such a critical analysis might be called for. In her memoirs, for instance, Kolonomos refers to the reluctance of some partisan units to accept Jews fleeing deportation. Kolonomos, *Dviženjieto na otporot*, 26–27; see also Čepreganov and Nikolova, "Učestvoto na evreite vo NOD vo Makedonija," 219–28.

138 One of the figures considered emblematic of the Macedonian Jews' national commitment is Rafael Kamhi, a Jew from Salonika, who joined the VMRO at the turn of the nineteenth century and became one of its couriers. In 1943, while residing in Salonika in the German zone, he escaped deportation thanks to the intercession of Bulgarian officials. Macedonian historiography has presented him as "a Macedonian Jew from Bitola, an active member of the VMRO." Since 2011, "Evenings in honor of the Jews, heroes of Ilinden" are co-organized by the Holocaust Fund and the Jewish Community of Macedonia on the occasion of the commemoration of the Republic of Kruševo—a short-lived political entity proclaimed in 1903 by rebels from the Secret Macedonian-Adrianople Revolutionary Organization (IMRO) during an anti-Ottoman uprising. The remembrance of Rafael Kamhi has a special place in this event. Karajanov, *Rafael Moše Kamhi*.

139 Email correspondence from Bruno Boyer, director of international relations at the Mémorial de la Shoah in Paris, February 20, 2023.

140 Fond na Holokaustot na Evreite od Makedonija, "Otkrivanje na obeležjeto za pogromot na makedonskite Evrei vo Treblinka," 2008, http://www. holocaustfund.org/index.php?option=com_content&view=article&id=528% 3Aotkrivanje- na-obelezjeto-za-pogromot-na-makedonskite-evrei-vo-treblin- ka&catid=112%3 Afotogalerii&Itemid=586&lang=mk (accessed February 19, 2020; no longer active).

on the occasion. "They were treated as Yugoslav Jews, in accordance with the qualification adopted by the Bulgarian occupation powers during the Second World War, or as Bulgarian Jews, the designation that appeared in the precise documentation on the basis of which the Germans accepted the 7,200 Jews of Macedonia."[141] In retrospectively affirming the exclusive Macedonian self-identification of all the Jews of this multicultural region, the Macedonian authorities too engaged in an attempt at nationalizing the past.

At the same time, together with associations such as the Monastir Immigrants' Committee and the Association of Macedonian Jews of the Next Generation in Israel (*Dor hemshech shel joztej Makedonia beIsrael*), the leaders of the Jewish community lobbied for the replacement of the count of victims appearing next to the word "Bulgaria" in the permanent exhibition at Yad Vashem—that glittering "0" that had aroused the admiration of many visitors—with 11,343. The change was obtained in 2009 when the permanent exhibition was renewed: the authority exercised by Bulgaria over the occupied territories and its role in the organization of the roundups were thus recognized. However, it is in the United States Holocaust Memorial Museum that the leaders of the Skopje Memorial Center and the Holocaust Fund have found their most influential ally.

Since its opening in 1993, the USHMM has become an influential actor in the debates relating to the compensation of looted Jewish property as well as in the documentation of the responsibilities of states in the Holocaust—Romania, among others.[142] With remarkable consistency, its leaders have also worked to publicize Bulgaria's role in the persecution and roundups of Jews in Yugoslavia and Greece. In the early 2000s, when the Claims Conference sought to document the conditions that prevailed in the Jewish forced labor camps in Bulgaria in order to assess the eligibility of Bulgarian Jews for compensation, the Washington museum made its collections available and helped to document the violence perpetrated against Jewish laborers.[143] In 2012, USHMM officials publicly called on the Bulgarian government to reevaluate its historical policy: the Bulgarian Embassy in Washington, DC, had proposed naming an intersection situated

---

141 Dimitar Čulev, "Vo Treblinka im se oddolži na svoite ubieni evrei," *Utrinski vestnik*, September 24, 2008. Under the Bulgarian decree of June 10, 1942, on citizenship in the territories under Bulgarian occupation, the Jews were denied the status of Bulgarian nationals. They were registered as "Yugoslav" or "Greek" citizens; that is, as "nationals" of states that did not have a legal existence at that time.

142 Radu Ionid, a historian specializing in the Holocaust in Romania who was long responsible for archival acquisition policy at USHMM, was a member of the Wiesel Commission on the Holocaust in Romania.

143 Steve Lipman, "Bulgaria Wasn't Second Denmark," *Jewish Week*, July 16, 2004.

in the vicinity of the Bulgarian diplomatic representation after the former wartime deputy speaker of the National Assembly, Pešev. When asked by the Washington, DC, City Council about the appropriateness of such a tribute, the museum issued an unfavorable opinion based on two reasons: first, in the request sent by the embassy to the DC City Council, Bulgaria was presented as a country "occupied" by Nazi Germany, and not as an "ally" of the Reich; second, by celebrating only one side of Bulgarian policy toward the Jews during the war, the public authorities hindered the beginning of a reflection on Bulgarian responsibilities in the Holocaust.[144] On March 12, 2018, during the seventy-fifth anniversary commemorative ceremonies in Skopje, the director of the Center for Advanced Holocaust Studies of the USHMM, Paul Shapiro, reiterated the museum's position: "The Holocaust had European dimensions and local dimensions. Here, it was the Bulgarians who were in charge."[145] From then on, each attempt to inscribe a univocal memorial account of the events of 1943 gave rise to opposing mobilizations and requests for additional information.

Remembering the Holocaust to Fight Anti-Semitism: Room for Convergence?

How can we assess the influence of these international efforts to raise awareness of the facts over Bulgarian-Macedonian controversies? One way to address this question is to look for their refraction in the positions adopted by the major American Jewish organizations, key actors in the exhortations to remember the destruction of the Jews of Europe. In this case, without questioning the exceptionality of the Bulgarian trajectory, a triple evolution has been observed in the statements of the most prominent Jewish institutions: first, a broadening of the range of positions; second, a more systematic call to evoke the deportations that, without subtracting anything from the account of the "rescue of the Bulgarian Jews," no longer omits the role of the Bulgarian authorities in the roundups; and third, a close association between the intelligence of the past and the present struggles against anti-Semitism. The change of line impelled by the young multilingual neurologist and ophthalmologist Aleksandăr Oskar, since his election as head of the Organization of the Bulgarian Jews Šalom in April 2016, the initiation of a dialogue with the director of the Skopje Memorial Center Goran Sadikarijo

---

144 Eric Tucker and Randy Hershaft, "Bulgarian Honor Bid in DC Stirs Holocaust Debate," *Associated Press*, May 7, 2013.
145 Paul Shapiro's statement to the Macedonian press, broadcast on the Bulgarian program *Svobodna zona* on TvEvropa, Sofia, March 13, 2018.

in the summer of 2017, and the aspiration of these two leaders to strengthen their ties with the WJC have helped to foster this new configuration.[146]

Following the demise of socialism, the leaders of Šalom had made the reestablishment of relations with American Jewish organizations a priority. In August 1990, the president of the American Jewish Joint Distribution Committee (JDC), Silvia Hassenfeld, visited Sofia; met with the president of the Central Israelite Spiritual Council, Josif Levi; and attended the inauguration of a Jewish library donated by the JDC. The heat of the summer was conducive to exchanges despite the victory of the ex-Communists in the first multiparty elections two months earlier.[147] Following in the footsteps of the Anti-Defamation League, the main American Jewish organizations were gradually going to promote in the United States the narrative of the "rescue of the Bulgarian Jews"—in the new version crafted by the anti-communist right wing.[148] On May 12, 1994, the US Congress thus adopted a declaration praising King Boris's contribution to the "rescue." Four years later, in February 1998, the ADL granted the new Bulgarian head of state Petăr Stojanov (SDS) a Courage to Care Award for "the heroism of his people under King Boris III."[149] On the occasion of the sixtieth anniversary of the "rescue," on March 12, 2003, in a second congressional statement, the range of contributions to the nondeportation of the Bulgarian Jews was expanded: the National Assembly, the Orthodox Church, the king, Bulgarian politicians, intellectuals, and citizens, as well as the "Bulgarian people" were all praised "for preserving and continuing their tradition of ethnic and religious tolerance." With regard to the deportations, Congress used modest wording, "acknowledging with sadness the deportation of more than 11,000 Jews from Thrace and Macedonia, territories administered by Bulgaria at the time, to Nazi concentration camps."[150]

Fifteen years later, the picture has undergone some tinkering, revealing a richer palette of assessments among American Jewish organizations. On March 10, 2018, the president of the American Jewish Committee (AJC),

---

146 "Aleksandăr Oskar: V Bălgarija započvat da duhat vetrovete na promjanata i veče se govori ne samo sa spasenieto, no i za deportacijata," *Marginalia.bg*, March 19, 2018.

147 "Djoint se vărna," *Evrejski Vesti*, September 25, 1990, 2.

148 Benatov, "Debating the Fate," 108–30.

149 "ADL Honors Bulgaria for Saving Jews from Holocaust," press release dated February 13, 1998.

150 108th US Congress, 1st Sess., H. Con. Res. 77, *Concurrent Resolution Commemorating the 60th Anniversary of the Historic Rescue of 50,000 Bulgarian Jews from the Holocaust and Commending the Bulgarian People for Preserving and Continuing Their Tradition of Ethnic and Religious Tolerance*, passed March 12, 2003.

David Harris, offered a statement sparse in references to the deportations, silent on the issue of Bulgarian state responsibility, but lightened by the reference to the king. On the other hand, his speech underlined two contemporary priorities that give the Bulgarian ally its full value, the resurgence of anti-Semitism and the precarious balance in the Middle East:

> Bulgaria occupies a very special place in our hearts, and it has for many years. Why? Two reasons in particular. The first reason has to do with the past, the second with the future. . . . Although Bulgaria was an ally of the Third Reich during the Second World War, this did not prevent some brave Bulgarians—most notably, members of Parliament and the Church—from standing up and refusing to comply with the deportation orders. As a result, nearly 50,000 Jews were saved from the death camps. No, sadly, not all Jews under Bulgarian rule were protected, but most were, and this act of bravery and brotherhood must never be forgotten. Rather, it needs to be remembered and taught not only as a history lesson, but also as an answer to the contemporary hatred, xenophobia, and anti-Semitism that is ominously reemerging today. . . . And who among us will ever forget the 2012 terrorist attack in Burgas that killed five Israelis and one Bulgarian, and wounded 32 others—and the courageous Bulgarian response? Though under pressure not to pursue the investigation thoroughly, the government pressed ahead and, correctly, pinned the blame on Hezbollah, a step that, in turn, led the European Union to overcome its reluctance to acknowledge the true nature of the group and place its "military wing" on the terrorism list.[151]

This juxtaposition between past and present is not unique to American Jewish organizations. Since the early twenty first century, the call for a remembrance of the Holocaust in Europe has been increasingly associated with a denunciation of current anti-Semitic acts. On January 27, 2005, in the wake of the second Organization for Security and Cooperation in Europe (OSCE) conference on anti-Semitism held in Berlin in April 2004 and the appointment of an OSCE representative for the fight against anti-Semitism, the European Parliament adopted a resolution explicitly correlating Holocaust

---

151 American Jewish Committee, "AJC Honors 75th Anniversary of Bulgarian Rescue of Nearly 50,000 Jews, Celebrates Friendship with Bulgaria Today," March 10, 2018, https://www.ajc.org/news/ajc-honors-75th-anniversary-of-bulgarian-rescue-of-nearly-50000-jews-celebrates-friendship. On July 18, 2012, a suicide bombing targeted Israeli tourists during their transfer from Burgas Airport to their vacation destination. The investigation was conducted in close cooperation among Bulgarian, Israeli, and US security services. A few months later, the Bulgarian Ministry of the Interior implicated Hezbollah in the attack. "Izvănredno: Avtobus s izraelski turisti beše vzriven na letište 'Burgas,'" *Kapital*, July 18, 2012.

remembrance and the fight against racism.[152] In fact, Bulgaria, a country long reputed to be free of anti-Semitism, has not been spared the (re)emergence of anti-Jewish attitudes. At the beginning of the new century, the Protocols of the Elders of Zion and other anti-Semitic works were published in Bulgarian. Shortly thereafter, a political party with the evocative name *Ataka* (Attack) made its way into parliament with anti-Roma, anti-Muslim, and anti-Semitic rhetoric. The attenuation in the National Assembly of the anti-Semitic rhetoric of its leader, the journalist Volen Siderov, followed by a split in the party in 2009, gave hope for a time that the so-called protest vote would be eroded. This was not the case. The nationalist constellation underwent a recomposition, not an erosion. Since 2003, a "Lukov march" has taken place every year in the streets of Sofia in tribute to the former leader of the Bulgarian Legionnaires, General Lukov, who was killed by the antifascist resistance on February 13, 1943. Over the years, this mobilization has grown, attracting a coterie of xenophobic and neo-Nazi European youth.

The new configuration favored an engagement of the World Jewish Congress on the terrain of the present—and then the past. In 2012, the organization asked the Bulgarian authorities to ban the parade. Several incidents further reinforced the coupling between the denunciation of anti-Semitism and the memory of anti-Jewish persecutions.[153] And it was around this pairing that a rapprochement with Šalom took place: in the fall of 2017, the Organization of the Bulgarian Jews joined the petition launched by the WJC to have the 2018 edition of the "Lukov march" banned. This international initiative gathered 175,000 signatures[154] without preventing some 1,500 participants from defying the order issued by the Sofia City Hall.[155] Bulgarian-American collaboration coincided with an inflection of Šalom's position on the issue of deportations. On August 29, 2017, after opening a dialogue with the director of the Memorial Center in Skopje, Šalom's executive committee amended its official statement of December 2011:

---

152 European Parliament, *European Parliament Resolution on Remembrance of the Holocaust, Anti-Semitism and Racism*, Brussels, January 27, 2005, P6_TA(2005)0018.

153 For example, the desecration of the monument to the "rescue of Bulgarian Jews" in Vidin in the summer of 2017. World Jewish Congress, "Holocaust Memorial in Bulgaria Defaced with Anti- Semitic Slogans," August 21, 2017.

154 World Jewish Congress, "WJC Petition Signed by 175,000 and Calling for Ban on Neo-Nazi March Delivered to Bulgarian PM," February 6, 2018. The petition was handed over to Prime Minister Borisov by the executive vice president of the WJC, Robert Singer, February 2, 2018.

155 World Jewish Congress, "World Jewish Congress Decries Neo-Nazi March Held in Sofia, Bulgaria despite Municipal Ban," February 20, 2018.

December 4, 2011. The deportation of the Jews from Thrace [Belomor-ska Trakija], Vardar Macedonia and the town of Pirot *during the Second World War* is a historical fact that cannot be denied. We, the Bulgarian Jews, pay tribute to the innocent victims, honor and will honor their memory. The German powers together with the pro-Nazi Bulgarian government are guilty of the deportation of the Jews from these territories, *as well as the lack of opposition from the local* [meaning: Macedonian] population. The Bulgarian government must, at the time and place of its choosing, assume moral responsibility for the acts of the pro-Nazi government toward the Jews during the years 1941–1943.[156]

August 29, 2017. The deportation of the Jews from Thrace [Belomor-ska Trakija], Vardar Macedonia and the town of Pirot, *during the period when these territories were under Bulgarian administration in the years of the Second World War*, is a historical fact that cannot be denied. We, the Bulgarian Jews, pay tribute to the innocent victims, honor and will honor their memory. The German powers together with the pro-Nazi Bulgarian government are guilty of the deportation of the Jews from these territories. The Bulgarian government must, at the time and place of its choosing, assume moral responsibility for the acts of the pro-Nazi government toward the Jews during the years 1941–1943.[157]

The evolution was discreet, but noticeable: at the request of the Macedonian side, reference to the weak solidarity shown by the non-Jewish population of Macedonia toward their Jewish fellow citizens disappeared. On the other hand, Bulgaria's sovereignty over the occupied territories was made explicit.

It would seem that the WJC leadership played a pivotal role in this shift, the president of which, R. S. Lauder, did not hesitate to reiterate in March 2018 his commitment to an acknowledgment of the role of the Bulgarian authorities in the deportations:

The unique story of the bravery shown by ordinary Bulgarian people and the members of the country's Orthodox Church is unfortunately not known well enough in America. . . . The Bulgarian story, and the Bulgarian people, are unique to what was Nazi-occupied Europe. Even as the Bulgarian government sided and collaborated with Hitler, the majority of civil society refused to give up their Jewish neighbors—and succeeded in rescuing them. . . . *Let's not forget, though, that at the same time ordinary Bulgarian citizens showed this courage in Bulgaria itself, the Bulgarian authorities de-*

---

156 *Stanovište na OEB Šalom po vъprosa na sъdbata na evreite pod bъlgarsko upravlenie v godinite na Holokosta v Evropa*, December 4, 2011 (emphasis in original); in author's possession.
157 Ibid., August 29, 2017 (emphasis in original).

cided to round up and deport to the death camps the Jews in the areas admin-
istered by Bulgaria during the war in northern Greece and southern parts of
Yugoslavia, today's Macedonia and eastern Serbia. This, however, by no means
diminishes the courage and kindness of the Bulgarian people who stood up in
defense of their Jewish friends and neighbors. In fact, it shows us that in difficult times, even when the leaders fail to act responsibly, there are ordinary
people who will do so. They are the real leaders, and it is their achievements
that should be celebrated.[158]

Could the decision of Bulgaria's prime minister Borisov to visit Skopje
on the occasion of the seventy-fifth anniversary of the deportation of the
Jews from Macedonia be illuminated in light of these statements? Perhaps, in
part. More specific diplomatic considerations also influenced the position of
the Bulgarian chief executive.

Confronted with the displacement of the interpretive dispute over anti-
Jewish persecution to the space of museums, the Bulgarian authorities had
initially sought to retaliate on this terrain by projecting an unaltered version
of the scheme of "saving Bulgarian Jews." On January 26, 2010, three years
after the International Auschwitz Council had announced, on the occasion of its fourteenth session on July 4–5, 2007, that the 1977 "thoroughly
outdated Bulgarian exhibition [would] be removed," and that it "[would]
accept, without reservation, Greek plans for a national exhibition,"[159] the
Speaker of the Bulgarian parliament Cecka Cačeva (GERB) donated to the
Auschwitz-Birkenau Museum seventeen documents tracing the main stages
of the "rescue."[160] In a second phase, Bulgaria initiated a rapprochement
with the International Holocaust Remembrance Alliance (IHRA), an organization created after the Stockholm Declaration (January 27–29, 2000)
with the aim of working for knowledge and remembrance of the Holocaust
and fighting against Holocaust denial and anti-Semitism. Over the years,
with its four commissions (Education, Research, Memory and Museums,
and Commemoration) and some thirty member states, the IHRA, whose

---

158   Imanuel Marcus, "Ronald S. Lauder: 'The Jews Will Never Forget the Bravery
of the Bulgarians,'" *Magazine 79*, March 10, 2018 (emphasis in original); in
author's possession. Ronald S. Lauder's public speech during the commemorations was much more subdued; see https://www.worldjewishcongress.
org/download/AngCXufSOhhn-ukHOaNy3w?utm_source=PRESS&utm_
campaign=e7c8c83964-EMAIL_CAMPAIGN_2018_03_09&utm_
medium=email&utm_term=0_c3b21e69b1-e7c8c83964-319166653.

159   Memorial and Museum Auschwitz-Birkenau, report, September 15, 2008, of
International Auschwitz Council Meeting XIV, July 4–5, 2007, https://www.
auschwitz.org/en/museum/auschwitz-council/iac-meetings/meeting-xiv-4-
5-july-2007,14.html.

160   http://www.parliament.bg/bg/gallery/ID/529.

honorary president is the Israeli historian Yehuda Bauer, had established itself as a key player.[161] In December 2012, Bulgaria became an observer member; five years later, the government entrusted a commission including the president of Šalom with the preparation of Bulgaria's application for liaison membership, which was obtained in June 2017.[162] The organization of the seventy-fifth anniversary celebrations coincided with the final stage of Bulgaria's journey toward full membership, which was approved in November 2018. In these circumstances, one can imagine the importance of symbolic gestures such as the invitation of the director of the Skopje Memorial Center and the Macedonian ambassador to the IHRA to the Bulgarian ceremonies or the visit of the Bulgarian prime minister to Skopje.

That the rapprochement with the IHRA was, from the point of view of the Bulgarian leaders, aimed at reinforcing, rather than questioning, the national interpretation of Jewish persecution during the war seems likely.[163] However, joining the alliance could also be expected to narrow down the range of public statements about the past the Bulgarian authorities could legitimately make. Among the conditions for joining the IHRA were the full opening of the Holocaust archives, critical examination of the past, and efforts to counter Holocaust denial and distortion. A delegation chaired by Ambassador Plamen Bončev, and including political scientist Albena Taneva and historian Rumjana Marinova-Hristidi, alongside a representative of Šalom, Clive Leviev-Sawyer, familiarized themselves with the alliance's key concepts and norms. At a roundtable organized in Sofia in July 2019 on Jewish forced labor, Marinova-Hristidi even suggested that "it is better to recognize ourselves [the pleasant and unpleasant facts of our history] than to let someone tell us and interpret them from outside."[164]

161 The IHRA comprised thirty-five members in February 2023 and ten observer states. https://www.holocaustremembrance.com/about-us/countries-membership.

162 "Bulgaria Is a Step Closer to Full Membership of the International Holocaust Remembrance Alliance," *Sofia Globe*, July 1, 2017.

163 One of Bulgaria's first initiatives as a new IHRA member was the organization of an exhibition dedicated to the "rescue of the Bulgarian Jews" at the Villa Seligmann in Hannover, whose artistic director Eliah Sakakushev–von Bismarck is a native of Plovdiv. Simon Benne, "Ausstellung der Villa Seligmann: Wie Bulgarien seine Juden rettete," *Hannoversche Allgemeine*, October 16, 2019.

164 "Pamet, zabrava i izopačavane: Evrejskite trudovi lageri po vreme na Vtorata svetovna vojna," *Librev.com*, February 5, 2020 (transcript of a discussion of July 11, 2019), https://www.librev.com/index.php/discussion/bulgaria/3692-pamet-zabrava-i-izopachavane-evreiskite-trudovi-lageri-po-vreme-na-vtorata-svetovna-voina.

Finally, Bulgarian authorities have insisted on their determination to repress any expression of anti-Semitism. In October 2017, Bulgaria incorporated into its national legislation the definition of anti-Semitism adopted by IHRA in 2016; meanwhile, Deputy Foreign Minister Georg Georgiev was appointed coordinator of the fight against anti-Semitism.[165] This decision came at a delicate time. Following the parliamentary elections of March 26, 2017, a governing coalition was formed around Bojko Borisov (GERB), which brought together proponents of Bulgarian radical nationalism—*Ataka*, the National Front for the Defense of Bulgaria (*Nacionalen front za spasenie na Bălgarija*, NFSB), and the Internal Macedonian Revolutionary Organization.[166] In May 2017, Deputy Minister for Regional Development Pavel Tenev was forced to resign after posting a photograph on his Facebook page in which he performed the Nazi salute in front of a wax effigy from the Grévin Museum.[167] A few weeks later, the government announced the appointment of Deputy Prime Minister and Interior Minister Valeri Simeonov, the leader of the NFSB, an organization that had built its electoral success on the stigmatization of minorities, particularly Roma, as head of the National Council for Cooperation on Ethnic and Integration Issues (*Nacionalen săvet za sătrudničestvo po etničeskite i integracionnite văprosi*).[168]

These contradictory indications, reflecting the tensions between the executive, the Šalom organization, and part of the scholarly community, suggest how complex the Bulgarian configuration was. Other parameters must therefore be considered if one wishes to explain the timid opening toward Macedonia.

In the Spotlight of Euro-Atlantic Integration

In the wake of the recommendations of the December 2012 European Council, Bulgaria and Macedonia had begun negotiating a good-neighbor treaty. The talks were conducted without enthusiasm so long as Prime

165 "Izbraha Georg Georgiev za nacionalen koordinator za borbata s anti-semitizma," *News.bg*, October 18, 2017.
166 In the run-up to the election, these three organizations had formed a coalition, United Patriots (*Obedineni patrioti*), which won 9.31 percent of the vote.
167 "Zamestnik-ministăr na regionalnoto razvitie e sniman v nacistki pozdrav," *Dnevnik*, May 17, 2018.
168 Bulgarian human rights organizations collected 15,000 signatures demanding the cancellation of this appointment. "15 hiljada glasa ot cjalata strana kazaha 'ne' na Valeri Simeonov kato šef na integracijata," *Marginalia.bg*, June 27, 2017.

Minister Nikola Gruevski (VMRO-DPMNE) exercised ungentlemanly control over Macedonia, its media, and its intelligence services. In May 2017, the formation of a new social democratic majority (*Socialdemokratski Sojuz na Makedonija*, SDSM) led by economist Zoran Zaev created a novel structure of opportunity: as soon as he took office on May 31, the new head of the executive relaunched the integration project into NATO and the EU.[169] Two months later, the good-neighborliness treaty with Bulgaria was concluded.[170]

The previous document governing bilateral relations was dated February 22, 1999: the two states had committed themselves to refraining from any irredentist claims or hostile actions. In return, Bulgaria had indirectly recognized the existence of a Macedonian language distinct from Bulgarian.[171] In the new treaty, the singularity of the latter is mentioned twice, instead of once, through reference to the "constitutional language of each of the states." The Macedonian authorities agreed that the preamble suggested the existence of a "common history" of Bulgarian and Macedonian territories separated by the postimperial borders.[172]

Three innovations, however, are noteworthy: the first concerns the creation of a "joint multidisciplinary expert commission on historical and educational issues" charged with "contributing to an objective scientific interpretation of historical facts, based on authentic historical sources and evidence" (Article 8, paragraph 2). The formula marks the entry of history into the field of interstate dialogue and the solicitation of historical expertise. The two states also envisage jointly organizing commemorative ceremonies "of common historical events and personalities" (Article 8, paragraph 3). The second novelty concerns the protection granted to nationals domiciled in the neighboring state (Article 11, paragraph 4), a clause intended to take note of the growing number of Macedonians who have acquired a Bulgarian passport since Bulgaria's accession to the EU in 2007.[173] Finally,

---

169 "Šekerinska: Nato i EU se edinstveniot protivotrov za nacionalizmot," *Deutsche Welle*, February 22, 2018.

170 http://www.parliament.bg/bills/44/702-02-13_ZP_ratifitsirane_Dogovora_priyatelstvo_ dobrosasedstvo_i_satrudnichestvo_RB-RMakedoniya.PDF (accessed February 19, 2020; no longer active).

171 AIM Sofia, "Bulgaria Recognises Macedonian Language: The End of Linguistic Controversy between Bulgaria and Macedonia," February 22, 1999, http://www.aimpress.ch/dyn/trae/archive/data/199902/90222-005-trae-sof.htm.

172 The treaty was strongly criticized by the VMRO-DPMNE, which did not take part in the ratification vote. Risto Nikovski, "The Harmonized Text of the Agreement with Bulgaria Is Humiliating for Macedonia," *Macedonian Political Highlights*, July 2017.

173 Neofotistos, "2009," 19–22.

the third novelty is that Article 12 provides for the formation of a committee to monitor the implementation of the treaty.

The conclusion of the agreement was interpreted in Bulgaria as a diplomatic success. For the first half of 2018, the country was to assume the rotating presidency of the Union. The Borisov government had focused its agenda on reactivating the enlargement process to the Western Balkans.[174] At the time the project was formulated—in the midst of Brexit—it seemed unrealistic: since Croatia's accession to the EU in July 2013, only Serbia and Montenegro had opened and closed EU accession chapters with silent obstinacy. However, by championing further enlargement and announcing the holding of an EU–Western Balkans summit in Sofia on May 17, 2018, Bulgaria sought to increase its regional (and European) influence. To realize this ambition, the Bulgarian elites had to demonstrate their ability, if not to settle, at least to mitigate bilateral disputes. Following shortly after the official visit of the Bulgarian head of state Radev to Macedonia in February 2018, Prime Minister Borisov's participation in the commemorations of the seventy-fifth anniversary of the deportation of the Jews from Macedonia is also illuminated in the light of this diplomatic agenda.[175]

On February 6, 2018, the European Commission published an ambitious strategy for the Western Balkans.[176] On April 17, it recommended the opening of accession talks with Albania and Macedonia and set the year 2025 as the horizon for the accession of Serbia and Montenegro to the EU. At the same time, Greek-Macedonian negotiations on the name of the state of Macedonia resumed under the aegis of the UN mediator Matthew Nimitz. On June 12, 2018, a compromise on the name—"Republic of North Macedonia"—put an end to twenty-seven years of controversy.[177] As a result, North Macedonia was invited to join NATO at the July 2018

---

174 Bulgarian Presidency of the Council of the European Union, "United We Stand Strong," https://www.cece.eu/news/2018/everyone/eu-news-bulgarian-presidency-united-we-stand-strong. See also the parliamentary decision adopted in relation to the draft program of the Bulgarian presidency: https://eu2018bg.bg/upload/614/EN_POSITION+OF+THE+NATIONAL+ASSEMBLY.pdf.

175 Katerina Blaževska, "Skopje i Sofija trasirat sorabotkata," *Deutsche Welle*, February 16, 2018.

176 European Commission, Communication from the Commission to the European Parliament, the Council, the European Economic and Social Committee and the Committee of the Regions, *A Credible Enlargement Perspective for and Enhanced EU Engagement with the Western Balkans*, Strasbourg, February 6, 2018, COM (2018) 65 final.

177 Andrew Rettman, "Macedonian Name Deal Opens Door to Western Expansion," *EUobserver.com*, June 12, 2018.

summit. The removal of the Greek veto, however, did not suffice to convince the EU Council to start up Macedonia's accession talks; France, Denmark, and the Netherlands blocked the process. North Macedonia would have to wait for four more years before it could open negotiations with the European Union.[178]

In concluding our examination of the Bulgarian-Macedonian historical controversies, a modest, trivial observation is in order: in Bulgaria as in North Macedonia, the writing of history continues to be "driven by the concern for the present."[179] But this dependence of the past on changing actualities constitutes a singular challenge here insofar as the establishment of facts and the patient administration of proof are in their infancy. Long hampered by the divisions of the Cold War, by the inaccessibility of certain archives, and by the disinterest of foreign and local researchers, the documentation of anti-Jewish persecutions has received an impetus over the past decade that leaves many areas still underresearched. These include the bureaucracy of anti-Semitism and its relationship to the historical sociology of the Bulgarian state; the entanglements between the conduct of the war, the Bulgarianization of the occupied lands, and anti-Jewish policy; and the implementation of mechanisms such as the identification of Jews, the administration of professional exclusions, the Aryanization of Jewish properties, the expulsion of Jews from Sofia and other cities in May 1943, and their experience of relegation to the province and to forced labor, among others.

The configuration under consideration bears resemblance to the sociotechnical debates examined by Yannick Barthe, Michel Callon, and Pierre

---

178 France's opposition in October 2019 to the opening of accession talks with North Macedonia (and Albania), already postponed twice, led to the resignation of Macedonia's prime minister, Zoran Zaev, in January 2020. On March 24, 2020, the EU members reached a political agreement on the start of negotiations. On July 15, Zaev's Social Democratic Union of Macedonia majority narrowly won the early elections, originally scheduled for April 12 (and postponed due to the COVID-19 pandemic). However, in November 2020, in an unexpected turnabout, Bulgaria vetoed the start of the negotiations, denouncing North Macedonia's failure to abide by the 2017 bilateral good-neighborliness treaty. It took much bickering before the Bulgarian veto of North Macedonia's EU accession talks was finally lifted on June 24, 2022. Three weeks later, on July 16, the Macedonian parliament approved a revised French proposal for a Bulgarian-Macedonian compromise, allowing accession negotiations to begin; they were officially announced three days later. By June 2023, however, little progress had been made as a result of continued Bulgarian-Macedonian contention.

179 Hartog, *Évidence de l'histoire*, 35.

Lascoumes.[180] The recognition that controversies serve as prodigious generators of societal dynamics rather than being mere record-keepers of ontological reality, and that such dissensus enables an assessment of both accepted and disputed facts, became evident in the Bulgarian public television broadcast *Istorija* on March 5, 2018, as described at the outset of the chapter. Despite the program's ostensibly targeted investigation into the architects behind and mechanisms of the "rescue," the debate demonstrated how it had become challenging to discuss the survival of the Bulgarian Jews without acknowledging their deportation from occupied territories. The two sets of events were no longer interchangeable; rather, they now were inextricably linked by tangible connections and situated at the very center of contemporary inquiry.

In what manner were these associations forged? Through a succession of gradual shifts, the full effects of which were only partially foreseen. Chapter 4 began by examining the 1990s, a time characterized by the denunciation of communism, which resulted in the transfer of the "savior" image from dictator Zhivkov and the Communist Party to the elites of the precommunist regime and to King Boris. This redistribution of roles seemed to leave intact the interpretive framework of anti-Jewish persecution that reimagined mass murder in Europe as mass rescue south of the Danube. However, in the early 2000s, as debates on the comparative crimes of communism and Nazism intensified during Bulgaria's path toward Euro-Atlantic integration, the relocation of memorial disputes to Israel and the launch of competing memorial initiatives by descendants of Balkan Holocaust survivors would ultimately facilitate a reformulation of the "rescue" narrative. The tutelary figures of Zhivkov and the king were replaced with the heroic image of a Bulgarian people, to whom the collective paternity of the "rescue" was then assigned.

The reappraisal of the conduct of the former parliamentarian Pešev was itself the product of mobilizations at multiple scales and provides an intriguing contribution in this regard. On the European legislative stage, his actions were recast as evidence of the virtues of parliamentary institutions, paving the way for the establishment of an interpretive consensus, first, by merging the merit-based lists; second, by depoliticizing actors through magnified individualities; and finally, by recasting "the Bulgarian people" as a synecdoche of moral commitment. The historicity of references to the notion of "Bulgarian tolerance," whose prodromes we had identified during the trials of 1945, favored the resurgence of "people" as a signifier, a term open to a plurality of interpretations. The collapse of communism resulted in the

---

180 Barthe, Callon, and Lascoumes, *Agir dans un monde incertain.*

displacement of the postwar concept of the "progressive people," as the new construct of the "people-nation" took hold.

A fortuitous divergence becomes apparent: by redirecting the focus toward the "good people," it became possible to disentangle the virtuous society from a government that, albeit no longer overtly labeled as "fascist," remained susceptible to being designated as "pro-Nazi." It is with the opening of this narrow passage that an investigation into Bulgarian responsibility in the Jewish predicament during World War II could be pursued. Initially, this did not impact the topic of the "rescue": demonstrating the determination of the public authorities to deport all Jews from the "old" and "new" territories only made the society's opposition to its leaders more admirable. Gradually, however, the issue of pinpointing Bulgarian responsibility became ever more pressing: should the responsibility lie with the government or the state?

This brief exposition may raise concerns that only reconfigured narrative fragments, shaped by the fluctuations of controversy, are presented. It is time to give form and substance to these words; indeed, examining the shifting entanglements in the discussions of the Holocaust and other issues offers an opportunity to reincorporate actors into the narrative. These dynamic groupings acted as powerful catalysts for change, ushering into debates new protagonists bearing distinctive methodologies, epistemologies, and agendas. Novel coalitions were forged, and with them, tactical reconfigurations. The passage of time, once more, manifested in a three-part cadence.

The first phase emerged following the demise of communism, as the discussions around anti-Jewish persecutions began to be conducted through the dual lens of the forced assimilation of the Turks of Bulgaria, on the one hand, and the lingering controversies over fascism, on the other. In both instances, the objective was to anchor democracy in Bulgaria and to lend credibility to its project on the international stage. The primary actors in these debates were essayists, publicists, elected officials, and community leaders.

A decade later, a second phase unfolded on the European and the global stage, where the Bulgarian politicians dealing with the matter of the Holocaust as a signifier of Europeanism and a means of achieving legitimacy. For those concerned about the potential dichotomy of a West—where the extermination of Jews is paradigmatic of public memory—set in opposition to an East, absorbed by a specter of Communist violence, the Bulgarian case offers a reassuring denial: here, memories of Communist and Nazi crimes do not collide. For the entrepreneurs of anti-communist memory, the appeal for remembrance of all twentieth-century suffering serves the production of a heroic narrative. Far from promoting a critical reading of national dogmas, the European institutions act as a sounding board for the establishment of an equivalence between the Holocaust in Europe and the "rescue" in Bulgaria. However, the discourse was soon challenged by voices from the Balkan Jewish communities who, due to political and national divisions, as well as disparate experiences of the past, saw some voices praising the "rescue" and others denouncing Bulgaria's complicity in the genocide of European Jews. Subsequently, historians and museums—notably the USHMM and Yad Vashem—gradually entered the debate.

Moving forward another decade, a third phase unfurls, one where debates about the history of the Holocaust are refracted through the lens of a present rife with anti-Semitism, racism, and intercommunal violence. The cultural diplomacy of the "rescue" narrative advanced, giving rise to mounting calls for greater factual precision—particularly from American and international Jewish organizations. Consequently, the theme of anti-Jewish persecution became intricately linked with that of contemporary expressions of anti-Jewish sentiment. In this complex milieu, the renewal of Šalom's leadership, Bulgaria's integration into the IHRA, and the advocacy of institutions such as the WJC facilitated the appropriation of this thematic association, leading to a narrowing of what is deemed acceptable for public discussion, what is deemed credible, and what is subject to public sanctioning.

For now, the heightened visibility of divergent interpretations of the past has not engendered an environment conducive to the resolution of contested issues and past grievances, but rather has facilitated the institutionalization of dissent. While it is not possible to speak of a unification of narratives of the past, one can observe the emergence of a reading slowly permeating academic, memorial and cultural circles on a global and a Southeast European scale, while leaving others to persist. The partial separation between the social worlds, within which these competing interpretations of the past circulate, may facilitate the coexistence of these discordant readings. Allowing the somewhat interlocking components of the past to come into play, this absence of unification among perspectives may have the potential to trigger a reformulation and eventual elucidation of historical issues deemed most sensitive. How this coexistence evolves will to a large extent depend on choices made by political and memory actors, in Bulgaria and beyond.

Conclusion

A fact both irrevocable and prodigious: about 48,000 Jews in Bulgaria, almost the entire Bulgarian Jewish community, were not deported during World War II. Beginning with Hannah Arendt, the first generation of those writing on the destruction of the European Jews consistently pointed out this historical exception.[1] A few years later, Raul Hilberg offered a more nuanced reading of the events. Territorial ambitions, strategic prudence, delay tactics—in his account, these were all to be situated within a state policy that considered the Jews a "pawn in the hands of an opportunistic power." He continued, "They were like a surplus commodity, to be traded for political advantage. The Reich could not completely destroy the Bulgarian Jews because it could not offer sufficient gain to the cautious Bulgarian rulers."[2] Yet the American historian added, "It was as though the degree of involvement had already been predetermined. The operation was brought to a halt as if stopped by an invisible sign which said, 'So far and no farther.'"[3]

In the Bulgarian State Archives, as if in a daze, one enters to discover a wealth of archival records showing the array of individual and collective protests that arose in autumn 1940 against the passing of the first anti-Jewish law.[4] To be sure, unlike in Vichy France, in Bulgaria the legislation on the "Jewish question" had been discussed in parliament and debated in the press, a setup propitious for public controversy. The diversity of the actors involved in these protests, in terms of social networks and resources, nonetheless seemed to defy the sociological rules of social movements. They included members of the intellectual and political elite, professional unions, the Orthodox Church, as well as ordinary citizens; certain of the latter who wrote were visibly not familiar with the art of lodging grievances. Let us recall that at the time Bulgaria was a personal monarchy with a predominantly rural population that had only recently achieved literacy. Then came the second wave of protests, in March 1943, in opposition to the deportation of Jews from the "old" kingdom. Despite a tightening of the political

---

1   Arendt, *Eichmann in Jerusalem*, 188.
2   Hilberg, *Destruction of the Jews*, 794.
3   Ibid.
4   Part of this documentation has been digitized by the Bulgarian Central State Archives.

channels—the executive had received full powers over the "Jewish question" in June 1942, and the authorities sought to keep the preparations for the deportations secret—this cluster of initiatives was no less striking. Even more so was their success: the deportation orders were called off, and the Bulgarian Jews who had been arrested were freed. The later attempts at deportation prepared by the Commissariat for Jewish Affairs failed to secure the approval of the government and the king.

Any investigation into the social production of knowledge about Bulgaria's Jewish policies during World War II is bound to start with this constellation of events and their reverberations across the world. A scholar must work with them, rather than against or without them. Yet, the fascination that such archival records exert cannot overdetermine the direction, much less the outcome, of the inquiry. Who has forgotten Georges Perec's luminous lines on puzzles: on how, in doing a puzzle, one reproduces the earlier moves of the puzzle's maker? Reflecting on this double process of assembly, he noted, "In isolation, a puzzle piece means nothing—just an impossible question, an opaque challenge. But as soon as you have succeeded . . . in fitting it into one of its neighbors, the piece disappears, ceases to exist as a piece. The intense difficulty preceding this link-up—which the English word *puzzle* indicates so well—not only loses its *raison d'être*, it seems never to have had any reason, so obvious does the solution appear. The two pieces so miraculously conjoined are henceforth one, which in its turn will be a source of error, hesitation, dismay, and expectation."[5] In writing the present volume, I have striven to accept Perec's invitation by bringing together contrasting, often contradictory, pieces, without attempting to resolve the tension between them or dissolve them into a single whole. The challenge was to adjust each piece to the problem at hand and allow meanings to emerge that—unlike Perec's jigsaw puzzle—have not been composed in advance.

Historiographical Disputes

Three historiographical disputes have wound their way through this investigation: the nature of the authority that Bulgaria exercised over its occupied territories; its autonomy with respect to the Third Reich; and the politics of citizenship. These interrogations converge on one critical issue: how to assess Bulgaria's and Germany's respective shares of responsibility for the deportation and extermination of the Jews from the "new" kingdom.

---

5   Perec, *La Vie mode d'emploi*, 17–18.

What was the legal status of the occupied territories and who ruled over them? Were these lands fully under Bulgarian jurisdiction? Were they regions under temporary military and civil administration, where Bulgarian law and bureaucracy nonetheless prevailed? Or were they spaces where the key decisions would ultimately depend on Nazi Germany?[6] While the Bulgarian government and public considered it a final and complete annexation, toward the end of the war Hitler toyed with the idea of creating a separate Macedonian state under the auspices of Vanče Mihajlov.[7] To this day, the most enlightening analysis of these jurisdictional dilemmas has been written by an associate law professor at the University of Sofia, Zdravka Krăsteva. At the intersection of Bulgarian law and the law of war, she offers a contrarian analysis of the arguments deployed during the Nuremberg trial to assert the nonsovereignty of the Croatian *ustaša* state and comes up with several decisive conclusions: Bulgaria was a sovereign state during the war; the signing of a bilateral agreement with the Third Reich for the deportation of Jews from the occupied territories proves that the Germans understood these populations as being under Bulgarian jurisdiction; finally, from the perspective of international law, the pressure that Nazi Germany exerted over its Bulgarian ally was not enough to constitute a case of force majeure (here the author distinguishes between the notions of "pressure" [*natisk*] and "constraint" [*prinuda*]).[8] One related question, however, remains. In terms of an internationally recognized annexation, was such de facto administration likely to reduce the perception held by the Bulgarian ruling elites of their own decision-making autonomy in these territories, vis-à-vis the Reich?

How should we characterize the alliance between the Third Reich and Bulgaria since this member of the Tripartite Pact did not send an expeditionary force to the eastern front and did not declare war on the Soviet Union? Even today, in Bulgarian public discourse, the relationship with the Reich is still sometimes presented as "de facto German occupation."[9] To what

---

6 We might recall the resolution adopted on March 8, 2013, by the Bulgarian parliament affirming that, unlike South Dobrudža, ceded by Romania in September 1940, the Yugoslav and Greek territories were not under Bulgarian jurisdiction in September 1940.

7 The author wishes to thank Maria Todorova for this reminder. On this episode, see Troebst, "Führerbefehl!," 491–501. This article was translated into Macedonian: "Naredbata na Adolf Hitler za proglasuvanje na nezavisna Makedonija (septemvri 1944)," *Glasnik na Institutot za nacionalna istorija* 46, no. 2 (2002 [2003]): 25–39.

8 Krăsteva, "Pravni aspekti na dăržavnata antievrejska politika," esp. 159–69.

9 On March 8, 2013, Maksim Benvenisti, then president of Šalom, spoke of a "de facto occupation (*praktičeska okupacija*) of Bulgaria by Nazi Germany." See Dima Kirilova, "V Kjustendil početoha tăržestveno spasjavaneto na

extent was the Bulgarian state subordinated to its protector and powerful ally? Bulgaria was certainly economically dependent on Germany, conducting over 60 percent of its foreign trade with the country by the end of the 1930s.[10] It was also indebted to the Reich for the fulfillment of its dreams of a "greater Bulgaria," dreams that had consumed national elites since the creation of a Bulgarian principality in 1878, and even more so in the wake of the Balkan Wars (1912–13) and World War I (1919 Treaty of Neuilly). The transport of Jews from the occupied territories was readily presented as the foil to such territorial gains, or as a measure of compensation for the refusal to deploy a Bulgarian contingent on the eastern front. This was alternatively interpreted as the sine qua non condition of the "rescue of the Bulgarian Jews," and as a concession intended to preserve as many lives as the unequal power relations between Bulgaria and the Reich would allow. It would be a hazardous exercise in counterfactual history to venture into this unfulfilled future—that is, the political and military consequences that the Bulgarian authorities' refusal to undertake the roundups might have had in 1943.

With these dilemmas addressed, the distribution of responsibilities in carrying out the acts remains to be discussed. Those who defend the Germans' power of initiative often juxtapose the Bulgarian deportations with the Nazi calendar of the Final Solution in central and southeastern Europe from the summer of 1942 to the spring of 1943. They point to the double chain of agents involved in negotiating the roundups with the Bulgarian authorities: the Reich Security Main Office (*Reichssicherheitshauptamt*, RSHA), on the one hand, and the German Foreign Office (*Auswärtiges Amt*, AA), on the other. In November 1941, at the time of the signing of the Anti-Comintern Pact, discussions began in Berlin between German Foreign Minister Joachim von Ribbentrop and his Bulgarian counterpart, Ivan Popov, at the latter's initiative. They continued throughout 1942, with Minister Plenipotentiary of the Reich Adolf-Heinz Beckerle serving as the liaison between the Bulgarian authorities and Martin Luther, the point person for Jewish Affairs within the AA, who was tasked with pressuring Nazi allies into handing over their Jewish population. Beyond possible reluctance among the Bulgarians, the irregular rhythm of these talks reflects the existence of inter- and intrainstitutional rivalries in Germany's management of the Final Solution.

---

bălgarskite evrei," *Dariknews.bg*, March 8, 2013, https://dariknews.bg/novini/obshtestvo/v-kyustendil-pochetoha-tyrzhestveno-spasqvaneto-na-bylgarskite-evrei-1052126.

10 John Lampe, aggregating Bulgarian trade with both Germany and Austria, calculates the total as 41 percent of exports and 30 percent of imports from 1929 to 1931; and 63 percent of exports and 59 percent of imports by 1938–39. Lampe, *Bulgarian Economy*, 90.

On the RSHA side, within a chain of command beginning with *Reichsführer-SS* Heinrich Himmler and continuing to *SS-Obergruppenführer* Ernst Kaltenbrunner (who after Reinhard Heydrich's assassination in the spring of 1942 led the office from January 1943) and Adolf Eichmann, *Referat IV B 4*, one can find that *SS-Hauptsturmführer* Theodor Dannecker, Eichmann's special representative, was dispatched to Sofia on January 21, 1943, to expedite the preparations for the deportations. Working with him was the SS and police attaché Adolf Hoffmann, assigned to the German legation in Bulgaria in March 1943 on the basis of an agreement between Himmler and Ribbentrop. These three names—Beckerle, Dannecker, and Hoffmann—bear witness to the direct involvement of Reich agents and their painstaking monitoring of the preparations for the arrests, the creation of temporary detention centers, and the transportation from Bulgaria, Vardar Macedonia, and Northern Greece to the extermination camps in Nazi-occupied Poland.

Those who, in contrast, favor an interpretation of the historical facts that accentuates Bulgaria's decision-making autonomy note how early Bulgaria and Germany began to discuss and seek a European "solution" to the problem of how to treat Jews with different citizenship statuses: for example, the meeting between Ribbentrop and the Bulgarian foreign minister mentioned above. They highlight the June 1942 vote by the Bulgarian National Assembly that granted the executive full powers over Jewish Affairs, as well as the range of decision-makers and bureaucrats involved in the anti-Jewish persecutions (the Council of Ministers; the Ministries of the Interior and Public Health, Foreign Affairs, War, Agriculture, and Public Property; the national railway company; the Bulgarian National Bank, and others). Moreover, they underline that government decisions were subject in the last instance to the king's approval. Beyond the existing state bureaucracy, specialized institutions were also created, including the Commissariat for Jewish Affairs (KEV). Reporting to the minister of the interior and endowed with broad prerogatives, KEV designed, coordinated, and implemented anti-Jewish policies. Article 7 of the August 26, 1942, decree stated that "Jewish municipalities" (*evrejskite obštini*)—those communal institutions now placed under the authority of the Commissariat—had the "task of preparing the deportation (*izselvaneto*) of the Jewish population." Article 29 envisaged the expulsion of Jews from Sofia "to the provinces or outside the Kingdom."[11] These documents are thus taken as evidence that at least part of the Bulgarian state apparatus—at a minimum, the Commissariat and the Ministry of the Interior—had in mind, beginning in 1942, the deportation

---

11 DV, no. 192, August 29, 1942.

of the Jews from the "old" and "new" kingdoms as the ultimate horizon for anti-Jewish policies.

This historical interpretation, in addition, showcases the role of the police, the army, and the Bulgarian administration in carrying out round-ups in the occupied territories—and, briefly, in the "old" kingdom—as well as in the management of the transit camps; conveyance by train through Northern Greece, Bulgaria, and Vardar Macedonia; dispatching (together with the German police) the Greek Jewish deportees by boat from Lom; and the subsequent organization of the confiscation of Jewish property. Such accounts further specify that the arrests, deportations, and appropriation of Jewish property were authorized by decrees passed by the Council of Ministers at the beginning of March 1943. Finally, those who underline Bulgarian decision-making autonomy point out that, when the government and King Boris refused to apply the new deportation plan submitted by Commissioner for Jewish Affairs Aleksandăr Belev, in May 1943, and "contented themselves" with authorizing the expulsion of Jews living in Sofia and other Bulgarian cities to the provinces, the German response was rather mild. The pressing demands of the Reich were not considered sufficient to impose the deportation of Jews of Bulgarian citizenship.

The third point of contention, the interpretation of citizenship policies, forms a subset within the discussions of the chain of events leading to the deportations. All accounts agree that the failure to grant Bulgarian citizenship to the Jews living in the occupied territories deprived them of state protection. But how to explain this situation? Article 4 of the decree published in the *State Gazette* on June 10, 1942, regarding citizenship in "the lands liberated in 1941," stated that "all Yugoslav and Greek citizens of non-Bulgarian origin who, on the day that this decree enters into force, resided in the lands liberated in 1941, become Bulgarian citizens. . . . This decree does not concern people of Jewish origin."[12] Should this be seen as the legal consequence of two prior texts: the Citizenship Law passed in December 1940[13] and the Law for the Defense of the Nation, in force from January 23, 1941?[14] The former denied Bulgarian citizenship to individuals who were "unworthy and dangerous to state security and the public order"[15] and stipulated that citi-

---

12 DV, no. 24, June 10, 1942.

13 DV, no. 288, December 20, 1940.

14 DV, no.16, January 23, 1941.

15 More specifically, article 21, part III of the December 1940 Law stated that 'Bulgarian citizens living abroad, who through their acts expose the Bulgarian state or place its security at risk. . . . Bulgarian citizens of non-Bulgarian origin, as well as those who were naturalized . . . , if they, with their children, have proved unworthy and dangerous for the security of the state and the public order" could be deprived of their Bulgarian citizenship.

zens who chose to emigrate would automatically lose their citizenship upon leaving the territory; the latter prohibited the granting of Bulgarian citizenship to people of Jewish descent. Or was it a political choice made between May and June 1942, under pressure from German authorities?

Two additional points should be taken into consideration as well: the first related to questions of periodization, the second to the level of protection granted to the Bulgarian Jews. Some documents suggest a different timeline of cooperation between Bulgarian and German authorities in Jewish arrests, one beginning significantly earlier than usually admitted. In November 1941, when the Jews had already begun to be exterminated on a large scale in Serbia under Nazi occupation, Serbian Jews who had sought refuge in Macedonia were arrested by the Bulgarian authorities, handed over to the Germans, and subsequently murdered in Serbia.[16] In addition, in the summer of 1942, Germans and Bulgarians agreed in an exchange of verbal diplomatic notes that Bulgarian Jewish citizens residing in Germany or in territories under German control—mainly in the Protectorate of Bohemia and Moravia—would have their Bulgarian citizenship revoked, with an eye to their subsequent deportation.[17] In July 1942, a report from Karl Klingenfuss, then employed with *Referat D III* of the Reich's Foreign Office, confirmed that the Bulgarian authorities had accepted all the Reich's anti-Jewish measures to be applied to those Jews holding Bulgarian citizenship who lived in regions under German control, including the "eastward transfers," and that the Bulgarian state had undertaken not to request their return.[18] At least 140 Bulgarian Jews living in France would thus be deprived of their

---

16 In October 1941, having been informed by the Gestapo of the presence of Serbian Jews in Skopje, the Bulgarian authorities demanded they be registered with the police. The 213 Serbian Jews who obeyed this order were arrested on November 25, 1941; 47 men over age eighteen were transported to the Beograd-Benjica camp in Serbia, where they were executed on December 3, 1941. CDA, F 2123K, op. 1, ae. 22 286, l. 56–57; Micković, *Logor Banjica, Logoraši*, 1:163–66. The author wishes to thank Milan Koljanin for making this source available.

17 On July 4, 1942, Dimităr Šišmanov, secretary-general of the Ministry of Foreign Affairs, confirmed that he had received approval from Prime Minister Bogdan Filov, indicating to the German authorities that "the Bulgarian government has nothing against deporting Jews who are Bulgarian citizens finding themselves in German territory." The Bulgarian government merely requested a list of the names of the deportees, their place of birth, and the address from which they were being displaced since their deportation may have legal consequences for the Bulgarian state. CDA, F 176K, op. 8, ae. 1110, l. 3.

18 Naučen Arhiv na Bălgarska Akademija na naukite, F 111, op. 1, ae. 14, l. 9 (translated into Bulgarian from German; reproduction of documentation kept at Yad Vashem under the call number 207505–207506).

citizenship, rounded up and held in the camp at Drancy before most were deported to the east.[19] This position was reiterated on June 11, 1943, in a letter from the Commissariat to the Bulgarian Ministry of Foreign Affairs, in response to a request sent by the German legation in Sofia: "The KEV is not interested in the situation of people of Bulgarian origin, citizens of Bulgaria, living in Germany and in the countries under German occupation."[20]

Each milestone in this debate leads to the ultimate question: who was responsible for the events of March 1943? If Bulgaria's shared responsibility in anti-Jewish persecutions is to be acknowledged, including in the roundups and deportations from the territories entrusted to the Bulgarian administration, should this responsibility be located in a specific government, in a political regime, or in the Bulgarian state?

As this investigation comes to a close, we have reconstituted a constellation of actors who contributed to the mobile, even metonymic, connections between the Holocaust in Europe and the "rescue of Bulgarian Jews" in Bulgaria. This, however, was an extraordinary act of translation. Until recently, World War II was typically described in Bulgarian public discourse through two stages: first, the persecution of the European Jews, in a narrative that centered on the Third Reich, Poland, and Soviet Union, while pushing the other European states, including those in the Balkans, to the margins. Then came an account of events in Bulgaria. Between the two frames—wide shot and close-up, to continue the cinematic metaphor—the meaning of the archival records was reshuffled. This rearrangement did not only concern the final outcome, the deportations in most of Europe versus nondeportation

---

19   Quoted in Klarsfeld, *Le calendrier de la persécution des Juifs*, 1126–27, 1227. Referring to the data collected by Georges Etlin, an internee in Drancy charged by the camp authorities with keeping statistical accounts, Klarsfeld notes, "This table is not entirely accurate, because it takes into account not only convoys going to the East, but also transfers of detainees from Drancy to other internment camps" (1126). Some victims were also classified with "unknown," "to be determined," or "stateless" nationality, thus limiting the possibility of providing exhaustive data on the deportees' origin (1127). Finally, it should be noted that the roundups of September 14, 1942, in the Paris region, which affected 208 people, including 27 children, specifically targeted Bulgarian, Yugoslav, Baltic, and Dutch Jews (1227). The last deportation of Bulgarian Jews from France occurred in July 1944: there were seven Bulgarian Jews in Convoy 77, the last French transport to Auschwitz. See Hoppe, "Juden als Feinde Bulgariens?," 233. The author wishes to thank Georges Mayer, president of the Convoi 77 Association, for sharing the number and names of the seven July 1944 Bulgarian deportees. Email correspondence, November 22, 2022.

20   Quoted in Grinberg, *Hitlerskijat natisk za uništožavaneto na evreite ot Bălgarija*, 32.

from Bulgaria's "old" kingdom; it also extended to deciphering the policies that had been implemented before the roundups began. The historiographical consequences of this way of narrating the past cannot be underestimated: apart from the planning and carrying out of deportations, the enforcement of most anti-Jewish policies in the "old" kingdom—identification of the Jews; professional exclusions and Aryanization of property; political, economic, and social marginalization; detention in camps and internal exile; forced labor, and more—has remained almost untouched territory.[21]

What We Talk about When We Talk about the Holocaust

If there is one unambiguous lesson to be drawn from this research, it is that the Holocaust in Bulgaria has, since the end of World War II, been unendingly associated with the discussion of other more or less loosely related issues. In 1945, denouncing the acts committed against the Jews served to demonstrate the scale of "fascist crimes" in the country, to rally a politically divided Jewish community to the project of the Fatherland Front (OF), and to propel revolutionary momentum. In the diplomatic realm, heralding the convictions of war criminals charged with anti-Jewish crimes helped lend credibility to the notion of Bulgarian opposition to the pro-Nazi regime, and thus solicit leniency from the victorious powers.

At the end of the 1950s, invoking the Holocaust within the context of Bulgarian–East German discussions on a joint film production became a way for elites from the two countries to draw on distinct symbolic reservoirs for legitimizing the past, in order to arm themselves for contemporary struggles. Through representing Jewish fates, they set the terms for establishing a socialist *and* national identity, as well as a belonging to the Eastern bloc. Meanwhile, their choices betrayed their position within a global moment in which certain modes of signifying the Holocaust were able to traverse the borders of East and West. By the middle of the 1960s, when the Federal Republic of Germany returned to the question of German responsibility for Nazism, Eastern Europe's denunciation of fascism, past *and* present, played out in a collaboration between legal professionals, Jewish organizations, and Holocaust survivors from West Germany, Israel, Bulgaria, the United States, Yugoslavia, and the Soviet Union. At the same time, the trial courtroom offered a space where interpretive conflicts about the past were made explicit and publicized. Some of these battles placed Jews and non-Jews who had

---

21   Only the dispossession of Jewish property has led to some pioneering research; see Avramov, *"Spasenie" i padenie.*

remained in Bulgaria after 1949 in opposition to anti-communist exiles and Bulgarian *olim* in Israel.

As we approach the 1980s, references to the Holocaust become increasingly interwoven with praise for the Bulgarian Communist Party, for its leader Todor Zhivkov, and for a state whose external image suffered from suspicion of involvement in the May 1981 assassination attempt on Pope John Paul II, followed by a dull reception of Gorbachev's perestroika. From the 1990s to the early 2000s, Jewish destinies became one arena in which partisan identities and national roots were both fostered and contested. In Macedonia (today North Macedonia), Jewish suffering became a metaphor for a fate of national nonrecognition; rediscovered in Bulgaria, the Jewish predicament was marshaled to denounce the right-wing pretense that the precommunist era had been faultless, allegedly embodying at once civilization and modernity. In dialogue with an expanded range of actors who felt empowered to speak their truth of the past (memory entrepreneurs, politicians, and scholars), the events of World War II turned into battlegrounds. As this book has endeavored to show, the centrality of anti-Jewish persecutions in these public debates resulted precisely from their incessant reformulations.

Jewish Voices in the Writing of the Past

If talk of the Holocaust always involved speaking of other issues by proxy, this by no means implies that the anti-Jewish persecutions were thereby not discussed, or that no Jewish voices took part in formulating narratives of the past that did not give Jewish agency its due. Jewish survivors were key players in the production of knowledge and representations of Jewish fates in the "old" and "new" kingdoms, under socialism, as well as following the end of the Cold War. Here lies undoubtedly one of the major insights of this study.

Each chapter has illustrated one facet of Jewish agency. The first restored the role of a network of Bulgarian Communist Jews, mostly lawyers by training, involved in the prosecution of perpetrators of anti-Jewish crimes. The second introduced the pivotal figure of Angel Wagenstein, coauthor of visual and print narratives of the Holocaust from the 1950s onward, alongside East German filmmaker Konrad Wolf. In the third chapter, we turned to other forms of Jewish advocacy, including the work of Nehemiah Robinson, the director of the Institute for Jewish Affairs of the World Jewish Congress, while also examining the way intra-Jewish fractures affected the work of the West German investigators in charge of the Beckerle case. In the fourth chapter, by examining internal debates at the Organization of the Jews of Bulgaria Šalom regarding the legacy of the "rescue of the Bulgarian Jews," competing definitions of Jewishness, and the reconnection to major Jewish organizations across the globe, we opened a window onto the social and generational divides within the Jewish community, as well as the structural opportunities created by the introduction of multiparty politics beginning in the 1990s.

Finally, the question of how to broach the tangle of human ties, the intimate yet divided family histories, came into focus in the memorial initiatives of chapters 4 and 5. As we have shown, the contrast in the diverse Jewish commitments cannot be attributed to competing demands of rival political and national entities alone. Rather, the various forms of engagement also bear witness to the existence of distinct prewar Jewish trajectories, diverging Jews' experiences of World War II, as well as to the multiple ways of building a new Jewish life after 1945. The choices made by Bulgarian and non-Bulgarian Jews additionally reflected the positions these protagonists occupied within the national party systems and communal organizations, as well as their intimate beliefs about the logics of wartime events. In 1990, Michael Pollak introduced the expression "memory entrepreneur," echoing sociologist Howard Becker's "moral entrepreneurs," to designate actors who wish to obtain public sanction for their own readings of the past. Pollak's wording was intended to emphasize the work of "framing memory" that accompanied the transformation of individual memories into collective recollections.[22] In the scholarly literature produced since then, however, the focus on advocacy has sometimes involved an essentially instrumental reading of the social uses of the past, omitting the "intransigent ethics" and the interrogation of the "truth" carried out by the memory entrepreneurs, as Pollak described them. The preceding pages have attempted to remain alert to the original thrust of Pollak's contribution.

Challenges of the Page:
Leafing through Time, Speaking the Seen

It is a dilemma shared by all scholars that take history as their object of study: how to narrate the past, that "foreign country" accessible only through mediation?[23] Moreover, how can we build a footbridge—rather than a seawall—toward the mid-twentieth century when the extreme violence of World War II is enjoined to hand over the keys of an illegible, and

---

22 Michael Pollak, "Mémoire, oubli, silence," in Pollak, *Une identité blessée*, 29–31.

23 Tony Judt, "The Past Is Another Country: Myth and Memory in Postwar Europe," *Daedalus* 121, no. 4 (1992): 83–118.

increasingly violent, present?[24] How are we to keep in view both the singularity of a moment *and* the profusion of narratives about that moment, all while hoping such multiple retellings will help us find our way in disoriented times? To tell this story of intricate and confusing transactions between time and space, I have opted for a diachronic structure, aimed at overcoming the pitfalls of linearity.

To this end, I employed several devices. First, almost all the chapters follow an obsessive structure of clockwork rhythm. They begin with the mention of dates; they are striated by calendar markings, arranged in numerical divisions. Such thorough dating echoes the scrupulous care with which Bulgarian state officials, aided by their German allies and mentors, embarked on the deportation plans, fixing the appointed times for the military to seal the Jewish quarters and for the police to make the arrests, coordinating transfers between transit camps and train stations, transfers from one train to another, from railway to maritime transport, to the end of the line. This obsession with facts and figures is also reminiscent of the requests for information from the Commissariat for Jewish Affairs to regional delegates, demands that became more urgent as the date set for the roundups drew near. In the gaps between them can be glimpsed the desperate chronology, compressed and crushing, of the petitions that Jews deprived of employment and resources filed with Jewish municipalities in the winter of 1942–43.

As one might presume, the writing choices made in this book also bear the imprint of other works in progress, in this case on the Holocaust in the "new" lands of Vardar Macedonia and Thrace.[25] They pinpoint the existence of a gap between the way time was experienced by Bulgarian administrators and by the victims of the anti-Jewish system, even while affinities among forms of inscription—numbers and dates—might hide this gulf. In his reflection on Aby Warburg's *Pathosformeln*, Carlo Ginzburg cites an observation by Joshua Reynolds: "[The] extremes of contrary passions are with very little variation expressed by the same action."[26] Yet a bygone era cannot be restored, no clarifying effects produced, by delicately smoothing out its pleats. To avoid such a snare, I constructed a mobile set of spatiotemporal frames among which the reader might tarry.

A similar aim underpinned the mise en abyme of the narratives and the historical events to which they presumably correspond. From the start of the investigation, I had committed to advancing the facts together with

---

24   Hamit Bozarslan, "Quand la violence domine tout mais ne tranche rien: Réflexion sur la violence, la cruauté et la Cité," *Collège international de Philosophie*, nos. 85–86 (2015): 19–35.

25   Ragaru, "Madding Clocks," 161–94; Ragaru and Le Noc, "Visual Clues."

26   Ginzburg, *Fear, Reverence, Terror*, ix.

the ways in which they were narrated, without presuming either their radical separation or the scholar's exclusive access and right to claim *the* truth. From this point of view, the recurring references to specific temporal points were intended as coordinates that might drill an opening into the bundle of research, allowing each—though related to the others—to retain its own unique logic.

In the hope of troubling any linear progression of the narrative, I chose to offer the reader the opportunity to return to the same episode on several occasions, each time equipped with a distinct set of instruments, data, and questions; for instance, the March 12, 2018, ceremony in Skopje commemorating the deportations, with which the book opens, reappears at the start of chapter 4. Between these two restitutions of the event, there occur shifts in the scene's protagonists, as well as in the balance between the Macedonian and Bulgarian speeches. Time swelled as new guests were welcomed to the table, while the temporal frame underwent revisions as well. In the introduction, the day March 12, 2018, serves as a brief prelude to a seventy-five-year-long process of shaping historical retellings. In chapter 4, by contrast, March 12—the commemoration of the deportation of Macedonia's Jews and the nondeportation of Bulgarian Jews—is stretched to encompass ten days, and this extension is used to think about discussions of memory and history in a three-decade-long postcommunist period.

The second writing dilemma I faced was how to restore visual materials that, for copyright reasons, could not be systematically included in the manuscript—particularly the visual archives of chapter 3. This was a paradoxical situation in an investigation that so insists on the singularity of each document, and that stresses the powerful effects of analyzing written, visual, and audio sources together. Such a visible absence, nevertheless, offered an opportunity to reflect on how to make images come alive, with the tools of block black-and-white letters and paper alone. Ekphrasis also proved a fruitful device in reenacting the 1945 trial hearings for anti-Jewish crimes out of photographic stills. In assessing the feature film *Zvezdi/Sterne*, I worked from two intermediary versions of a cardinal scene as well as from the version of the sequence retained in the final montage: Jews arriving in Bulgaria after having been deported from Northern Greece. The first two sources—screenplay and storyboard—constitute distinct kinds of textual products: in order to turn the script into a storyboard, the creators of the movie had to do away with parts of the written text. Technical terms replaced some of the poetic wording of the screenplay. An intermediate object, the storyboard enables both proximity to and distance from the scene filmed. In the sequence actually shot, words incarnate into flesh—in bodies, gestures, and landscapes. Colors, light, and camera angles add to (and substitute for) the initial wordy script. In a final attempt at exploring the kind of knowledge the confrontation between images and words may deliver, I described, with my own words, the scene that was finally shown to the audience. At each level, through various connections and operations of translation, the visual and the written were intermingled, and came to complement one another.

Has such a method borne fruit? Line after line, the imperfect overlap between juxtaposed sequences lent itself to visualizing *and* interpreting images together. The choice was not an easy one: reflecting on images of the final film cut in *Zvezdi/Sterne* amounted to blanketing them with a new layer of language, at the risk of hiding them from view. To understand the reasons behind this choice, we might recall Siegfried Kracauer's reflections on photography,[27] alongside Ginzburg's interpretation of Kracauer's work.[28] The first refutes the idea that images would only serve a documentary function; the second reflects on the role of the photographer in the selection of a point of view and its ability to create a feeling of estrangement, thereby stimulating doubt, imagination, and thought.

For the visual archives of the 1943 deportations, three archival inventories respectively located in Bulgaria, the United States, and Germany were initially given responsibility for making the images speak. In addition to analyzing differences among their written depictions of this iconographic source, I explored the contrasts and similitudes between the 1943 moving images and the photograms extracted from them in 1967. Finally, multiple beams of testimony were laid down in this analytical framework: those of Bulgarian operators contemporary to the events as well as East German archivists who took notes on a reel they watched several decades later. Bringing together these multiple documentary sources, the manifold practices of transcription and translation, and the uses of the 1943 film footage by protagonists located at distinct points from this visual object delivered some fruitful insight into the origins and nature of the 1943 deportation film. Here, the aim was to identify, rather than resolve, the tensions among the sources and to follow the interpretive avenues these tensions opened.

One more decision lay at the core of this research: to cite at length the original archival material, and thus give this documentation breathing space, rather than suffocate it in a stifling interpretive framework. The (nearly exhaustive) transcription of the July 2000 parliamentary debate on the proposal to remove the Speaker of the National Assembly, Blagovest Sendov, was emblematic of this approach. In sound and in writing, the amazingly graphic exchanges in the Bulgarian assembly illustrated the richness of this archival source, once apprehended in its totality. Much of our understanding of the

---

27 Kracauer, *Theory of Film*, and *History*.
28 Carlo Ginzburg, "Details, Early Plans, Microanalysis: Thoughts on a Book by Siegfried Kracauer," in Ginzburg, *Threads and Traces*, 180–92.

situation would have been missed had only short excerpts from this document been deployed to support a single argument. Attention, for instance, might have been driven away from the applause and jeers preserved in the session's stenographic report. By reading thoroughly, one comes to hear the procession of sounds and to grasp that their volume was set differently within smaller and larger parliamentary groups. Through their exclamations and interjections, the parties with the larger contingents literally gave voice to their political influence and, thereby, exerted power.

The patient transcription of sources was not only motivated by the object of inquiry: a study of discordant, polyphonic knowledge. More generally, the goal was to find a way of writing that would bring little-known social worlds and situations to life, with the belief that readers would come to see and feel them. The condition of this encounter? That senses and sensibility be brought into the description of past events. Thus, the author would also avoid adopting *une position de surplomb*, a position of superiority, guarding the keys to the interpretive process, and only conferring them on the reader at the end of the journey. Instead, throughout the book, I took the risk of letting readers judge the evidence put before them—giving them a place in this history of stories so often told (and mistold)—in the hope that one day, perhaps, one of them will feel the need to recount it anew.

Appendix

The March 1943 Deportations from Territories Occupied by Bulgaria

Sources and Statistical Estimates

On the number of Jews rounded up in March 1943 in the territories of the kingdoms of Yugoslavia and Greece occupied by Bulgaria, four archival sources are available to date: two Bulgarian and two German. Most of the reports do not mention the Jews from the Pirot region of Serbia, 158 of whom were transferred to the port of Lom before being deported by boat.

1. The first estimate—the one most often cited in academic writings and in public commemorations of the events—was provided by the German police attaché to Sofia, Adolf Hoffmann, in a report dated April 5, 1943, to the Reich Main Security Office (*Reichssicherheitshauptamt*, RSHA); it mentions the deportation of 11,343 Jews, including 4,221 Thracian Jews (Kingdom of Greece) from the port of Lom, and 7,122 Macedonian Jews (Vardar Macedonia, Kingdom of Yugoslavia) from the provisional internment camp in Skopje.

    Source: Hoffmann an das RSHA – Attachégruppe, 05.04.1943, PAAA (*Politisches Archiv des Auswärtigen Amtes*), R 10863, Bl 178–83. The document appears in Nuremberg trial archives under the reference number NG–4144, as well as in the Yad Vashem archives (K 207604/9). A Bulgarian translation was published in David Koen, eds., *Oceljavaneto: Sbornik ot dokumenti, 1940–1944* (Sofia: Iz. centăr Šalom, 1995), 234–38.

2. The second estimate comes from a report penned by the commissioner for Jewish Affairs, Aleksandăr Belev, on March 23, 1943, referring to the arrest of 4,256 Jews in the Belomorie, including 37 who held

foreign citizenship and were later released, and four who died during the journey or in the camps; as well as 7,303 arrests in Vardar Macedonia. The number of arrests during the raids in the city of Pirot (Serbia) was estimated at 158. This data, compiled before the transfers from Skopje were completed, provides no information on foreign Jews who were released from the Skopje internment camp. A list with the names of 76 foreign Jews, dated March 29, 1943, can be found in the archives of the Commissariat for Jewish Affairs: 57 Spaniards, 14 Italians, 3 Hungarians, and 2 of unspecified citizenship.

Sources: Doklad po izselvaneto na evreite ot Trakija i Belomorieto, Aleksandăr Belev, March 23, 1943, CDA, F 2123K, op. 1, ae 4096, l. 162–64; Spisăk na osvobodenite ot lagera lica ot evrejski proizhod čuždi podanici, CDA, F 190K, op. 3, ae 171, l. 1–2.

3. An activity report from the Commissariat for Jewish Affairs covering the period January 1–March 31, 1943, contains the figure of 11,357 deportees: 4,219 from the Danube port of Lom (from Northern Greece and Pirot) and 7,138 from the temporary internment camp in Skopje, Vardar Macedonia (Kingdom of Yugoslavia).

Source: Otčet za dejnostta na KEV za perioda ot 1 januari do 31 mart 1943, CDA, F 190K, op. 3, ae 103, l. 9.

4. Finally, in a report to the Reich Main Security Office at the end of March 1943, Adolf-Heinz Beckerle, minister plenipotentiary of Germany in Sofia, reported that 7,123 were deported from Vardar Macedonia and 4,211 from Northern Greece: 11,334 Jews in all.

Source: Jevrejski Istorijski Muzej Beograd, no. 2479, k. 23–6–1/7, Belgrade (Serbia).

Nadja Danova and Roumen Avramov have offered estimated ranges for the number of Jews rounded up and deported from the three administrative regions (the Belomorie in occupied Greece, Bitola and Skopje in occupied Vardar Macedonia) created in the "new" kingdom of Bulgaria (April 1941 borders) and published a list of the names of those arrested in all the occupied territories.

Table 1: Planned Arrests and Actual Deportations of Jews from Bulgaria's "New" Kingdom

Region of Origin	Listed for Arrest	Deported
Belomorie (Thrace)	4,224–4,269*	4,025–4,039
Bitola (Vardar Macedonia)	3,342	3,264
Skopje (Vardar Macedonia)	4,039**	3,825**
Total	11,605–11,650	11,114–11,128

* These are estimated ranges.

** The Jews from Pirot in Serbia (158) are included in the numbers for the Skopje region, since Pirot was included in that territorial unit at the time.

Source: Nadja Danova and Roumen Avramov, eds., *Deportiraneto na evreite ot Vardarska Makedonija, Belomorska Trakija i Pirot, mart 1943 g. Dokumenti ot bălgarskite arhivi*, 2 vols. (Sofia: Obedineni izdateli, 2013), 1:859.

Table 2: Jews Deported from the "Limits of the Kingdom" (*predelite na carstvoto*)

Place of Departure	Number
Lom	4,219–4,221*
Skopje	7,122–7,138*
Total	11,343–11,357**

* These are estimated ranges.

** The preceding lines actually add up to 11,341–11,359.

Source: Nadja Danova and Roumen Avramov, eds., *Deportiraneto na evreite ot Vardarska Makedonija, Belomorska Trakija i Pirot, mart 1943 g. Dokumenti ot bălgarskite arhivi*, 2 vols. (Sofia, Obedineni izdateli, 2013), 1:861.

Bibliography

Archival Sources

Bulgaria

Arhiv na Bălgarska nacionalna filmoteka (BNF) – Archives of the Bulgarian
National Film Library, Sofia
Arhiv na Bălgarsko nacionalno radio (BNR) – Archives of the Bulgarian
National Radio, Sofia
Bulgarian National Library
National
Centralen dăržaven Arhiv (CDA) – Central State Archives, Sofia
Dăržaven voenno-istoričeski arhiv – Central Military-Historical Archives, Veliko
Tărnovo
Ieroham, David. Private archive, Sofia
Komisija za razkrivane na dokumentite I za objavjavane na prinadležnost na
bălgarski graždani kăm Dăržavna sigurnost I razuznavatelnite službi na
Bălgarskata narodna armija (Comdos) – Committee for disclosing the docu-
ments and announcing affiliation of Bulgarian citizens to the State Security
and intelligence services of the Bulgarian National Army, Sofia
Naučen Arhiv (NA) na Bălgarska Akademija na naukite (BAN) – Scientific
Archives of the Bulgarian Academy of Sciences, Sofia
Rahamimov, Emil. Private archive, Sofia
University Library at the University Sveti Kliment Ohridski

United States

New York Public Library, New York City
Simon, Andrea. private archive, New York City
United States Holocaust Memorial Museum (USHMM) Film and Video
Archives & Photo Archives, Washington, DC
World Jewish Congress (New York Office), Records at the American Jewish
Archives, Cincinnati

Germany

Bundesarchiv-Filmarchiv, German Federal Archives, Berlin
Hauptstaatsarchiv Darmstadt, Central archives of the Land of Hesse in Germany, Darmstadt
Library of the Institute for East and Southeast European Studies in Regensburg
Regional Library of Munich

Israel

Beit Lohamei HaGhetaot Archives, Kibboutz Lohamei HaGetaot
Rahamimov, Iris. Private archive, Tel Aviv
Yad Vashem Archives, Jerusalem

Republic of North Macedonia

Državen Arhiv na Republika Severna Makedonija – State archives of the Republic of North Macedonia, Skopje
National and University Library Sv. Kliment Ohridski, Republic of North Macedonia, Skopje

Serbia

Jevrejski istorijski Muzej Beograd – Archives of the Jewish Historical Museum in Serbia, Belgrade

France

Archives du Mémorial de la Shoah, Paris
Bibliothèque nationale de France, Paris
Grinberg, Ilya. Private archive, Paris

News Agencies, Radio Outlets, and Information Websites

Bulgaria

Agencija Fokus – Focus News agency
Alternativna informativna mreža (AIM) – Alternative Information Network
Bălgarska telegrafska agencija (BTA) – Bulgarian Telegraphic News Agency

Bălgarsko nacionalno radio (BNR) – Bulgarian National Radio
Dariknews.bg
Mediapool.bg

Germany

Deutsche Welle
Radio Free Europe/Radio Liberty (in the Czech Republic since 1995)

Israel

Jewish Telegraphic Agency News (JTA)

Republic of North Macedonia

Macedonian Information Agency (MIA)

United Kingdom

BBC

Newspapers and Periodicals

Before 1989

Bulgaria

Cionističeska tribuna – *Zionist tribune*, weekly of the United Zionist Organization (ECO)

Evrejski Vesti – *Jewish News*, weekly, later bimonthly, publication of the Jewish section of the Fatherland Front (OF), later of the Central Consistory of the Bulgarian Jews

Godišnik na Obštestvena kulturno-prosvetna organizacija na evreite v Narodna Republika Bălgarija (OKPOE) – *Almanac of the OKPOE*, annual publication of the Societal Educational-Cultural Organization of the Jews of the People's Republic of Bulgaria

Kino i vreme – *Cinema and time*, theoretical periodical about the filmic art

Kinoizkustvo – *Cinematographic art*, monthly

Kinorabotnik – *Cinema worker*, periodical targeting technical movie professionals as an audience

Naroden săd – People's Court, 1944–45, periodical covering the trials before the
  Thirteen Chambers of Sofia's People's Court
Narodna Kultura – People's culture, weekly
Otečestven front – Fatherland Front, daily, publication of the National Commit-
  tee of the Fatherland Front (OF)
Rabotničesko delo – Workers' deeds, daily, publication of the Central Commit-
  tee of the Workers' Party/Communists (renamed the Bulgarian Communist
  Party in 1948)

After 1989

Bulgaria

Demokracija – Democracy, daily of the Union for Democratic Forces (SDS,
  anti-communist coalition)
Dnevnik – Daily, daily, unaffiliated
Duma – Word, daily of the Bulgarian Socialist Party (BSP)
Kapital – Capital, economics weekly, unaffiliated
Kultura – Culture, cultural weekly, unaffiliated
Literaturen vestnik – Literary journal, cultural weekly, unaffiliated
Marginalia.bg – online publication of the association for human rights
  Sdruženie za čoveški prava "Marginalija"
Obektiv – Objective, monthly publication of the Bulgarian Helsinki Committee
Sega – Now, left-wing daily
24 časa – 24 heures, daily

Israel

Jerusalem Post

Italy

Corriere della Sera – Evening Courier, daily

Republic of North Macedonia

Fokus – Focus, political weekly
Nova Makedonija – New Macedonia, daily close to the right-wing VMRO-
  DPMNE
Utrinski vesnik – Morning newspaper, daily

United States

New York Times

Diaries, Memoirs, Published Archival Collections, and Documentary Films

Aroesti, Jakov, Duško Konstantinov, and Miloš Konstantinov. "Bitoljski jevreji, Bitola" (unpublished manuscript, 1959). Typescript. Yad Vashem, O.10/15.

Baeva, Iskra, and Evgenija Kalinova, eds. *"Văzroditelnijat proces": Bălgarskata dăržava i bălgarskite turci (sredata na 30-te-načaloto na 90-te godini na XX vek)*. Sofia: D. A. Arhivi, 2009.

Biljarski, Cočo, and Ivanka Gezenko, eds. *Diplomatičeski dokumenti po učastieto na Bălgarija v Vtorata svetovna vojna*. Sofia: Sineva, 2006.

Comforty, Jacky. *Monument of Love*. Comforty Media Concepts, United States, 2023, 83 min.

———. *The Optimists: The Story of the Rescue of the Bulgarian Jews*. Comforty Media Concepts, United States, 2001, 82 min.

Dăržavna Agencija Arhivi (DAA). *Iz ličnija arhiv na Kimon Georgiev*. 3 vols. Poredica "Arhivite govorjat" no. 58. Sofia: DAA, 2009.

———. *Truden izbor s goljamo značenie: Sădbata na bălgarskite evrei, 1943, dokumentalna izložba*. Sofia: DAA, 2013.

Dejanov, Dejan. *Iz spomenite na Dejan Dejanov*. Sofia, July 4, 1959. Typescript.

Dimitrov, Georgi. *Dnevnik: 9 mart 1933–6 fevruari 1949*. Sofia: U. I. Sv. Kliment Ohridski, 1997.

Drugata Bălgarija: Dokumenti za organizaciite na bălgarskata političeska emigracija, 1944–1989. Sofia: I. K. Anubis, 2000.

Filov, Bogdan. *Dnevnik*. Sofia: Iz. na OF, 1990.

Gaffney, Ed. *Empty Boxcars: Persecution, Murder and Rescue in Bulgaria and Its Occupied Territories in World War II*. Gamut Media, United States, 2012, 83 min.

Grinberg, Natan. *Dokumenti*. Sofia: Centralna konsistorija na evreite văv Bălgarija, 1945.

Hutzelmann, Barbara, Mariana Hausleitner, and Souzana Hazan, eds. *Die Verfolgung und Ermordung der europäischen Juden durch das nationalsozialistische Deutschland 1933–1945*, vol. 13: *Slowakei, Rumänien, Bulgarien*. Berlin: De Gruyter Oldenbourg, 2018.

Institut po istorija na BAN, ed. *Obrečeni i spaseni: Bălgarija v antisemitskata programa na Tretija Rajh. Izsledvanija i dokumenti*. Sofia: Sineva, 2007.

Institut za nacionalna istorija. *Izvori za Osloboditelnata vojna i Revolucijata vo Makedonija: 1941–1945*. 4 vols. Skopje: Institut za nacionalna istorija, 1968–83.

Kalderon, Gitta. *Mishloach Manot: A Life Story; The Sammy-Kalderon Family from Bitola, Macedonia*. Skopje: Holocaust Fund for the Jews of Macedonia, 2017.

Kazasov, Dimo. *Burni godini, 1918–1944*. Sofia: Naroden Pečat, 1949.

Keshales, Haim. *Tova se sluči prez onezi godini: Beležki za života na bălgarskoto evrejstvo prez godinite 1944–1950.* 3 parts. Jerusalem, Yad Vashem Archives, Record Group O.13, Bulgaria collection, File nos. 1, 2, 3.

Koen, David, ed. *Oceljavaneto: Sbornik ot dokumenti, 1940–1944.* Sofia: Iz. centăr Šalom, 1995.

Komisija za razkrivane na dokumentite i za objavjavane na prinadležnost na bălgarski graždani kăm Dăržavna sigurnost i razuznavatelnite službi na Bălgarskata narodna armija (Comdos). *Dăržavna sigurnost i evrejskata obštnost v Bălgarija (1944 g.–1989 g.): Dokumentalen sbornik.* Sofia: Comdos, 2012.

Lulčev, Ljubomir. *Tajnite na dvorcovija život: Dnevnik (1938–1944).* Sofia: Veselie, 1992.

Mermall, Gabriel, and Norbert J. Yasharoff. *By the Grace of Strangers: Two Boys' Rescue during the Holocaust.* Jerusalem: Yad Vashem and The Holocaust Survivors' Memoirs Project, 2006.

Mitakov, Vasil. *Dnevnik na Pravosădnija ministăr v pravitelstvata na Georgi Kjosejivanov i Bogdan Filov.* Sofia: Trud, 2001.

Načeva, Vera. *Vremeto e v nas: Spomeni i razmisli.* Sofia: Partizdat, 1984.

Natan, Žak. *Pametni vremena: Spomeni.* Sofia: Iz. na BKP, 1970.

Nikolova, Elka. *The Dressmaker.* United States, 2023 (working version of a documentary film).

Niselkova, Nina, and Suzana Hazan, eds. *Nikola Mušanov: Dnevnik, Spomeni, avtobiografija.* Sofia: Iz. Iztok-Zapad, 2018.

Oliver, Haim. *Transportite na smărtta ne trăgnaha.* Studija za naučno-populjarni filmi, Bulgaria, 1977, 38 min.

Passi, Rosalija. *Imalo edno vreme.* Sofia: Prosveta, 1994.

Paunovski, Vladimir, and Josif Iliel, eds. *Evreite v Bălgarija meždu uništoženieto i spasenieto.* Sofia: Adasa Press, 2000.

Pešev, Dimităr. *Spomeni.* Sofia: I. K. Gutenberg, 2004.

Poppetrov, Nikolaj, ed. *Socialno naljavo, Nacionalizmăt—napred: Programi i organizacionni dokumenti na bălgarski avtoritaristki nacionalističeski formacii.* Sofia: I. K. Gutenberg, 2009.

Simon, Andrea. *Angel Wagenstein: Art Is a Weapon.* United States and Bulgaria, 2017, 85 min.

Taneva, Albena, and Vanja Gezenko, eds. *Glasove v zaštita na graždansko obštestvo: Protokoli ot Svetija sinod na Bălgarskata Pravoslavna cărkva po evrejskija văpros (1940–1944).* Sofia: Galiko and Centăr za evrejski izsledvanija, 2002.

Todorov, Vărban, and Nikolaj Poppetrov, eds. *Sedmi săstav na narodnija săd: Edno zabraveno dokumentalno svidetelstvo za antisemitizma v Bălgarija prez 1941–1944 g.* Sofia: Iz. Iztok-Zapad, 2013.

Toškova, Vitka, ed. *Iz dnevnika na Bekerle – pălnomošten ministăr na Tretija rajh v Bălgarija.* Sofia: Iz. Hristo Botev, 1992.

Toškova, Vitka, Nikolaj Kotev, Nikolaj Stoimenov, Rumen Nikolov, and Stilijan Nojkov, eds. *Bălgarija, svoenravnijat săjuznik na tretija rajh.* Sofia: Voennoizdatelski kompleks Sv. Georgi Pobedonosec, 1992.

Vagenštajn, Anžel. *Predi kraja na sveta: Draskulki ot neolita.* Sofia: I. K. Colibri, 2011.

Ziok, Ilona. *Fritz Bauer–Tod auf Raten.* CV Films, Germany, 2010, 110 min.

Interviews

Boyer, Bruno. Head of the International Relations' Department at the French Mémorial de la Shoah. By telephone, March 17, 2018; email correspondence, February 24, 2023.

Chary, Frederick. American historian. Email correspondence, October 1 and 3, 2016.

Ieroham, David. Grandson of jurist David Ieroham. Sofia, February 26, 2016.

Ioanid, Radu. Historian and diplomat, then head of international archive acquisition policy at the USHMM. By telephone, June 20, 2017.

Oliver, Dik. Son of the writer and documentarist Haim Oliver. Sofia, December 13 and 15, 2016.

Rahamimov, Emil. Son of the jurist Mančo Rahamimov. Sofia, December 15 and 17, 2016.

Rahamimov, Iris. Granddaughter of physician Persiado Rahamimov. Email correspondence, March 8, 9, 22, and 27, 2019.

Ruckhaberle, Dieter. Artist, museum curator and director of the Staatliche Kunsthalle in West Berlin (1978–93). By telephone, June 24 and 25, 2017.

Simon, Andrea. Documentarist. Email correspondence, January 19, 21, and 27, 2020; February 2, 7, and 18, 2020.

Wagenstein, Angel. Scriptwriter and novelist. Sofia, December 12, 2016.

Zieseke, Christiane. Former assistant to Dieter Ruckhaberle at the Staatliche Kunsthalle, West Berlin. By telephone, June 21, 2017.

Published Secondary Sources

About, Ilsen, and Clément Chéroux. "L'histoire par la photographie." *Études photographiques* 10 (2001): 8–33.

Agocs, Andreas. "Divisive Unity: The Politics of Cultural Nationalism during the First German Writers' Congress of October 1947," in Mary Fulbrook and Andrew Port, eds., *Becoming East German: Socialist Structures and Sensibilities after Hitler.* New York: Berghahn Books, 2013, 56–78.

Aït-Touati, Frédérique. *Fictions of the Cosmos: Science and Literature in the Seventeenth Century*. Trans. Susan Emanuel. Chicago: University of Chicago Press, 2011.

Alboher, Shlomo. *The Jews of Monastir, Macedonia*. Skopje: Holocaust Fund of the Jews from Macedonia, 2010.

Aleksiun, Natalia. "The Central Jewish Historical Commission in Poland, 1944–1947." *Polin: Studies in Polish Jewry* 20 (2008): 74–97.

Angelov, Veselin. *Strogo poveritelno! Asimilatorskata kampanija sreštu turskoto nacionalno mălcinstvo v Bălgarija, 1984–1989*. Sofia, 2008.

Appadurai, Arjun, ed. *The Social Life of Things: Commodities in Cultural Perspective*. Cambridge: Cambridge University Press, 1986.

Arasse, Daniel. *On n'y voit rien: Description*. Paris: Gallimard Essais, 2003.

Arditi, Benjamin. *Hasifrut haantishemit beBulgariya: Reshima bibliografit*. Holon, Isr.: B. Arditi, 1972.

———. *Rolijata na Car Boris III pri izselvaneto na evreite ot Bălgarija*. Tel Aviv: Kooperativen pečat O. P., 1952.

———. *Yehudei Bulgariya bishnot hamishtar hanatzi, 1940–1944*. Holon: Israel Press, 1962.

Arendt, Hannah. *Eichmann in Jerusalem: A Report on the Banality of Evil*. New York: Viking-Compass, 1965.

Arié, Gabriel, Esther Benbassa, and Aron Rodrigue. *A Sephardi Life in Southeastern Europe: The Autobiography and Journal of Gabriel Arié, 1863–1939*. Seattle: University of Washington Press, 1998.

Arnold, Jasmin. *Die Revolution frisst ihre Kinder: Deutsches Filmexil in der UdSSR*. Marburg, Ger.: Tectum, 2003.

Assa, Aaron. *Makedonija i Evrejskiot narod*. Skopje: Makedonska revija, 1992.

Avramov, Roumen. "Anchialo 1906: The Political Economy of an Ethnic Clash." *Études balkaniques* 4 (2009): 31–115.

———. "Četejki arhivite na deportacijata." In Danova and Avramov, *Deportiraneto*, 1:11–35.

———. *Ikonomika na "văzroditelnija proces."* Sofia: Riva, 2016.

———. *"Spasenie" i padenie: Mikroikonomika na dăržavnija antisemitizăm v Bălgarija, 1940–1944*. Sofia: U. I. Sv. Kliment Ohridski, 2012.

Avramov, Roumen, and Jérôme Sgard. "Bulgaria: From Enterprise Indiscipline to Financial Crisis." *Documents de travail*, vol. 96. Paris: CEPII, 1996.

Baev, Jordan. "The Establishment of Bulgarian–West German Diplomatic Relations within the Coordinating Framework of the Warsaw Pact." *Journal of Cold War Studies* 18, no. 3 (2016): 158–80.

Balalovska, Kristina, Alessandro Silj, and Mario Zucconi. "Minority Politics in Southeast Europe: Crisis in Macedonia." *Ethnobarometer Working Paper Series* no. 6, 2002.

Bankier, David, and Dan Michman, eds. *Holocaust and Justice: Representation and Historiography of the Holocaust in Postwar Trials.* Jerusalem: Yad Vashem; and New York: Berghahn Books, 2010.

Bar-Zohar, Michael. *Beyond Hitler's Grasp: The Heroic Rescue of Bulgaria's Jews.* Holbrook, AZ: Adams Media Corporation, 1998.

Barna, Ildikó, and Andrea Petö. *Political Justice in Budapest after World War II.* Budapest: Central European University Press, 2015.

Barthe, Yannick, Michel Callon, and Pierre Lascoumes. *Agir dans un monde incertain: Essai sur la démocratie technique.* Paris: Seuil, 2001.

Baruch, Marc-Olivier. *Des lois indignes? Les historiens, la politique et le droit.* Paris: Tallandier, 2013.

Baruh, Eli. *Iz istorijata na bălgarskoto evrejstvo: Našite stradanija v evrejskite trudovi lageri prez fašistkija režim v Bălgarija, 1941–1944.* Tel Aviv: Yafor Printing House, 1960.

Baruh, Nir. *Otkupăt na Car Boris i sădbata na bălgarskite evrei.* Sofia: U. I. Sv. Kliment Ohridski, 1991.

Bathrick, David. "Holocaust Film before the Holocaust: DEFA, Antifascism and the Camps." *Cinéma, revue d'études cinématographiques* 18, no. 1 (2007): 109–34.

Baulland, Paul, and Isabelle Gouarné, eds. "Communismes et circulations internationales." *Critique internationale* 66 (2015): 9–104.

Bazyler, Michael J., and Frank M. Tuerkheimer. *Forgotten Trials of the Holocaust.* New York: New York University Press, 2014.

Beauwallet, Willy, and Sébastien Michon. "L'institutionnalisation inachevée du Parlement européen: Hétérogénéité nationale, spécialisation du recrutement and autonomisation." *Politix* 89 (2010): 147–72.

Becker, Howard. *Art Worlds.* Berkeley: University of California Press, 1982.

———. "Visual Sociology, Documentary Photography, and Photojournalism: It's (Almost) All a Matter of Context." *Visual Sociology* 10, nos. 1–2 (1995): 5–14.

Behr, Valentin. "Genèse et usages d'une politique publique de l'histoire: La 'politique historique' en Pologne." *Revue d'études comparatives Est-Ouest* 43, no. 3 (2015): 21–48.

———. "Science du passé and politique du présent en Pologne: L'histoire du temps présent (1939–1989), de la genèse à l'Institut de la mémoire nationale." PhD diss., University of Strasbourg, 2017.

Belting, Hans. *Pour une anthropologie des images.* Paris: Gallimard, 2004.

Benatov, Joseph. "Debating the Fate of Bulgarian Jews during World War II." In Himka and Michlic, *Bringing the Dark Past to Light,* 108–30.

Benbassa, Esther, and Aron Rodrigue. *Sephardi Jewry. A History of the Judeo-Spanish Community, 14th–20th Centuries.* Berkeley: University of California Press, 2000.

Benjamin, Walter. *The Arcades Project.* Cambridge, MA: Belknap Press of Harvard University Press, 1999.

Benveniste, Rika. *Those Who Survived: The Resistance, Deportation, and Return of the Jews from Salonika in the 1940s.* Jerusalem: Yad Vashem, 2022.

Benvenisti, David. "The Unfavourable Conditions for the Dissemination of Antisemitic Propaganda in Bulgaria (1891–1903)." *Annual: Social, Cultural and Educational Organization of the Jews in the People's Republic of Bulgaria* 15 (1980): 177–220.

Berenbaum, Michael. "The Holocaust Memorial Museum of Macedonian Jewry: How to Present the Experience of Macedonian Jews to Macedonians and the World." In Ragaru, *La Shoah en Europe du Sud-Est*, 178–95.

———. *The Jews in Macedonia during World War II / Evreite vo Makedonija za vreme na vtorata svetska vojna.* Skopje: Holocaust Fund of the Jews from Macedonia, 2012.

Berghahn, Daniela. "Resistance of the Heart: Female Suffering and Victimhood in DEFA's Antifascist Films." In *Screening War: Perspectives on German Suffering*, ed. Paul Cooke and Mark Silberman (Rochester, NY: Camden House, 2010), 165–86.

Bessone, Magali. "La réconciliation par l'histoire en Bosnie-Herzégovine: L'impossible réception d'un modèle multiculturel européen." *Revue d'études comparatives Est-Ouest* 45, no. 3 (2014): 149–75.

Bevers, Jürgen. *Der Mann hinter Adenauer: Hans Globkes Aufstieg vom NS-Juristen zur Grauen Eminenz der Bonner Republik.* Berlin: Christoph Links, 2009.

Billig, Joseph. "Le procès de Franz Rademacher (la diplomatie homicide)." *Centre de documentation juive contemporaine "Le Monde Juif"* 2, no. 50 (1968): 27–36.

Bilsky, Leora. "Rachel Auerbach: Re-imagining the Victim as 'Eyewitness' to the Nazi Camera." In *Jewish-European Emigré Lawyers: Twentieth Century Humanitarian International Law as Idea and Profession*, ed. Leora Bilsky and Annette Weinke (Göttingen, Ger.: Wallstein, 2021), 74–102.

Bindenagel, James D., ed. *Washington Conference on Holocaust-Era Assets, November 30–December 3, 1998: Proceedings.* Washington, DC: US Government Printing Office, 1999.

Bjuksenšjutc [Büchsenschütz], Ulrih. *Malcinstvenata politika v Bălgarija: politikata na BKP kăm evrei, romi, pomaci i truci 1944–1989.* Sofija: Meždunaroden Centăr po Problemite na Malcinstvata i Kulturni Vzaimodejstvija, 2000.

Blais, Hélène. "Les enquêtes des cartographes en Algérie ou les ambiguïtés de l'usage des savoirs vernaculaires en situation coloniale." *Revue d'histoire moderne et contemporaine* 54, no. 4 (2007): 70–85.

Blaive, Muriel, Christian Gerbel, and Thomas Linderberger, eds. *Clashes in European Memory: The Case of Communist Repression and the Holocaust.* Innsbruck: Ludwig Boltzmann Institute for European History and Public Spheres, 2011.

Bloxham, Donald. *Genocide on Trial: War Crimes Trials and the Formation of Holocaust History and Memory.* Oxford: Oxford University Press, 2000.

Bobeva, Daniela, Ivan Chalakov, and Jordan Markov. *Migracijata—evropejskata integracija i izticaneto na mozăci ot Bălgarija.* Sofia: Centar za izsledvane na demokracijata, 1996.

Bohus, Kata. "Parallel Memories? Public Memorialization of the Antifascist Struggle and Martyr Memorial Services in the Hungarian Jewish Community during Early Communism." In Bohus, Hallama, and Stach, *Shadow of Antifascism*, 87–108.

Bohus, Kata, Peter Hallama, and Stephan Stach, eds. *Growing in the Shadow of Antifascism: Remembering the Holocaust in State-Socialist Eastern Europe.* Budapest: Central European University Press, 2022.

Boyadjieff, Christo. *Saving the Bulgarian Jews in World War II.* Ottawa: Free Bulgarian Center, 1989.

Boucheron, Patrick. "On nomme littérature la fragilité de l'histoire." *Le Débat* 165 (2011): 41–56.

Braham, Randolph L. *The Politics of Genocide: The Holocaust in Hungary.* 1981. Revised and augmented in 1994. Reprint, Boulder, CO: East European Monographs, 2016.

Brown, Keith. *The Past in Question: Modern Macedonia and the Uncertainties of a Nation.* Princeton, NJ: Princeton University Press, 2003.

Browning, Christopher R. *The Final Solution and the German Foreign Office: A Study of Referat D III of Abteilung Deutschland, 1940–43.* New York: Holmes & Meier, 1978.

Brunnbauer, Ulf. "Historiography, Myths and the Nation in the Republic of Macedonia." In Brunnbauer, *(Re)writing History*, 165–200.

Brunnbauer, Ulf, ed. *(Re)writing History: Historiography in Southeast Europe after Socialism.* Münster: Lit-Verlag, 2004.

Brustein, William I., and Ryan D. King. "Balkan Anti-Semitism: The Cases of Bulgaria and Romania before the Holocaust." *East European Politics and Societies* 18, no. 3 (2004): 430–54.

Bruttman, Tal, Stefan Hördler, and Christoph Kreuzmüller. *Die fotographische Inszenierung des Verbrechen: Ein Album aus Auschwitz.* Darmstadt, Ger.: WBG Academic, 2019.

Buffet, Cyril. *Défunte DEFA: Histoire de l'autre cinéma allemand*. Paris: Cerf, 2007.

Byford, Jovan. "Remembering Jasenovac: Survivor Testimonies and the Cultural Dimension of Bearing Witness." *Holocaust and Genocide Studies* 28, no. 1 (2014): 58–84.

Case, Holly. "The Combined Legacies of the 'Jewish Question' and the 'Macedonian Question.'" In Himka and Michlic, *Bringing the Dark Past to Light*, 352–76.

Cekov, Borislav, and Albena Taneva. *Antievrejskoto zakonodatelstvo v Evropa i Bălgarija*. Sofia: IMP/Centăr za evrejski izsledvanija, 2015.

Čepreganov, Todor, and Sonja Nikolova. "Učestvoto na evreite vo NOD vo Makedonija." In *Evreite vo Makedonija: Istorija, tradicija, kultura, jazik i religija*, ed. Berta Romano Nikolikj (Skopje: Jewish Community in the Republic of Macedonia, 2015), 219–28.

Cesarani, David, and Eric Sundquist, eds. *After the Holocaust: Challenging the Myth of Silence*. London: Routledge, 2012.

Chartier, Roger. *On the Edge of the Cliff: History, Language and Practices*. Baltimore: Johns Hopkins University Press, 1997.

Chary, Frederick. *The Bulgarian Jews and the Final Solution, 1940–1944*. Pittsburgh, PA: Pittsburgh University Press, 1972.

Chéroux, Clément. *Mémoire des camps: Photographies des camps de concentration et d'extermination nazis 1933–1999*. Paris: Marval, 2001.

Chevalier, Dominique. "Musées and musées-mémoriaux urbains consacrés à la Shoah: Mémoires douloureuses and ancrages géographiques: Les cas de Berlin, Budapest, Jérusalem, Los Angeles, Montréal, New York, Paris, Washington." 2 vols. Habil. thesis [Habilitation à diriger des recherches, HDR], University of Paris 1–Panthéon Sorbonne, 2012.

Claverie, Élizabeth. "Sainte indignation contre indignation éclairée: L'affaire du Chevalier de la Barre." *Ethnologie française* 3 (1992): 271–90.

Cohen, Albert, and Anri Assa, eds. *Saving of the Jews in Bulgaria, 1941–1944*. Sofia: State Publishing House "Septemvri," 1977.

Cohen, Boaz. "Doctor Jacob Robinson, the Institute for Jewish Affairs and the Elusive Jewish Voice in Nuremberg." In *Holocaust and Justice: Representation and Historiography of the Holocaust in Postwar Trials*, ed. David Bankier and Dan Michman (Jerusalem: Yad Vashem; New York: Berghahn Books, 2010), 81–100.

———. "Rachel Auerbach, Yad Vashem, and Israeli Holocaust Memory." *Polin* 20 (2008): 121–97.

Cohen, Lea. *You Believe: Eight Views on the Holocaust in the Balkans*. Skopje: Holocaust Fund of the Jews from Macedonia, 2013.

Cohen, Mark. *Last Century of a Sephardic Community: The Jews of Monastir, 1839–1943*. New York: Foundation for the Advancement of Sephardic Studies and Culture, 2003.

Cole, Tim. *Traces of the Holocaust: Journeying in and out of the Ghettos*. London: Continuum, 2011.

Colonomos, Ariel. "L'exigence croissante de justice sans frontière: Le cas de la demande de restitution des biens juifs spoliés." *Études du CERI* 78 (July 2001).

Comforty, Jacky, with Martha Aladjem Bloomfield. *The Stolen Narrative of the Bulgarian Jews and the Holocaust*. Lanham, MD: Rowman & Littlefield, 2021.

Conze, Eckart, Norbert Frei, Peter Hayes, and Moshe Zimmermann. *Das Amt und die Vergangenheit: Deutsche Diplomaten im Dritten Reich und in der Bundesrepublik*. Munich: Blessing, 2010.

Costa, Olivier, and Paul Magnette. "Idéologies et changement institutionnel dans l'Union européenne: Pourquoi les gouvernements ont-ils constamment renforcé le Parlement européen?" *Politique européenne* 1, no. 9 (2003): 49–75.

Crampton, Richard. *A Short History of Modern Bulgaria*. Cambridge: Cambridge University Press, 1987.

Crane, Susan A. "Choosing Not to Look: Representation, Repatriation, and Holocaust Atrocity Photography." *History and Theory* 47 (October 2008): 309–30.

Cüppers, Martin, Annett Gerhardt, Karin Graf, Steffen Hänschen, Andreas Kahrs, Anne Lepper, and Florian Ross. *Fotos aus Sobibor: Die Niemann-Sammlung zu Holocaust und Nationalsozialismus*. Berlin: Metropol Verlag, 2020.

Danova, Nadia. "La Bulgarie et l'Holocauste: État des recherches sur le problème et perspectives." *Études balkaniques*, no. 4 (2012): 18–44.

Danova, Nadja. "Dălgata sjanka na minaloto: Deportacijata na evreite ot Zapadna Trakija, Vardarska Makedonija i Pirot: săstojanie na proučvaneto na problema." In Danova and Avramov, *Deportiraneto*, 1:36–65.

———. "La déportation des Juifs des territoires sous administration bulgare: Savoir et mémoire en Bulgarie actuelle sur le mois de mars 1943." In Ragaru, *La Shoah en Europe du Sud-Est*, 120–30.

Danova, Nadja, and Roumen Avramov, eds. *Deportiraneto na evreite ot Vardarska Makedonija, Belomorska Trakija i Pirot, mart 1943 g. Dokumenti ot bălgarskite arhivi*. 2 vols. Sofia: Obedineni izdateli, 2013.

Daskalov, Rumen. *Ot Stambolov do Živkov: Golemite sporove za novata bălgarska istorija*. Sofia: I. K. Gutenberg, 2009.

Daston, Lorraine, and Peter Galison. *Objectivity*. New York: Zone, 2010.

David-Fox, Michael. "The Iron Curtain as Semi-Permeable Membrane: The Origins and Demise of the Stalinist Superiority Complex." In *Cold War Crossings: International Travel and Exchange across the Soviet Bloc, 1940s–1960s*, ed. Patryk Babiracki and Kenyon Zimmer (College Station: Texas A&M University Press, 2014), 14–39.

David-Fox, Michael, Peter Holquist, and Alexander Martin, eds. *Fascination and Enmity: Russia and Germany as Entangled Histories, 1914–1945*. Pittsburgh, PA: University of Pittsburgh Press, 2012.

Deák, István. *Europe on Trial: The Story of Collaboration, Resistance, and Retribution during World War II*. Boulder, CO: Westview Press, 2015.

Dean, Martin, Constantin Goschler, and Philipp Ther, eds. *Robbery and Restitution: The Conflict over Jewish Property in Europe*. New York: Berghahn Books, 2007.

de Blic, Damien, and Cyril Lemieux. "Le scandale comme épreuve: Éléments de sociologie pragmatique." *Politix* 71 (2005): 9–38.

Dejanova, Liljana. "The Non-Saved Jews: Recent Controversies and Political Uses in the Bulgarian Public Space." In Ragaru, *La Shoah en Europe du Sud-Est*, 162–72.

———. *Očertanija na mălčanieto: Istoričeska sociologija na kolektivnija pamet*. Sofia: Kritika i Humanizăm, 2010.

———. "Spasjavaneto. 60 godini po-kăsno: Medijnite obrazi na edno tăržestvo." *Trimesečen informacionen bjuletin za antisemitizma v Bălgarija*, no. 2 (2003): 18–32.

Deyanova, Liliana. "Des condamnations locales du communisme à la condamnation internationale de janvier 2006: Les guerres des élites bulgares pour le monopole de la mémoire du communisme." In *Expérience et mémoire*, ed. Bogumil Jewsiewicki and Erika Nimis (Paris: L'Harmattan, 2008), 193–213.

———. "Kăm konstruiraneto na evreina kato vrag: Medijni strategii na izobrazjavane na evreina kato drug i 'obrazi na vraga' prez 2003-a godina v Bălgarija." In *Antisemitizmăt v Bălgarija dnes. Ima li?*, ed. Alfred Krispin (Sofia: I. K. Kolibri, 2004), 47–78.

———. *Nacionalno minalo i golemija dekor*. Sofia, 2008. Typescript.

di Bulgaria, Giovanna. *Memorie*. Milan: Rizzoli, 1964.

Didi-Huberman, Georges. *Images in Spite of All. Four Photographs from Auschwitz*. Chicago: University of Chicago Press, 2008.

Di Lellio, Anna, and Stephanie Schwander-Sievers. "The Legendary Commander: The Construction of an Albanian Master-narrative in Post-war Kosovo." *Nations and Nationalism* 12, no. 3 (2006): 513–29.

Dimovski-Colev, Gjorgji. *Bitolskite evrei*. Skopje: Društvo za nauka i umetnost Bitola, 1993.

Dobčev, Petko. *Antievrejskoto zakonodatelstvo i negovoto preodoljavane (1942–1945)*. Sofia: Feneja, 2010.

Dojnov, Plamen. *Bălgarskijat socrealizăm, 1956, 1968, 1989: Norma i kriza v literaturata na NRB*. Sofia: Siela, 2011.

Döscher, Hans-Jürgen. *Seilschaften: Die verdrängte Vergangenheit des Auswärtigen Amts*. Berlin: Propyläen Verlag, 2005.

Douglas, Lawrence. *The Memory of Judgment: Making Law and History in the Trials of the Holocaust*. New Haven, CT: Yale University Press, 2001.

———. *The Right Wrong Man: John Demjanjuk and the Last Great Nazi War Crimes Trial*. Princeton, NJ: Princeton University Press, 2016.

Dragostinova, Theodora. *The Cold War from the Margins. A Small Socialist State on the Global Cultural Scene*. Ithaca, NY: Cornell University Press, 2021.

———. "The East in the West: Bulgarian Culture in the United States of America during the Global 1970s." *Journal of Contemporary History* 53, no. 1 (2018): 212–39.

———. "The 'Natural Ally' of the 'Developing World': Bulgarian Culture in India and Mexico." *Slavic Review* 77, no. 3 (2018): 661–84.

Dragostinova, Theodora K., and Malgorzata Fidelis. "Beyond the Iron Curtain: Eastern Europe and the Global Cold War." *Slavic Review* 77, no. 3 (2018): 577–684.

Droit, Emmanuel. "Le Goulag contre la Shoah: Mémoires officielles et cultures mémorielles dans l'Europe élargie." *Vingtième siècle, Revue d'histoire* 94 (2007): 101–20.

Džulibrk, Jovan. *Istoriografija Holokausta u Jugoslaviji*. Belgrade: Univerzitet u Beogradu, 2011.

Earl, Hilary. *The Nuremberg SS-Einsatzgruppen Trial, 1945–1958: Atrocity, Law and History*. Cambridge: Cambridge University Press, 2009.

Ebbrecht-Hartmann, Tobias. "Echoes of the Archive: Retrieving and Reviewing Cinematic Remnants from the Nazi Past." In *Archive and Memory in German Literature and Visual Culture*, ed. Dora Osborne (Rochester, NY: Boydell & Brewer, 2015), 123–40.

———. "Filmdokumente von Deportationen: Zum Umgang mit Filmaufnahmen von Tätern der Deportationen aus Stuttgart und Dresden." March 2012, https://www.yadvashem.org/de/education/newsletter/5/films-about-deportations.html.

———. "Trophy, Evidence, Document: Appropriating an Archive Film from Liepaja, 1941." *Historical Journal of Film, Radio and Television* 36, no. 4 (2016): 509–28.

Eder, Jacob. *Holocaust Angst: The Federal Republic of Germany and American Holocaust Memory since the 1970s*. New York: Oxford University Press, 2016.

Elenkov, Ivan. *Kulturnijat front: Bǎlgarskata kultura prez epohata na komu-nizma; političesko upravlenie, ideologičeski osnovanija, institucionalni režimi.* Sofia: Ciela, 2008.

———. "The Science of History in Bulgaria in the Age of Socialism: The Prob-lematic Mapping of Its Institutional Boundaries." *CAS Sofia Working Papers,* 2007.

11 Mart 1943–1958 Bitola: Na 3 013 Bitolski evrei—žrtvi na fašizma. Skopje: Opštinski odbor na Sojuzot na borcite od NOB Bitola, 1958.

Elsaesser, Thomas. "Histoire palimpseste, mémoires obliques: À propos de *Sterne* de Konrad Wolf." *1895: Revue de l'association française de recherches sur le cinéma* 58 (2009), https://journals.openedition.org/1895/3953.

———."Vergebliche Rettung: Geschichte als Palimpsest in Sterne." In *Konrad Wolf—Werk und Wirkung,* ed. Michael Wedel and Elbe Schieber (Berlin: Vis-tas Verlag, 2009), 73–92.

Eškenazi, Žak, and Alfred Krispin, eds. *Evreite po bǎlgarskite zemi: Anotirana bibliografija.* Sofia: IMIR, 2002.

Estraikh, Gennady. "The Life, Death, and Afterlife of the Jewish Anti-Fascist Committee," *East European Jewish Affairs* 48, no. 2 (2018): 139–48.

Evrei zaginali v antifašiskata borba. Sofia: Nacionalnija sǎvet na Otečestven Front, 1958.

Faure, Justine, and Sandrine Kott, eds. "Le bloc de l'Est en question." *Vingtième siècle, Revue d'histoire* 109 (2011): 2–212.

Feinstein, Joshua. *The Triumph of the Ordinary: Depictions of Daily Life in the East German Cinema, 1949–1989.* Chapel Hill: University of North Carolina Press, 2002.

Feldman, Jackie. "Marking the Boundaries of the Enclave: Defining the Israeli Collective through the Poland 'Experience.'" *Israeli Studies* 7, no. 2 (2002): 84–114.

Finder, Gabriel N., and Alexander V. Prusin. *Justice behind the Iron Curtain: Nazis on Trial in Communist Poland.* Toronto: University of Toronto Press, 2018.

Flanzbaum, Hilene, ed. *The Americanization of the Holocaust.* Baltimore: Johns Hopkins University Press, 1999.

Fleiter, Rüdiger. "Die Ludwigsburger Zentrale Stelle—eine Strafverfolgenbe-hörde als Legitimationsinstrument? Gründung und Zuständigkeit 1958 bis 1965." *Kritische Justiz* 35, no. 2 (2002): 253–72.

Frei, Norbert. *Adenauer's Germany and the Nazi Past: The Politics of Amnesty and Integration.* New York: Columbia University Press, 2002.

———. "Fritz Bauer oder: Wann wird ein Held zum Helden?" In *Zwischen Stadt, Staat und Nation: Bürgertum in Deutschland,* ed. Stefan Gerber, Wer-ner Greiling, Tobias Kaiser, and Klaus Ries (Göttingen, Ger.: Vandenhoeck & Ruprecht, 2014), 273–80.

Frodon, Jean-Michel, ed. *Cinema and the Shoah: An Art Confronts the Tragedy of the Twentieth Century*. Albany: State University of New York Press, 2010.

Frommer, Benjamin. *National Cleansing: Retribution against Nazi Collaborators in Postwar Czechoslovakia*. New York: Columbia University Press, 2005.

Fulbrook, Mary. *German National Identity after the Holocaust*. Cambridge, UK: Polity Press, 1999.

———. *Reckonings: Legacies of Nazi Persecution and the Quest for Justice*. Oxford: Oxford University Press, 2018.

Garbolevsky, Evgenija. *The Conformists: Creativity and Decadence in the Bulgarian Cinema 1945–1989*. Newcastle, UK: Cambridge Scholars Publishing, 2011.

Garcia, Patrick. "Vers une politique mémorielle européenne? L'évolution du statut de l'histoire dans le discours du Conseil de l'Europe." In *Un espace public européen en construction*, ed. Robert Frank (Brussels: Peter Lang, 2010), 179–201.

Genčeva, Galina. *Bălgarski igralni filmi*, vol. 2: *1948–1970*. Sofia: Iz. Dr. Petăr Beron, 1988.

Genov, Nikolai, and Ulrike Becker, eds. *Social Sciences in Southeastern Europe*. Paris: Conseil international des sciences sociales/Informationszentrum Sozialwissenschaften, 2001.

Gensburger, Sarah. "Voir et devoir voir le passé: Retour sur une exposition historique à visée commemorative." *Critique internationale* 68 (2015): 81–99.

Genton, Bernard. *Les Alliés et la culture, Berlin 1945–1949*. Paris: PUF, 1998.

Germa, Antoine, and Georges Bensoussan, eds. "Les écrans de la Shoah: La Shoah au regard du cinéma." *Revue d'histoire de la Shoah* 195 (2011): 21–620.

Geva, Sharon. "Documenters, Researchers and Commemorators: The Life Stories and Work of Miriam Novitch and Rachel Auerbach in Comparative Perspective." *Moreshet* 16 (2019): 56–91.

Gezenko, Ivanka. "Zakonodatelnata i izpălnitelnata vlast v izgraždaneto na anti-evrejskoto zakonodatelstvo 1940–1944 g." In *Obrečeni i spaseni: Bălgarija v antisemitskata programa na Tretija rajh; Izsledvanija i dokumenti*, Institut po istorija na BAN (Sofia: Sineva, 2007), 162–76.

Giannakos, Symeon. "The Macedonian Question Reexamined: Implications for Balkan Security." *Mediterranean Quarterly* 3 (1992): 26–47.

Gigova, Irina. "The Feeble Charm of National(ist) Communism: Intellectuals and Cultural Politics in Zhivkov's Bulgaria." In *Beyond Mosque, Church, and State: Alternative Narration of the Nation in the Balkans*, ed. Theodora Dragostinova and Yana Hashamova (Budapest: Central European University Press, 2016), 151–80.

Ginsburgs, George. *Moscow's Road to Nuremberg: The Soviet Background to the Trial*. The Hague: Martinus Nijhoff, 1996.

Ginzburg, Carlo. *Fear, Reverence, Terror: Five Essays in Political Iconography.* Calcutta: Seagull Books, 2017.

———. *Threads and Traces: True, False, Fictive.* Berkeley: University of California Press, 2012.

Glick Schiller, Nina, and Georges Eugene Fouron. *Georges Woke up Laughing: Long-Distance Nationalism and the Search for Home.* Durham, NC: Duke University Press, 2001.

Goda, Norman J. W., ed. *Rethinking Holocaust Justice: Essays across Disciplines.* New York: Berghahn Books, 2018.

Godet, Martine. *La Pellicule et les ciseaux: La censure dans le cinéma soviétique du Dégel à la perestroïka.* Paris: CNRS Éditions, 2010.

Goschler, Constantin, ed. *Compensation in Practice: The Foundation "Remembrance, Responsibility and Future" and the Legacy of Forced Labor during the Third Reich.* New York: Berghahn Books, 2017.

———. "The Politics of Restitution for Nazi Victims in Germany West and East (1945–2000)." Working Paper OP-3, University of California, Berkeley, Institute of European Policies, 2003, https://escholarship.org/content/qt7bz5801b/qt7bz5801b.pdf?t=kro5qk.

Gradvohl, Paul. "Orban et le souverainisme obsidional." *Politique étrangère* 1 (2017): 35–45.

Green, Andrew. "Counterfeiting the Nation? Skopje 2014 and the Politics of Nation Building in Macedonia." *Cultural Anthropology* 28, no. 3 (2013): 161–79.

Grinberg, Natan. *Dokumenti: Părvata kniga za deportiraneto na evreite ot Trakija, Makedonija i Pirot.* With a foreword by Tatjana Vaksberg. Sofia: I. K. Gutenberg, 2015. 1st edition, 1945, Central Consistory of the Bulgarian Jews.

———. *Hitlerskijat natisk za uništožavaneto na evreite ot Bălgarija.* Tel Aviv: Amal, 1961.

Grínperg, Natán. *Dokouménta, isagoyí–epistimonikí epimélia Vasílis Ritzaléos.* Komotiní: Paratiritís tis Thrákis, 2013.

Grosescu, Raluca. "State Socialist Endeavours for the Non-Applicability of Statutory Limitations to International Crimes: Historical Roots and Current Implications." *Journal of the History of International Law* 21, no. 2 (2019): 239–69.

Groueff, Stephane. *Crown of Thorns: The Reign of Boris III of Bulgaria, 1918–1943.* Lanham, MD: Madison Books, 1987.

———. *My Odyssey.* New York: Writers' Advantage, 2003.

Grozev, Kostadin, and Rumjana Marinova-Hristidi, eds. *Evreite v iztočna Evropa i Săvestksi săjuz v godinite na Vtorata svetovna vojna i studenata vojna (1939–1989).* Sofia: U. I. Sv. Kliment Ohridski, 2013.

Gruev, Mihail, and Aleksej Kaljonski. *Văzroditelnijat proces: Mjusjulmanskite obšnosti i komunističeskijat režim.* Sofia: IIBM, 2008.

Gundermann, Christine. "Real Imagination? Holocaust Comics in Europe." In *Revisiting Holocaust Representation in the Post-Witness Era,* ed. Tanja Schult and Diana Popescu (Basingstoke, UK: Palgrave Macmillan, 2016), 231–50.

Hacohen, Dvora. *Immigrants in Turmoil: Mass Immigration to Israel and Its Repercussions in the 1950s and After.* New York: Syracuse University Press, 2003.

Hadžijski, Ivan. *Sădbata na evrejskoto naselenie v Belomorska Trakija, Vardarska Makedonija i Jugozapadna Bălgarija prez 1941–1944.* Dupnitsa, Bul.: IIA DevoraBi, 2004.

Hallama, Peter. *Nationale Helden und jüdische Opfer: Tschechische Repräsentationen des Holocaust.* Göttingen, Ger.: Vandenhoeck & Ruprecht, 2015.

Hartog, François. *Évidence de l'histoire: Ce que voient les historiens.* Paris: Gallimard, 2005.

Haskell, Guy H. *From Sofia to Jaffa: The Jews of Bulgaria and Israel.* Detroit: Wayne State University Press, 1994.

Heller, Kevin Jon. *The Nuremberg Military Tribunals and the Origins of International Criminal Law.* Oxford: Oxford University Press, 2011.

Hicks, Jeremy. *First Films of the Holocaust: Soviet Cinema and the Genocide of the Jews, 1938–1946.* Pittsburgh, PA: University of Pittsburgh Press, 2012.

———."'Soul Destroyers': Soviet Reporting of Nazi Genocide and Its Perpetrators at the Krasnodar and Khar'kov Trials." *History* 98 (2013): 530–54.

Hilberg, Raul. *The Destruction of the European Jews.* 3 vols. New York: Holmes & Meier, 1985.

———. *Perpetrators, Victims, Bystanders: The Jewish Catastrophe, 1933–1945.* New York: HarperCollins, 1992.

Himka, John-Paul, and Joanna Beata Michlic, eds. *Bringing the Dark Past to Light: The Reception of the Holocaust in Postcommunist Europe.* Lincoln: University of Nebraska Press, 2013.

Hirsch, Francine. *Soviet Judgment at Nuremberg. A New History of the International Military Tribunal after World War I.* Oxford: Oxford University Press, 2020.

Hirsch, Marianne. *The Generation of Post-Memory: Writing and Visual Culture after the Holocaust.* New York: Columbia University Press, 2012.

Hix, Simon, and Bjørn Høyland. "Empowerment of the European Parliament." *Annual Review of Political Science* 16, no. 1 (2013): 171–89.

Hoeft, Brigitte, ed. *Der Prozess gegen Walter Janka und andere: Eine Dokumentation.* Reinbek, Ger.: Rowohlt Taschenbuch Verlag, 1990.

Hoppe, Jens. "Juden als Feinde Bulgariens? Zur Politik gegenüber den bulgarischen Juden in der Zwischenkriegszeit." In *Zwischen großen Erwartungen und bösem Erwachen: Juden, Politik und Antisemitismus in Ost- und Südosteuropa 1918–1945*, ed. Dittmar Dahlmann and Anke Hilbrenner (Paderborn, Ger.: Schöningh, 2007).

Hristova, Natalija. *Spesifika na "bălgarskoto disidentstvo": Vlast i inteligencija, 1956–1989*. Sofia: Letera, 2005.

Ioanid, Radu. *The Holocaust in Romania: The Destruction of Jews and Gypsies under the Antonescu Regime, 1940–1944*. Chicago: Dee, 2000.

———. *La Roumanie et la Shoah*. Paris: CNRS éd., 2023.

Ivanov, Mihail. *Kato na praznik: Dokumentalni stranici za "văzroditelnija proces" (1984–1989)*. https://www.omda.bg/public/biblioteka/mihail_ivanov/praznik_1.htm.

Ivanova, Evgenija. *Othvărlenite "priobšteni" ili procesa, narečen "Văzroditelen" (1912–1989)*. Sofia: Institut za Iztočnoevropejska Humanistika, 2002.

Jablonka, Ivan. *L'Histoire est une littérature contemporaine: Manifeste pour les sciences sociales*. Paris: Seuil, 2014.

Jalămov, Ibrahim. *Istorija na turskata obštnost v Bălgarija*. Sofia: Ilinda Evtimov, 2002.

Janakiev, Aleksandăr. *Cinema.bg: Sto godišen filmov proces*. Sofia: Titra Film, 2003.

———. *Enciklopedija Bălgarsko kino*. Sofia: Titra Film, 1999.

Jockusch, Laura. *Collect and Record! Jewish Holocaust Documentation in Early Postwar Europe*. Oxford: Oxford University Press, 2012.

Joly, Laurent. *Vichy dans la "solution finale": Histoire du Commissariat général aux questions juives, 1941–1944*. Paris: Grasset, 2006.

Jotov, Stiljan. "Spasenieto na bălgarskite evrei—70 godini vojna na interpretaciite." *Sociologičeski problemi* 3–4 (2013): 193–206.

Jurgenson, Luba. "La représentation de l'effacement dans des dispositifs muséographiques." In *Muséographie des violences en Europe centrale et en ex-URSS*, ed. Delphine Bechtel and Luba Jurgenson (Paris: Éditions Kimé, 2016), 175–90.

Jurgenson, Luba, and Alexandre Prstojevic, eds. *Des témoins aux héritiers: L'écriture de la Shoah et la culture européenne*. Paris: Petra, 2012.

Kafka, Franz. *The Zürau Aphorisms of Franz Kafka*. New York: Schocken Books, 2006.

Kalderon, Gitta. *Mishloach Manot: A Life Story; The Shammy-Kalderon Family from Bitola, Macedonia*. Skopje: Holocaust Fund for the Jews from Macedonia, 2017.

Kalinova, Evgenija. *Bălgarskata kultura i političeskijat imperativ (1944–1989)*. Sofia: Paradigma, 2011.

Kanušev, Martin. *Prestăplenie i nakazanie v nacionalnata dăržava: Istoričeska sociologija na nakazatelnite politiki v Bălgarija.* Sofia: Nov bălgarski universitet, 2015.

Karajanov, Petar. *Rafael Moše Kamhi: Ilindenski deec ot evrejsko poteklo.* Skopje: Veda, 2003.

Kărdžilov, Petăr. "Filmi razdeli: Părvi stăpki na socrealizăm v bălgarskoto kino." In *Socialističeskijat realizăm: Novi izsledvanija,* ed. Plamen Dojnov (Sofia: Nov bălgarski universitet, 2008), 96–111.

Kassow, Samuel D. *Who Will Write Our History? Emanuel Ringelblum, the Warsaw Ghetto, and the Oyneg Shabes Archive.* Bloomington: Indiana University Press, 2007.

Kerenji, Emil. "Jewish Citizens of Socialist Yugoslavia: Politics of Jewish Identity in a Socialist State, 1944–1974." PhD diss., University of Michigan, 2008.

Keshales, Haim. *Korot yehudei Bulgariya.* 5 vols. Tel Aviv: Davar, 1969–73.

Kitanoski, Mišo, and Biljana Loteska, eds. *Skopskite evrei.* Skopje: Kitano Press, 2002.

Klarsfeld, Serge. *Le calendrier de la persécution des Juifs en France, 1940–1944.* Paris: Les fils et filles des deportés juifs de France and Beate Klarsfeld Foundation, 1993.

———. *Vichy-Auschwitz, la "solution finale" de la question juive en France.* Paris: Fayard, 2001. Originally published in 1983.

Kleinberger, Alain, and Philippe Mesnard, eds. *La Shoah: Théâtre et cinéma aux limites de la représentation.* Paris: Éditions Kimé, 2013.

Kochavi, Arieh J. *Prelude to Nuremberg: Allied War Crime Policy and the Question of Punishment.* Chapel Hill: University of North Carolina Press, 1998.

Koen, David, Todor Dobrianov, and Rajna Manafova, eds. *Borbata na bălgarskija narod za zaštita i spasjavane na evreite v Bălgarija prez Vtorata svetovna vojna: Dokumenti i materiali.* Sofia: BAN, 1978.

———. *Evreite v Bălgarija, 1878–1949.* Sofia: Iz. Fakel-Leonidovi, 2008.

Koen, Lea. *Spasenie, gonenija i holokost v carska Bălgarija (1940–1944).* Sofia: Enthusiast, 2021.

Koleva, Daniela. *Bălgarija – Izrael: Razkazi za dve strani i dve epohi.* Sofia: Siela and IIBM, 2017.

Koleva, Daniela, and Ivan Elenkov. "Did 'the Change' Happen? Post-socialist Historiography in Bulgaria." In Brunnbauer, *(Re)writing History,* 94–127.

Kolonomos, Žamila-Andžela. *Dviženjieto na otporot i evreite od Makedonija.* Skopje: Fond na Holokaustot na Evreite od Makedonija, 2013.

Kolonomos, Žamila, and Vera Vesković-Vangeli, eds. *Evreite vo Makedonija vo Vtorata svetska vojna (1941–1945): Zbornik na dokumenti.* 2 vols. Skopje: MANU, 1986.

Komisar, Efrat. "Filmed Documents: Methods in Researching Archival Films from the Holocaust." *Apparatus: Film, Media and Digital Cultures in Central and Eastern Europe* 2–3 (2019), https://doi.org/10.17892/app.2016.0002-3.85.

Konrad, Gyorgy. *Antipolitics: Pushing the State Out of Our Nightmares; An Essay.* San Diego: Harcourt Brace Jovanovich, 1984.

Koposov, Nikolay. "Populism and Memory: Legislation of the Past in Poland, Ukraine, and Russia." *East European Politics and Societies* 36, no. 1 (2021), https://doi.org/10.1177/0888325420969786.

Kornbluth, Andrew. *The August Trials: The Holocaust and Postwar Justice in Poland.* Cambridge, MA: Harvard University Press, 2021.

Kostyrchenko, Genadiy. "Politika sovetskogo rukovodstva v otnoshenii yevreyskoy emigratsii posle XX s"ezda KPSS (1956–1991)." In *Yevreyskaya emigratsiya iz Rossii. 1881–2005: Materialy mezhdunarodnoy nauchnoy konferentsii (Moskva, 10 – 12 dekabrya 2006),* ed. Oleg Vital'evich Budnitskiy (Moscow: ROSSPEN, 2008), 202–19.

Kracauer, Siegfried. *History: The Last Things before the Last.* Oxford: Oxford University Press, 1969.

———. *Theory of Film: The Redemption of Physical Reality.* New York: Oxford University Press, 1960.

Krăsteva, Zdravka. "Pravni aspekti na dărăvnata antievrejska politika v carstvo Bălgarija (1940–1944)." In *Antievrejskoto zakonodatelstvo v Evropa i Bălgarija,* ed. Borislav Cekov and Albena Taneva (Sofia: IMP/Centăr za evrejski izsledvanija, 2015), 77–192.

Krispin, Alfred, ed. *Antisemitizăm v Bălgarija dnes: Ima li?* Sofia: I. K. Colibri, 2004.

Kudryashov, Sergey, and Vanessa Voisin. "The Early Stages of 'Legal Purges' in Soviet Russia (1941–1945)." *Cahiers du monde russe* 49, nos. 2–3 (2008): 263–96.

Kulenska, Veselina. "The Antisemitic Press in Bulgaria at the End of the XIXth Century," *Quest: Issues in Contemporary Jewish History* 3 (July 2012).

———. *"Dass wir unser Land vom ökonomischen Joch der Juden Befreien": Antisemitismus in Bulgarien am Ende des 19. Jahrhunderts.* Berlin: Metropol Verlag, 2020.

Kulka, Otto Dov. *Landscape of the Metropolis of Death: Reflections on Memory and Imagination.* Cambridge, MA: The Belknap Press of Harvard University Press, 2013.

Laczó, Ferenc. "From European Fascism to the Fate of the Jews: Early Hungarian Jewish Monographs on the Holocaust." In Laczó and Puttkamer, *Catastrophe and Utopia,* 175–204.

Laczó, Ferenc, and Joachim von Puttkamer, eds. *Catastrophe and Utopia: Jewish Intellectuals in Central and Eastern Europe in the 1930s and 1940s.* Berlin: De Gruyter, 2018.

Lampe, John. *The Bulgarian Economy in the Twentieth Century.* London: Croom Helm, 1986.

Latour, Bruno. "Si l'on parlait un peu politique?" *Politix* 58 (2002): 143–65.

Laurent, Natacha. "Le Conseil artistique du ministère soviétique du Cinéma, 1944–1947." In *Le Cinéma "stalinien": Questions d'histoire,* ed. Natacha Laurent (Toulouse: Presses universitaires du Mirail and La Cinémathèque de Toulouse, 2003), 71–80.

Le Bourhis, Eric, Irina Tchervena, and Vanessa Voisin, eds. *Seeking Accountability for Nazi and War Crimes in East and Central Europe: A People's Justice?* Rochester, NY: University of Rochester Press, 2022.

Levin, Judith, and Daniel Uziel. "Ordinary Men, Extraordinary Photos." *Yad Vashem Studies* 26 (1998): 265–93.

Lewis, Ingrid. *Women in European Holocaust Films: Perpetrators, Victims and Resisters.* Basingstoke, UK: Palgrave Macmillan, 2017.

Liebmann, Stuart. "Les premiers films sur la Shoah: Les Juifs sous le signe de la Croix." *Revue d'histoire de la Shoah* 195 (2011): 145–82.

Lindeperg, Sylvie. *Clio de 5 à 7: Les actualités filmées de la Libération, archives du futur.* Paris: CNRS Éditions, 2000.

———. *"Night and Fog": A Film in History.* Minneapolis: University of Minnesota Press, 2014. Originally published in French, 2007.

———. *Nuremberg: La bataille des images.* Paris: Payot, 2021.

Lindeperg, Sylvie, and Annette Wieviorka, eds. *Le Moment Eichmann.* Paris: Albin Michel, 2016.

Lipstadt, Deborah E. *The Eichmann Trial.* New York: Schocken, 2011.

Littoz-Monnet, Annabelle. "Explaining Policy Conflict across Institutional Venues: European Union-Level Struggles over the Memory of the Holocaust." *Journal of Common Market Studies* 52, no. 3 (2013): 489–504.

Lory, Bernard. "Strates historiques des relations bulgaro-turques." *Cemoti* 15, no. 1 (1993): 149–67.

Maeck, Julie. *Montrer la Shoah à la télévision de 1960 à nos jours.* Paris: Nouveau Monde Éditions, 2009.

Maeck, Julie, and Matthias Steinle, eds. *L'image d'archives: Une image en devenir.* Rennes, Fr.: Presses universitaires de Rennes, 2016.

Mais, Yitzchak, and Rajna Koska-Hot, eds. *Macedonian Chronicle: The Story of Sephardic Jews in the Balkans.* Skopje: Holocaust Fund of the Jews from Macedonia, 2011.

Marinov, Tchavdar. "Ancient Thrace in the Modern Imagination: Ideological Aspects of the Construction of Thracian Studies in Southeast Europe (Romania, Greece, Bulgaria)." In *Entangled Histories of the Balkans*, ed. Rumen Daskalov and Alexander Vezenkov (Leiden: Brill, 2015), 3:10–117.

———. "Historiographical Revisionism and Re-articulation of Memory in the Former Yugoslav Republic of Macedonia." *Sociétés politiques comparées* 25 (May 2010): 1–19.

———. *Nos Ancêtres les Thraces: Usages idéologiques du passé en Europe du Sud-Est*. Paris: Éditions L'Harmattan, 2016.

———. *La Question macédonienne de 1944 à nos jours: Communisme et nationalisme dans les Balkans*. Paris: L'Harmattan, 2010.

Marinova-Christidi, Rumyana. "From Salvation to Alya: The Bulgarian Jews and Bulgarian-Israeli Relations (1948–1990)." *Southeast European and Black Sea Studies* 17, no. 2 (2017): 223–44.

Mariot, Nicolas. "Faut-il être motivé pour tuer? Sur quelques explications aux violences de guerre." *Genèses: Sciences sociales et histoire* 53 (2003): 154–77.

Marrus, Michael R. "The Nuremberg Doctors' Trial in Historical Context." *History and Medecine* 73 (1999): 107–23.

———. *Some Measure of Justice: The Holocaust Era Restitution Campaign of the 1990s*. Madison: University of Wisconsin Press, 2009.

Marrus, Michael R., and Robert O. Paxton. *Vichy France and the Jews*. Stanford, CA: Stanford University Press, 1995. Originally published in 1981.

Matkovski, Aleksandar. "The Destruction of the Macedonian Jewry in 1943." *Yad Vashem Studies* 3 (1959): 203–58.

———. *Istorija na Evreite vo Makedonija*. Skopje: Makedonska revija, 1982.

———. *Tragedijata na Evreite od Makedonija*. Skopje: Kultura, 1962.

Mazower, Mark. *Salonica, City of Ghosts: Christians, Muslims, and Jews, 1430–1950*. New York: Alfred A. Knopf, 2005.

Mendelsohn, Daniel. *The Lost: A Search for Six of Six Million*. New York: HarperCollins, 2006.

Meškova, Polja, and Dinjo Šarlanov. *Bălgarskata gilotina: Tajnite mehanizmi na narodnija săd*. Sofia: Agencija Demokracija, 1994.

Metodiev, Momčil, and Marija Dermendžieva. *Dăržavna sigurnost—predimstvo po nasledstvo: Profesionalni biografii na vodešti oficeri*. Sofia: IIBM and Siela, 2015.

Meusch, Matthias. *Von der Diktatur zur Demokratie: Fritz Bauer und die Aufarbeitung der NS-Verbrechen in Hessen (1956–1968)*. Wiesbaden, Ger.: Historische Kommission für Nassau, 2001.

Miller, Marshall Lee. *Bulgaria during the Second World War*. Stanford, CA: Stanford University Press, 1975.

Milton, Sybil. "Images of the Holocaust—Part I." *Holocaust and Genocide Studies* 1, no. 1 (1986): 27–61.

———. "Images of the Holocaust—Part II." *Holocaust and Genocide Studies* 1, no. 2 (1986): 193–216.

Mink, Georges, and Laure Neumayer, eds. *L'Europe et ses passés douloureux.* Paris: La Découverte, 2007.

Micković, Evica, ed. *Logor Banjica, Logoraši: Knjige zatočenika koncentracionog logora Beograd-Banjica (1941–1944).* 2 vols. Belgrade: Istorijski arhiv Beograda, 2009, 1:163–66.

Mitrevski, Boro. *Skopje 1941 niz bugarskata upravno-policiska arhiva i ustaško-domobranskata dokumentacija.* Skopje: Napredok, 1973.

Moine, Caroline. "RDA (1946–1990): Gels et dégels à l'Est: le cinéma est-allemand." In *Cinéma et régimes autoritaires au xxᵉ siècle: Écrans sous influence,* ed. Raphaël Muller and Thomas Wieder (Paris: PUF, 2008), 167–72.

Molho, Michael. *In Memoriam: Hommage aux victimes juives des nazis en Grèce.* Salonique: Imp. N. Nicolaidès, 1948.

Mouralis, Guillaume. *Le Moment Nuremberg: Le procès international, les lawyers et la question raciale.* Paris: Presses de Sciences Po, 2019.

———. "Le Procès de Nuremberg: Retour sur soixante-dix ans de recherche." *Critique internationale* 73 (2016): 159–75.

Mückenberger, Christine. "The Anti-Fascist Past in DEFA films." In *DEFA: East German Cinema, 1946–1992,* ed. Sean Allan and John Sandfiord (New York: Berghahn Books, 1999), 58–76.

Mutafčieva, Vera, ed. *Istorija naselena s hora.* Sofia: I. K. Gutenberg, 2006.

Mutafčieva, Vera, Vesela Čičovska, Dočka Ilieva, Elena Nončeva, Zlatina Nikolova, and Cvetana Veličkova. *Sădăt nad istoricite: Bălgarskata istoričeska nauka; Dokumenti i diskusii, 1944–1950.* Sofia: A. Iz. Prof. Marin Drinov, 1995.

Nedeva, Irina. *Misija Pariž: Razgovori s Evgenij Siljanov.* Sofia: Semarš, 2007.

Neofotistos, Vassilikis. "2009: Bulgarian Passports, Macedonian Identity; The Invention of EU Citizenship in the Republic of Macedonia." *Anthropology Today* 25, no. 4 (2009): 19–22.

———. *The Risk of War: Everyday Sociality in the Republic of Macedonia.* Philadelphia: University of Pennsylvania Press, 2012.

Neuburger, Mary. *The Orient Within: Muslim Minorities and the Negotiation of Nationhood in Modern Bulgaria.* Ithaca, NY: Cornell University Press, 2004.

Neumayer, Laure. *The Criminalisation of Communism in the European Political Space after the Cold War.* London: Routledge, 2018.

Nissim, Gabriele. *Čovekăt kojto sprja Hitler: Istorijata na Dimităr Pešev, kojto spasi evreite na cjala edna nacija.* Sofia: Nar. Săbranie na Republika Bălgarija, 1999; reissued: Sofia: Iz. na NBU, 2018.

———. *Der Mann, der Hitler stoppte: Dimităr Pešev und die Rettung der bulgarischen Juden.* Berlin: Siedler, 2000.

———. *L'Uomo che fermò Hitler.* Milan: Mondadori, 1998.

Nissim, Gabriele, and Gabriele Eshkenazi. *Ebrei invisibili: I sopravvissuti dell' Europa Orientale dal comunismo a oggi.* Milan: Mandadori, 1995.

Nojkov, Stilijan, and Valentin Radev. *Tsar Boris III v tajnite dokumenti na Tretija rajh 1939–1943.* Sofia: U. I. Sv. Kliment Ohridski, 1995.

Novick, Peter. *The Holocaust in American Life.* Boston: Houghton Mifflin, 1999.

Ofer, Dalia. "Tormented Memories: The Individual and the Collective." *Israeli Studies* 9, no. 3 (2004): 137–56.

Ognjanov, Ljubomir, Mitka Dimova, and Milčo Lalkov. *Narodna demokracija ili diktatura: Hristomatija po istorija na Bălgarija, 1944–48.* Sofia: Literaturen Forum, 1992.

Oliver, Haim. *Nie, Spasenite (ili kak evreite v Bălgarija bjaha iztrăgnati ot lagerite na smărtta).* Sofia: Sofia Press, 1967.

Onken, Eva-Clarita. "The Politics of Finding Historical Truth: Reviewing Baltic History Commissions and Their Work." *Journal of Baltic Studies* 38, no. 1 (2007): 109–16.

Oren, Nissan. *Bulgarian Communism: The Road to Power, 1934–1944.* New York: Columbia University Press, 1971.

———. "The Bulgarian Exception: A Reassessment of the Salvation of the Jewish Community." *Yad Vashem Studies* 7 (1968): 83–106.

———. *Revolution Administered: Agrarianism and Communism in Bulgaria.* Baltimore: Johns Hopkins University Press, 1973.

Organizacija na evreite v Bălgarija Šalom, ed. *75 godini: Nezabravenite lica na spasenieto.* Sofia: Iz. centăr Šalom, 2018.

Oschlies, Wolf. *Bulgarien—Land ohne Antisemitismus.* Erlangen, Ger.: Ner-Tamid-Verlag, 1976.

Pašova, Anastasija, and Petăr Vodeničarov. *Văzroditelnijat proces i religionznata kriptoidentičnost na mjusjulmani ot Blagoevgradski okrăg: Izsledvanija i dokumenti.* Sofia: Semarš, 2011.

"Passing through the Iron Curtain." Special issue: "Imagining the West in Eastern Europe and the Soviet Union." *Kritika: Explorations in Russian and Eurasian History* 9, no. 4 (Fall 2008): 703–9.

Paunovski, Vladimir, and Josif Iliel, eds. *Evreite v Bălgarija meždu uništoženieto i spasenieto.* Sofia: Adasa Press, 2000.

Paxton, Robert O. *Vichy France: Old Guard and New Order 1940–1944.* 1972. Reprint, Columbia University Press, 2001.

Pendas, Devin O. *The Frankfurt Auschwitz Trial, 1963–1965: Genocide, History, and the Limits of the Law.* Cambridge: Cambridge University Press, 2006.

Perchoc, Philippe. "Un passé, deux assemblées: L'assemblée parlementaire du Conseil de l'Europe, le Parlement européen et l'interprétation de l'histoire (2004–2009)." *Revue d'études comparatives Est-Ouest* 45, no. 3 (2014): 205–35.

Perec, Georges. *Penser/Classer.* 1985. Reprint, Paris: Seuil, 2003.

———. *La Vie mode d'emploi.* 1978. Reprint, Paris: Fayard, 2010.

Perego, Simon. "Les commémorations de la destruction des Juifs d'Europe au Mémorial du Martyr juif inconnu du milieu des années 1950 à la fin des années 1950." *Revue d'histoire de la Shoah* 193 (2010): 471–507.

Perry, Duncan. *The Politics of Terror: The Macedonian Revolutionary Movements, 1893–1903.* Durham, NC: Duke University Press, 1988.

Person, Katarzyna. "Rehabilitation of Individuals Suspected of Collaboration: The Jewish Civic Court under the Central Committee of Jews in Poland, 1946–1950." In Le Bourhis, Tcherneva, and Voisin, *Seeking Accountability,* 261–82.

Pešev, Dimităr. *Spomeni.* Sofia: I. K. Gutenberg, 2004.

Petrov, Valerij, and Marko Behar. *Naroden săd: Horova agitka.* Sofia: Bălgarska rabotničeska partija/komunisti, 1944.

Phillips Cohen, Julia. *Becoming Ottomans: Sephardic Jews and Imperial Citizenship in the Modern Era.* Oxford: Oxford University Press, 2014.

Phillips Cohen, Julia, and Sarah Abrevaya Stein, eds. *Sephardi Lives. A Documentary History 1700–1950.* Stanford, CA: Stanford University Press, 2014.

Pinkert, Anke. *Film and Memory in East Germany.* Bloomington: Indiana University Press, 2008.

———. "Tender Males: Jewish Figures as Affective Archive in East German DEFA film." *Studies in Eastern European Cinema* 3, no. 2 (2012): 193–210.

Piskova, Marijana. *"Geroite na Šipka": Arhiven pročit na edin film za rusko-turskata vojna (1877–1878) ot vremeto na studenata vojna.* Blagoevgrad, Bul.: U. I. Neofit Rilski, 2015.

———. "Iz dokumentalnoto nasledstvo na Fondacija 'Bălgarsko delo.'" *Izvestija na dăržavnite arhivi* 80 (2000): 8–102.

Pollak, Michael. *Une identité blessée: Études de sociologie et d'histoire.* Paris: Éditions Métailié, 1993.

Poppetrov, Nikolaj, ed. *Socialno naljavo: Nacionalizmăt—napred; Programi i organizacionni dokumenti na bălgarski avtoritaristki nacionalističeski formacii.* Sofia: I. K. Gutenberg, 2009.

Pozner, Valérie. "Le 'réalisme socialiste' et ses usages pour l'histoire du cinéma soviétique." *Théorème* 8 (2005): 11–17.

Pozner, Valérie, Alexandre Sumpf, and Vanessa Voisin, eds. *Filmer la guerre: Les Soviétiques face à la Shoah, 1941–1946*. Paris: Éditions du Mémorial de la Shoah, 2015.

Priemel, Kim Christian. *The Betrayal: The Nuremberg Trials and German Divergence*. Oxford: Oxford University Press, 2016.

Priemel, Kim Christian, and Alexa Stiller, eds. *Reassessing the Nuremberg Military Tribunals: Transitional Justice, Trial Narratives, and Historiography*. New York: Berghahn Books, 2012.

Ragaru, Nadège. *Assignés à identités: Violence d'État et expériences minoritaires dans les Balkans post-ottomans*. Istanbul: Isis Press, 2019.

———. "Bordering the Past: The Elusive Presences of the Holocaust in Socialist Macedonia and Socialist Bulgaria." *Südost-Forschungen* 76 (2017): 1–32.

———. "Bulgarie, 1989 au prisme de 1997: Une 'révolution' en palimpseste." In *1989 à l'Est de l'Europe: Une mémoire controversée* (La Tour d'Aigues, Fr.: Éditions de l'Aube, 2009), ed. Jérôme Heurtaux and Cédric Pellen, 172–202.

———. "Les dossiers de la Sûreté d'État bulgare: Le communisme dans les pliures du temps." *Revue des études slaves* 81, nos. 2–3 (2010): 205–27.

———. "East-West Encounters at the Adolf-Heinz Beckerle Trial (1967–1968): How Holocaust Knowledge and Remembrance Went Global." In *Remembering across the Iron Curtain: The Emergence of Holocaust Memory in the Cold War Era*, ed. Stephan Stach and Anna Koch. Berlin: De Gruyter, forthcoming.

———, ed. "Écritures visuelles, sonores et textuelles de la justice: Une autre histoire des procès à l'Est." *Cahiers du monde russe* 61, nos. 3–4 (2020): 275–498.

———. "En quête de notabilité: Vivre and survivre en politique dans la Bulgarie postcommuniste." *Politix* 67 (2004): 71–99.

———. "Figure de l'accusé en témoin de l'accusation: Les circulations internationales des poursuites judiciaires des crimes de la Shoah en Bulgarie." *Revue d'histoire de la Shoah* 214 (October 2021): 121–48.

———. "The Jews of Bulgaria and the Yugoslav and Greek Territories Occupied by Bulgaria during World War II." In Ragaru, *Assignés à identités*, 139–75.

———. "Justice in Mantle Coats: Shooting the Bulgarian People's Courts in Revolutionary Times (1944–1945)." In Le Bourhis, Tcherneva, and Voisin, *Seeking Accountability*, 31–77.

———. "The Madding Clocks of Local Persecution: Anti-Jewish Policies in Bitola under Bulgarian Occupation (1941–1944)." In *Reconsidering the History of the Second World War in South-Eastern Europe*, ed. Xavier Bougarel, Hannes Grandits, and Marija Vulesica (London: Routledge, 2019), 161–94.

———, ed. *La Shoah en Europe du Sud-Est: Les Juifs dans les territoires sous administration bulgare, 1940–1944*. Paris: E-Éditions du Mémorial de la Shoah, 2014.

———. "La spoliation des biens juifs en Bulgarie pendant la Seconde Guerre mondiale: Un état des lieux historiographique." In Ragaru, *Assignés à identités*, 176–218.

———. "Symbolic Time(s) of Violence in Late Socialist Bulgaria." *Slavic Review* 82, no. 2 (2023, 82 , no. 1 (2023), 48–68.

———. "The Unbearable Lightness of Bulgarian Socialism: The Movie *Life Goes Quietly By—1957*." In *Cold Revolution: Central and Eastern European Societies in the Face of Socialist Realism (1948–1959)*, ed. Jérôme Bazin and Joanna Kordjak. Milan: Mousse, 2020.

———. "Viewing, Reading, and Listening to the Trials in Eastern Europe: Charting a New Historiography." *Cahiers du monde russe* 61, nos. 3–4 (2020): 297–316.

Ragaru, Nadège, and Maël Le Noc. "Visual Clues to the Holocaust: The Case of the Deportation of Jews from Northern Greece." *Holocaust and Genocide Studies* 35, no. 3 (Winter 2021): 376–403.

Redlich, Shimon, ed. *War, Holocaust, and Stalinism: A Documented History of the Jewish Anti-Fascist Committee in the USSR*. Luxembourg: Harwood Academic Publishers, 1995.

Reuter, Elke, and Detlef Hansel. *Das kurze Leben der VVN von 1947 bis 1953: Die Geschichte der Verfolgten des Nazi-Regimes in der SBZ und DDR*. Berlin: Ed. Ost, 1997.

Rich, David Alan. "Law and Accountability, Secrecy and Guilt: Soviet Trawniki Defendants' Trials, 1960–1970." In Le Bourhis, Tcherneva, and Voisin, *Seeking Accountability*, 221–56.

Rickman, Gregg. *Swiss Banks and Jewish Souls*. New Brunswick, NJ: Transaction, 1999.

Ritzaleos, Vassili. "Bulgarian Foreign Policy and the Deportation of Greek Jews." In Ragaru, *La Shoah en Europe du Sud-Est*, 111–19.

Rodrigue, Aron. *Jews and Muslims: Images of Sephardi and Eastern Jewries in Modern Times*. 2003. Seattle: University of Washington Press, 2015.

———. *Sephardim and the Holocaust*. Washington, DC: United States Holocaust Memorial Museum, Center for Advanced Holocaust Studies, 2005.

Romano, Albert. "Yahadut Bulgariya." In *Enziklopediyah shel galuyot: Sifrei zikaron learzot hagolah veedoteyha*. Jerusalem: Encyclopedia of the Diaspora, 1968.

Rosskopf, Annette. *Friedrich Karl Kaul: Anwalt im geteilten Deutschland (1906–1981)*. Berlin: Verlag Spitz, 2002.

Rousso, Henry. *The Haunting Past: History, Memory, and Justice in Contemporary France*. Philadelphia: University of Philadelphia Press, 2002. Originally published in French, 1998.

———, ed. *Juger Eichmann: Jérusalem 1961*. Paris: Éditions du Mémorial de la Shoah, 2011.

———. *Vichy, an Ever-Present Past*. With a foreword by Robert Paxton. Hanover, NH: University Press of New England, 1998. Originally published in French, 1994.

———. *The Vichy Syndrome: History and Memory in France since 1944*. Cambridge, MA: Harvard University Press, 1991. Originally published in French 1987.

Rozen, Minna, ed. *The Last Ottoman Century and Beyond: The Jews in Turkey and the Balkans 1808–1945*. Vol. 1. Tel Aviv: Goren-Goldstein Diaspora Research Center, Tel Aviv University Press, 2005.

Ruckhaberle, Dieter, ed. *Wege zur Diktatur, Ausstellung, Staatliche Kunsthalle Berlin und Neue Gesellschaft für bildende Kunst, vom 9.1 bis 10.2.1983*. Berlin: Staatliche Kunsthalle, 1983.

Ruckhaberle, Dieter, and Christiane Ziesecke, eds. *Rettung der bulgarischen Juden 1943: Eine Dokumentation*. Berlin: Staatliche Kunsthalle Berlin, 1984.

Sage, Steven. "Sedmi săstav na Narodnija săd v Sofija, mart–april 1945: Părvijat v sveta Holokost proces v sobstvenija i v našija kontekst." In *Evreite v iztočna Evropa i Săvetski săjuz v godinite na Vtorata svetovna vojna i studenata vojna (1939–1989)*, ed. Kostadin Grozev and Rumjana Marinova-Christidi (Sofia: U. I. Sv. Kliment Ohridski, 2013), 159–70.

Sands, Philippe. *East West Street: On the Origins of Genocide and Crimes against Humanity*. New York: Alfred A. Knopf, 2016.

Sarkisova, Oksana, and Péter Apor, eds. *Past for the Eyes: East European Representations of Communism in Cinema and Museums after 1989*. Budapest: Central European University Press, 2008.

Šarović, Liljana, et al. *Štipskite evrei: Zbornik na trudovi i sećavanja*. Skopje: Fondacijata "11 mart 1943-Štip," 1999.

Schaffer, Simon. "Natural Philosophy as Public Spectacle." *History of Science* 21 (1983): 1–43.

Schandler, Jeffrey. *While America Watches: Televising the Holocaust*. Oxford: Oxford University Press, 1999.

Schenk, Ralf. "Auferstanden aus Ruinen: Von der Ufa zur Defa." In *Das Ufa-Buch: Kunst und Krisen, Stars und Regisseure, Wirtschaft und Politik*, ed. Hans-Michael Bock and Michael Töteboerg (Frankfurt: Zweitausendeins, 1992), 476–81.

Schmidt, Fabian, and Alexander Oliver Zöller. "Filmography of the Genocide: Official and Ephemeral Film Documents on the Persecution and Extermination of the European Jews 1933–1945." *Audiovisual Traces* 4 (February 22, 2022), https://film-history.org/issues/text/filmography-genocide.

Schraftstetter, Susanna. "The Diplomacy of *Wiedergutmachung*: Memory, the Cold War, and the Western European Victims of Nazism, 1956–1964." *Holocaust and Genocide Studies* 17 (2003): 459–79.

Šealtiel, Šlomo. *Ot rodina kăm otečestvo: Emigracija i nelegalna imigracija ot i prez Bălgarija v perioda 1939–1949*. Sofia: U. I. Sv. Kliment Ohridski, 2008.

Segev, Tom. *The Seventh Million: The Israelis and the Holocaust*. New York: Hill and Wang, 1993.

Semkova-Dimitrova, Zornica. *Promeni v sădebnata vlast na Bălgarija*. Sofia: U. I. Sv. Kliment Ohridski, 2004.

Serres, Michel. *Éclaircissements: Cinq entretiens avec Bruno Latour*. Paris: Flammarion, 1994.

Shapira, Anita. "The Eichmann Trial: Changing Perspectives." *Journal of Israeli History* 23, no. 1 (2004): 18–39.

Shea, John. *Macedonia and Greece: The Struggle to Define a New Balkan Nation*. Jefferson, NC: McFarland, 1997.

Shneer, David. *Grief: The Biography of a Holocaust Photograph*. Oxford: Oxford University Press, 2020.

———. *Through Soviet Jewish Eyes: Photography, War and the Holocaust*. New Brunswick, NJ: Rutgers University Press, 2011.

Söhner, Jasmin. "Der heiligen Rache darf nicht ein Auschwitz-Henker entgehen! Die erste sowjetische Zeugenaussage in Westdeutschland zwischen Propaganda und Vergeltung." *Jahrbuch 2017 zu Geschichte und Wirkung des Holocaust*, 2017, 157–72.

Söhner, Jasmin, and Máté Zombory. "Accusing Hans Globke, 1960–1963: Agency and the Iron Curtain." In Le Bourhis, Tcherneva, and Voisin, *Seeking Accountability*, 351–86.

Sorokina, Marina. "People and Procedures: Toward a History of the Investigation of Nazi Crimes in the USSR." *Kritika: Explorations in Russian and Eurasian History* 6, no. 4 (Fall 2005): 797–831.

Spittmann, Ilse. "Dr 17: Juni im Wandel der Legenden." *Deutschland Archiv* 17, no. 6 (1984): 594–605.

Stach, Stephan. "'The Jewish Diaries . . . Undergo One Edition after the Other': Early Polish Documentation, East German Antifascism, and the Emergence of Holocaust Memory in Socialism." In Bohus, Hallama, and Stach, *Shadow of Anti-Fascism*, 273–301.

Stefoska, Irena, and Darko Stojanov. "Remembering and Forgetting the SFR Yugoslavia: Historiography and History Textbooks in the Republic of Macedonia." *Südosteuropa: Journal of Politics and Society* 64, no. 2 (2016): 206–25.

Stengel, Katharina. "Mediators behind the Scenes: The World Jewish Congress and the International Auschwitz Committee during the Preparations for the First Auschwitz Trial in Frankfurt." In Le Bourhis, Tcherneva, and Voisin, *Seeking Accountability*, 320–49.

Steur, Claudia. *Theodor Dannecker: Ein Funktionär der "Endlösung."* Essen: Klartext Verlag, 1997.

Struk, Janina. *Photographing the Holocaust: Interpretations of the Evidence.* London: I. B. Tauris, 2004.

Sujecka, Jolanta, ed. *The Balkan Jews and the Minority Issue in South-Eastern Europe.* Warsaw: La Rama, 2020.

Sumpf, Alexandre, and Vincent Laniol, eds. With Denis Rolland. *Saisies, spoliations et restitutions: Archives et bibliothèques au XXᵉ siècle.* Rennes, Fr.: Presses universitaires de Rennes, 2012.

Szymaniak, Karolina. "On the Ice Floe: Rachel Auerbach—the Life of a Yiddishist Intellectual in Early Twentieth Century Poland." In Laczó and Puttkamer, *Catastrophe and Utopia*, 302–51.

Tamir, Vicki. *Bulgaria and Her Jews: The History of a Dubious Symbiosis.* New York: Sepher-Hermon Press for Yeshiva University Press, 1979.

Taneva, Albena. "Liderskijat obštestven model: Spasjavaneto na evreite v Bălgarija v političeskija diskurs." PhD diss., Universitet Sv. Kliment Ohridski, 2007.

Terzioski, Rastislav. *Denacionalizatorskata dejnost na bugarskite kulturno-prosvetni institucii vo Makedonija.* Skopje: Institut za nacionalna istorija, 1974.

Todorov, Nikolaj. "Evrejskoto naselenie v balkanskite provincii na osmanskata imperija prez XV–XIX vek." In Todorov, Damjanov, and Koen, *Proučvanija za istorijata na evrejskoto naselenie v bălgarskite zemi,* 7–20.

Todorov, Nikolaj, Simeon Damjanov, and David Koen, eds. *Proučvanija za istorijata na evrejskoto naselenie v bălgarskite zemi (XV–XX vek).* Sofia: Izdatelstvo na Bălgarskata akademija na naukite, 1980.

Todorov, Tzvetan, ed. *La fragilité du bien: Le sauvetage des Juifs bulgares.* Paris: Albin Michel, 1999.

———, ed. *The Fragility of Goodness: Why Bulgaria's Jews Survived the Holocaust.* Princeton, NJ: Princeton University Press, 2004.

Todorov, Vărban, and Nikolaj Poppetrov, eds. *VII săstav na narodnija săd: Edno zabraveno dokumentalno svidetelstvo za antisemitizma v Bălgarija prez 1941–1944 g.* Sofia: Iztok-Zapad, 2013.

Todorova, Maria. "The Mausoleum of Georgi Dimitrov as *Lieu de mémoire.*" *Journal of Modern History* 78 (2006): 377–411.

Todorova, Maria, Augusta Dimou, and Stefan Troebst, eds. *Remembering Communism: Private and Public Recollections of Lived Experience in Southeast Europe.* Budapest: Central European University Press, 2014.

Todorova, Olga. "Evreite v bălgarskata slovesnost ot načaloto na XIX vek do Osvoboždenieto." *Librev.com*, July 12, 2012, https://www.librev.com/index.php/2013-03-30-08-56-39/discussion/bulgaria/1759--ix-.

———. "Obrazăt na 'nečestivija' evrein v bălgarskata knižnina ot XVIII–načaloto na XIX vek i văv folklor." *Bălgarski folklor*, no. 3 (1994): 10–22.

Tošev, Lăčezar. "Kratka hronika na priemaneto na rezolucija 1481 na PACE." *Edin zavet* 54 (2006).

Touykova, Marta. "Conversion partisane et usages politiques du passé: Le cas du Parti socialiste bulgare." *Revue d'études comparatives Est-Ouest* 37, no. 3 (2006): 67–96.

Traverso, Enzo. *L'Histoire comme champ de bataille: Interpréter les violences du XXᵉ siècle.* Paris: La Découverte, 2011.

Troebst, Stefan. "Antisemitismus im 'Land ohne Antisemitismus': Staat, Titularnation und jüdische Minderheit in Bulgarien, 1878–1993." In *Antisemitismus im östlichen Europa*, ed. Mariana Hausleitner and Monika Katz (Wiesbaden: Harrassowitz, 1995), 109–25.

———. *Die bulgarisch-jugoslawische Kontroverse um Makedonien 1967–1982.* Munich: Oldenbourg, 1983.

———. "'Führerbefehl!'—Adolf Hitler und die Proklamation eines unabhängigen Makedonien (September 1944): Eine archivalische Miszelle." *Osteuropa* 52, no. 4 (2002): 491–501.

———. "Macedonian Historiography on the Holocaust in Macedonia under Bulgarian Occupation." *Südosteuropäische Hefte* 2, no. 1 (2013): 107–14.

Troeva-Grigorova, Evgenija. "Prinuditelnijat trud prez Vtorata svetovna vojna v spomenite na bălgarskite evrei." In *Prinuditelnijat trud v Bălgarija (1941–1962): Spomeni na svideteli*, ed. Ana Luleva, Evgenija Troeva-Grigorova, and Petăr Petrov (Sofia: Ak. Iz. Marin Drinov, 2012), 39–54.

Vagenštajn, Anžel. *Tri scenarija: Zvezdi; Zvezdi v kosite, sălzi v očite; Boris părvi.* Sofia: I. K. Colibri, 2002.

Val, Perrine. *Les relations cinématographiques entre la France et la RDA: Entre camaraderie, bureaucratie et exotisme (1946–1992)*. Paris: Presses universitaires du Septentrion, 2021.

Vasileva, Bojka. *Evreite v Bălgarija, 1944–1952*. Sofia: U. I. Sv. Kliment Ohridski, 1992.

Verdery, Katherine. *National Ideology under Socialism: Identity and Cultural Politics in Ceaușescu's Romania*. Berkeley: University of California Press, 1991.

———. *The Political Lives of Dead Bodies: Reburial and Postsocialist Change*. New York: Columbia University Press, 1999.

Veyne, Paul. *Comment on écrit l'histoire*. Paris: Seuil, 1971.

Vezenkov, Aleksandăr. *9-i septemvri 1944 g*. Sofia: Siela, 2014.

Voisin, Vanessa, Éric Le Bourhis, and Irina Tcherneva. "Introduction." In Le Bourhis, Tcherneva, and Voisin, *Seeking Accountability*, 1–26.

Wahnich, Sophie. "Trois musées de guerre du XXe siècle: Imperial War Museum de Londres, historial de Péronne, mémorial de Caen." In *Muséaux de guerre and mémoriaux: Politiques de la mémoire*, ed. Jean-Yves Boursier (Paris: Éditions de la MSH, 2005), 53–64.

Wedel, Michael, and Elke Schieber, eds. *Konrad Wolf—Werk und Wirkung*. Berlin: BFF Vistas Verlag, 2009.

Weinke, Annette. "Der Kampf um die Akten: Zur Kooperation zwischen MfS und osteuropäischen Sicherheitsorganen bei der Vorbereitung antifaschistischer Kampagnen." *Deutschland-Archiv* 32, no. 4 (1999): 564–77.

———. *Die Verfolgung von NS-Tätern im geteilten Deutschland: Vergangenheitsbewältigungen 1949–1969 oder; Eine deutsch-deutscher Beziehungsgeschichte im Kalten Krieg*. Paderborn, Ger.: Ferdinand Schöningh, 2002.

———. *Eine Gesellschaft ermittelt gegen sich selbst: Die Geschichte der Zentralen Stelle Ludwigsburg 1958–2008*. Darmstadt, Ger.: WGB, 2008.

———. *Law, History, and Justice: Debating German State Crimes in the Long Twentieth Century*. Oxford: Berghahn Books, 2018.

Werner, Paul, ed. *Konrad Wolf—Aber ich sah ja selbst, das war der Krieg: Kriegstagebuch und Briefe 1942–1945*. Berlin: Die Möwe, 2015.

White, Hayden. *Metahistory: The Historical Imagination in Nineteenth-Century Europe*. Baltimore: Johns Hopkins University Press, 1973.

Wiesel, Elie, Tuvia Friling, Radu Ioanid, and Mihail E. Ionescu, eds. *Comisiă internațional pentru studierea Holocaustului în România: Raport final*. Iași, Rom.: Polirom, 2004.

Wieviorka, Annette. *Auschwitz, 60 ans après*. Paris: Robert Laffont, 2005.

———. *Déportation et génocide: Entre la mémoire et l'oubli*. Paris: Plon, 1992.

———. *The Era of the Witness*. Ithaca, NY: Cornell University Press, 2006. Originally published in French, 1998.

Wittmann, Rebecca. *Beyond Justice: The Auschwitz Trial*. Cambridge, MA: Harvard University Press, 2005.

———. "Tainted Law: The West German Judiciary and the Prosecution of Nazi War Criminals." In *Atrocities on Trial: Historical Perspectives on the Politics of Prosecuting War Crimes*, ed. Patricia Heberer and Jürgen Matthäus (Lincoln: University of Nebraska Press, 2008), 211–29.

Wojak, Irmtrud. *Fritz Bauer 1903–1968: Eine Biographie*. Munich: Buxus Edition, 2016.

Wóycika, Zofia. *Arrested Mourning: Memory of the Nazi Camps in Poland, 1944–1950*. Frankfurt: Peter Lang, 2013.

Yablonka, Hanna. *The State of Israel vs. Adolph Eichmann*. Trans. Ora Cummings with David Herman. New York: Schocken, 2004.

———. *Survivors of the Holocaust: Israel after the War*. London: Macmillan, 1999.

Young, James. "America's Holocaust: Memory and the Politics of Identity." In *The Americanization of the Holocaust*, ed. Hilene Flanzbaum (Baltimore: Johns Hopkins University Press, 1999), 68–82.

———. *At Memory's Edge: After-Images of the Holocaust in Contemporary Art and Architecture*. New Haven, CT: Yale University Press, 2000.

Železčeva, Ivanka Gezenko. "Novi strihi kăm săzdavaneto i dejnostta na Komisarstvoto po evrejskite văprosi." *Istorija* 21, no. 1 (2015): 20–37.

Zerubavel, Yael. *Recovered Roots: Collective Memory and the Making of the Israeli National Tradition*. Chicago: University of Chicago Press, 1995.

Znamierowska-Rakk, Elżbieta. "Bulgaria's Territorial Revisionism as the Driving Force for Its Rapprochement with the Third Reich." In *Territorial Revisionism and the Allies of Germany in the Second World War*, ed. Marina Cattaruzza, Stefan Dyroff, and Dieter Langewiesche (New York: Berghahn Books, 2013), 102–25.

Zubrzycki, Geneviève. *The Crosses of Auschwitz: Nationalism and Religion in Post-Communist Poland*, Chicago: University of Chicago Press, 2006.

Zweig, Ronald. *German Reparations and the Jewish World: A History of the Claims Conference*. London: Frank Cass, 2014.

Index

"Meticulously researched and beautifully written, Dr. Nadège Ragaru's *Bulgaria, the Jews, and the Holocaust: On the Origins of a Heroic Narrative* should put to rest once and for all the myth of the World War II Bulgarian government as the altruistic savior of Bulgarian Jewry. Using print, visual, and sound sources from numerous countries, Dr. Ragaru analyzes and demonstrates how the perceptions—some intentionally erroneous—of what happened during World War II have been created and transmitted over the course of the past 78 years. This includes the deliberate downplaying if not utter omission in the Bulgarian historical canon of the fact that Bulgarian troops and police proactively rounded up and deported 11,343 Jews from Bulgarian-occupied territories to their death in the Nazi Treblinka death camp."

—Menachem Z. Rosensaft, adjunct professor of law, Cornell Law School; General Counsel Emeritus, World Jewish Congress

"The Bulgarian state both persecuted and rescued Jews during World War II. Neither narrative is complete without acknowledgement of the other. In a highly original volume, Nadège Ragaru traces the evolution of two divergent narratives across geographical, chronological, and ideological space from the events in 1943 to the present. Using diverse venues, historical scholarship, criminal trials, contemporaneous deportation footage, fictional film, museum representation, and political debate, she reveals how regional, national, European, and global politics impacted the narratives within Cold War and post-communist frameworks and suggests guidance for responsibly integrating them without sacrificing awareness of individual agency in persecuted and persecutor."

—Peter Black, historian and consultant

"This powerful book traces Bulgaria's difficult path toward accounting for its contradictory implication in the Holocaust: while Bulgarian authorities helped the Germans to murder the Jews from its occupied territories, a diverse coalition managed to prevent the deportation of Jews from pre-1941 Bulgaria. Ragaru provides a nuanced, exhaustively researched analysis of the interplay between silencing and selectively articulating the memory of these events. A must-read that highlights the centrality of the Holocaust and its (non)memory for Bulgaria's twentieth-century history."

—Ulf Brunnbauer, director of the Leibniz Institute for East and Southeast European Studies, Regensburg

Printed and bound by CPI Group (UK) Ltd, Croydon, CR0 4YY

09/06/2025

14685698-0002